W9-APY-952

SCOTLAND UNDER CHARLES I

ALEXANDER HENDERSON

[*Frontispiece*

SCOTLAND
UNDER CHARLES I

by

David Mathew

EYRE & SPOTTISWOODE
London

*This book, first published in 1955, is printed in Great Britain for
Eyre & Spottiswoode (Publishers) Ltd., 15 Bedford Street, London, W.C.2,
by The Chiswick Press, New Southgate, N.11*

FOR ROSE MACAULAY
in memory of a long friendship

CONTENTS

ILLUSTRATIONS

PREFACE

THE reign of Charles I in Scotland bore little resemblance to the same sovereign's rule in the southern kingdom. Politically it was the aftermath of the long and successful epoch of James VI, who had been King of Scotland as long as any one living could remember. The accession of Charles I had marked the coming of a stranger in place of the most native of all the rulers of the Stewart dynasty since that House had first attained the Scottish Crown. The framework of the State belonged to an old model and was deep-rooted in the past. The magnates who stood about the throne had always stood there, they and their ancestors as far back as the reign of James I of Scotland two centuries previously. The ties with France were enduring and had only partially been transformed by the Reformation. The alignment of the forces of the great lords around James VI had borne a recognisable resemblance to that which the emissaries of Charles VII would discern at the court of the Dauphin's father-in-law the King of Scotland.

The sixteenth century had left a legacy of religious strife and of political neutrality. There had been no external enemy save England and peace had been maintained with that kingdom since the Treaty of Edinburgh in 1560. The Spanish Armada meant no more to Scotland than the periodic interest of the House of Argyll in the salving of the Tobermory galleon. Philip II had never been an enemy and Scotland was immune from the Elizabethan legend. Her former subjects did not like to think back to the Queen of Scots and to her death at Fotheringhay on foreign soil.

On the side of social life there was no artificial barrier to prevent the transforming effects of foreign contacts. Admittedly these only affected the few; the lords; the members of the chief legal families; certain ministers. These, however, formed the climate of opinion in the ruling groupings. France was a background for all that world and especially for those who followed Calvin's teaching. Buchanan had come from there and Andrew Melville had sought refuge in that country with the Duke of Bouillon at Sedan. Throughout the Presbyterian circles Saumur was a household name. On the other hand James VI had owed much to his half-French cousin Esmé Stuart of Aubigny.

It is true that in the early stages of the Reformation period the influence of France in Scotland had been at least politically Catholic. Mary of Guise, widow of James V, had introduced a French garrison into Edinburgh to which the bishops gave some support. After the murder in 1546 of Cardinal Beaton, who however independent had held the French bishopric of Mirepoix *in commendam*, Scots Catholics in fact came to be associated with either a "French" or a "Spanish" interest. Very soon the English party became identified with a victory for political Protestantism and for Genevan theology in its French dress.

There is a striking contrast between the course of the Reformation in England and in Scotland. Thus in England the Reformation had, except under Queen Mary, the strong support of the Crown, while in Scotland it was imposed on a most reluctant monarchy. James V had seen the Auld Kirk as a chief support for the royal policy. His daughter Mary Queen of Scots received a Catholic upbringing in France, but a distaste for the mechanics of the New Religion also affected his grandson James VI. The Reformation in the shape that it took in Scotland was alien to him. It had been fostered by the majority of the great houses and had found its leaders among their cadets and dependents. A group of lords had led the Congregation of Jesus Christ. The death of Mary of Guise had been followed by the meeting in August 1560 of the Parliament which had abolished the papal jurisdiction in Scotland and had established a Calvinist Confession of Faith. John Knox had issued the Book of Discipline in the next year.

In Scotland this movement was essentially regional spreading mainly from burgh to burgh. It was only at a much later date that part of the Highlands gained their Presbyterian colouring. The opposition aroused by the innovators was very different from the strong reaction symbolised in England by the mission of Campion and Parsons and the spearhead of the Counter-Reformation. In Scotland the adherence to the Old Faith had a conservative character; it was tenacious and bound up with the enduring structure of clan life. This would also apply in the south-west where the Maxwells would follow their chief's leadership. Apart perhaps from Aberdeen, Catholicism was by the end of the sixteenth century very weak in the Scottish towns. Many factors make it difficult to penetrate the degree of attachment to Catholic doctrine and the possibilities of sacramental practice. Much spade-work must be done before the nature of the Catholic survival can be assessed; at present the necessary preliminary studies are lacking. It may be that the strength of the fear of Rome in Scotland as well as in England was a measure of the surviving power of the Old Faith. A recent survey describes[1] that northern area which would always retain its allegiance. "The Catholic part

[1] *West Highland Survey*, 1955, ed. F. Fraser Darling, p. 315.

of the Highlands runs from Banffshire through Inverness-shire, down the Great Glen, out to the west coast in Knoydart and Moydart, across the small isles of Eigg and Canna to South Uist and Barra." The whole subject awaits its historian.

As always it is the victorious side which is well-documented.[1] From the first there had been three tendencies among the leading stocks who accepted the Reformation ungrudgingly; they may be divided into those who desired to approximate to Geneva, those who were naturally Conservatives and finally that mass of the indifferent who were determined to maintain the church lands which had thus come to them. It was from the second grouping that opposition to the Covenanters would spring either immediately or more gradually by reaction. Difficult as it is to be precise it would seem that almost from the first there was a section of the lords of the Reformed Faith whose traditional preferences led them to support the institution of episcopacy.

Against these conflicts here can be set the background of the daily life which in many regions is known to us with accuracy. Over a great part of Scotland, everywhere in fact to the south and east of the Highlands we can gain a firm impression; in the ports along the Moray Firth and eastwards through Buchan and then down through the Garioch and Mar, Mearns, Angus, Strathearn and Mentieth as far west as the Lennox on the Firth of Clyde, and all that lay to the southwards of these lands away from the "hill clans".

The inventories, whether copious or sparse, give a clear view provided only that they are complete. The instructions for the laying out of the gardens and policies at Ancram are very detailed. The library of the third Earl of Lothian has survived quite intact. In many respects it is easier to envisage the setting of life in seventeenth-century Scotland than that in France or England at the same time. Culross, although some of the principal features are of a later date, gives an impression of a small Scottish burgh on the shores of Forth; it has no southern counterpart. This also applies to some Edinburgh wynds. Certain works seem characteristic of different aspects of this period, although not necessarily created in it; the castle garden at Edzell; the dower house and chapel at Stobhall; the decorated south front of Strathbogie; the earlier portion of the house now known as Argyll's Lodging on the slope to the north east of Stirling Castle.

As an example of the working of some economic factor we can see the place of the miller in the local structure; the loans that he

[1] Except in the case of mass migrations of the defeated groupings as in the case of those leaving France at the Revocation of the Edict of Nantes.

might be prepared to make; the long continuance of the mill servants.[1] The holders of burgh roods and occupiers of common lands are all listed. A detailed picture can be obtained of such a small town as Inverurie in the Garioch. There is evidence[2] as to the least fortunate.

"1624. Annes Davidson, dep.; deid there out at the fauld dykes of Netherton being ane cauld stormie nicht.

1626, 4 July. Walter Cheyne, son to William Cheyne, tailyeour[3] in Inverury, being in service with George Grubb in Inverury, coming from the peat moss with his master. The said Walter drowned coming over Don in ane salmon coble upon the back pot of Artoneis."

These facts are set out to indicate the bearing of the local happenings.

The variations between the value of Scottish and English money should be set down. Thus £400 Scots was the equivalent of £33 6s. 8d. sterling and five hundred merks was worth £27 15s. 6d. in the southern currency. These figures underline the richness of the South.

The present volume should be placed in its setting. It is one of a series of studies which stem from *The Celtic Peoples and Renaissance Europe* published in 1933. This book dealt primarily with the moulding effect of the Elizabethan polity on Irish and Welsh affairs and on the relationship with Spain which these involved. It closed with the Essex Rising in 1601 and the flight of Tyrone and Tyrconnell six years later, events which may be held to mark the end of the old-fashioned system of local alliance in Wales and Ireland.

The Jacobean Age and *The Age of Charles I*, both confined to English matters, dove-tailed into each other and between them covered certain aspects of the forty years which separated the accession of James I from the outbreak of the Civil Wars. A volume concerning Welsh and Irish affairs over the same period will follow and the present study deals with Scotland. It is a survey of life in Scotland during the first sixteen years of the reign of Charles I and ends with the King's final departure from Edinburgh in 1641. For two generations the Scottish scene had been dominated by the figure of James VI and I, a sovereign whose lines of policy had so profound an influence in his native country.

[1] Thus William Snape was miller's man from 1611 till 1631 to George Glennie and Gilbert Johnstone successively millers at Aquohorties, notes by James Mill, minister of Inverurie printed in *Inverurye and the Earldom of Garioch* by the Rev. John Davidson, p. 181.

[2] Notes by James Mill printed *ibid.*, p. 212.

[3] For the sake of consistency the letter "z" is printed as "y".

After a general description of the Scottish polity an account is given of the Presbyterian outlook and the nature of the opposition to King Charles is examined in detail. The points of similarity and difference between the English Puritans and their Scottish counterparts are essential for an understanding of the troubled history of their alliance. The theocratic and political aspects of the Presbyterian world are studied through the lives and thought of Johnston of Wariston and Sir Thomas Hope. This leads on to an examination of the Episcopalian tradition. An analysis of the position of the magnates completes the survey of the active forces then dominant in Scottish politics.

A picture is then given of the social and economic life of the country region by region. This involves an examination of the "old" forces represented among others by the Huntlys, father and son. The surviving Catholic element in the north east of Scotland and in the Lowlands is then analysed. Chapters are given to the northern earldoms and to the islands and the West. The importance of the contacts with France are then assessed.

The last part of the book is concerned with the emergent figures, Argyll and Hamilton. Their respective positions are considered in detail and the King's ties with his cousin Lennox are indicated. At this point the influence of Archbishop Laud in Scottish affairs is examined. The final chapters contain a consideration set out in narrative form of some aspects of the National Covenant and the Glasgow Assembly. The parts played by Rothes and Leven are studied, as is that of Montrose in his period as a Covenanter. The book ends before Montrose's work became of independent significance. It is in fact a record of the royal defeat.

I express my gratitude to the Marquess of Lothian for the use of the manuscripts in his possession and for the opportunity to examine the seventeenth-century library collected by the third Earl of Lothian, to the Marquess of Tweeddale for the chance to study Yester and for permission to reproduce three portraits there, to the Earl of Haddington for permitting an examination of the books assembled by the first Earl of Haddington, to the Countess of Darnley through whom I examined the Lennox portraits at Cobham Hall, to Lord Sempill who enabled me to study Craigievar and its furnishings, and to Major Maxwell Stuart for the use of the manuscripts at Traquair. I thank the authorities of the General Register House, the Advocates Library and Blairs College for their courteous assistance. I am grateful to Mr Norman Daniel with whom I visited many sites in different parts of Scotland, and to Sir Compton Mackenzie for his vivid appreciations given to me across the years. I have a similar debt to my cousin the late Janet

Mathew and her sister Miss Knox with whom I visited the kirk of Kilbirnie. I express my gratitude to Dr Gordon Donaldson, the late Dr Agnes Muir Mackenzie, the Rev. J. M. Bulloch, the Rev. Anthony Ross, the Rev. David McRoberts and Mr John Durkin for judgments on different aspects of the subject. I have been stimulated by discussions with Lady Hesketh and Miss C. V. Wedgwood. I am always conscious of my great debt to Dr A. L. Rowse, who has developed the study of national history along regional lines.

Finally, my brother Gervase has worked out the whole book with me and has helped me in every section.

DAVID MATHEW

OXFORD,
May, 1952.
STONOR PARK,
February, 1955.

CHAPTER I

THE SCOTTISH POLITY

IN the seventeenth century the climate of Scottish opinion and the organisation of Scottish social life bore little resemblance to the habits of thought and the money-conscious stratified class system which characterised the southern kingdom. In considering Scotland and England in the years before the Civil Wars it is difficult to find a common factor. Even after the conflict had opened, the methods and the aims of the Royalists in Scotland had little in common with those of the King's English supporters. The Covenanters had even less in common with those who rallied to the Parliament and its army. It is natural that the policies of the leaders of the two nations should diverge, it is more remarkable that the opposition groups in either country should have succeeded in acting in concert.

The personal union of the Crowns, which had come about when James VI succeeded Elizabeth I, had given the English Court experience of Scotsmen. It had not, however, provided the English political world with any direct knowledge of Scotland. In some ways this range of understanding was notably diminished as compared with that possessed by Walsingham and Burghley and Robert Cecil. Until 1603 successive English ambassadors in Scotland had provided useful and coherent data.

The Scottish and English leaders were dissimilar in their background, their education and their outlook. The Scots were without that proud insularity marked by its own traditional culture with which Queen Elizabeth's policy and legend had combined to stamp all except a very small minority of the English governing classes. Perhaps the only Scotsman among the leaders who was consciously attuned to English life was the Earl of Rothes, one of the most prominent of the Covenanting peers. He died in the early stages of the conflict, but he was the only Scottish leader with the capacity and perhaps also the inclination to play the Mirabeau.

The Englishmen who either sat in Parliament or else were concerned with local administration had passed through a range of experience very different from that of their Scottish equals. They were conditioned in the first place by the nature of the English Reformation and also very markedly by their emergence from successful external war. In Scotland external wars were only a memory, and such struggles had always been waged against the

English. Internal conflict on the other hand was common enough. England, which was so rich and great a country, was in many respects self-sufficient. It developed its own commerce with the Continent, but had little need of that foreign employment and foreign education which were both essential elements in the economy of the northern kingdom. Under one aspect it may be said that the beginning of the Civil War in Scotland was determined by the great mass of Scottish soldiers then available in the armed camps of Europe.

The Elizabethan Age had a powerful effect on the imagination and in great measure determined the thought of such men as Strafford. There was a sense in which the Jacobean Age and the early part of the reign of Charles I were in the nature of an Elizabethan aftermath. The great Queen formed a standard of reference for both sides in the English conflict. In Scotland the memory of Elizabeth I aroused scant sympathy and the situation was in fact reversed. Few men cared to dwell on the reign or on the imprisonment and death of the Queen of Scots. Those years which in England had seen the defeat of the Armada and the last Elizabethan glories had witnessed in Scotland the patience and indeed the cunning of King James's policies. In the religious field, which in Scotland was so closely intertwined with politics, the Presbyterian movement was dynamic. It was approaching its logical climax in the perfect victory of the Kirk of Scotland. The Kirk belonged to the Scottish people; it was manifestly the creation of their leaders. The majority of Scottish captains abroad were determinedly Calvinist. It was the idea of the defence of the Covenant which drew them home.

This need not be considered in a too narrowly religious sense. It was also an exercise in Scottish patriotism. Under Gustavus Adolphus the Presbyterian officers had come to appreciate the value of politico-military power when used in defence of the Protestant interest. It is probable that they considered the political organisation which grew around the Covenant as the most useful national expression of inherent Scottish authority.

In this connection a study of the career of the Earl of Leven is useful. He was the inevitable *Condottiere* like some great soldier in the service of Milan or Venice in earlier times. Unlike such men he did not arouse jealousy. This was because he did not break the solidarity of the governing class but came to reinforce it. In this he was characteristic of all the other captains who returned to Scotland intent on working for the extension of the power of their respective families. Abroad they had been accustomed to lay stress on their ancestry and on their noble blood. In consequence in so far as the National Covenant and later the Solemn League and Covenant were revolutionary, they marked the most conservative of revolutions. The Scottish veterans returned to their own country determined to secure authority in Scotland for those who had always held it. This was not an objective which could commend itself to Charles I or to Archbishop Laud.

Hitherto the great change in Scottish history had been the establishment of Presbyteranism; but this Faith, although in many respects the antithesis of Catholicism, had certain affinities with the Old Religion. The Church of Scotland was a convert-making and an apostate-rejecting body. It is remarkable how early in the history of the Kirk, and with what sincere abhorrence, the word "apostate" was brought into use. Quite apart from the civil effects of excommunication, the psychological consequences were very real. It is impossible to understand such a career as that of the Marquis of Montrose without meditating upon the nature of the weapons wielded by the Church of Scotland. In the Highlands the position was very different, but in the God-fearing Lowlands there was little support forthcoming for an excommunicated man. Scotland was marked by an intransigent conformity.

The northern kingdom was in many ways an old-fashioned polity. The feuds and jealousies and to a less extent the alliances were hereditary. The Reformation had thrown up no substantial body of "new men". Nearly all the families which manœuvred about the throne were only repeating the transient groupings of friendship and hostility which their ancestors had formed and dissolved throughout the last two centuries. In the middle of the fifteenth century the Earls of Douglas had been forfeited and early in the reign of James IV the power of the Macdonalds, Lords of the Isles, had been destroyed. For the rest the ancestral dynasties continued, aided by the fact that the great earldoms normally passed to the heirs-general thus ensuring the continuation of the entity even if in the hands of another stock. In this way the Gordons had acquired the earldom of Sutherland.

There was in general no lack of male heirs. The loyalty of the heads of cadet branches to their chief was very marked. There is ample evidence for such an admiring friendship towards the head of the house in the material that Mark Napier collected for the life of the young Montrose. It is worth noting that over the years a long subsisting rivalry was often an enduring factor like that which separated the House of Huntly from the Earls Marischal. Great Scottish families were in such cases polarised in opposition to one another; by contrast their attitude to the occupant of the throne and his policies was much more flexible.

B

The Highland clans remained remote from most men's calculations. They had played little part in the sixteenth century history of Scotland in so far as that centred upon the Stuart dynasty. They were hardly considered as a factor by those who framed the National Covenant. To the Earls of Argyll they were an ever-present preoccupation. With the exception of the Campbells no other considerable Covenanting leaders appear to have given thought to them until Montrose began his campaigning in the North. Current politics hardly reached them; they remained apart from these various conflicting forces which were brought to bear on the measures taken by King Charles I in Scotland. An exception must however be made in the case of those few chiefs of clans who had become hereditary Lords of Parliament. These, like the Frasers of Lovat, were inevitably involved with Lowland policies.

In the Western Highlands the chiefs had little contact with the South of Scotland and until the second half of the seventeenth century they remained largely untouched by those continental influences which in one shape or another did so much to mould the outlook of the governing classes that centred about Edinburgh.[1] Neither the French and Genevan Calvinist, nor the older French Catholic influence can be said to have affected them. Just as they were remote from continental education so also they were untouched by architectural developments and the whole southern manner of living. They were beyond the reach of that come-and-go of the rich lords who rode between Edinburgh and Aberdeen and onwards to Strathbogie or Dunrobin. Thus Torcastle had been built by Lochiel when James VI required him to erect a dwelling-house with an orchard, garden, pidgeon house, and other policies. This small castle and Ewen Cameron's spreading timber house in Lochaber reflected the withdrawn Highland life.

The Lowlands were represented in the Scottish Parliament on a fairly extensive scale, but this body bore very little resemblance to its English counterpart. Its work has not been made the subject of any authoritative modern study and the Scottish records appear to contain no body of comment on its influence and standing which can be compared with the mass of information relating to the contemporary English House of Commons.

The significant factor was not membership of the Scottish Parliament, but of the committee known as the Lords of the Articles which emerged from it. Professor C. S. Terry sets out[2] this point

[1] The Highland leaders had even less contact with England. Argyll had proposed that Ewen Cameron of Lochiel (b. 1629) should study at Oxford, but the plan did not materialise.

[2] *The Scottish Parliament,* Its Constitution and Procedure 1603-1707, by Charles Sanford Terry (1905), p. 155.

clearly. "The fact that until nearly the middle of the seventeenth
century Parliament was neither a deliberative nor a legislative
assembly supports the conclusion that its members were not called
upon individually to vote, except upon the election of the Lords
of the Articles."

The Scottish Parliament in the period between the Union of the
Crowns and the Act of Union consisted of a single chamber.
Before the outbreak of the Civil Wars the peers and higher clergy
sat by right of summons, while the officers of state attended as
nominees of the Crown. Under this ruling the High Treasurer,
Lord Privy Seal, Lord Clerk Register, Advocate, Lord Justice
Clerk and Treasurer Depute were almost invariably in attendance.[1]

The position of the barons of the shires and burgesses of the
royal burghs was very different from that of the other groupings.
The representatives of both shires and burghs were elected annually
irrespective of whether a Parliament was summoned or imminent.
The pocket borough was unknown for only the royal burghs enjoyed the franchise and their representation was confined to *bona
fide* burgesses and merchants.[2] It appears improbable that prior to
the Parliament of 1640 the private member either claimed or was
allowed to vote upon the measures ratified in his presence. The
situation is described[3] by Professor Terry. "He, or rather the
Estate of which he was a member, had delegated authority to
the Committee of the Articles and thereby stood committed to its
resolutions. The general members of the House remained merely
passive spectators of the Crown's assent to the legislative programme of the Articles." With this may be compared the judgment
formulated[4] by Professor Rait. "Throughout almost the whole
existence of Parliament, the Privy Council arranged the main
business which a Parliament or General Council was summoned to
transact." As late as the seventeenth century the Council is
described[5] as performing the functions of a lawgiver.

As a consequence there was no great prestige attached to
membership of Parliament except in the case of peers. Election did
not involve a widespread body of support. By the Act of 1587 a
county member could be elected by as few as six freeholders.
Further the northern and western shires had no representation
until about the middle of the seventeenth century.[6] Attendance at

[1] *Ibid.*, pp. 4 and 6.   [2] *Ibid.*, p. 17.
[3] *Ibid.*, p. 156.
[4] *The Parliaments of Scotland*, by Robert S. Rait (1924), p. 9.
[5] *Ibid.*, p. 10.
[6] In regard to the barons of the shires Orkney, Argyllshire, Sutherland and
Ross had no representation before 1612, 1630, 1639 and 1649 respectively.
Caithness appears to have been represented for the first time in 1644.
Cf. Terry, *op. cit.*, p. 20.

the convention of royal burghs was of more consequence to the mind of the burgesses than presence in a parliament. Over against both there stood the General Assembly of the Kirk of Scotland; but it seems clear that, apart from these bodies, the attention of the politically conscious section of the community was concentrated on the privy councillors. Under one aspect the history of the Scottish Kingship was that of a monarchy supported, frustrated or strangled by its hereditary advisers.

At the same time the placing of the various groups can be assessed exactly; it was not haphazard. Thus it may be said that the Earls of Argyll stood in a special relation to the Crown through the office of Justiciar of Scotland which they held. Heads of other great houses had some grant of regality like that accorded to the Earls of Huntly. Such nobles were concerned to maintain against more recent sovereigns the privileges with which they had been favoured by earlier kings.

In all the bonds of "man-rent" by which lesser chiefs bound themselves and their followers to some lord, the duty owed to the King was invariably excepted. Still it was a source of weakness for the dynasty that no lord could be defeated save at the hands of some equal, who had received a royal commission for this purpose. Especially in the long minorities there was a constant jealousy of any lord or group of lords under whose influence or control the King might fall. There was a constant seeking of alliances against one another and implicitly against their sovereign. The Lords had to bind themselves together so that none of their number might attack them on the King's behalf.

The question of religion must be envisaged against this complex background. Whatever were the wishes of the central government, it was hardly practicable to penetrate to the tenantry who served the great lords or the Highland chiefs. Thus we find in the circle of established leadership the existence of a Catholic "interest", politically conservative, allergic to the ethos of the New Religion but in the last analysis singularly indeterminate. This quality was the natural outcome of a politico-religious preference which could not issue in regular sacramental practice owing to the great scarcity of priests.

It is unlikely that the materials exist for any satisfactory account of the religious life of the north-western Highlands in the century that followed the Reformation. The question of the survival of priests and the degree to which they continued to officiate has never been studied. How, for instance, were funerals conducted in this region in the long years which elapsed between 1560 and the introduction of ministers of the Reformed Faith?

In the Lowlands the situation was quite different. There the existence of the Old Religion in such country districts as those under Maxwell influence and the survival of urban Catholicism in Edinburgh and Glasgow can both be traced. A strong Catholic life existed in the counties dominated by the House of Huntly.

There was, however, a marked unity among members of the ruling class in contact with government whether the individuals had a Catholic or a Protestant preference. Various factors contributed to this result. In the years before the Reformation the greater families had united in gathering to themselves the wide monastic properties. The practice of holding monasteries *in commendam* on the French model was very common. Twenty out of a total of twenty-seven members who sat in the Parliament of 1560 in virtue of the headship of religious houses were laymen and commendators. In consequence neither the Protestant nor the Catholic "interest" would permit the abrogation of the rights of abbots and priors to their seats. The retention of church lands so obtained was a dominant class interest.

While there was little religious neutrality in Scotland, the mentality of the *politiques* within the ruling group formed a bridge between the Catholic and Presbyterian positions. In the first period of the Reformation the career of Maitland of Lethington is a case in point. Here, too, the influence of French practice can be seen reflected. The political life of the Earl of Dunfermline, who was chancellor under James VI, provides an example of this standpoint. He was a statesman of continental sympathies whose dimmed Catholic preferences were combined with a sufficient measure of Presbyterian conformity.

The routine of contact among the great families, the long ceremonies of funeral and bridal which meant so much to them, were carried forward within a Presbyterian setting. It was only an occasional laird in a Catholic district who would, like Gordon of Gight, arrange a burial with the illegal rites of the Old Faith. The French alliance was now seen principally in terms of the Huguenot grouping. In the provinces a Calvinist governor like Duplessis Mornay at Saumur exerted an influence on the young Scots lords coming to his *château* and to the university which he had founded. Cardinal de Richelieu would not refuse a welcome to Scots gentlemen who accepted the Genevan Discipline. The wealthy Catholic families in the Lowlands, like the houses of Douglas and Seton, tended to acquiesce in the policy of the majority. The Catholic "interest" was dead in so far as it was linked with Spain or with the Spanish Netherlands.

The long reign of James VI had certainly contributed to this result. The need for conciliating Elizabeth I had always prevented any royal support for those lords who were inimical towards the Queen of England. In spite of feuds between the rival houses, King Charles was in the first place confronted by a relatively united body of Scottish peers.

One of the factors that brought them together was the King's project for endowing the bishoprics with land and the diocesans with office. The idea of the episcopate, regarded in its political aspect, had passed through distinct phases. In the first years after the victory of the Reformed Church the bishops served the purpose of a convenient administrative vehicle for conveying church lands to the noble families from which they sprang. It is true that the opposition to the bishops as such came in with Andrew Melville and not with Knox, who gave but little attention to this subject. Further the bishops, if regarded as visiting superintendents, aroused little political feeling. It was their re-introduction into Parliament as a separate entity upon which the King could rely and above all their new position on the privy council which ranged the body of the peers against them. As a result of contact with the English Court a very small number of peers were anglicised. There seem, however, to have been very few "episcopalian" peers in the sense of men who supported the politically privileged episcopate which Charles I and Archbishop Laud envisaged. Support for an explicit episcopalian tradition was for the most part centred on Aberdeen and came from quite another social grouping.

A significant element in the Scottish polity was the body of advocates practising at Edinburgh at the apex of whose profession stood the Court of Session. This court had been established by Parliament[1] in 1532, and since 1584 beneficed clergymen were no longer eligible for judgeships. The senators of the College of Justice were regarded as councillors and until 1626 were frequently summoned to take part in business that was not judicial in character. In this year the appointment of peers as ordinary lords of session was forbidden. It is, perhaps, from this period that there can be traced the gradual emergence of a Scottish *noblesse de robe*. The term is appropriate since the leading advocates both represented a distinct class and were closely associated with the peers. They were their agents in legal matters and in a wide sense their representatives in the capital. The profession was homogeneous and in time became at least in part hereditary.[2] Its members were con-

---

[1] Cf. "Foundation of the College of Justice" by R. K. Hannay, *Scottish Historical Review*, vol. xv (1947), pp. 30-46.

[2] Lord Cranstonriddell, appointed in 1597, seems to have been the first of the judges to be the son of a king's advocate. Sir James Skene, Lord Curriehill, appointed in 1612, was the son of a judge who bore the same title. His sister

nected by blood both with the Lowland lairds and with the Edinburgh burgess stocks. They were wholly within the Presbyterian cultural pattern. In a sense they were born intermediaries and under Charles I leading lawyers served as the chief link between the Covenanting peers and the Kirk. They gained from the ministers a trust that was accorded to no peer except Argyll. It follows that such men were inaccessible to the Court and that the King's methods were repugnant to them. Nevertheless they received their appointments from the fount of honour. It was, perhaps, their influence which enabled the Scottish leaders to support throughout the struggle the abstract concept of monarchy.

In contrast to the position of the lawyers the town middle class in Scotland had during these years a very limited political significance. Its activities were channelled within the convention of royal burghs and there was little contact between the various centres apart from these gatherings. At the same time even such a considerable town as Aberdeen was in effect dominated by the great families in that neighbourhood. On the other hand certain links bound together all literate Scotsmen and the Presbyterian ministers in part sprang from and in great measure relied on the allied burgess groupings. In general the middle class, except in Aberdeenshire, can be considered as acting on behalf of the claims of the Church of Scotland.

Although the Court was not closed to the members of the burgess stocks, no one from that grouping, churchmen apart, had played a significant *rôle* in the development of the Scottish monarchy. In Scotland there had been no counterpart either to Thomas Cromwell or to Gresham and Cranfield. By comparison with the standing of such men the political position of George Heriot, the goldsmith to James VI, was quite subordinate. Further, the class which in England provided the justices of the peace had not emerged north of the Border.

The King of Scotland was left alone with the magnates and their adherents. Although the line of the royal Stewarts was not sacrosanct, it had in fact not been assailed. Since the days of David Bruce Scotland had never been without her legitimate sovereign. The great lords acted always in the name of the King and in rare instances, such as the last period of the reign of James III, on behalf of the heir apparent. For more than two hundred years there had been a tradition of lawful kings and long minorities.

married Lord Foresterseat. Lord Durie, appointed in 1621, was a nephew of Lord Wrightlands and Patrick Nisbet Lord Eastbank, son of James Nisbet, a merchant in Edinburgh, was a cousin to both these lords of session. Cf. *An Historical Account of the Senators of the College of Justice* by George Brunton and David Haig (1836), *passim*.

The fortunes of the dynasty were sharply influenced by the changing policy of individual magnates. The position of the Campbells is a case in point. Until the reign of Charles I they had acted as hereditary and almost viceregal supporters of the royal house. It was the achievement of the Marquis of Argyll to bring the monarchy almost under tutelage and to foreshadow the later policy of his Whig successors.

During the seventeenth century the distinction between the Highlands and the Lowlands was less marked than had been the case in earlier centuries. Thus the recruitment for foreign service affected both sections of the country. From one angle Scotland could be divided into those regions whose chiefs had access to the central government and those occupied by stocks who were deprived of spokesmen. The McGregors and many of the Macdonalds were in this position. In these and similar instances the group of ruling but often mutually antagonistic families had succeeded in preventing any effective appeal by their enemies to the seat of power.

In a sense that hardly applied to any other sovereign state, the great lords from all parts of Scotland were of interest to the neighbouring foreign governments. In England throughout the reign of Elizabeth I this concern was limited to those powerful leaders who belonged to or were ready to come within the Protestant affiliation. This was likewise the case in regard to the contacts made by Henry IV, when King of Navarre; but the French government was in no way affected by any question of religious allegiance. Like other Powers they tended to woo the disaffected and, under Charles I, the disaffected lords were the leaders of the Covenant.

These contacts with magnates conceived as semi-independent were something very different from the routine bribery of privy councillors as practised by the Count of Gondomar in dealing with the English advisers of James I. Further, ease of communication with the Scottish leaders was assisted by the fact that for a century they had been the most travelled aristocracy in Europe. Links with the universities of Paris and Orleans and the presence of Scots guards and archers had preceded the connection formed through the two French marriages of James V; later this contact had been rendered closer since the reigning Queen of Scotland had resided for fourteen years at the Valois Court. The Scottish leaders placed value on both social and economic privileges and a course of travel to Paris and through the Huguenot towns was a normal conclusion of a Scottish peer's education. Padua and Venice and also sometimes Rome were visited by those whose fathers permitted extended travel. If Italy was included in the tour, Geneva was visited on the homeward journey.

There was a sense in which the Calvinism of the French lords
of the Religion was more akin to the attitude of the bulk of the
Scottish peers than was the religious standpoint of the English
Puritans. Neither the French nor the Scottish group could be
described as Puritan in the Sabbatarian sense of that expression;
they shared a tenacious and acquisitive conservatism; both sets
approved of much mundane display. What they had in common
with the English Parliamentarians and indeed also with the
Lutheran world upon the Continent was a resolute opposition to
the grant of political power to any churchman.

Compared to England or France, Scandinavia exerted a very
subordinate influence[1] on Scotland, but the extent has not yet
been assessed. To give one example, the effect of the architecture
of late sixteenth century Danish castles on Scottish building awaits
examination. It is possible that ideas were brought back by the
embassy that went to fetch Queen Anne of Denmark. There was
regular traffic to the Sound and between East Scotland and the
Baltic ports.

The Scottish staple had been long established at Campvere, but
contacts with the Netherlands appear to have meant little in
Scottish life apart from specifically commercial exchanges. The
influential Scotsmen abroad were not the members of the small
merchant body but the officers in foreign service, and principally
those who had enlisted to support the Protestant cause. The
soldiers of fortune in Vienna were few when compared with all
those who followed the King of Sweden.

Scotland, viewed from the political angle, was an uneasy
amalgam of great lords and their supporters, chief among whom
were the gentlemen with military experience. In their search for
the increase and maintenance of power and landed wealth the
chiefs took up varying positions. The greatest among them were
in conflict with one another or in jealous and uncordial alliance.
They were confronted by a kingship which was relatively weak
and had always been compelled to rule through the instrumentality
of various members of their own group. The middle class bureau-
cracy, which during the seventeenth century was emerging in
France and England, did not exist in Scotland. On the other hand
there had come into this situation the organised power of the
Scottish Kirk, whose ministers were coming to fulfil some of the
functions of a *bourgeoisie*. Thus they had often both a determined
capacity for self-expression and a legalistic background which

[1] As far as the Court contacts were concerned, James V had married successively Madeleine of Valois and the Duchess of Longueville, James II
married Marie of Gueldres, James I and James IV made English marriages,
James III and James VI married princesses of Denmark.

alike pre-supposed a considerable standard of education. They also received the support of lawyers.

Perhaps there could be no peace between an authoritarian Crown and the magnates with their bastard feudalism and a Kirk which was theocratic in its principles. It is possible that peace was impracticable between any two of these three interests.

An examination of the King's attitude towards his Scottish subjects, and an indication of the very strict limits of his experience and understanding of Scottish matters, will throw light on the whole course of the coming conflict. Although born at Dunfermline and created Duke of Albany[1] on the day of his baptism, Charles I had little knowledge of conditions of life in Scotland. He was brought south at the age of four and did not return for nearly thirty years. In different ways both the sons of James I were absorbed into the English life. It may be said that the Prince of Wales lost his sense of Scotland in his absorption in his Elizabethan heritage. The younger brother was primarily affected by the religious and political teachings which his father encouraged him to adopt; he was moreover insulated by his shyness and reserve.

He had a reverence for his father's practices and it seems that he conceived of himself as completing his work, but he had none of the old King's fatigued hard-won experience. He was driven by an implacable sense of duty and his conception of kingship was never in accord with the actual shape of affairs in Scotland. Some comments may be made upon the tangled background.

At the accession of Charles I the heads of the two Scottish houses most nearly related to the sovereign were both minors,[2] James fourth Duke of Lennox and James third Marquis of Hamilton. As the only surviving adult male of the line of the Stuarts of Lennox the King was according to Scots law the guardian and tutor of the Duke and his brothers. Sir Philip Warwick remarked[3] in comparing these two young lords that Lennox was the "greater man," a comment which is accurate in so far as it refers to the prestige of a Scottish, and later of an English dukedom. In all other respects the Marquis of Hamilton was the more significant

[1] Prince Charles was born on 19 November 1600 and created Duke of Albany on 23 December 1600; his elder brother Prince Henry was born on 19 February 1594 and became Duke of Rothesay at birth. Their father King James VI and I succeeded to the English throne on 28 April 1603.

[2] The Duke of Lennox was born on 6 April 1612 and succeeded on his father's death on 30 July 1624. The Marquis of Hamilton was born on 19 June 1606 and inherited on 2 March 1625. Charles I came to the throne on 27 March of the same year.

[3] Warwick, *Memoirs of the Court of Charles I*, p. 105.

figure with the wide friendship and alliance possessed by his family in the northern kingdom.

It is, perhaps, as well to set out in some detail the rather complicated position in regard to the right of succession to the Crown of Scotland. The head of the House of Hamilton was recognised as the next heir after the King's sister and her children. This claim originated in the marriage of Lord Hamilton with the daughter of James II, and between the death of the Duke of Albany in 1536 and the birth of Henry Duke of Rothesay in 1594, the head of the Hamiltons, the Duke of Chatelherault and then his eldest son, had been the next heir[1] to the throne.

This situation had drawn the Hamilton kinship close together, but it had likewise aroused a constant suspicion in the minds of their rivals. At the same time their own position had been challenged. The complicated marriages and liaisons of Chatelherault's father had thrown a measure of doubt on the former's legitimacy. Could this legitimacy be successfully impugned, the claim would pass to Chatelherault's aunt the Countess of Lennox[2] and thence to the Stuarts of the Lennox line.

It would seem that Charles I had learned from his father that deference to the great Scottish families which neither would accord to the leaders of the English peerage. The prestige of the Scots monarchy had not recovered from the double failure of the old royal house and of the male line of Robert Bruce. The Stuarts were only one among other noble families and they were hemmed round by those who shared their ancestry, Stewarts of Atholl, Ochiltree, Traquair, Blantyre.[3] The monarchy had not recovered from the weakness of the early Stuarts and the long captivity of James I. Throughout the fifteenth and sixteenth centuries parties drawn from among the noble families had ruled during seven

[1] Except for a few days in December 1542 and again in 1566-7. James second Earl of Arran, great-grandson of James II, was known after 1549 by his French title of Duke of Chatelherault or Châtellerault. On his death in 1575 his claim passed to his son the third Earl of Arran.

[2] Elizabeth Countess of Lennox was a grand-daughter of James II. Among her grandsons were Matthew fourth Earl of Lennox, the father of Darnley, and John Stuart d'Aubigny, the father of Esmé first Duke of Lennox.

[3] The Stewarts of Avandale and Ochiltree were descended from a legitimated son of Murdoc second Duke of Albany (d. 1402). The Stewarts of Atholl, extinct in 1625, were descended from the eldest son of Sir James Stewart, the Black Knight of Lorne, by his marriage to Joanna widow of James I. The Stewarts of Buchan, extinct in 1580, were descended from Sir James Stewart's second son. The Stewarts of Traquair were descended from a natural son of the first Earl of Buchan. The mother of the first Earl of Traquair was a Stewart of Ochiltree. The Stewarts of Blantyre were cadets of the Garlies family later Earls of Galloway, but the ancestry of their progenitor Sir William Stewart (d. 1402) of Jedworth is uncertain.

successive royal minorities. No sovereign since the fourteenth
century had come as an adult to the Scottish Throne.

The tradition of royal authority had been further weakened by
the respect with which King James VI and I regarded the legal
rights of the high baronage. Thus from 1585 until 1590 he was
engaged in a suit at law to claim the position of heir-general to the
Earls of Angus. He made this claim as the representative of his
grandmother the Countess of Lennox, who was the only surviving
child of Archibald sixth Earl of Angus. The case was decided
against the King on the grounds that Lady Lennox had surrendered
her rights in order to conciliate the Earl of Morton[1] when her
son Darnley married the Queen of Scots. The mere fact of bringing
the case throws a light upon King James's attitude. He had been
surrounded by great families who never ceased to count upon the
royal forbearance.

It was a consequence of this situation that the relations between
the first Marquis of Argyll and his eldest son with the successive
Stuart Kings had a detachment which has no counterpart in
English politics. McCailein Mor could not forget that he was
"eighth man from Robert Bruce".[2]

Besides, the general position was affected by that family feeling
which in different ways was so strongly marked a characteristic
of both James I and his second son. They were united in a sense
of responsibility towards and affection for the Stuarts of Lennox-
Aubigny. It was not in James I to forget how much he owed to
Esmé Stuart, who came from France when the young King was
sixteen and taught him all that he would ever know about the
customs and manners of the Valois Court. At the same time King
James differed from his successor in having an abiding and
proprietary affection for those of his intimates whose fortune he
had created. The right to the Lennox lands in Scotland, the
dukedom of Richmond, the earldoms of Richmond and Newcastle-
upon-Tyne and March, the barony of Settrington[3] and every acre
of the estates in England had been the direct fruit of his goodwill.

---

[1] The Regent Morton and his elder brother David Earl of Angus were sons
of George Douglas of Pittendriech and first cousins to Lady Lennox.

[2] The first Marquis was in fact fifth in descent from Archibald second Earl
of Argyll, grandson of John Steward second Lord Lorne. He was eighth *man*
in descent if the distaff generations are omitted.

[3] The earldom of Richmond and the barony of Settrington were created in
1613 and the dukedom of Richmond and the earldom of Newcastle-upon-
Tyne in 1623 all in favour of the second Duke of Lennox, and became extinct
on his death. The earldom of March was created in 1619 for the third Duke
of Lennox and the dukedom of Richmond was revived in favour of the fourth
Duke of Lennox in 1641.

Both the Stuart sovereigns were in turn guardians to a generation of the House of Lennox. Both generations were partly French;[1] Royalist to the core; in religious matters pliable and accommodating. The youngest generation had a gallantry and a vivacity, an air of the Court,[2] which was very different from the outlook of their Scottish neighbours. The Stuarts of Lennox had younger sons, but they had no cadet branches, no supporting lairds or kinsmen. Neither the sons nor the daughters were really acclimatised in Scotland with the sole exception of the Countess of Mar. They brought into the Erskine and Gordon families a direct French inheritance as well as that Stuart blood which Charles I, like his father, so greatly prized. In examining the Scottish scene it is noteworthy that it was this family alone that Charles I received into a deep protective intimacy.

In all other cases the King approached the circle of the rich Scottish lords not as a series of family groups but as a succession of individuals, giving, retracting and re-conferring his aloof confidence according to his view of their use and merit. Except for the few peers of the second rank who came with some regularity to the English Court,[3] the King was without knowledge of the personal background and family history of his great Scottish subjects. King James had intervened familiarly in the question of their marriages, but his son had no contact with such matters. The marriages in which he interested himself were within the closed and private circle of his own courtiers; the brother and sisters of the fourth Duke of Lennox married in England.[4]

The third Marquis of Hamilton was for long the King's chosen instrument in Scottish affairs, but this did not imply any appreciation of the *rôle* of the Hamilton kindred or any comprehension of the ties by which the Marquis was assisted or hampered. Men always came before King Charles as individuals to be evaluated by the impression made in the series of interviews which it was his royal duty to conduct. It would have helped the King if he could have understood any of those who upheld the Presbyterian system. In this he was at a disadvantage when compared with his father for any personal attachment to Presbyterian values proved a barrier to his confidence. A link with Hamilton and Lanark was the fact

[1] The first Duke of Lennox was the son of John Stuart by Anne de la Queille and married Catherine daughter of Guillaume de Balsac, Seigneur d'Entragues. The Stuarts of Aubigny were thus cousins to Henriette de Balsac d'Entragues, Marquise de Verneuil, mistress of Henri IV.
[2] Cf. Vandyck's well-known portrait of Lord John and Lord Bernard Stuart.
[3] There were often English connections to explain these contacts. Roxburgh and his second wife had been attached to the Court of James I. Carnwath's second wife was English as was Lady Nithsdale, a relative of Buckingham's.
[4] Except Anne who became the wife of Lord Angus.

that their religious attitude was diffusedly Protestant. Both
brothers seem to have viewed the Kirk and kirkmen with a care-
lessness which the King could understand. It was the Presbyterianism of their fierce old mother and some of their kindred which
remained beyond his grasp. It is doubtful if the King understood
any man who stood by a firm adherence to the General Assembly
of the Kirk of Scotland.

In this respect the outlook of Queen Henrietta was rather
different. As a daughter of Henry of Navarre she had been
familiar from childhood with the great Calvinist families of her
own country. Her friend Lady Derby came from just that *milieu*
and in later life she showed much kindness to such a resolute
Presbyterian as the Countess of Balcarres. It did not seem strange
to her that the Scots should be unwilling to welcome Archbishop
Laud. This point is merely noted. Except perhaps after Naseby,
it was without effect on the royal policies. The standpoint originated in a lack of seriousness in the Queen's attitude towards the
Church of England.

Under one aspect the failure of understanding between the King
and his influential Scottish subjects was the result of almost complete absence of contact. Except for his coronation journey in
1633, the King did not go north in the earlier part of his reign and
for some years prior to his accession a Scotsman could hardly
hope to make his fortune in England. Since the rise to favour of
the Duke of Buckingham the chances open to Scotsmen had been
restricted; the Court of Charles I was singularly devoid of opportunities for their advancement.

A study of this period leaves the impression that the King as a
person was a cypher as far as the Scottish leaders, Hamilton always
excepted, were concerned. Even his own agents, like Traquair,
fumbled in their dealings with him. The bishops, at least those
who had been appointed by King James, had an understanding of
their old master but very little knowledge of the new sovereign.
It was, perhaps, Hamilton's misfortune that he knew the King
too well.

This failure of contact has its bearing upon the revolutionary
character of the Scottish action. During the long royal minorities
groups of the chief lords had ruled and pillaged Scotland, while
when the sovereign was an adult there were different methods of
exerting pressure. For both King and nobles it had been a tangled
life with plotting at close quarters such as the detail of the Gowrie
Conspiracy indicates. It may be said that James VI was adept at
this in-fighting. Such methods entailed go-betweens; interviews;
sharp bargaining. There was, however, no traditional method by

which the baronial leaders could bring leverage to bear upon an absent monarch.

For his part Charles I ruled through the Privy Council of Scotland without seemingly giving much thought to precedents and anomalies. He had a fatal capacity for giving offence in ignorance. It is very doubtful if it occurred to him how deeply he was wounding the Scottish peers when he appointed Archbishop Spottiswoode as chancellor in 1635. The same effect resulted when he nominated additional bishops to the privy council. All groups of laymen were united when their sphere of influence and profit was narrowed by this action on the part of the Crown.

It was hard for Charles I to understand the reaction of the laity to the confidence which he reposed in the episcopate. The attitude of respect which he maintained towards the bishops seemed to the great lords to be unkingly and unnatural. He did not use them as his own high servants according to the traditions of mediæval kingship; he treated them with a serene consideration which was inexplicable. It is very doubtful if any of the bishops, except those three or four whom he nominated towards the end on Laud's advice, could feel at ease with the reverence which the distant King accorded them. Those who survived from his father's reign had little in common with their grave sovereign. They were for the most part men of birth who had inherited or acquired some landed property. Their interests were bound up with whatever group of the great families they were linked to by patronage or kinship.

The career of George Graeme or Graham, successively Bishop of Dunblane and Orkney[1] from 1602 to 1638, is characteristic of this somewhat ancestral type of Scottish churchman. It is worth setting out the detail. Graeme was a younger son of Inchbrakie, one of the cadet branches of the House of Montrose. After his father's death his mother had married another laird of the same stock, Graham of Balgowan. The Bishop's wife was a daughter of Sir Robert Crichton of Clunie and throughout his life Inchbrakie and Balgowan aided his children. The third Earl of Montrose was cordial and granted him certain lands within the lordship of Huntingtower.[2] Bishop Graeme's predecessor in the diocese of Dunblane

---

[1] Neither the dates of his birth nor death are known, but he graduated at St. Andrews in 1587. He was translated to Orkney from Dunblane on 26 August 1615 and, according to the *Handbook of British Chronology*, Royal Historical Society 1939, died before 19 December 1643.

[2] *Some Letters and Correspondence of George Graeme*, ed. L. G. Graeme, Miscellany of the Scottish History Society, vol. ii, p. 234. Graeme's stepfather John Graham of Balgowan was one of those who pressed him to accept the bishopric of Dunblane in 1602, *ibid*, p. 233.

had been his grand-uncle Andrew Graham.[1] A maternal uncle Peter Rollock, a cadet of the Rollos of Duncrub, held the diocese of Dunkeld, but in this case merely as administrator of the temporalities of that dilapidated see. The Bishop had a hearty concern for the care of his family. He appointed guardians and accepted guardianships; he was tutor to the Smyths of Braco.[2] At the beginning of King Charles's reign he purchased the barony of Gorthie in Strathearn from his kinsmen the Murrays of Tullibardine[3] as a provision for his heir. Later he bought the estates of Graemeshall and Breckness for his two younger sons.[4] He hoped that his uncle the former Bishop of Dunkeld, who had become a lord of session and had no legitimate children, would provide for his youngest daughter Jean.[5] He was a cheerful contentious parent[6] anxious about his daughters' marriages.[7] Bishop Graeme appears as a shrewd and kindly man in no way rigorist,[8] very generous to his neighbours and fully appreciating the assured place which he held in the social fabric. He was cordial towards the bishops of his own standing and was an intimate friend in his later years of Alexander

[1] From 1487 until the Reformation the see of Dunblane had been held in succession by three members of the Chisholm family. From 1575 until 1594 the temporalities of the diocese had been administered by Andrew Graham the youngest son of the first Earl of Montrose, *ibid.*, p. 233 and H.B.C., p. 221.

[2] *Correspondence of George Graeme*, pp. 249-54. Patrick Smyth eventually became the Bishop's son-in-law, *ibid.*, p. 238.

[3] The purchase of Gorthie is dealt with in three letters written between 8 January and 26 March 1630, a fourth letter on the same subject is undated, *ibid.*, pp. 253-66. Lord Tullibardine was cautioner for Sir David Murray who was then lately dead. The lands of Gorthie were in the possession of the latter's brother Sir William Murray of Abercairny. Sir William Murray of Tullibardine and Sir Andrew Murray of Arngask, father of Bishop Graeme's friend Lord Scone, both married daughters of the second Earl of Montrose.

[4] Between 1621 and 1630 he purchased Graemeshall which was inherited by his second son Patrick Graeme, minister of Holm, and Breckness which passed to the fourth son John, *ibid.*, p. 239.

[5] In the letter will made on his translation to Orkney the Bishop states "Item my doghter Jeane to Mr Jhon Rollok and to the consideratione of My L of Piltone my Unkill, for he vantis bairnis and scho is my datir", *ibid.*, p. 249.

[6] In the postscript of a letter dated 2 March 1630 to his eldest son David Graeme the Bishop wrote "wret man, to reid your letters all the clerks in the towne must be convende, wret better and spell better in Gods name", *ibid.*, p. 258.

[7] Letter to David Graeme dated 8 January 1630, "I knaw not how your sister Marion her tocher can be used to that purpose of Gorthe, for I wold wish to be quyt of her, *primo quoque tempore*", *ibid.*, p. 254.

[8] When staying at Glasgow the Bishop was attacked by the Presbyterian party for curling on the ice on Sunday, *ibid.*, p. 237. In referring to the cargo of a Dutch vessel bound for Kirkwall he wrote, "I luike for a punschen of sak, some resinges, Tobacco and sik uther trittel trattelles", *ibid.*, pp. 238-9.

THE MARQUIS OF ARGYLL

Lindsay of Dunkeld.[1] The impression which both Graeme and Lindsay leave is that of magistrates and administrators of Christian principles conscious of their standing among the middle baronage. In matters of social custom they seem to have held by the traditions of an older Scotland. Such characters would have had but little in common with the English Primate, nor with the sovereign who had brought him to Canterbury.

It was the King's constant tendency to underestimate the solidarity of Scottish life; he was without experience of the clan system or of that pattern of entrenched alliances that bound together the great Lowland families. The relationship of a cadet to the head of his house was foreign to the King's whole outlook. A letter from Bishop Graeme to his eldest son bears on this point. "I beseik thee," he wrote,[2] "medill (meddle) not with ony thing that direcly, or indirekly, may tuich my lord Tulybarin; for thou knawis it hes ever bene my mynd to serve and desyr all myne to serve thos (people) quhen I am dead." This open profession of a determination to serve the House of Tullibardine was not what the King looked for from his bishops. Charles I seems never to have grasped the degree in which Scotsmen of the ruling class would stand together.

They were bound together like a grape vine and the matters which united them lay beyond his sympathies. Their ties and loyalties drew them into coherent groups even when these were opposed to one another. These groups were linked by blood or by ancestral service. Even before the strife it was clear that leaders like Huntly and Argyll could call many swordsmen. This was a very different matter from that self-chosen affinity which bound the Opposition Lords together in the southern kingdom. The King was not trained to appreciate these Scottish factors.

Sometimes the men of rank who supported their sovereign's policies were themselves outside the main stream of privileged Scottish life like the Marquis of Douglas, who was separated from the majority of his equals in the Lowlands by his Catholicism. In general Charles I could best understand those who, like himself, were immune from the effects of Presbyterian conviction. He could not appreciate the appeal that the General Assembly of the Kirk made to many Scotsmen; in consequence he was never really on terms with its steadfast supporters. He could more easily grasp the standpoint of those who may be called the marginal Presbyterians, men of a general Protestant conviction who were yet

[1] Alexander Lindsay, Bishop of Dunkeld from 1611 until 1638, was a younger brother of Lindsay of Evelick, a cadet of the Crawford family. The Bishop's sons inherited the estates of Evelick and Kilspindie and his daughters were married to John Lundie of Lundie and Sir Patrick Balfour of Hay.

[2] *Ibid.*, p. 401.

C

ready to harbour that suspicion of the Kirkmen which their sovereign found so natural.

Like many religious men he understood those who were indifferent in doctrinal questions better than he did those who were opposed to his own system. Thus the King was on easy terms with the second Marquis of Huntly who had something of that scepticism which was a characteristic of a section of the English courtiers. Besides, Charles I appreciated his withdrawn dignity.

It was alleged by Patrick Gordon of Ruthven that Huntly had yielded to what he termed "that English divell, keeping of state".[1] His friends and clansmen resented[2] the distance at which he kept them. "He was knowen," wrote Gordon,[3] "to be both affable, courteous and sociable before he was called to court; his breiding in Ingland, the habit and longe custom he gott there, owercam and whollie changed his naturall inclination." The King's understanding of the Marquis of Huntly has a bearing on his failure in other quarters. Gordon's comment on both men is also revealing as indicating the impression created on one group among his near contemporaries. "Never two," he writes[4] of Charles I and Huntly, "lived in an age that went neirer to be one in abilities, both of bodie and mynd; they warr both near about one pitch, of one stature, of one strength, of one activitie, of one constitution, both melancholians, borne under Saturne."

In spite of his birth in Scotland, Charles I represented English life in its most complicated and unappealing form. It probably did not occur to him that his northern subjects regarded England as a rich and ruthless country. The rudimentary character of the Scottish constitution, the failure to assess support or to appreciate the clan and kinship system were relatively minor matters. The root cause of the King's failure lay in his inability to estimate the nature, the appeal or the intentions of the Church of Scotland.

[1] A Short Abridgment of Britain's Distemper from the yeare of God MDCXXXIX to MDCXLIX. By Patrick Gordon of Ruthven, Spalding Club, 1844, p. 75. This account was written under the Commonwealth.

[2] "With a certaine kynde of reserved inclinatione, he seemed desyrous to keip a distance with his inferiours, without distinctione of qualitie; for freinds and followers were equalled with domestickes", ibid., p. 229.

[3] Ibid., p. 230.   [4] Ibid., p. 231.

CHAPTER II

THE PRESBYTERIANS

IT is not altogether easy to reconstruct the lineaments of the Church of Scotland in her heyday. The Calvinism of the early seventeenth century had never known disaster; many men had been seized by its unfailing convictions of Reprobation and Election, very few had as yet withdrawn their adhesion to these twin doctrines. Presbyterianism was essentially a creed that was victorious. The Presbyterian polity carried with it a conscious recognition of its own truth. It had an assurance which was bound up with the fact that it had kept itself unspotted from the world. Its ministers had not as yet accepted a defeat. They were united in an angry contempt for all Erastian compromises. It was, perhaps, this factor which made the struggle between Andrew Melville and the Crown so deeply significant. The essential point in the conflict was that he had not yielded.

The Presbyterian attitude to the Old Religion was unequivocal. It does not seem that it admitted of shades of feeling. Popery was symbolised by the Beast of the Apocalypse. The Pope was anti-Christ. These views were held with an evangelical fervour. It would appear that individual ministers and elders who had a kindly feeling for their Catholic neighbours are not found among those who gave unfeigned support to the Solemn League and Covenant. Such more friendly thoughts are found in individuals at a later period when the Church of Scotland had undergone the chastening experiences consequent upon her political downfall.

The attitude towards Anglicans and Lutherans was coloured by a sharp distaste for the Erastian elements present in the leadership of both these creeds. The Church of England neither possessed nor desired to possess the political power wielded by the Presbyterians at the zenith of their influence. The fact that excommunication, when exercised by the Church of Scotland, carried civil effects equivalent to outlawry[1] gave the ministers an unassailable position. The strength of this position and the popular

---

[1] A comment by William Law Mathieson bears on this point. "But the most effective way in which the State assisted the spiritual Power was by attaching civil penalties to the sentence of excommunication. In this respect the Reformed Church merely served itself heir to the legal endowment of its Catholic predecessor", *Politics and Religion*, vol. i, p. 187. This parallel omits various essential factors.

support that it received, especially in the south-west of Scotland, gave rise to a confident intransigence. Still this was a Christian intransigence enlightened by enthusiasm. The fatigue which later in the seventeenth century was to assail all the Churches was not yet apparent. In the days of the Solemn League and Covenant the doctrine of Election imparted a dynamic quality into the Kirkmen's attitude.

A very clear impression of the religious outlook of the period is given in *The Last and Heavenly Speeches and glorious Departure of John, Viscount Kenmure,* an account by Samuel Rutherford of the deathbed of the young head of the Gordons of Lochinvar, who had been all his life a devoted Presbyterian. The short nervous sentences recall vividly the scenes in the Place of Kenmure in the first days of September, 1634.

"I dare speak nothing to you," began[1] the minister on approaching the dying man, "but one thing, the wrath and ire of God Almighty." The next sentence sets the tone for the whole passage. "My Lord hearing this with tears cried out so, that they heard him in the withdrawing room (of the Place of Kenmure) and in all the houses about." It seems that Lord Kenmure was troubled in conscience owing to what he held to be his weakness in withdrawing from Parliament to avoid opposing the King about religion. His own attitude in regard to his sovereign's innovations was crystal-clear. "Being asked what was his judgment anent the ceremonies now entered in the Kirk of God, he answered,[2] 'I think, and am persuaded in my conscience, they are superstitious, idolatrous and antichristian, and come from hell; and I repute it a mercy that my eyes shall not see the desolation that shall come upon this poor church. It's plain Popery that is coming among you'."

The remarks on his deathbed are very pithy and throw an interesting light on social custom. "To two gentlemen neighbours.[3] 'It is not rising soon in the morning, and running out to the park and stone dyke, that will bring peace to the conscience when it comes to this part of the play.' To his cousin[4] he said, 'Serve the Lord, and follow not the footsteps of your father-in-law (for he had married the Bishop of Galloway's daughter). Learn to know that you have a soul'." Among his visitors were his sister Lady Herries and her husband, the latter a Catholic. His comments to these relatives were explicit.[5] "To a lord, that was his brother-in-law.

---

[1] *The last and heavenly speeches of John Viscount Kenmure* in Select Biographies, vol. i, edited for the Wodrow Society by the Rev. W. K. Tweedie (1845), p. 392. An edition was printed at Edinburgh in 1649.
[2] *Ibid.,* p. 397.   [3] *Ibid.,* p. 401.
[4] *Ibid.,* p. 394.   [5] *Ibid.,* pp. 398, 399.

'Mock not at my counsel, My Lord. . . . Your soul is builded upon a sandy foundation. When you come to my estate, you will find no comfort in your religion.' To a lady, that was his own sister. 'Who knows, sister, if the words of a dying brother may prevail with a living sister. Alas! you incline to a rotten religion.[1] . . . The half of the world is ignorant and goeth to hell, and knoweth not that they have a soul; it is a wonder to see any to know that they have a soul: read the Scriptures. They are plain Scottish language to all who desire wisdom from God.' "

Lord Kenmure's speeches to his coachman and to his household servants are most revealing. "He said to his coachman.[2] 'You will go now to any man that will give you most hire; but do not do so. Go where ye may get best company: though you get less wages, yet will you get the more grace (he made him hold up his hand and promise before God to do so) because your calling is subject to drunkenness and company.' He spoke ordinarily to all the boys of the house,[3] servants, butlers, cooks, omitting none saying 'Learn to serve and fear the Lord. . . . Your pastors and guides mislead you. They are but a pack of dumb dogs. Use the means yourself, and win to some sense of God, and pray as you can morning and evening'."

His final words[4] to the general body of those around him are in the classic Christian tradition. "After he had exhorted many friends and servants, as they were going out of the chamber, he said to them, 'Stay, Sirs, I have somewhat yet to say. Be not deceived with the world; for me I have played the fool, and brought the House of Kenmure to the perfection of a complete fabric, as it was never before, and busied myself exceedingly; and when I came to the top of my hopes, and thought to enjoy them, the Lord came and plucked me from my hopes; thereafter I did see my own folly'."

There is a record[5] of what was almost his last sentence. "The devil and temptations took me such a nick as I could not win by unhurt; but, oh! strong, strong Jesus. O the deep of his love that would not want (fail) me." He then called to his Lady, and a gentleman who was a friend to his Lady and had come from the East country a good way to visit him with the pastor. Lord Kenmure departed this life on 12th September about the setting of the sun.

This account suggests some points of interest. Kenmure had lived as a youth with John Welch at St. Jean d'Angély. He was

---

[1] Lady Herries is referred to as "a Papist", *ibid.*, p. 406.
[2] *Ibid.*, p. 403. [3] *Ibid.*, p. 405.
[4] *Ibid.*, p. 404. [5] *Ibid.*, p. 397.

familiar with the Reformed Church in France. His thought was
impregnated with a strict Calvinism. He had built up his house
and had obtained his viscountcy; he was dying without a son.[1] He
did not consider that his household would be kept up to the
standard which he had developed;[2] he was leaving his wife to a
devout widowhood. Lady Kenmure was one of the sisters of the
great Marquis of Argyll and the reference of Samuel Rutherford
to the gentleman who was her friend would appear to suggest one
of those spiritual intimacies which were becoming a pattern for a
Presbyterian lady of quality. This was a world in which there was
a strong tradition of marital fidelity among the women and in
which men thought no evil.

The relation of the minister to the patroness owed something to
the example of French Calvinism. The spiritual friendship between
Jeanne d'Albret and her religious advisers can be regarded as its
prototype. It was ministers who could speak most freely to the
Queen of Navarre. A letter of roughly the same date can be set
beside the Rutherford account to indicate the gentler manner of
certain preachers when dealing with a great lady confirmed in
Grace. "The Lords worke prospereth gratiouslie in this countrey,"
wrote[3] the Reverend Josias Welch to the Countess of Eglinton, "it
flourisheth indeed lyke the palme tree: and even this last sabath
in Antrim, ane English congregation, the superstitious forme of
kneelyng at the sacrament put away and the true paterne of the
institution directlye followed." He went on to point out that "in
this little church (of Templepatrick), Sunday was senyght, wee had
above fourteen or fifteen hundreth at the sacrament." The conclusion sets the tone. "As for you, elect ladye, what shal I say to
you but what the Apostle sayeth to the Thessalonians I, 5 ch.,
24 v."

Undoubtedly much of the spiritual direction was given by word
of mouth, but a clear impression of the general standpoint can be
obtained from that section of the letters of Samuel Rutherford
which deal with this subject. The greater number are addressed
either to Lady Kenmure, both during her married life and widowhood, or to Marion M'Naught, a cousin of Kenmure's, who was
the wife of William Fullerton, Provost of Kirkcudbright. A freedom from constraint may be noted in his letters to Marion

[1] His widow gave birth to a posthumous son who was christened on 10
December 1634 and died as a child of five.

[2] Lord Kenmure does not seem to have considered that his widow would
require the luxury of a permanent coachman.

[3] Letter dated 1630 printed in *Memorials of the Earls of Eglinton* by Sir
William Fraser, vol. i, p. 225.

M'Naught, which was not always present[1] in his correspondence with the richer woman. Rutherford moved seldom; his childhood had been passed in the Border country; his studies made at Edinburgh.[2] The whole series was in fact composed either at Anwoth, where he had become minister in 1627, or at Aberdeen, where he was removed by order of the Court of High Commission in August, 1636. The last letter of this group was dated[3] from the latter city on 4 January, 1638. Some quotations will indicate the line of thought.

It will be simplest to begin with the letter on Lord Kenmure's death which Rutherford addressed to his widow. It breathes the spirit of his own account of the Viscount's last days. "Your Lord and lover," he wrote,[4] "hath graciously taken out your husband's name and your name out of the summonses that are raised at the instance of the terrible, sin-revenging Judge of the world against the house of the Kenmures." Later he was more consoling. "I verily think[5] that Christ hath said, 'I must needs-force have Jean Campbell for myself'; and He hath laid many oars in the water to fish and hunt home-over your heart to heaven." The *motif* of a legally binding act in the spiritual order is recurrent.[6] "The great Messenger[7] of the Covenant preserve you in body and spirit," and again "Fasten your[8] grips upon the heritage; and our Lord Jesus make the charters sure, and give your Ladyship to grow as a palm-

[1] "Madam", Rutherford wrote to Lady Kenmure from Anwoth on 15 November 1633 about nine months before her husband's death, "it is a part of the truth of your profession to drop words in the ears of your noble husband continually of eternity, judgment, death, hell, heaven, the honourable profession, the sins of his father's house. He must reckon with God for his father's debt: forgetting of accounts payeth no debt", *Letters of Samuel Rutherford*, ed. by Rev. Andrew I. Bonnar (1894), Letter xxx, p. 91.

[2] Much obscurity surrounds Rutherford's early years. He was born at Nisbet in the modern parish of Crailing in Roxburghshire about 1600. He was about fifteen years younger than Marion M'Naught. He is said to have been educated at Jedburgh and he certainly entered the University of Edinburgh in 1617. Cf. *Life of Samuel Rutherford* by Thomas Murray (1828) and *D.N.B.* vol. 1, pp. 7-9.

[3] Letter cclxxxi, addressed to Lord Loudoun, *ibid.*, p. 545.

[4] Letter xxxvii, dated 14 September 1634, *ibid.*, pp. 100-1. Rutherford seems always conscious that she was Lady Jean Campbell with the political significance that this implied.

[5] Letter ccv. from Aberdeen in 1637, *ibid.*, pp. 402-3. It is superscribed "For the Right Honourable my Lady Viscountess of Kenmure.

[6] Cf. Letter xxix, addressed to Marion M'Naught from Anwoth on 20 August 1633. "Christ got a charter of Scotland from His Father; and who will bereave him of His heritage, or put our Redeemer out of His mailing, until his tack be run out", *ibid.*, p. 89.

[7] Letter vii, for Lady Kenmure dated at Anwoth 1 February 1630, *ibid.*, p. 48.

[8] Letter xxxv, dated from Anwoth on 29 April 1634, *ibid.*, p. 99.

tree on God's mount Zion, howbeit shaken with winds, yet the root is fast." It seems that analogies were suggested by the open country of his native Teviotdale and the burns which came down from the moors. "I desire not to go[1] on the lee-side or sunny side of religion, or to put truth betwixt me and a storm: my Saviour did not so for me, who in His suffering took the windy side of the hill." The key phrase is, perhaps the following passage.[2] "Be content to wade through the waters betwixt you and glory with him, holding his hand fast, for he knoweth all the fords."

Another aspect of this spiritual guidance is made clear in a long letter to Marion M'Naught written[3] at Anwoth in the peaceful years. "You are not ignorant what our Lord in His love-visitation is doing with your soul, even letting you see a little sight of that dark trance you must go through ere you come to glory." A little later he gave encouragement. "Indeed our fair morning is at hand, the day-star is near the rising, and we are not many miles from home." In the final portion of the same letter[4] it is seen how his views were shaped by his distaste for the practice of fasting and what the Presbyterians of his generation called will-worship. "Welcome Lord Jesus. But it is a fearful sin in us, by hurting the body by fasting, to loose one stone or the least piece of timber in it, for the house is not our own."

"I know," he wrote[5] later to Lady Boyd from Aberdeen, "He (Christ) hath other things to do than to play with me and to trundle an apple with me, and that this feast will end." A letter[6] to Robert Gordon of Knockbreck is in this vein. "Nay, since I came to Aberdeen, I have been taken up to see the new land, the fair palace of the Lamb; and will Christ let me see heaven, to break my heart, and never give it to me." At times he would return to the orchard metaphor. "But as a child cannot hold[7] two apples in his little hand, but the one putteth the other out of its room, so neither can we be masters and lords of two loves." The idea

[1] Letter xl, for Lady Kenmure dated at Anwoth 26 November 1631, *ibid.*, p. 105.

[2] Letter xix, to the same dated at Anwoth 26 November 1631, *ibid.*, p. 68.

[3] Letter xxvi dated 19 September 1632, *ibid.*, pp. 83-5. Writing to Marion M'Naught from Aberdeen in 1637 these sentences occur. "That burning bush in Galloway and Kirkcudbright shall not be burnt to ashes for the Lord is in the bush . . . chosen and greatly beloved woman, faint not", *ibid.*, p. 513.

[4] *Ibid.*, p. 85.

[5] Letter lvii dated 7 March 1637, *ibid.*, p. 222.

[6] Letter xcii dated at Aberdeen on 9 February 1637, *ibid.*, p. 195.

[7] Letter cxcv. for Lady Largirie wife of the proprietor of Castermadie in the Stewartry of Kirkcudbright, *ibid.*, p. 383.

recurs[1] in a letter to Lady Gaitgirth. "The owner of the orchard," Rutherford explained, "may take two or three apples off his own trees before midsummer, and ere they get the harvest-sun." Finally a letter to Earlston the younger sums[2] up the motive of his pastorate. "But God be thanked for many spilled salvations, and many ill-ravelled hesps (hanks of yarn) hath Christ mended, since first He entered Tutor to lost mankind."

These quotations describe one aspect[3] of Samuel Rutherford's approach, but an objective survey of his thought would be incomplete if the degree to which he was oppressed by the menace of Rome was left unmentioned. He was not a travelled[4] man and had no experience of Anglicanism; he was not aware of the cold distaste for the Papacy which marked the Church of England. He feared that an episcopate on the Laudian model would soon conform to the Tridentine prototype. His mind ran much upon the Whore of Babylon.[5]

Rutherford feared that the Kirk of Scotland would be subverted by an acceptance of prelacy.[6] He was dominated by the thought of the evils that had come upon Jerusalem. "This is the day[7] of Jacob's visitation, the ways of Zion mourn, our gold is become dim, the sun is gone down upon our prophets." It was a peril that he had foretold when he was a young minister. "We are in great fears," he had written[8] to Lady Kenmure in 1630, "of a great and fearful trial to come upon the Kirk of God; for these, who would build their houses and nests upon the ashes of mourning Jerusalem, have drawn our King upon hard and dangerous conclusions

[1] Letter ccxxxviii dated at Aberdeen 7 September 1637, *ibid.*, p. 474. The same letter contains one of Rutherford's rare mechanical parallels. "All the saints, because of sin, are like old rusty horologues (watches) that must be taken down, and the wheels scoured and mended, and set up again in better case than before", *ibid.*, p. 471.

[2] Letter cxcvi written at Aberdeen in 1637, *ibid.*, p. 386.

[3] Cf. two sentences, the first written to Marion M'Naught and the second to Lady Kenmure. "From Him is the Shepherd and the Stone of Israel", letter xxxviii, dated at Anwoth 25 September 1634, *ibid.*, p. 102. "And therefore be content . . . every day to be adding and sewing a pasment to your wedding garment", letter xlii, undated, *ibid.*, p. 109.

[4] Cf. Letter cxcix, for John Gordon of Cardoness the younger written at Aberdeen in 1637. "The instinct of nature makes a man love his mother-country above all countries", *ibid.*, p. 392. At this date he had probably not visited either England or the Continent.

[5] Cf. Letter lxxiii to the Earl of Lothian written at Aberdeen in 1637. "The knavery and perfidious treachery to Christ of the accursed and wretched prelates, the Antichrist's first-born and the first-fruit of his foul womb", *ibid.*, p. 176. In spite of the gender he had clearly the Whore of Babylon in mind.

[6] Letter civ, to Lady Kenmure dated at Aberdeen 7 March 1637, *ibid.*, p. 216.

[7] Letter clxi, to John Stuart Provost of Ayr written at Aberdeen in 1637," *ibid.*, p. 301.

[8] Letter xi dated from Anwoth on 26 June 1630, *ibid.*, p. 53.

against such as are termed Puritans, for the rooting of them out. Our prelates (the Lord take the keys of his house from these bastard porters) assure us that, for such as will not conform there is nothing but imprisonment and deprivation."

It was Rutherford's strength that his thought and that of so many of his brethren was channelled upon the welfare of his own country. "I know," he wrote[1] to Hugh Henderson, then minister of Dalry, "of no bar in God's way but Scotland's guiltiness; and He can come over that impediment, and break that bar also, and then say to guilty Scotland, as he said 'Not for your[2] sakes'." It was soon clear that he was on the side that would be victorious.[3] Rutherford was very human. "The ministers are raging," he wrote[4] one of his adversaries, "but I love a rumbling and roaring devil best." It is evident that he wrote with urgency and frequency:[5] his letters have a tone that is both confident and personal.[6] At times he had a touch which was curiously Salesian. "This great idol-god the world," he told[7] John Gordon of Cardoness, "will be lying in white ashes on the day of your compearance; and why should night-dreams, and day-shadows, and water-froth, and May-flowers run away with your heart?" Certainly Samuel Rutherford was single-minded.

In regard to the life of the Presbyterian ministers there is a wealth of material. Certain aspects can be well illustrated from the sermons and papers of Robert Bruce, who became a leading figure among Scottish divines during the early manhood of James VI. He had been moderator of the General Assembly in 1589 and 1592 and had crowned and anointed Anne of Denmark as Queen of Scotland. He was deprived of his pastoral charge in 1603 and may be taken as a type of the Presbyterian opposition to the King's

[1] Letter cxciv written at Aberdeen in 1637, *ibid.,* p. 382.

[2] Ezek. xxxvi, 22, 23.

[3] Letter xcviii. "Ere it be long we shall see the white side of God's Providence", *Letters of Samuel Rutherford,* p. 205.

[4] Letter ccxliii, to Marion M'Naught on 7 September 1637 in reference to the bishop's supporters in Aberdeen, *ibid.,* p. 480.

[5] The metaphor of "the dry wind coming, but neither to fan nor to purge" was recurrent cf. letters xxxiv, lxx and clxi, *ibid.,* pp. 96, 152 and 301. Among Rutherford's surviving letters, five, to Lords Boyd and Lindsay, Lady Gaitgirth, Lady Rowallan and Marion M'Naught, were written on the same day 7 September 1637, *ibid.,* pp. 457-81.

[6] Cf. Letter xcviii dated at Aberdeen 19 February 1637. "He hath an hiding place for Mr. Alexander Colville against the storme: go on and fear not what man can do", *ibid.,* p. 205. A letter to the Earl of Cassilis, no. cclxviii, dated 9 September 1637, is characteristic. "One of our tribes, Levi's sons, have sold their mother and their father also, and the Lord's truth, for their new velvet-world and their satin-church", *ibid.,* p. 520.

[7] Letter cxxiv, *ibid.,* p. 249. Although writing from Aberdeen Rutherford signed himself "your loving pastor". To Lady Cardoness he signed as "Your lawful and loving pastor" to make plain his rights in Anwoth, *ibid.,* p. 379.

policies. He was also characteristic of the stricter ministers of his generation in being a formidable opponent of episcopal government under all its aspects. Robert Bruce remained one of the most influential preachers in the Scottish Kirk until his death in 1631 in his own house of Kinnaird not far from the Forth in Stirlingshire. The country parts of the midlands were by that time strongholds of the New Faith; the farms and lairds' houses from Forfar and Coupar Angus to the Braes of the Carse of Gowrie; the seaport burghs from Montrose to Dundee; the greater part of Fife and Kinross; the rich lands between Stirling and the Pentland Hills.

This is the stage in the account to set out the Presbyterian beliefs in some detail. Side by side with the Genevan teaching on the election and predestination of each individual, which arose from Calvin's interpretation of the doctrine of the absolute sovereignty of God, much practical stress was laid upon the preaching of the Evangel. This was the first duty of a minister to which all else was subordinate. With this there went the view that the office of a bishop was unscriptural, a standpoint propagated by Andrew Melville when he returned to Scotland from Geneva in 1574. As a consequence "the call of the people and the approval of his peers replaced episcopal consecration[1] in the making of a minister." It may be remarked that elders were chosen by the general body of the membership and specially ordained to their own office. By this means there was secured the preservation of the doctrines of the parity of ministers and the priesthood of all believers.

These postulates are reflected in Calvin's teaching on the subject of the two sacraments that he admitted,[2] Baptism and the Lord's Supper. They were conceived as instituted by Christ for men in accordance with the pattern of the Jewish Passover. In this connection article xxi in the Scots Confession of 1560 sets out the position with exactness. "As the Fatheris under the Law," explained[3] John Knox, "besydis the veritie of the sacrifices, had two cheaf Sacramentis, to witt, Circumcisioun and the Passover, the despysaris and contemnaris whairof war not reputed for Godis people; so (do) we acknawledge and confesse that we now, in the tyme of the Evangell, have two Sacramentis onlie, instituted be the Lord Jesus, and commanded to be used of all those that will be reputed members of his body to witt, Baptisme and the Supper,

---

[1] Article on "Presbyterianism" by the Rev. John Dall in *Encyclopaedia of Religion and Ethics*, vol. x, p. 248. In the context the use of the term "ordination" would have been clearer.
[2] Cf. Calvin's statement that "a sacrament is so separated from the reality by the unworthiness of the partaker that nothing remains but an empty and useless figure", *Institutes*, Book iv, ch. xiv, par. 16.
[3] Article xxi. Cf. The *Shorter Catechism*, question 91.

or Table of the Lord Jesus." There was thus a determination to eradicate from among the people the memory of the Mass and of the Catholic priesthood.

With this there went the practice of much private prayer, a constant searching of the Scriptures and a reliance on the symbolism of the Old Testament. The leading Presbyterians, both ministers and in certain cases others,[1] were accustomed to offer guidance. They were singularly literal-minded. Study of the Old Testament taught them how God dealt with His enemies. These comments may serve to indicate the general tenor of the beliefs sustained by Robert Bruce and the other ministers, who were his contemporaries.

The testimony of John Livingston quoted by Wodrow will give the note and flavour of Bruce's preaching. "No man," he wrote,[2] "in his time spake with such evidence and power of the spirit. No man had so many seals of conversions; yea many of his hearers thought no man, since the Apostles, spoke with such power. He had a notable faculty of searching deep in the Scriptures, and making the most dark mysteries most plain; but especially in dealing with people's consciences. He was much exercised in conscience himself, both in public and in private. He was very short in prayer when others were present, but every sentence was like a strong bolt shot up to heaven." A comment made by Robert Fleming in his *Fulfilling of the Scriptures* is interesting.[3] "He (Bruce) was a man that had much inward exercise about his own personal case, and had been oft assailed anent that great foundation truth, the being of a God, which cost him many days and nights wrestling."

Mr. Livingston, in his manuscript account already cited, gives a vivid impression of the preacher's minatory style. The narrative relates[4] to a conference which he held with him at Larbert in 1627. "Mr. Bruce told him in private that he had dreamed a dream (and severall of his extraordinary communications have been during his sleep, and in the night season) and had seen a great long book, with black boards, flying in the air, and many black fowls flying about it. That, as it touched any of them, they fell down dead. That he heard a voice audibly as Mr. Livingston heard him speak, 'This is the ire of God upon the ministry of Scotland'. That he

---

[1] As for example Johnston of Wariston.
[2] *Sermons by the Rev. Robert Bruce with collections for his life* by the Rev. Robert Wodrow, ed. Rev. William Cunningham, Wodrow Society (1843), p. 142. John Livingston or Livingstone (1603-1672) was a disciple of Robert Bruce. Like Josias Welch he, for a time, accepted a call in Northern Ireland.
[3] *Fulfilling of the Scriptures*, p. 358, printed *ibid.*, p. 144. Robert Fleming was born in 1640 and his evidence is therefore not contemporary.
[4] *Ibid.*, p. 147.

presently fell a-weeping and crying to God, that he might be keeped faithful, and not be one of those who were stricken down dead; and when he awoke he found all the pillows wet with his tears."

Robert Fleming and John Wemyss give details[1] of his bearing in the pulpit. "He was not a Boanerges, yet being, as Mr. Fleming observes, of a slow and grave delivery, he spake as becometh the oracles of God, with great authority, composure and weight." The other comment is very telling. "That great and learned man, Mr John Wemyss[2] of Lathocker, was occasionally present at that meeting with Mr Bruce, and when he came out, said, 'O! What a strange man is this, for he knocked down the spirit of God upon us all,' alluding to a motion Mr Bruce used with his hands upon the table at which he stood."

An account of a Sunday preaching at Larbert evokes the atmosphere surrounding the gentlemen of serious intention during these years. The little room here mentioned appears to have resembled that built into the church of Kilbirnie[3] in Ayrshire about this time. "When he preached," so runs[4] the narrative, "at Larbert Kirk (near where he owned the estate of Kinnaird) there was nearby a chamber, where he used to go in betwixt sermons. One day, some noblemen and gentlemen who had been hearing him, wearied betwixt sermons, when he stayed longer than he used. They having got a good way to ride after the sermon, they called the bellman, and desired him to go to him in the little room, where he was retired, and knock softly at the door, and, if he opened, to acquaint him they desired he might begin as soon as conveniently he could because some of them had far to ride. The bellman did as he was commanded, but Mr. Bruce was taken up so in wrestling that he did not hear him."

Robert Bruce's outlook was luminously positive. In the third sermon upon the Lord's Supper preached when he was a young man he is seen taking up his stand.[5] "Now quhat doe they (the Papists)? They, in place of a minister, pastor, or bishop, call him as thou pleases, quha is called lawfully of God, they substitute a priest, and surrogate ane hireling, quha hes na calling or office

[1] *Ibid.*, p. 154 and p. 152.

[2] John Wemyss of Lathnockar (1579?-1636) had fairly close contacts with Bruce.

[3] When the Crawfurd gallery was constructed in Kilbirnie church by Sir John Crawfurd in 1642 a small private apartment for the minister was also added.

[4] An account in *Sermons and collections*, pp. 150-1.

[5] A sermon preached the fifteen of Februarie, *ibid.*, p. 77. Bruce uses the phrase "the auncients of the Latin and Orient Kirks", *ibid.*, p. 61.

now in the Kirk of God." A statement which has not the same authority[1] purports to describe a visit made by Archbishop Spottiswoode to the old minister at Kinnaird. The prelate is described as saying, " 'Mr Bruce, do you not know me, and who I am?' The other answered, 'Sir, I know you to be a traitor to God, and to the Church of Scotland'."

A final passage[2] will give the quality of his preaching. Bruce was speaking about the passage relating to the woman who had an issue of blood. He is describing the words of Christ. "Sa soone as he felt it ga from him he sayis, 'Quha is this that hath twitched me?' Peter, quho was ever maist sudden, answers and sayis: 'Thou are thrumbled and thrusted be the multitudes, and yit thou speeris quha hes twitched thee'."

Certain points arise in connection with these various comments. Robert Bruce of Kinnaird was a landowner with the prestige that his rank carried. For the last thirty years of his life he was consciously in opposition to the royal policy. He suffered for this independence, but the mere fact that he maintained his standpoint alienated his friends and disciples from any attachment to monarchy as opposed to a theoretic acceptance of that institution.

Scottish Presbyterianism at that period had both a theocratic and an oligarchic character. Scotland was fruitful soil for conflicting groups of lords, but not in the last analysis for theocracy. As far as the political sphere was concerned it was the landowners who remained in possession of the field. As long as the leading ministers were drawn in great part from the landed gentry this divided outlook and purpose was to some degree masked. Put in another way the emergent conflict within Presbyterianism, considered as a political force, lay between the First Estate and the Second Estate. Just as in France, the Second Estate of the clergy had much in common with the nobles from whom many of their leaders sprang. It would be an anachronism to suggest that at this date there was any "popular" element among the leading clergy, although some moved towards a classless theocracy. There was a certain popular or mob opinion, but this was only used as an engine to support policy; there was no influential Presbyterian demagogue. It was true that there was popular enthusiasm in certain parts of Scotland, but this was because, especially in the West Country, large sections of the people had been seized with a profound belief in Presbyterian doctrine. The lay elders had weight within the Reformed Kirk, but these were usually chosen

[1] Wodrow states that he received this account from Bruce's successor, a minister of Larbert, *ibid.*, p. 153.
[3] *Ibid.*, p. 68.

from what were broadly the possessing classes. Both Argyll and Montrose were content to be enrolled among the ruling elders. There was on the whole a remarkable unanimity between the views of ministers and elders. Those Presbyterian lords who came in time to oppose the theocratic conceptions of leading ministers and their supporters were for the most part men who had passed outside the effective ranks of eldership.

It was principally the emphasis on the sermon in the Reformed worship which, together with their rights in the Presbytery and Kirk-Session, gave the elders their status in the Presbyterian community. Both the content and the manner of the sermon were subjects in regard to which an elder would feel able to pronounce judgment. It should be mentioned that within the Catholic system there was no parallel to such co-operative responsibility. On the other hand the leading ministers, such as Andrew Melville, were greatly aided by the inherent social authority which they derived from their own background and alliances. This made it easier for them to accept the position occupied by the ruling elder.

Finally Presbyterianism was conceived not only in its early stages but also as late as the seventeenth century as essentially a liberating force. It retained in Scotland that dynamism which had proved so effective in France in securing adherents to the Calvinists. Certain converts from Catholicism, such as the sixth Earl of Eglinton,[1] would give a determined and indeed enthusiastic support to their new Faith. This was in part due to the fact that Catholicism in most parts of the Lowlands had been gravely weakened and was often a traditional allegiance unsupported by regular sacramental observance. The mass opinion also had its influence. Wherever it was strongly planted Presbyterianism may be said to have been the mood of the Scottish people expecting victory. It was seen as God's gift to Scotland, which the Scots were to offer to the sister kingdom.

It is by no means easy to form a clear impression of the lives of the ministers in the generations immediately following the Reformation. The material is copious, but much of it is hagiography; in consequence it requires those modifying interpretations to which all hagiography must be submitted. A mass of detail, and indeed much of the surviving correspondence, deals with a relatively restricted area of dispute. It is inevitable but unfortunate that so much attention should have been concentrated on

[1] Lord Eglinton used to describe David Dick, who was appointed minister of Irvine 1618, as "the instrument to reclaim him from Popery".

the struggle against prelacy. This was the principal controversial issue in which the Presbyterian ministers opposed the sovereign and his Anglican advisers. Still the attitude of the leaders of the Kirk towards the "fourteen bellie gods," as the bishops were described, does something to mask the more sympathetic aspects of the outlook of the ruling Presbyterians. For they possessed certain qualities, notably an egalitarian simplicity and a touching and immediate trust in God, that are bound to make a strong appeal. This is not always recognised because attention is seldom focused on those characteristics which the leaders shared with the rank and file of those who gave their lives to spread the Reformed doctrine. Like every other religious body the Church of Scotland had its share of ecclesiastical politics and manipulation.

The ministers of that time were in theory and to a great extent in fact very consciously a scholarly body. This is borne out in a statement in regard to Andrew Melville made[1] by John Row in his *Historie*. He is referring to the supplication sent by Melville in 1611 to the English Privy Council. "Being requested, by many who loved him . . . he put pen to paper, and wrote this Suppli- catorie Confession following, in Latine, becaus he could utter his mynd and affection better in that language nor in English." Their sometimes pragmatic love of learning won them the respect of the wealthier classes, to whom their readiness to teach school[2] would prove congenial. In a period when private tutors were rare, they were the schoolmasters of a whole generation.

It was to a great extent from their learning, using this term broadly, that the ministers derived their innate authority. In this they were helped by the desire of the Lowland Scots for self- advancement. Moreover their position was consolidated by the fact that they so frequently themselves belonged to substantial families. The established Lowland gentry who adhered to the Reformed religion were ready to marry their daughters to young ministers. Such a practice was only rarely acceptable to their equals in England or in the Lutheran parts of Germany. Finally it was an element of strength in the situation of the ministers that they were not separated from their flock by a special status.

---

[1] *The Historie of the Kirk of Scotland* by John Row, Maitland Club, 1842, p. 108.

[2] The following comment on John Davidson is made by Row: "He wes . . . placed Minister of Preston-pans, quhair he erected and built a kirk and schoole; to that end sold his owne patrimonie (having no children) and dedicat all the meanes that he had, with the charitable contribution that he obtained from others, to so good and profitable a worke, for the mainteinance of that ministrie and schoole in all tyme coming", *Coronis being a continua- tion of the Historie of the Kirk of Scotland* by William Row, Maitland Club, 1842, p. 222.

It was a result of the essential equality of ministers and elders that serious objection was always taken to the use of the expression "layman". This is made clear by William Row in his *Coronis*. He states[1] that the "shifting of the Ruleing-Elders aff Judicatories of the Kirk, Presbytories and Assemblies" was partly due to the "pryde and ill-conscience of some Prelaticall Ministers, quho wold not have lay-men (as they popishlie termed them) to be either witnesses or opposers of their actions".

Such a standpoint led on naturally to sympathy with the English Puritans. "Conformitie," John Row explains,[2] "wes more urged in England then before, quhilk made sundrie both Ministers and other good professours leave the countrey, and went and lived in Nova Anglia." As the reverse of the medal, contact with English bishops or with the world of Court favour aroused antipathy. This is apparent in two comments[3] made on Archbishop Patrick Adamson, one dealing with his alleged recantation and the other with his death. The phrases are quoted as evidence of the ministers' outlook. "Moreover, I confesse I wes busie with some Bischops in England, in prejudice of the discipline of our Kirk (partlie when I wes there, and partlie by mutuall intelligence since), nor became a good Christian, meikle lesse a faithfull pastor." The following words are attributed to Mr Adamson, as he is carefully styled, when on his deathbed. "I gloried in the favour of my Prince, and now he loveth any of the dogges of his kennell better nor me."

Two passages throw light upon the standpoint of the Presbyterian ministers. Both indicate, the first in a rather idealised form, the motive power which lay behind their actions. "Yet, in the generall," wrote[4] William Row, "I say in the worke of the Reformation, the rooting out of idolatrie, and the planting of the sinceritie of the Gospell, wes chieflie looked unto; insomuch that the faithfull servants of God, quho were the first preachers of His blessed word in this kingdome, had little mynd of themselves, or how they might be intertained; but paused how this great worke might be effectuate to God's glorie, and the salvation of His people's soules." The second comment[5] forms part of a tribute to John Murray, sometime minister of Dunfermline. "Now, for Mr John Murray, all the tyme he wes lying upon his deathbed, he profest that this wes his rejoyceing, that he never consented to the blecking and diffigureing of that faire, well favoured face of this Kirk of Scotland."

[1] *Ibid.*, p. 202.   [2] John Row, *op. cit.*, p. 157.
[3] *Ibid.*, pp. 29 and 36.
[4] *Additional Illustrations to the Historie of the Kirk of Scotland* by William Row, Maitland Club, 1842, p. 315.
[5] John Row, *op. cit.*, p. 188.

D

The spirit of this time is reflected in the account of the last days and death of Patrick Simson, who was minister at Stirling for twenty-seven years. His father Andrew Simson was one of the considerable number of Presbyterian ministers of the first generation who had begun life as teachers; he was master of the grammar school at Perth. His mother Violet Adamson was sister to the Archbishop of St Andrews. Some of the details of the setting are very vivid and the whole forms a companion panel to the description of Lord Kenmure's deathbed.

"In the beginning of March, 1618," writes[1] William Row in the *Coronis*, "he (Mr Patrik Symson) said to his wife, 'Spouse, this wallie March will make ane end of all thir things.' And so it was, for he deceased March 31. Upon the 11 day of March, Helen Gardiner (a gracious woman), spous to John Sherer, bailie of Stirlin, said to him, 'Sir, remember the tenth day of August.' He ansuered, 'It sall never slip out of my mynd'." A little later Row sets[2] out to explain this allusion.

"The true relation of that mater is this: His first wife, Martha Barron,[3] a gracious woman, the wife of his youth, with quhom he had lived in great love and contentment, being visited with seeknes long befor her death, quho had often confessed that the Devill had often suggested to her, and cast in her teeth, that he sould be about with her, and that shee sould be given over in his hand. Her husband replyed. That any quho had such markes of saving grace as he had sein in her these eighteen yeares, wold certainlie be objects of Satan's malice and hatred: but the gates of hell cannot prevaile, as against the Kirk, so neither against any member thereof. Upon a Sabboth, August 8 (1601), shee altered and begouth to speake to her daughter Lilias Symson (quho being about ten or eleven yeares of age, had the whole charge of that great familie the whole two yeares her mother was tyed to her bed) in ane uncouth strane, and in a distracted way. It wes in the morning, and her father being to preach twyse that day, shee was loath to goe and awake him; but he lying in the roume above, that quhilk he heard beneath did awake him; and quhen he came downe hearing her distracted speaches, speaking unreverentlie to him (farr contrair to her custome), and sieing her distracted behaviour . . . he kneeled downe and prayed. But shee tooke no notice of the prayer; yet, notwithstanding, he prophesied that those quho were witnesses of that sad houre should sie a gracious worke of God upon this His owne servant."

[1] *Coronis*. p. 232.
[2] *Ibid.*, pp. 234-5.
[3] She was daughter of James Baron, Provost of Edinburgh.

Mr Simson's wife continued in this state through the Monday. "On Tuesday,[1] by the first breake of day, he went over the streete to his yeard, bare-footed and bare-headed, (as David did, quhen he went up Mount Olivet, flieing out of Jerusalem from his sonne Absalom). He locked the yeard-doore behind him; having charged them that were in the house with Helin Gardiner, the bailie's wife, to attend her, sitting quyet beside her. Helin Gardiner, a woman that loved him dearlie, fearing he had bein fallen dead, through waking, fasting and greife, about thrie houres in the morning, went to sie if shee could winne in to the yeard; but shee, finding the doore locked, came in againe. After foure a clocke, being impatient of his stay, shee went againe, and with the helpe of a barrow did climb up and gott over the dyke into the yeard; and coming up the alley, shee began to be affrayed, hearing (doubtles at the departing of these heavenlie ministering spirits) a wonderfull, strange, loud, confused sound and noyse. . . . Then she came softlie to the head alley, quhair she found him lying on the ground, bare-footed, bare-legged, and bare-headed."

To her enquiries as to what had happened he made this reply. " 'Helin, women are weake; they are not good secretars. I will, provyding yee never divulge it. What wes I? What es I, being dust and ashes, that the holy ministering spirits sould have bein sent to delyver me my message?' By this she understood clearlie that he had sein a vision of Angels." Mr Simson then returned to the house. He went to pray at his wife's bedside and in his supplications mentioned Jacob. "She satt straight upp in bed, cast the cannobie asyde with her hands, and said, 'And thou art Jacob today, who has wrestled and prevailed'." She lived two days longer, dying on Friday, August 13. The incidental information builds up a clear impression: the manse with a bedroom on either floor; the yard in which the minister used to meditate; the alley way running beneath the house; the wheelbarrow standing beside the wall.

Now seventeen years later and aided by his second wife, Patrick Simson prepared to die. In his last sickness he was visited by his brother Archibald, who was minister at Dalkeith. It is recorded[2] that the latter asked the meaning of various symbols painted in the wall. The questions and replies were much in character. "Asked anent the Hawke? Ansuered, in Latine, *Solus inter aves, accipter fertur recto cursu sursum.* Everie Christian should be a hawke. his course should be upward and upright, or right up. Lord save us from her fierceness. but grant that we walke not in circular or oblique courses. What meanes the Torch burning at both ends, and both burning upward? Ansuered, Christians' hearts sould be heaven-ward; both in prosperitie and adversitie, love and seal sould kyth." One query is very curious. "What meant the Armenian Whyte[1] Mouse? Ansuered, The hunters can find no meanes to take it. . . . Such a mouse was Daniel, the Thrie Children, and Eleazar; such a mouse sould everie Christian be, quho sould choose affliction rather nor sin."

There are many references during these years to the gift of prophecy with which the leading ministers were graced,[2] nor were heavenly portents wanting. "Mr John Makbirnie," we read,[3] "first at the South Ferrie, over against the Castle of Broughtie, and then at Aberdein, a most zealous and painfull Pastor, a great opposer of Hierarchie. He was a shineing torche and a burning starre; quhairfor the Lord miraculouslie made, at his death, a starre to appeare in heaven at the noone-tyde of the day; quhilk many yet alyve testifies that they did evidentlie sie it, at Witsonday 1609."

Although all gear was to be used in God's service, there was no tendency to despise prosperity[4] as such. From the early days there was an intimate contact between the ministers and their wealthy neighbours. This appears in the episode of the visit of Lady Faudonside to the manse at Prestonpans. "The Lady Faddinsyde," we are told,[5] "came with one of her sonnes, Mr John Ker, to visite Mr Davidson, and to take their leave of him. Mr John Ker, the Ladie's sonne, wes then ane young gentleman latelie come from France, pransing in his French garb, with his short skarlet cloake and his long caudie rapier, according to the mode of those tymes. After the Ladie Fadinsyde had for a space conferred with Mr Davidson, her sonne, the yong gentleman, standing by, discoursing with some of his comerads, shee did take her leave of Mr Davidson; lykewayes Mr John her sonne did: But

---

[1] *Ibid.*, p. 232.

[2] e.g., "This Mr John Davidson wes a verie zealous, honest man, and indeed a verie prophet of God; for it is ordinar with God to give his servants, quhom he stirres up and employes in extraordinar employments, with extraordinarie gifts and endowments, such as the gift of prophesie. Such prophets ther were many, in Scotland, about and shortlie after tyme of the Reformation; viz. Mrs Wischart, Knox, Welsh, Row, Craig, Davidson, Ferguson, etc. Thir foir-prophecied many things, quhereof some fulfilled in their owne dayes, and all of them after their death . . . Mr John Davidson . . . yea, a verie prophet of God", *ibid.*, pp. 220 and 219.

[3] *Ibid.*, p. 223.

[4] "Of Mr John Row's two daughters, the eldest was married to Wm. Rig, a rich merchand in Edr., of quhom came ane numerous offspring and posteritie of many rich people", *ibid.*, p. 212.

[5] *Ibid.*, pp. 221-2.

after Mr Davidson had narrowlie looked upon the yong gentleman, he sayes to him: 'What meanes this long caudie rapier, this
short skarlet cloake, and all this gay graith (gear) of yours? Away,
away with these things. I know you, Sir, to be a good scholer:
Cast away these daft conceits."[1] This story is enshrined in an
edifying tale of prophecy, but it throws a clear light on social
relations. It is in keeping that this same Mr Davidson should have
a sharp comment[1] on the proposal that certain ministers should
be selected to vote in Parliament. "I sie the loune Bischops creep-
ing in into our Kirk by this meane."

Inventories of manses of this period would certainly yield items
of interest. An impression may be obtained from the inventory[2]
of the goods found in James Melville's house at his decease. The
Presbyterian leader was at that time living in exile at Berwick-
on-Tweed, where he had married the vicar's daughter as his second
wife. The only rooms mentioned are the hall, the chamber and
the parlour; apart from furnishings the only goods listed are six
silver spoons and certain books, whose titles are not given. In the
hall stood a fir table and frame, two small fir tables, two short fir
forms, and a little old corner cupboard. There were also two old
little green chairs, six "thrume" cushions and a Scots needle-
work carpet. In the chamber and parlour the sparse furniture was
of better quality and included six leather chairs, ten Scots needle-
work cushions and six green "carsey" cushions.

A study of the autobiographical material left by John Row,
who was minister of Carnock in the presbytery of Dunfermline
from 1592 until 1646, reveals a similar very frugal setting. "In his
yonger yeares," it is explained,[3] "his father being a great Hebrean,
and the man that first brought the knowledge of the Hebrew
letters to Scotland, tooke paines upon him. . . . His father died
quhen he wes twelve yeares of age, learning his gramer." John
Row was then brought up by his uncle the young Laird of
Balfour.

An account is given[4] of the lodging arrangements at Edinburgh,
where his uncle sent him to study at the College. "He wes tabled
in the house of ane advocate, called Mr John Russell, whose wife
wes his aunt (quho had received thrie horse loads of law bookes
which were his father's and some silver)." At the end of the year
he fell sick with the plague, but Mr Russell refused him his room

---

[1] *Ibid.*, p. 222.
[2] *Autobiography and Diary of James Melvill*, ed. Robert Pitcairn, Wodrow
Society, 1842, pp. liii-lv. It is stated to have been taken on 24 February 1615,
but Melville died on 13 January 1613-4.
[3] *Coronis*, p. 243.   [4] *Ibid.*, p. 245.

on his return "because he had gotte a greater offer with another.
. . . So his brother (in-law), Wm. Rig, tooke him in to his house,
and intertained him the other thrie yeares he was at the Colledge.
And so he passed his course, and was laureat 1590."

He had not yet decided on his future. "Some of his friends[1]
advysed him to be prentise to his brother-in-law, to be a merchant;
some advysed him to be prentise to Gilbert Primerose, a notable
Chirurgian; but he, dislyking those employments, and resolving to
prosecute his studies, his master, the Principall of the Colledge,
Mr Rollock, tooke him to wait upon himselfe, and to studie with
him." His training completed, the young man's first call was to
Carnock. At that time the kirk, subsequently repaired by Sir
George Bruce of Culross and his son, was thatched with heather,[2]
lacked lights and had no seats. It was only after he married
Grissell Ferguson that John Row was able to settle in a manse.[3]
He stayed in the same charge[4] throughout his life. Mrs Row was
the daughter of David Ferguson, minister of Dunfermline, and
four of her five sons entered[5] the service of the Kirk. It was from
parishes like Carnock that there would come some of the
strongest opposition to King Charles's measures.

The ministers can therefore be envisaged as very solidly entrenched, politically powerful, respected by their flocks and often
feared. It is worth considering their attitude to those groups that
they found alien. Undoubtedly the most unamenable factor was
that represented by those who were attached to Popery. In this
connection an important point should be made. The Presbytery
did all that it could to extirpate what it conceived to be the ancient
errors; but it did not persecute to blood. Father Ogilvie was the
only priest to suffer execution and he came before a court presided over by Archbishop Spottiswoode. It would be interesting
to penetrate to the reason for what would appear to be a policy
of mercy. The best explanation seems to be that the Presbyterians
trusted implicitly in God's justice. They regarded the Papists as
the followers of anti-Christ. They were in their eyes the lasting
opponents of the True Evangel. God was not mocked and this led

---

[1] *Ibid.,* p. 246.

[2] Cf. for a description of the Kirk, *ibid.,* p. 247.

[3] After his marriage ane old Freir (friar) dying that possets the halfe of
his gleib, he gott the whole gleib and some more stipend than he had at
first; but still the stipend wes verie small", *ibid.,* p. 240.

[4] "that verie small charge, thair not being above one hundred communicants."

[5] John Row became principal of King's College, Aberdeen, Robert minister
of Abercorn, William minister at Ceres and James minister at Monivairs and
Strowan. Their uncles James and William Row were ministers at Kilspindie
and Forgandenny respectively.

them to the conviction that each Papist would go in time to his own place.

Witchcraft was a very different matter and in their mind this involved the actual entertainment of the Devil in person. It was the calling down of Satan to sit in the but-and-ben on a Scottish hillside that cried out for exemplary punishment. This is a suitable point at which to comment on this question of witchcraft which exercised so much effect upon the Scottish mind. The population had certain deep fears in this matter which were compounded of very ancient superstitions incoherently allied to a very practical fear of poison. This last point affected the rich and in a quite special sense the mind of James VI.

The question of the trials for witchcraft in Scotland during this period raises a number of interesting points. In the first place there is no real counterpart in Ireland or south of the Border to the Scottish preoccupation with this subject. It is significant that trials for witchcraft appear to have been practically unknown in Ireland and were extremely rare in Wales. In England there were elaborate accusations relating to the Pendle witches and these were by chance linked up with the journey of Charles I to Scotland for his coronation; but, apart from the Pendle series which related to a remote part of Lancashire, accusations of witchcraft were at most spasmodic. It is also the fact that James VI had come to take possession of his southern kingdom with clear and well-formed opinions upon this subject.

It would seem that in Scotland there were two main trends corresponding to white and black magic respectively. The idea of unusual powers, when correlated with the belief in their diabolic origin, was almost equally unsatisfactory whether these were used for healing or for destruction. The fact that in the records of the trials so many women are described as long suspected of witchcraft suggests that these accused had been practising herbal remedies over a period.

Under one aspect this could be regarded as the poor invading the private life of the rich for diverse purposes varying between the case of the woman who was alleged to have transferred Archbishop Adamson's disease to the body of a white pony and that of those who were burned for killing the Earl of Angus with their spells. In this connection the accusation of witchcraft was invoked where the death of a man of standing was either difficult to explain or in some way discreditable. Thus Robert second Earl of Lothian appears to have died by his own hand. A petition was delivered to the Council on behalf of his brother and sisters requesting that two suspected witches might be kept in prison "that

God may be glorified, justice ministrat upoun the offendouris and the honnour and reputatioun of that nobleman vindicated and relieved." This was by no means an isolated[1] case and it is probable that behind such accusations lay a mixture of calculated shrewdness and fear.

It was always desirable to remove any suspicion of suicide for the taking of a man's own life was held to be both a criminal and an abhorrent act. It suggested to the mind of that age a state of despair which involved the subject's eternal damnation. It is possible that the tendency to brood upon the doctrines of election and reprobation was not without its influence on the lives of some of those caught up in the network of the witchcraft trials.

It is difficult to find a common factor linking the regions affected by the witchcraft trials since it is clear that they were fairly numerous across the whole length of the East of Scotland. Accusations appear to have been less common in the west country and in Galloway. Some of the principal centres are unexpected. An assertion in one survey[2] bears on this point. "Dalkeith and its neighbourhood, as is well-known, was a veritable nest of warlocks and witches." This was a rich countryside, accessible to the capital and very deeply Protestant. The accused came from all sections of the population with the exception of the gentry and the wealthier burgess stocks. As an example, in 1630 accusations were brought[3] against a group of townspeople of small means living at Cousland, four miles east of Dalkeith. These included a tailor and his wife and daughter and the wives of a weaver and a piper. A woman living at Easthouses, in Newbattle, was accused, as was the wife of a cordiner at Longniddry on the coast. In the following year the trial[5] of a warlock John Neill throws a light on the whole circle of his highly respectable acquaintances; farmers, millers and their families, all living in the parishes of Paxton, Eyemouth and Mordington in Berwickshire. They were for the most part tenants of either Sir David Home of Wedderburn or Sir James Douglas, who were made responsible in their capacity of "master and landlore" for their journeys to Edinburgh to take part in this unsavoury investigation.

[1] Thus James Borthwick of Newbyres petitioned that Meg Unes, under sentence of death for witchcraft, be examined as to her knowledge of the death of the late Lord Borthwick and of the suppliant's wife and children, *Register of the Privy Council of Scotland,* ii, p. 442.
[2] Introduction, *ibid.,* ii, p. xlii.
[3] The group also included two other women from Cousland, Christian Steill and Giles Swintoun, *ibid.,* iii, p. 544.
[4] For these cases cf. ii, p. 471. Margaret Cowan was described as the wife of Henry Fentoun, maltman in the Canongate, *ibid.,* ii, p. 470.
[5] Instructions under 10 March 1631, *ibid.,* iv, pp. 164-5.

What can be said of such cases and especially of those in which carnal dealings with the Devil were alleged? It is clear that absorption in the question of the fate of the reprobate was likely to develop fantasies in the minds of certain lonely women. Once they were convinced that they were destined to reprobation it was a short step to imagine these carnal acts that set a seal upon their own damnation. It is possible that the cases regarded by contemporaries as most nauseating were those which were very evidently the fruit of a disordered mind. On the other hand the position was complicated because in England, as the Overbury case showed, dealings with spells and incantations were the stock-in-trade of a certain stamp of poisoner.

A very different type of witchcraft arose from what may be called the practice of herbalist remedies and white magic with a view to profit. This appears in the case of George Fraser and his wife Giles Chalmers, who were both unsuccessfully indicted for sorcery. The husband had been visited in his sickness by a warlock named Philp, who was later burned for witchcraft in Banff. "John Philp," so runs[1] the evidence, "came and remained with the sick man several days and having obtained a quantity of lax water from a south-running well in a white pitcher . . . washed him therewith twice every day until he was cured." This was surely merely the use of immemorial remedies. In his examination at the court house of Banff before Lord Deskford, John Philp, who was described as a vagabond, admitted[2] that he used charms and spells to cure the sick in Fintray parish. He confessed that he had charmed James Maltman's son when he had the fever by the aid of the queen of fairies.

With what may be considered as this simpler form of witchcraft there also went accusation of associating with the Devil, but this was often a question of alleged simple companionship. There was, too, a constant effort to do good by magic, to increase and strengthen the sheep or to secure fine catches for the fishermen. An example from the Orkneys may be cited as typical. This particular case[3] resulted in the condemnation of Marion Richart for witchcraft, sorcery and divination. It was alleged at her trial in 1633 that six or seven times her grandson James Fischer, who was then keeping Manse Smythi's swine, went up into an old house called the house of Howing Gremay to shelter from a shower and that when he came within the broken building he saw Katharine

[1] Heard on 27 August 1633 and reported *ibid.*, vol. v, pp. 565-6.
[2] Report dated 22 February 1631, *ibid.*, iv, p. 638.
[3] Reported under 29 May 1633, *ibid.*, v, p. 552. As regards Marion Richart's movements in the islands it is noted that she came "to Stronsay to Margret Thomson's house", *ibid.*, v, p. 553.

Miller and Marion Richart sitting there with the Devil in the likeness of a black man seated between them. The sequel is pathetic. Katharine Miller cried out fiercely, "Take him for he will tell on us," but Marion would not suffer this interference with her grandchild, saying, "Let him alone for nobody will believe him."

This matter of witchcraft raises other questions such as the nature of the covens and the witches' sabbaths and the possible existence of an enduring organisation. Pre-Christian practices which had survived through the mediæval centuries played their part together with the factors already mentioned. These problems are linked with occurrences in the southern and central parts of Scotland. Such cases of a more elaborate witchcraft do not, however, fall within the period of King Charles's rule. Moreover, this matter was one which while it caused the ministers concern hardly affected the general tenor of responsible Scottish life.

Public opinion regarded the existence of such phenomena as inevitable. There were of course great areas, especially in the North West, to which the Reformed Faith had not yet penetrated, but in general where the Kirk was well planted the flock possessed a sound respect for the parish minister. He was, as the times went, a learned Scotsman whose history and background all men knew.

The characteristic of the Presbyterian outlook was inevitably the conviction of Election. That men should be confirmed in Grace gave rise in those who conceived themselves as God's creatures to a sense of gratitude which was both sober and disinterested. Within the liturgical forms of the Church of Scotland, great emphasis was laid upon the corporate Communion which was conceived of in pentecostal terms. At such times, carefully chosen so as to be remote from what were considered as the man-made festivals of the Catholic Church, the Christians of the Reformed Faith came together to wait upon God's spirit. Their day of preparation had some resemblance to the developed practice of the Quakers and so far as it had a Catholic parallel was linked with Quietist ideals. This would seem to have issued in a spirituality characterised by a deep desire to wait upon God and to do Him service with a grateful heart. Marked as their lives were by a clear spring of energy, the faithful members of the Kirk were seldom without a sense of guidance. They were convinced of God's immediate presence and that in the Communion they received from Him direct the gifts of Pentecost.

CHAPTER III

JOHNSTON OF WARISTON

ALTHOUGH the outlook of the Presbyterian leadership was theocratic, it was not necessarily clerical. In Catholic countries the layman of clerical views is known by his respect for the clergy and his dependence upon their judgments; but in Scotland a marked equality existed between ministers and laymen of strong opinions provided that they shared the best education of that day. Thus the Marquis of Argyll and Lord Wariston had an influence on the Presbyterian leadership to which none of the ministers attained. They felt themselves, and rightly, to be at the very core of those who tolerate no backsliding and whose support would only be given to a Covenanted King.

The group of the legal families centring on Edinburgh had only been formed in the course of the two previous generations, but, as has been suggested, it had already come to occupy something of the position of a *noblesse de robe*. It had, however, a closer connection with the landed interests than had its French counterpart; the judges almost invariably acquired estates in the Lothians within easy riding distance of the capital. The education of the judges' sons was similar to that given to the children of Scottish peers. Their families would join in time that group of the greater Lowland lairds which in this century was only in process of formation. In a country where social cleavages hardly existed they maintained close links both with the peers and with the Edinburgh merchant groupings. A high proportion of their marriages took place within their own network of legal families. They can, perhaps, best be studied in the career of Lord Wariston.[1] We possess enough detail as to his life for it to be worth while to make a very close examination.

Archibald Johnston, who became a lord of session in 1641 and lord clerk register in 1649, was baptised on 28 March, 1611, and was born and brought up in Edinburgh. On his father's[2] side he

---

[1] This name is spelt Warriston in the *D.N.B.*, xxx, pp. 56-8, but the form Wariston is used throughout the editions of Archibald Johnston's *Diary* edited by Sir George M. Paul, Dr. David Hay Fleming and Mr. James D. Ogilvie for the Scottish Historical Society.

[2] They had however continuing links with Edinburgh. By the will of Lord Wariston's grandfather Archibald Johnstone, merchant, of Kirkpatrick Juxta a legacy of one hundred marks was bequeathed "to help the repairing and completing of ye Kirk callit Kirkpatrick Juxta where my predecessoris bonis lyes", quoted in the introduction, p. 3, to *The Diary of Sir Archibald Johnston Lord Wariston 1639*. ed. George M. Paul, Scottish History Society, 1896.

was linked to the Johnstones Earls of Annandale and Hartfell, while his mother was a daughter of Sir Thomas Craig, the authority on Scottish feudal law, and a sister to Sir Lewis Craig, Lord Wrightlands. He was distantly related to George Buchanan and was a kinsman of Robert Baillie, under whom he studied at Glasgow University. The clearest impression of Wariston's outlook and background is obtained from his own diaries. These are among the mass of notebooks and papers which passed to Baillie of Jerviswood and then to the Earls of Haddington when they inherited Mellerstain.

Wariston was only fourteen years of age at the accession of Charles I, but he matured early; he assisted in framing the National Covenant when he was only twenty-seven. Henceforward he was central to the developing politico-religious situation in Scotland. As far as his public actions were concerned he never knew infirmity of purpose. His friends and enemies are agreed that he possessed a driving energy. He was wholly devoted to the public service conceived as the victory of the Church of Scotland. His diaries reflect his own misgivings and his sense of weakness which was overborne by his knowledge of his election, that is to say the fact that he was elected to Eternal Glory. James Kirkton, who was married to a daughter of George Baillie of Jerviswood, recalls[1] a comment familiar in Wariston's family circle. "He could never doubt of his own salvation he has so often seen God's face in the house of prayer."

He would spend long periods at prayer in his own chamber. In later life he seldom slept more than three hours in the twenty-four. The tradition among Wariston's supporters is reflected in a comment in Robert Wodrow's *Analecta*.[2] Baillie of Jerviswood was passing his house in the High Street of Edinburgh situated to the east of what is now known as Wariston's Close. Looking up at the windows he turned to his sister-in-law Lady Graden and said, "Many a sweet day and night with God had your now glorified father in that chamber." It was a sanctified life for the Lord Clerk Register.

As a consequence of this intense preoccupation Wariston was inaccessible; remote with his own family; unwilling to admit the claims of friendship. Although at the centre of political movements, he would accept no man as his political associate. He was dedicated to the cause of God's victory. His attitude to Rome was that of his class and period. It is clearly expressed in an entry in his

[1] *The Secret and True History of the Church of Scotland from the Restoration to the year 1678*, ed. C. P. Sharpe, p. 173.
[2] Analecta, iii, pp. 78-80, quoted by George M. Paul, introduction p. 3.

Diary made[1] in 1637. "Quhairin it came in to mynd that, if we licked up this vomit of Romisch superstition again, the Lord in his wrayth would vomit us out. The Lord ingraived in my mynd that of the prophet, 'Their is poison in the pot'."

All his life Wariston shunned worldliness and excessive drinking. The reference to the Earl of Sutherland in the quotation that follows shows that he was always ready to rebuke a man of fashion. It should be noted that in his writings Wariston refers to himself indifferently in the first and in the second person. One entry, made[2] when he was twenty, is illuminating. It relates to God's dealings with him. "His wonderful calling me unto the communion of the West Kirk, quherat he gaive me many tears (it being my first communion) even quhil I was drouned in al kynd of licentiousnes by Sutherlands compagnie . . . then by going to the communion in Kirkadie, and in Mr Jhon Chalmers kirk; and thairafter thos od motions thou got in ane little bak chalmer in Dalkeith,—al this being in thy 15 year of age; as also in thy 16 year thy going to the Panes, Musselbrugh, Westkirk, Carnok, thairafter in Foulden, once in Cashie[3] and tuyse in Paris—as many communions as many comforts."

In these years he formed a habit of solitary prayer which never left him. He was in some ways insular, certainly never at home except within the framework of the Genevan discipline. Apart from his flight to Hamburg in his last years, after Charles II had been restored, he only once went abroad. This was to complete his studies after leaving Glasgow University, and then he lived in strictly Huguenot surroundings, for a time in Paris but for the most part at Castres, where his future brother-in-law Robert Burnet had preceded him. Wariston's mother's family had had its share of that French education[4] which may be regarded as a mark of one section of the ruling grouping. At the same time Wariston was at home wherever Calvin's *Institutes* were venerated. He was content and only content where Predestinarian Calvinism was accepted as an axiom. The character of his religious sympathies, at once supranational and rigid, was very remote from that of his own sovereign. It was not in Lord Wariston to approve in any way of Charles I.

His singlemindedness made him uneasy at all festivities. The

[1] *Diary of Sir Archibald Johnston Lord Wariston 1632-9,* ed. George M. Paul, Scottish History Society 1911, p. 369.
[2] *Ibid.,* pp. 125-6.
[3] The towns mentioned are Prestonpans and Castres.
[4] His grandfather Sir Thomas Craig studied for six years at the University of Paris, while his uncle John Craig, physician to James I, graduated M.D. at Basle.

Diary has a note[1] relating to the marriage feast arranged by his brother-in-law John Rae, an Edinburgh advocate. "I straive to be merrie with Sir Antonin Alexander in sports and scornings (rallying) of the bryde, for the quhilk, first quhen I went to my awin chalmer, then at night, my mynd was tormented and wes oppressed with heaviness." His chosen occupations were very different. There is an entry relating to December 1633 when he was twenty-two. At this time he was much disturbed by the loss on the road from Cranston of his small Bible,[2] which he had marked with great pains. "On Sunday[3] in the morning never did mor humbly confesse nor mor ardently pray nor then, with rivers of tears. Betwixt sermons, siklyk (in like manner) afternoon in the Lady Currihils dask,[4] also som tears. After sermon I enjoyed the lyk libertie of tears, groans and crys: by Gods providence we sang 118 and the 119 Ps; we reed fra the 5 to the 9 of Romans."

In the following years there are suggestive entries. "On Sunday morning haiving read Sathans Stratagem in Doumanns wearfarre.[5] . . . On Sunday morning before I rais, I read Granado of the last jugement.[6] . . . I studyed the preparations contained in the Practise of[7] Piety. . . . On Foorsday, Frayday, Saturday reading in the Practical Catechisme[8] thou got good. . . . On Wednesday afternoone after a great dumpe of melancholy I got some libertie in prayer."[9]

It is not surprising that Wariston derived great comfort from the deathbeds of the Elect. "After both sermons," we read[10] in an entry under 20 August 1634, "by Gods comfortable providence I was led to Mr Patrik Nisbet's house (Patrick later Lord Eastbank, father of Sir John Nisbet, Lord Dirleton), quhair I saw to

---

[1] Entry under 27 April 1637, *Diary 1632-9*, p. 254.

[2] Entry under 15 December 1633, *ibid.*, p. 185

[3] Entry under 22 December 1633, *ibid.*, p. 185

[4] This reference to Lady Curriehill's desk is to his aunt's private sitting, Sir James Skene, Lord Curriehill had married Janet Johnston.

[5] Entry under 19 January 1634, *Diary 1632-9*, p. 194. The book referred to is *The Christian Warfare* by John Downham printed at London in 1609.

[6] Entry under 23 February 1634, *ibid.*, p. 198. It appears that Wariston used the translation of Luis de Granada *Of Prayer and Meditation* made by Fr. Hopkins in 1582.

[7] Entry under 3 March 1634, *ibid.*, p. 202. There are various references to Lewis Bayly's *Practice of Piety*. This work had reached its twenty-fifth edition in 1630. Wariston constantly studied *The Marrow of the Oracles of God, or diverse treatises about six of the weightiest things can concern a Christian in this life* by N. Bifield late Preacher of God's word at Isleworth in Middlesex. This book which is mentioned in the *Diary 1632-9*, pp. 104, 118-20, etc., was printed in London in 1625.

[8] Entry under 6 April 1634, *ibid.*, p. 202. The second edition of *A Practical Catechisme* was issued by Daniel Rogers, minister of Haversham, in 1633.

[9] Entry under 6 July 1634, *ibid.*, p. 233.

[10] *Ibid.*, p. 344.

my admiration the powerful presence of Gods spirit in the most
heavenly depairture of Helein Nisbet."[1]

In this close grouping of like-minded families Wariston grew up
and within the same circle he made his first and second marriages.
Inevitably the idea of the ministry occurred to him and this notion
came with special force when he lost his first wife in her sixteenth
year. He was just twenty-two and believed that God had taken
her from him as a punishment for his backsliding. He notes[2] that
he "roared", "youled pitifully" and "skirled" seeking for reconciliation and for God's pardon. As a boy he had been solitary and
highly-strung. It seems that it was at this time that he began those
communings with God in his "high chalmer" that he continued
throughout his adult life. He was dominated by a sense of his duty
to his Creator. In the period of his widowerhood he seems to have
lived in the Sheens or the Sciennes, an old house at the south-east
corner of the Meadows formerly the property of the Convent of
St Catherine of Siena and at that time in the possession of his
uncle Samuel Johnston. Casting up his assets and defects he noted
at this time that he had never been a good linguist, neither in
Scots, French, nor Latin.[3] On one occasion he spent the whole
afternoon pacing the long alley at the Sheens and considering
whether he should apply himself to the ministry or to the law.
"I fand[4] my gifts not so fitted for the first as for the last, becaus
my gift is rather dialecktik, nor didaktical, fitter for disputing *pro*
and *contra,* nor for teatching solid grounds."

It seems that he had no desire to preach, but he liked to discourse
privately on religious matters and the idea of explaining the
Catechism remained with him. In this connection there is a phrase
that has survived from Wariston's middle life. "The Lord was
pleased," he noted[5] on 26 May 1654, "in this sermon to bring to
my mynd my old dreame at London in 1646, that I would be
chased in over the hilles to Argyle; that S. J. CH(eisly) would
follow me, that, being depryved of other callings, I would taik me
to be a schoolmaster to teach any the Catechisme." His taste for
theological study was likewise constant. "I read[6] al daye on
Gerard *De Ecclesia.*" In the period before his second marriage,
when he was engaged to Helen Hay, he would explain Bolton's

[1] The Nisbets provide another example of mercantile-legal affiliations.
Lord Eastbank was the third son of James Nisbet, merchant of Edinburgh
by Margaret sister of Thomas Craig of Riccarton.
[2] Introduction to *Diary 1632-9,* p. xv.
[3] *Ibid.,* p. 135.
[4] *Ibid.,* p. 135.
[5] *Diary of Sir Achibald Johnston of Wariston, vol. II, 1650-4,* ed. David
Hay Fleming, Scottish History Society, 1919, pp. 262-3.
[6] *Diary 1632-9,* p. 206. A work by John Gerhard, professor of divinity
at Jena.

Discourse of True Happiness to her. Later they went through[1] Calvin's *Institutes* together.

In his notes Wariston girds against his own pre-occupation about money, but such self-accusations should be treated with reserve. He was disappointed of expectations from his uncle Samuel Johnston; he lost his first wife's slender fortune when she died childless; he purchased the small estate of Wariston, from which he took his title, from his second wife's family.[2] His diaries reveal that he was almost over scrupulously honest in money matters. He had no thought for tomorrow, nor for his children's tomorrow. Religion mastered him. A prayer made in later life[3] is much in character. "I desyred to hold up my nayme and my wyfes and every on(e) of my children, Elizabeth, Archbald, Rachel, Hellin, Margret, Jhon. Sanders, Janet, Catherin, James, and I begged of the Lord to look upon every on(e) of us and al our necessityes inward and outward."

He was severe on his own infirmities and on the infirmities of his colleagues. He gave to certain ministers the respect which they had earned through a strict adherence to those principles they shared with him. He was always wary in approaching his lay allies like the Marquis of Argyll.[4] The *Diary* records that Wariston held that the desire not for money but for power was his own temptation. He was quick to detect in other men that element of self-seeking from which he did not feel himself to be exempt. He was never surprised at any man's failure, nor at his own. He judged all men by their attachment to that Presbyterian tradition which the Covenant enshrined. Friends he seems hardly to have possessed except in the sense that some men's names were linked with his in public estimation. To this general statement there is an exception. Wariston took pleasure in the religious direction of women. This was an exercise which can be traced when he was only twenty-eight and it was one which grew upon him constantly.

It is of some political significance that the Countess of Loudoun came to Wariston for guidance. She was some six years his senior, a devout and ill-used wife, who had brought the Loudoun title and fortune to her extravagant husband George Campbell of

[1] *Ibid.,* p. 175.
[2] His first wife was Jane daughter of Sir Lewis Stewart and his second wife was a daughter of Lord Foresterseat.
[3] *Diary of Sir Archibald Johnston of Wariston, vol. III, 1655-60,* ed. James D. Ogilvie, Scottish History Society, 1940, p. 37.
[4] Cf. *ibid., introduction* pp. xxv-xxx *passim.* For Argyll's attitude to Wariston cf. introduction *Diary 1650-4.* In *Baillie's Letters,* ed. Laing, iii, p. 244. Argyll described Gillespie and Wariston as "tuo mad-headed youths that would ruyne the Kirk and Kingdom of Scotland".

SIR THOMAS HOPE

Lawers.[1] From his early manhood Wariston had established a close
and ambivalent relationship with the two Campbell chiefs. His
eldest surviving son Archibald was named after Argyll, but he
had from the beginning a strained attitude towards the head of
that great house. In some ways the purposes of Wariston and
Argyll were too akin. Loudoun he despised. In both cases the
wives had come to him for religious counsel. "That night," he
noted in an entry made[2] in 1639, "my Lady (Loudoun) and I
discoursed till tuo hours of the morning and I got good in the
praying with hir and seeing hir moved." It was a relationship well
known to Lady Wariston and discussed with[3] her; there is an indication that the prudent wife felt that it might injure her husband[4] in
some way. "I did wryte," Wariston notes,[5] "a very large and free
letter to my Lady Loudoun, both anent publik busines and their
privat case; and wairnd therin both the Chancellor and Argyle of
their sines and snares, and jugments like to befall them."

The first of these intimate disciples appears to have been his
cousin Lady Philiphaugh[6] and then Lady Riccarton. It was a
small group bound together without jealousy.[7] The Marchioness
of Argyll was favoured with less frequent[8] letters. It was essentially a Lowland circle and centres upon Edinburgh. If the first
Viscount Arbuthnott and his second wife be counted as members of
this affinity, they were the only representatives of the North[9] East.

It appears that when gathered together with one or two intimates Wariston would be moved to speak of God's attributes. It

[1] An entry under 28 July 1651 indicates both Wariston's attitude to the
Loudouns and also the political sense in which he used the word friendship.
"The Lord pity that poor woman, and give mercy to that miserable unclean
man, if it be al treu that is sayd, whereof I feare too much be treu, and that
I suffer in my nayme for my friendship to him", *Diary 1650-4*, p. 93.
[2] *Diary, 1632-9*, p. 369.
[3] "I told often my wyfe my poor Lady Loudoun was to gett som great
flappe", *Diary 1650-4*, p. 93.
[4] In regard to this correspondence Lady Loudoun is described as "angry at
my wife for hindering me", *ibid.*, p. 141.
[5] *Ibid.*, p. 141.
[6] "Upon the 4 Junii, Sunday, I got good by recommending tuyse, with
motion and tears unto God, the Lady Philiphaugh in Riccarton", *Diary
1632-9*, p. 259. Anne wife of James Murray of Philiphaugh was a daughter of
Sir Lewis Craig, Lord Wrightlands.
[7] "The Lady Riccarton had told me of my Lady Loudoun's melting in
teares upon the receate of my former letter, and of his blissing God for the
daye that ever shoe knew me, and that my freedome of wryting had been
most comfortable to hir", *Diary 1650-4*, p. 141.
[8] "I had wryten yesternight to my Lady Argyle to remember hir husband
of first tuo and foor last verses of 29 Proverbes, which did me good", *Diary
1650-4*, p. 156.
[9] "I got a letter from my Lord Arbuthnott shewing that the Lord had saifly
delivered his ladye", *ibid.*, p. 227. The loss of Wariston's diaries for the years
between 1639 and 1650 makes it difficult to trace the development of this
friendship.

E

was a pleasing trait that he attended and even on occasion praised the discourses of Presbyterian leaders who were politically opposed to him. One of his entries made on a Sunday[1] is characteristic. "God's consolations never run drye, ar ay tastye and keeps men ever fresh, for they are a fountayne, not a pudle or pond. . . . The restitution of Israel shal watter many nations. . . . I was drawen by my Lady Loudoun to repeate the sermons which I did and got liberty in both the prayers and in the grace after supper." This last passage recalls the tradition of the English Evangelicals like Bishop Bedell.

Under a different aspect there are certain resemblances to the world of Port Royal. Both groups were self-contained: Port Royal and the contemporary Presbyterians alike shared an Augustinian inheritance. There is also a certain parallel with the Arnauld family and the Duchesse de Longueville and her intimates. Wariston and the Arnaulds, he was only ten months older than Arnauld *le Grand,* both belonged to the *noblesse de robe* and the religious direction was in both cases given primarily to women of fashion. Among Jansenists and Presbyterians such exhortation was interlaced with political purposes and excitements. A comment by Wariston[2] is most convincing in its reference to God's assistance to him. "Thou putt it in my heade to wryte: Thou hast dyted (indited) it all: Thou hes maid me but a channel to let Thy liquor runne throu."

Two examples taken from his middle[3] life represent Wariston in his family. "I prayed on the 20 of Job, and keeped afternoone the exercise in our high chalmer . . . and I closed the exercise and got liberty in recommending the case of my wife (who was begun to crye) and of my chyld, and of my familye to the Lord, and then the publik business. . . . This night I sate up, and when my wyfe cryed I presented to the Lord 37 Isay 3 v., and 66 Isay 9 v., and 13 Hosea 13 v." Another entry dates from the same period. "On Thursday morning, 15 Apryle, I . . . heard from my Lady Loudoun, St John's hard taiking with hir. Was at Tho. Magdugal's son Thomas' baptisme, wheir I presented to my Lord roote and branch of our family to be His."

Wariston's career was very rapid and he came early to a clear ascendancy among the ministers of his own party. In his writings he accuses himself of ambition and of coveting,[4] from the time of the Treaty of Ripon in 1640, the post of lord clerk Register. There is something in this contention, and Wariston was finally destroyed because he agreed to return to this post under Crom-

---

[1] *Ibid.,* p. 267.
[3] *Ibid.,* pp. 151 and 157.
[2] *Ibid.,* introduction p. xxxviii.
[4] *Diary 1655-60,* p. 39.

well, but the driving force of his wish to keep in power was his determination to maintain the Covenant.

It was only in 1637 just at the beginning of his career that Wariston was concerned about the legal business brought to him. He offered his thanksgiving[1] because various important lairds, among them Philorth, Dunbar and Morphie, had engaged him to act for them in their processes. In the same year he lifted up his heart[2] to the Lord because of "My L. Cranstoune's intention to imploy me." After that he looked to his legal offices to sustain him and not to clients.

There had been a moment when Wariston was a young widower of twenty-three when he had not been sure of himself. He has left a comment in regard to the marriage he was contemplating with Lord Prestongrange's daughter. He held[3] that he would not be accepted since the Morisons of Prestongrange were "verie greadie and looked cheifly unto gear. . . . They lippened (trusted) to be barons of good qualitie."

Within a short time this mood had passed. From the signing of the National Covenant, for whose framing he had been in part responsible,[4] he gained an assurance in his public actions which he was never to lose.

Severity grew[5] on him. He took a stern view of private and of public shortcomings. In later life he saw himself as on a pinnacle. Thus Wariston could write[6] of the House of Hamilton "who hate me as if I had wronged the King and the Duke." He was, indeed, separated from nearly all his Scottish neighbours by a coldness towards the very idea of kingship. He made very free with the failings of all the members of the House of Stuart. He never agreed that any of them could measure up to his conception of a Covenanted King. A comment that he made[7] in the hard years sets out this standpoint. "My desyre, if it may stand with His (God's) pleasur, to live and dye with His covenant, work and remnant in poor but covenanted Scotland."

There is little hint of Wariston's recreations except fishing. "I find myself," he notes[8] on one occasion, "dull and heavy with too much eating." It is noticeable that his dreams reflect his own abiding seriousness. "This night[9] I dreamed of my being drawen

[1] Entry under 20 May 1637, *Diary 1632-9*, p. 267.
[2] *Ibid.*, p. 258.   [3] *Ibid.*, p. 178.
[4] *Diary 1650-4*, p. 72.
[5] This was noticeable in Wariston's dealings with his discipleship. "I was with Lady Stenhous and got libertye to recomend hir to God and begged to hir a view of hir 67 yeirs sines in the on(e) hand, and of God's 67 yeirs heaped kyndnesses to hir in the uther", *ibid.*, p. 224.
[6] *Diary, 1655-60*, p. 31.   [7] *Diary 1650-4*, p. 262.
[8] *Ibid.*, p. 208.   [9] *Ibid.*, p. 273.

in to serve my Lord Craighal (Craighall), and I thought he was
an Advocat, and would haive me as his man to taik the dolor
(dollar) of drynk-sylver, and could not gett that digested as
unsutable to my former calling." With this seriousness there went
a strain of simplicity which was perhaps the outcome of
his self-communing. He would always see himself as solitary.
"Pity my simplicity," he wrote,[1] "preyed upon by subtility of
uthers. In dealing with nimble, witty, untender men diffidence is
necessary to a statesman."

In another fashion the same quality is reflected in Wariston's
account[2] of a conversation with his wife. She told me that she
had not slept that night because she had lain down heavy and
was tossing in her thoughts the appearance of everybody's doing
us wrong, the judges there, Robert Baillie of Walston pressing to
turn the loss of Scotscraig's money upon us, Osborne's carriage to
her and then her woman Bessy Johnston (whom we had bred
both soul and body) dealing with Lady Kilbirnie to go home to
her and saying that my wife did now wear her clothes so long
and made them up again for her children, and that we had so many
children that it was a great burden to any servant who could expect
no profit from working for us.

There is a pleasing reference to the house of Wariston. One
night the Lord Clerk Register had prayed often that God might
"prevent or sanctifie" the reported intention of his enemies to
burn down Wariston. "The Lord knows[3] it is the only place I
haive to reteir to if the countrey wer peaceable. And my estate is
not aible to interteane my familye in this towne (Edinburgh); and
it is the place which He maid a Penuel and a Bethel unto me, and
wherin He promised to doe me good and deale weal with me."

Wariston was not without his encouragements, but the satis-
factions that he admitted were of a spiritual order. "I hoope[4] for
an harvest in Fyfe if their wer a spiritual ministery; multitude of
honest faces at comunions refreshes me." On one occasion he
refers to a journey into the Campbell country. "We sang[5] the
107th psalm from the 17th verse and I blessed God for the five
circles in the psalm instamped on me in the Sheins Yards and in
riding by Roseneath to Inverary up the loch side." He often
reverted to God's dealings with him in the alleyway of Sheins as
a young man.

It was, perhaps, in keeping with Wariston's severe mentality
that he should note[6] that sin was very loose in Atholl and retail[7]

[1] *Diary 1655-60*, p. 12.   [2] *Diary 1650-4*, p. 282.
[3] *Ibid.*, pp. 252-3.   [4] *Ibid.*, p. 314.
[5] *Ibid.*, pp. 252-3.   [6] *Ibid.*, p. 313.
[7] *Ibid.*, p. 314.

James Guthrie's statement about Stirling that Satan had a high throne there. He always retained an immaculate and religious patriotism. "I blissed[1] (blessed) God heartily and intreated Him to goe on in that conquering work as a greater proofe that He is God and is Scotland's God."

Two quotations may conclude this impression of Lord Wariston's character. "This night[2] I dreamed of Chryst, and ejaculations to Him, as being my freind and at Court near the Fayther, to speak for me." And again the prayer written in his notebook.[3] "O Fayther, Saviour and Sanctifyer taik Archye Jhonston—a poor, silly, imprudent, ignorant, improvident, passionat, humorous, foolish, ungrate, diffident body—in unto Thy thoughts, and know him by nayme and surnayme, and maik him knowe yet that Thou are the Lord God and his God and the God of his seed both in Thy words and workes."

The very strength of Wariston's ideas and the character of his self-revelation place him in a unique position. Markedly different tendencies are apparent in the careers of Sir Thomas Hope and the first Earl of Haddington, who reflected two other aspects of the approach of the great lawyers. As opposed to Wariston these men shared a more mundane and therefore more widely shared reaction to the problems that confronted them.

[1] *Ibid.*, p. 265. [2] *Ibid.*, p. 286.
[3] *Ibid.*, p. 254.

CHAPTER IV

THE LORD ADVOCATE

IT may be said that there was a permanent state of jealousy and friction between the great lawyers and the bishops. In England the episcopal bench was in possession of its privileges; but in Scotland the bishops were only moving into their place. Their pretensions would be regarded with an unfriendly eye by all the upholders of the Common Law. The career of the Lord Advocate provides an example of a legal figure of the elder generation who remained deeply attached to the prerogatives of the Church of Scotland and to the conception of the General Assembly. A study of the public life of Sir Thomas Hope of Kerse will serve to indicate the nature of the opposition which King Charles would arouse whenever he sought to use the bishops as instruments of royal policy. Sir Thomas Hope, whose shrewdness founded the fortunes of the Hopetoun family, held the office of lord advocate from 1626 until his death twenty years later. He was thus a nominee of Charles I, who never felt himself strong enough to dispense with his services.

He came of burgess stock settled in Edinburgh for some generations; his brother Henry founded the well-known mercantile family of Hope of Amsterdam. The date of his birth is unknown, but it was probably about 1580 or 1581.[1] Together with his brother James, he was servitor or pupil to John Nicolson of Lasswade, the well-known advocate. Thomas Hope had influential connections and enjoyed a lucrative practice for many years. When he became lord advocate he was admitted, according to an ancient privilege of that office, to sit with the judges in cases in which he was not himself employed.

Sir Thomas Hope had few close links with other legal families; he and his son married into landowning stocks[2] in Lothian; his own legal profits were ploughed back into the land. In the last ten years of the reign of James I he acquired the estates of

---

[1] He was only admitted as an advocate on 7 February 1605, but he became prominent as early as the following year through his defence of the six ministers at Linlithgow. His eldest son John Hope, Lord Craighall, was born about 1605.

[2] Except for his fourth son Sir James Hope of Hopetoun who in 1638 married the only child and heiress of Robert Foulis of Leadhills, a rich goldsmith in Edinburgh.

Prestongrange and Wester Granton;[1] a barony was erected from the properties of Kinnimouth and Craighall. It is only from 1633 that his career can be traced easily. In that year he began the diary that he kept until his death. In many ways it is a revealing document,[2] but it only starts when he was already middle-aged and established in power. By that time his opinions were fixed and his associations had been formed. The note of piety is that suitable to the head of a God-fearing Scottish family; it does not, as in Lord Wariston's case, derive from a force that seems to mould his thought and conduct. Sir Thomas Hope had a very clear sense of station, his own and others. He was a friend to the Presbyterian party so long as laymen and ministers should hold together. He did not make notes of sermons, nor did he offer to the ministers his personal friendship. One has the impression that it was to the establishment of the earldom of Hopetoun that he looked forward.

Among Hope's alliances two stand out as semi-permanent. He had long been a *protégé* of Sir John Murray,[3] who became in 1625 first Earl of Annandale. The latter was a minor Scottish favourite of James I and, in this case, Buckingham endorsed his sovereign's goodwill. This influence sufficed to secure for Hope the post of lord[4] advocate, but it was not a passport to the young King's favour.[5] At about the same time there began Sir Thomas Hope's lifelong association with Lord Haddington to whom Annandale had sold the estate of Tyninghame in East Lothian for two hundred thousand marks. It was to the lord advocate that the rich peers addressed themselves not only for a legal opinion in

[1] By the charter dated 11 January 1620 he had the privileges of an open park at Wester Granton.

[2] The earlier portions of the journal contain notes on business transactions which sometimes reflect his opinions. "Note of the Pacquets and Letteris sent and resauit from Court. 29 July 1633, Mr James Gordoun, quha promisit to send the samyn with Mr Patrick Dicksonne servitor to the Marquis of Douglas. 27 August 1634, Deluerit to the Erl Stirling, in his awin hous in Alexander Clerk's lodging, the new soapsignator dockettit be me. 27 November 1634, a nott of the Rosse his outragious speeches", *Sir Thomas Hope's Diary of his public correspondence 1633-1645*, edited for the Bannatyne Club (1814), pp. 6, 14, 15.

[3] Cf. Letter to the Earl of Annandale dated at Edinburgh on 1 November 1628. "We expectit dayly good newis anent the Rochell. God send them good", *Letters of Sir Thomas Hope 1627-46, Miscellany of the Scottish History Society*, vol. i (1893), p. 103.

[4] Letter from Haddington to Annandale, "He (the lord advocate) euer will acknowledge what he owes you for the help he had from you and your friends to promoue him and establish him in his place", *ibid.*, introduction p. 77.

[5] In 1627 Hope had applied to Charles I through Lord Annandale for a vacancy in the Court of Session for his son John, but met with a refusal on the ground that the candidate was only twenty-two or twenty-three years of age, *ibid.*, introduction, p. 88.

their litigation, but also in all those problems that later would be grouped under the general heading of conveyancing. All Hope's sympathies were with the Lords in their opposition to the King's proposals that the Crown should resume possession of alienated church property. Among his principal clients there were few whose interests were not affected by the scheme to endow an English-style episcopate in such a fashion. Thus Annandale, in addition to his lands in Dumfries and in the stewartry of Kirkcudbright, had invested in certain baronies belonging to Dundrennan Abbey and had acquired the bailliary of that monastery and of Lincluden. Lord Haddington in a letter which will be quoted in some detail makes clear the signal importance that the grandees attached to maintaining the lord advocate in his position. He also stressed the fact that in his delicate situation as the King's personal representative he must be allowed to act as he thought best if he were to protect the interest of the great houses with effect. The wording is worth noting carefully.

The Earl of Haddington began[1] by giving Lord Annandale his assurance that "my lord advocat will give him (an unnamed adversary) no advantage against you nor to any other, so far as his great sufficiencie can resist it". He then defines the state of the case. "Out of the necessitie of the time that forces men to provide meanes to maintaine them against the envie and calumnies that puts all men to their defences, he (the Lord Advocate) must gain the favour and protection of such as are powerfull to support. . . . His employments for his Maiesties seruice, wherby he procures to himself much dislike, which might breed him vexation, if he were not assisted by friends of prime credit, compels him to get and keepe their fauour, so as he must be excused to use the meanes. But I find him so faithfull, and considering that he knows more of your estate in this countrie nor yourself does, and that ye are not able so long as ye leeve to find any that can learne so much, or advyse your affaires so well,[2] I entreat your lordship to cherish his friendship." Sir Thomas's own comments should be read against the background of these sentences.

The letter displays a class consciousness very rare in Scotland. This was partly the result of the fact that at these interviews

[1] Letter dated 8 January 1631, now preserved among the Laing MSS. in the library of Edinburgh University and printed *ibid.,* introduction, pp. 77-8.

[2] An example of the nature of this advice is provided by a letter written to Lord Annandale by the Lord Advocate and dated at Edinburgh 29 December 1630. "The Erll of Monteth is to come up within 8 dayis at furthese, and quhen he is thair, if ye ply cannely the bussines agains your party Sir Archibald (Acheson), it may be ye find both freindschip and success beyond your expectatioun, quhilk I recomend to your lordship now as the gretest bussines ye haif ado heir", *ibid.,* p. 105.

money passed or sums were promised. In all the negotiations between equals, the plots and bands and associations, this did not occur. A note made by Sir Thomas bears on this matter. He records[1] that on 1 April 1634 at six o'clock in the evening a visit was paid to him in his chamber by the Countess of Home, the Earl of Lauderdale, the Lord Doune and Lord Maitland with his lady. It was a family party. Doune was the Earl of Moray's heir and Maitland would become the celebrated Duke of Lauderdale. Lady Home was an Englishwoman and the mother-in-law of the young peers. They were in treaty in regard to the succession to the Home estates.[2] "And ther," explains Sir Thomas in recording this interview, "first the Countess apart in the window, and then scho, the Erl Lauderdaill and Lord Doune, promisit to me, if thai get any thing be the process, to give me two thousand merkis. The Countess called it pundis. Item, this promise renewit by hir and the Earl of Murray and Lord Doune, on Weddinsday the 6 of August, 1634, at 6 hors at nycht."

The Diary contains numerous similar entries.[3] Fees were also paid for more regular consultations.[4] One note is rather curious. "This day," wrote[5] Sir Thomas Hope on 4 July 1635, "the Erll of Stirling came from Court, and in his chamber in Mr. John Layng his house, the Erll Traquhair promisit in the Erll of Stirling his presence to advance to me my pension for a zeir (year) if I prevaillit in the matter of Bancreiff against Sir P. Murray." Stirling was at that time secretary of state and Traquair treasurer depute. The Lord Advocate set down the witnesses to each transaction; he was always very careful that his just claims should not fail through his own negligence.

Meanwhile his position grew more substantial year by year. His eldest son had now attained the Court of Session and taken his seat as Lord Craighall. His younger sons were sent south for further education, Alexander to Court and James to study at

[1] Sir Thomas Hope's *Diary*, p. 10.

[2] James second Earl of Home had died in the previous year and a dispute sprang up between his two sisters and the heir male Sir James Home of Coldingknows. Lady Home was the daughter of Edward ninth Lord Dudley.

[3] Cf. Under 15 February 1639. "William Seytoun of Marry, desyrit me not to be agains him in the reduction of Meldrum's horning and promisit, if he wan the caus, fiftie doubill pieces of gold." Under 1641. "Item, on 5 November, the Earl of Abercorn promisit 50 dol", *Diary*, pp. 86, 154.

[4] In the account books of George third Earl of Winton there occurs this note. "Item, the 6 Februari (1628) to Mr Thomas Houpe and Nikolsonne, with Mr Robert Burnett at ane consultatioune, 93 *lib*, 6s, 8d." This is one of several entries of fees paid to Sir Thomas Hope. Burnet was brother-in-law to Lord Wariston, *Cal. Forbes Leith MSS*, H.M.C., Appendix to Second Report, p. 199.

[5] *Diary*, pp. 26-7.

Bourges[1] and at the University of Orleans. Alexander, to whom he was attached, persuaded him to have his portrait painted by Jameson.[2] He kept up relations with his brother's family.[3]

It was about this time that the Dowager Countess of Mar became a factor in his life. She was a turbulent and litigious widow at odds with her step-son. The Lord Advocate guided and humoured and made use of her; he saved up great portions for his two daughters so that they might marry into the Erskine family.[4] Finally Lady Mar came to live in his house in the Cowgate in Edinburgh and stayed there until she died.[5] Through her he strengthened his ties with the Court[6] and with Tyninghame.[7]

A man who takes up Hope's position must have his enemies, and those who would for one reason or another serve the King sought to remove him. He was too close in to the great lords of a Presbyterian colour, and both Traquair and Hamilton would consider whether he might not be driven from his place. It accorded with the Lord Advocate's interest and also with his inherent judgment to see as legal the various steps that would be taken to preserve the independence of the Scottish nation and the privi-

[1] They had left Scotland in February 1636. There is an entry under 5 July 1637. "Item . . . a letter to my sone Mr Alexander, and within it one to be sent to his brother Mr James, to Bourges in France, quhairin I haif dorectit him to return about Michaelmas next", *ibid.*, p. 62.
[2] On 20 July 1638. "This day William Jamesoun, painter, (at the earnest desyre of my sone Mr. Alexander) wes sufferit to draw my pictur." On 27 July. "Item, a second draucht be William Jamesone", *ibid.*, pp. 75, 76.
[3] On 5 August 1637. "Hary (Hope), my nephew, went by sea to Calis, and gevin him fyve twelff pund pieces off gold; and at his return he promisit to serve sum merchand in Amsterdam", *ibid.*, p. 65.
[4] Except for his son Charles (b. 1627), who died young, his daughters came at the end of the family. Mary (b. 1620) married in 1632 Charles Erskine of Bandeath, who was Lady Mar's fourth son, and Anne (b. 1625) married in 1646 David Erskine, Lord Cardross, who was Lady Mar's grandson.
[5] Two quotations will indicate Lady Mar's standpoint. Both letters were dated from Stirling and were preserved in 1893 among the Erskine-Murray MSS. On 30 July 1639 she wrote to her son Charles: "Tell your good father (Sir Thomas Hope) he knawis best whatt to doe. . . . Bott I would forgive nothing which may be gotten by law." On 22 November 1640 she wrote to Sir Thomas Hope: "My verie good Lord—New when necessitie compelle theme I am forced to have my recourse to your helpe. And if evrie one had kepit als good duetie to me as ever I did and shall doe to all with whome I have to doe. I neidit not now be oppressed with griefe as this day I am." *Letters of Sir Thomas Hope 1627-46*, pp. 110, 112. Entry under 11 may 1644. "Dame Marie Steuart, Countes of Mar, deceissit in my hous in the Cowgait", *Diary*, p. 205.
[6] Entry under 25 March 1637. "Letters to the Lord Duik (of Lennox) from the Countess of Mar in my favors", *ibid.*, p. 57.
[7] Apart from other references to the family Hope refers to the deaths of the first, second and third Earls of Haddington. "29 May 1637, Mononday. This day about 3 efternoone, Thomas Erl of Hadingtoune, Lord Privie Seille deceissit. God prepare me", *Diary*, p. 61. Catherine Countess of Haddington was Lady Mar's youngest daughter.

leges of that nation's leaders. For the rest he lived with some simplicity, planning and buying for his children rather than spending.

The references to Lady Hope are few. Sir Thomas committed himself to the statement[1] that his father-in-law Mr Bennet had been town clerk of Musselburgh, which suggests that he did not lay much store by his wife's relatives. There is also a comment which seems to give some indication of his attitude. After referring to the death of his infant grandson James Hope, he adds this phrase.[2] "And my wiff was angrie at my greif."

His affection for his sons was marked, especially perhaps for James Hope, who was provident and had a study in his father's house retained for his use[3] when he rode in to Edinburgh, and for Alexander, "carver to his Sacred Majestie".[4] The latter caused him much anxiety. The Lord Advocate was fond of his younger daughter Anne.[5] He kept a good establishment;[6] there was nothing especially ascetic about the Presbyterians of his tradition.[7] It is noticeable that he had the arms which would be appropriate to a landowner.[8] He was accustomed to quote Latin and occasionally Greek.[9]

He had always a clear sense of the duties owed to him and also of those owed by him to others. As he grew old he had a rather pleasing recollection of his more homely relatives.[10] For the last seven years of his life there are frequent references in his Diary

---

[1] Cf. *Scots Peerage*, vol. viii, p. 577, note 10.

[2] Entry under 6 November 1641, *Diary*, p. 154.

[3] Entry under 24 June 1644, *ibid.*, p. 191.

[4] Endorsement dated 17 February 1641, *Letters of Sir Thomas Hope*, p. 116.

[5] Entry under 7 June 1644, "To Anne my daughter, to pay a velvet cassikin too myself 80 lb", *Diary*, p. 207.

[6] There are references to his son's great coach which was "putt in the hall of the castell of Edinburgh"; to his son Mr. Alexander's coachman; to Robert Tait gardener at Granton, *ibid.*, pp. 77, 196, 203.

[7] An entry runs, "Resavit from Francis van Hoff ane barrell of Malvesie and ane uther of reid sack wyne". Cf. under 25 August 1643, "My deire sone (Sir Thomas Hope, Lord Chief Justice General) was buryat in the Grayferis. This day I vowit to my Lord, himilitie, patience, abstinence, sobrietie, and not to eat but one kynd of meit at denner, and above two drinks of wyne. The Lord gif me grace to performe it", *ibid.*, pp. 194, 195.

[8] In 1639 he gave his son James "my sword and twa pistoles" and to his son Sir Thomas "my petronell or carabin, indentit of rowat work; reserving the use thairof to myself, quhen I call for it". The Lord Advocate also had a carbine with a mother-of-pearl stock, *ibid.*, pp. 90, 93, 96.

[9] Cf. *ibid.*, pp. 154, 203.

[10] Entry under 2 November 1635. "Mr John Rig deceissit. The Lord prepare me for I am now the only and last of that stok of mankynd." Under 2 January 1644. "This day my worthie cousing William Rig off Athernie, departit at his hous of Athernie", *ibid.*, pp. 31, 201. A note made in 1640 reads, "17 May, Sounday, at 2 houres afternoon, good Elizabeth Nicolsoun deceissit, and left me the only levand of the stok of John Hope, my guid-schir in the degrie off thrid from him. The Lord prepare me", *Ibid.*, p. 113.

to God's Judgment Seat. One of his very few notices relating to
the clergy is inspired by the death of a contemporary. "This day,"
wrote[1] Sir Thomas on 16 February 1644, "worthie Mr John Ker,
minister at Prestoun, deceissit. The Lord prepare me, for we were
off one age."

His notes reveal a deep belief that God in His Providence
would guard His Kirk. This conviction should be stressed for it
was a sustaining element that lay behind Hope's caution and his
worldly prudence. "Item," he noted[2] on 2 April 1639, "as I
awaked on Weddinsday in the morning, I fell in ane earnest in-
calling of the Lord, that his Majestie wold pittie his peopell, and
vindicat them from the power and rage of their adversaries, and
wold establische the glorie of his blissit trewth in the land. And
quhill I wes praying, thir wordis wer spokin, but quhither be
me or some other I dar not say, but the wordis wer, 'I will preserve and saiff my peopell'." Like Saint Teresa of Avila, the
Lord Advocate referred to God as "his Majestie".

His thought lacked the theocratic element which marked that
of the Presbyterian ministers and Lord Wariston. There was in
consequence nothing to disturb his due reverence for earthly
sovereignty, a sentiment which was becoming in one who was the
King's agent in all legal questions. The Lord Advocate always
retained his wide support in Scotland because his line of reasoning was one which Scotsmen of position could comprehend. He
was determined that no harm should come to Scotland or to the
established interests in that kingdom either from the English
bishops or from the English Parliament.

In this connection it is of interest to trace the gradual liquidation
of the ties which had bound so many Scotsmen to James VI and I.
So far as the new King himself was concerned it may be regarded
as a personal question, the substitution in his life of Laud for
Buckingham. The notion of a personal favourite, through whom
application should be made, had long been familiar in Scotland,
and George Villiers was very ready to respond to that mixture
of self-confidence and flattery with which the Scottish lords
approached him. It was Archbishop Laud whom they could not
abide. Those who are attached to the clergy seldom realise how
very few laymen are not in their hearts opposed to clerical
influence.

Charles I was not accustomed to pay much heed to those who
had received his father's easy friendliness. There is a note of dis-
couragement in Sir Thomas Hope's reference to the death of Lord
Annandale, who had been much neglected by the Court in his

[1] *Ibid.*, p. 203.   [2] *Ibid.*, p. 98.

last years. "This day," he wrote[1] on 8 October 1640, "I gott word of the death of my good Earl of Annandaill, at Londoun, quho wes my dearest lord and freind: God prepare me." This experience was similar to that of all those who had once been close to their old sovereign. It is reflected in the outlook of the great political and legal family of the Earls of Haddington with whom the Lord Advocate was always in close relations.

Sir Thomas Hamilton, the founder of that house, had acquired the greatest legal fortune of the preceding generation and had also benefited from his master's generosity. He was a slightly older contemporary[2] and friend of James VI; he had been his trusted adviser and one of the Octavians in the years before he came to the English throne. His career had begun early for he was a lord of session under the title of Drumcairn at twenty-nine. He had served King James and his own interests in equal measure. During many years he had combined the office of lord advocate with his judicial functions. The new King had decreed that no nobleman or officer of state should have a seat on the bench of the Court of Session. In 1626 he had in consequence resigned both his presidentship of that court and his post as secretary of state. He had been named lord privy seal. He had by this time become Earl of Melrose, a title that he was later to exchange[3] for that of Haddington.

Sir Thomas Hamilton had early decided to take to the land and had concentrated on former ecclesiastical holdings. These were relatively easy to acquire either by direct grant from the Crown or by purchase from the actual holder. His father had passed over to him the kirklands of Dalmeny and the life-rent of Priestfield. Later Hamilton obtained the kirklands of Easter, Wester and Middle Binning.[4] In 1614 he bought the abbey lands of Melrose from Sir John Ramsay. His estates at Tyninghame, Coldstream and Luffness were also to some extent ecclesiastical[5] in origin.

This is an impressive list and sufficiently explains the progress of the family towards a quiet dynastic opposition to any

[1] Sir Thomas Hope's *Diary*, p. 120.

[2] He was born in 1563.

[3] His title was changed to that of Earl of Haddington in 1627, the year before he purchased Tyninghame. He belonged to a cadet branch of his family not descended from the royal marriage which gave the Hamiltons their special place in Scottish politics.

[4] He was created Lord Binning in 1613 and was known by that title until he became Earl of Melrose in 1619.

[5] His barony of Drom was also partly formed out of kirk lands. He had made extensive purchases from Lord Maxwell and Lord Lindsay of the Byres.

re-establishment of an endowed episcopate. Hamilton himself had been brought up at the University of Paris and was, perhaps, then a Catholic.[1] It is a point about which we can have no assurance. Later he seems to have been detached in religious matters and ready to follow King James's preferences without nostalgia. The portrait by Jameson painted when Sir Thomas Hamilton had become Earl of Haddington is now at Tyninghame. He is represented in ceremonial dress with the gold-braided gown and carrying gloves. The face framed in the ruff is ageing and instinct with caution. It has much of the spirit of the Elizabethan statesmen. It is not surprising that the ministers were never certain[2] of him; it needed the new King and Archbishop Laud to bring the Hamiltons of Tyninghame to a firm support of Presbyterianism.

The first Earl of Haddington was something of a scholar with that old-fashioned and discursive erudition[3] that his master could appreciate. The memorandum books at Tyninghame contain the

[1] He was educated at the High School at Edinburgh under William Robertson, who was suspected as a Catholic, and then studied at the University of Paris from 1581 until 1587. His uncle John Hamilton was Rector of that University from 1584 and returned to Scotland as a priest in 1600. A Pasquill presented to the King in 1597 refers to "Mr Thomas Hamiltoun, brought up in Parise with that apostat Mr Johne Hamiltoun, and men say the dregs of stinking Roman professioun sticke faste to his ribbes", Calderwood, *Historie of the Kirk of Scotland*, vol. v, p. 542. Cf. Fraser, *Memorials of the Earls of Haddington*, vol. i, p. 64. The first Earl of Haddington does not appear to have belonged to a Catholic family and his uncle is termed "apostat". There seems to be no evidence of Catholic sympathies in his later life. A letter to the Earl of Menteith dated 24 March 1629 relates to strong measures against Huntly. "It is," writes Haddington, "an exercise worthie of the care of all noblemen at court professedlie inclined to our (Protestant) religion", printed from the original in the Duke of Montrose's charter chest in Fraser, *Memorials*, vol. ii, p. 163.

[2] Cf. Andrew Melville's speech to him at the Hampton Court Conference in 1606. "My Lord, you would do God and His Majesty better service if ye bended your forces and speeches against your uncle, Mr John Hamilton, a seminary priest, and one Mr Gilbert Borown, abbot of Newabbey, who have infected a great part of Scotland with their superstitious dregs of popery.... But these men ye have clapped (fondled), and shut up the faithful servants of Jesus Christ into prison", *Original Letters relating to the Ecclesiastical Affairs of Scotland*, Bannatyne Club, vol. i, pp. 56-67. Cf. Fraser, *Memorials*, i, pp. 92-3.

[3] Among the more interesting books at Tyninghame are the following: *Cases collected by James Dyer*, London, 1601. *The Commentaries and Reports of Edmund Plowden*, 1595. *Il Furioso di Lodovico Ariosto*, 1556. *The History of Lewis the Eleventh* by F. Mathieu, London, 1614. Camden's *Britannia*. Machiavelli *Historie Fiorentini*, 1551. Bernard de Girard, *L'Histoire de France*, 1557. Calvin *Institutio Christianae Religionis*, 1618. *Plaidoyre de M. Jacques de Montholon pour les Pères Jesuites*, Paris 1612. All these have the signature "Melros" on the title page. *A Catholik Approach for Protestants* by George Bishop and John Norton, London, 1613. *Abissini Regis Historie*, 1628. *La Théorie des Planettes* by Charles Faye printed in 1637. These bear the signature "Hadinton". *La Nouvelle Historie d'Alexandre le Grand*, 1639, bears the same signature, but in this case it is presumably that of the third Earl of Haddington.

notes that he made on Seneca, and on the antiquaries Stow and Camden, on the Essays of Montaigne, the works of d'Aubigné, de Thou's *History* and Bodin's *La République*. There is, understandably, an analysis of the writings of Sir Edward Coke.

King James always showed Haddington quite special favour and a real confidence. He valued his quickness of mind and his adaptability. The royal comment on the marriage of his heir to the youngest daughter of the House of Mar throws light on all the parties. "The Lord haud a grup o' me. If Tam o' the Cowgate's son marry Jock o' Sklates' dochter, what's to come[1] o' me." This was not the sort of statement that his severe young successor liked to recall.

The Earl of Haddington was linked with many groupings; with the Jacobean Court for his third wife was sister to Robert Carr[2] the favourite; with the Scots peers for his sons-in-law included Airlie, Boyd, Carnegie, Cassilis and Lindsay of the Byres; with the legal families[3] and, perhaps, most significant, with the small knot of wealthy Lowland merchants. The Earl's mother was a daughter of James Heriot of Trabroun and his first wife was a daughter of James Foulis of Colinton, who was related to the wealthy goldsmith of that name. Both Haddington and his first wife were cousins of George Heriot,[4] "His Majesty's Jeweller" and the founder of Heriot's Hospital.

Since he occupied such a central position, a biographical study of Lord Haddington would throw light on many aspects of Scottish life during the years when James I reigned in England. He survived until 29 May 1637, dying in the month that the new Prayer Book was brought up to Scotland. His figure does not emerge with any clarity. By comparison with Wariston and Hope he may be regarded as a statesman who truly sought to serve the Scottish kingship. We can now consider the Episcopalian tradition to which in general he may be said to have adhered, the episcopate as it had shaped itself before Laud and his disciples came to trouble Scotland.

---

[1] Fraser *Memorials*, i, pp. 189-90. The marriage took place in 1622. The nickname arose from Lord Haddington's house in the Cowgate in Edinburgh.

[2] His marriage contract with the widowed Lady Home of Polwarth was signed on 16 September 1613, the day after the death of Sir Thomas Overbury. This tragedy in time destroyed the influence of Lady Home's brother.

[3] Both his father Thomas Hamilton, Lord Priestfield and his half-brother Andrew Lord Redhouse were judges. Another half-brother Sir John Hamilton of Magdalens became lord clerk register in 1622. He was also related to the various judges belonging to the Foulis family.

[4] George Heriot (1563-1624) was Haddington's exact contemporary. Heriot's second wife was a daughter of James Primrose, clerk of the privy council of Scotland, who belonged to the same grouping.

CHAPTER V

THE EPISCOPALIAN TRADITION

IT would be an error to read into the Episcopalianism of the early seventeenth century that clear-cut distinction between the Episcopalian and Presbyterian traditions which was manifested after the Revolution of 1688. The traditions were at first closely interwoven and it is at times difficult to disentangle them. Some earlier bishops, in particular, could claim and with justice a Presbyterian cast for their own thought.

Further, in a matter in which the varying judgments of the King held such significance, there were three stages in the opinion of the sovereign to be distinguished; the view held by James VI, before he succeeded to the English throne; the same king's views in the last twenty years of his life; the very different outlook of Charles I. There was again a parallel and clear distinction between the outlook of the Jacobean episcopate in Scotland and that of the few Scottish prelates nominated by Charles I under Laud's influence.

As far as church organisation is concerned, there is some reason for supposing that James VI favoured a system analogous to that obtaining in the Lutheran states in Germany. His view of the controlling power possessed by the sovereign in religious matters resembled that held by the Elector Augustus of Saxony, and his bishops were in the first place conceived along the lines of Lutheran superintendents. Examined from this angle, his practice in Scotland may be considered as an attempt to curb political Calvinism.

Such reasoning made the King an opponent of the representation of the Kirk in Parliament, a proposition to this effect having been brought forward in 1596 by Lord Menmuir. The King's relentless harrying of the House of Gowrie was, perhaps, bound up with the devotion of the leaders of the Kirk to the Ruthven family. The movement against the Gowrie Conspiracy, whether intended for this purpose or not, had the effect of removing the third Earl of Gowrie, who was the disciple[1] of Theodore Beza. The gradual

[1] John third Earl of Gowrie was described as a young man "of great expectation and much respected by the professors", Calderwood, *op. cit.*, vi, p. 27. He was killed at Gowrie House, Perth, on 5 August 1600 aged twenty-two and had stayed at Geneva with Beza for three months in the previous year.

establishment of an episcopal system seems to have been intended primarily to prevent the political ascendancy of the Kirk leaders. Various causes made the relationship between the Ruthvens and their sovereign difficult. It is nevertheless the case that until the emergence of the Marquis of Argyll as a political factor there was among the great Scottish lords no other family which had the entire confidence of the Presbyterian opposition.

In this question of the episcopate the King moved slowly. The selection by the King of an ecclesiastical commissioner as a member of the First Estate when a vacancy should occur was accepted by the General Assembly at Montrose in 1600. It was from this time that Calderwood notes[1] the beginning of the changes. "The trojan horse, the Episcopacy, was brought in busked and covered with caveats, that the danger and deformity might not be seen." At the Assembly, which met at Holyrood two years later, a resolution was accepted favouring the tenure of the dioceses by individual ministers. In consequence the three most recently nominated bishops[2] were named, in two cases jointly with another minister, to visit the districts of Ross, Caithness, Sutherland and Moray. Melville's comment[3] sets out the position clearly. "Thus under the guise of a mere commission of visitation there were three bishops put in possession of their bishoprics." In 1604 John Spottiswoode, minister of Calder, was designated Archbishop of Glasgow and as such took his seat in Parliament and on the Privy Council.

This stage of the proceedings was completed by three enactments. The Assembly of 1606 was a clerical convention whose members were nominated by the King in letters missive. At this gathering it was agreed that there should be constant moderators in the Presbyteries; this act was then extended to include Provincial Synods. In July 1607 the King instructed every synod to elect a bishop as its constant moderator if one resided within the area. At the Linlithgow meeting in 1608 all the bishops were commissioners of Assembly. So far each step in the royal action may be interpreted as an element in a secular policy which had also achieved the perpetual banishment of the Melvilles.

It is at this stage that the influence of his English experience and his now permanent residence in England began to affect the

[1] Calderwood, *op. cit.*, vi, p. 20.
[2] These were David Lindsay, minister of South Leith, provided to the see of Ross on 1 November 1600, George Gladstanes, minister of St. Andrews, provided to Caithness on 5 November 1600 and Peter Blackburn, minister in Aberdeen, provided to that see on 2 September 1600. They did not receive episcopal consecration until some years later. Cf. *H.B.C.*, pp. 215, 219 and 233.
[3] James Melville, *Autobiography and Diary*, p. 546.

F

King. In 1609 the bishops were granted jurisdiction in spiritual causes and in the following year two Courts of High Commission were established on the English model. At the Glasgow Assembly in 1610 Spottiswoode was elected moderator.[1] At this meeting it was decided that the provincial synods should become diocesan synods under the chairmanship of the local bishop and that excommunications and absolutions must be ratified by the diocesan. On the other hand it was asserted that the bishops were subject in all matters to the General Assembly, although this proviso remained a dead letter. Archbishop Spottiswoode and Bishops Lamb and Hamilton received episcopal consecration in England. By May 1611 the other Scottish bishops had been consecrated by the returning prelates.

This last group of changes was the fruit of the King's experiences since his accession to the English throne. It is doubtful how far they commended themselves in Scotland even to the bishops. Patrick Forbes in particular, who was ordained in the winter of 1611-2 at the age of forty-seven, seems to have come very slowly to the acceptance of episcopacy. This is the view set out[2] by his recent biographer. "The simple truth is that Forbes came to accept traditional episcopacy because of his deep concern for the Protestant position in Scotland." Bishop Forbes's own later comment[3] on the institution is very temperate. "Yet they (the Bishops) now being established and set at the rudder of our Church, I am so far from the judgement of them who would have no godly nor singularly gifted men to accept them, that I think it so far from a well-informed zeal, as it is rather in my judgement a sort of transportation with the love of their own opinion . . . they will put us rather in peril to have no church at all." It is a corollary to this somewhat restrained appreciation that the bishops made no attempt to impose episcopal ordination upon ministers who had received only the laying-on of hands of the Presbytery.

It is notable that most members of the Jacobean episcopate were united in a profound antipathy to the Church of Rome which served to make them tolerable to their own ministers. They were united in a vehement defence of Protestantism which must have given satisfaction to their zealous followers. Even those bishops

---

[1] Archbishop Spottiswoode was translated from Glasgow to St. Andrews on 6 August 1615. He succeeded Archbishop Gladstanes, who had been translated from Caithness on 12 October 1604 and had been consecrated on 23 January 1611 by the bishops who had returned from England.

[2] *The Life, Times and Thought of Patrick Forbes, Bishop of Aberdeen 1618-1635.* By the Rev. W. G. Sinclair Snow, Church Historical Society, 1952, p. 48.

[3] *Funerals,* p. lviii quoted by Snow *op. cit.,* p. 49.

who preached seldom and made few public utterances belonged by descent and through association to the strongly Protestant stocks among the landed families. There was here nothing of Laud's cold distaste for Rome. With rare exceptions the Scottish bishops and ministers worked solidly together to destroy the influence of the Papacy conceived as an anti-Christ. This was a uniting factor among the supporters of the Reformation in Aberdeenshire. A comment by Bishop Forbes bears on this point. "The clear light and powerful ministry of the Gospel," he explained,[1] "now in a degree both showing clearly and working powerfully anti-Christ, his fall."

It is difficult in considering this period to distinguish plainly between the parties, although the doctrine of "parity" among ministers was widely held. Still, the episcopal tradition which was gradually becoming re-embodied had many Presbyterian elements. Until they were men in middle life, all the elder generation of the bishops had held that the binding element in their religious life was the Ministry of the Word. It is not certain that those who returned to Presbyterianism in their old age did so unwillingly. The emergence of the episcopate was a symbol of the King's political victory. It was the substitution of Spottiswoode for Melville. In the sphere of doctrine the Confession of Faith which emerged from the Assembly held at Aberdeen in 1616 laid especial emphasis on the matter of predestination. There was at this stage no dissent from the Calvinist position which united bishops and ministers and all their flocks.

It is in these years that the effect of the King's residence in England showed its full influence on his religious policy. But two elements in the situation made its impact less severe than that of his son would prove to be. In the first place James I was moved by arguments in the sphere of policy and administrative convenience, perhaps also by what he saw as seemliness; his son was moved by deep religious faith. In the second place it is true that both made the mistake of bringing Anglican bishops with them into Scotland. Here also there was a difference. Those with James I accompanied him as advisers; Bishop Laud came with Charles I as his guide. Finally the actions of the old King were confined to measures. Charles I not only introduced new measures but he changed radically the character and personnel of the episcopate.

James I adopted the Anglican practice in regard to communicating on feast days and celebrating church festivals, both of which were repugnant to the Genevan conceptions which dominated religious life in Scotland. Confirmation by the bishop, the reception

[1] Patrick Forbes, *A Learned Commentarie,* p. 180.

of Holy Communion kneeling and the administration of Communion and Baptism in private houses in cases of necessity, all
alike derived from the system of the Church of England. These
proposed changes were embodied in five articles submitted to the
General Assembly which met at Perth in 1616. They were paralleled by the introduction of the Anglican Service into the Chapels
Royal. The articles were placed before Parliament in 1621. They
were always opposed[1] by the Presbyterians and remained one of
their standing grievances. These innovations were indeed contrary
to all that the black Geneva gown had come to mean for Scotland.
Yet the practical effect of the articles should not be exaggerated;
the administration of the sacraments in private houses was a
privilege which none need use,[2] and the bishops in fact may have
seldom administered Confirmation.

At the same time the defence of the five articles which was
brought forward by the Jacobean bishops would in time open
up a profound division of another character between the episcopate
and the strict Presbyterians. A quotation from a speech made by
Bishop Forbes in the Parliament of 1621 bears on this point.
"Seeing His Majesty," declared[3] the prelate in reference to the
five articles, "will have them brought in, I protest upon my salvation and condemnation there is no danger in using them. They are
indifferent in themselves, and therefore whosoever refuses to give
His Majesty obedience in using them are contentious and troublers
of the peace and unity of the Kirk." It is evident that such an
argument would be regarded from the Presbyterian standpoint as
Erastian. The Jacobean bishops were essentially moderate; they
were supporters of compromise within the ranks of the Reformed
Churches. In one matter they were, perhaps, farther removed
from the Presbyterians than any Laudian; their master was the
King.

Naturally this statement must not be pressed too far. The
bishops would not in fact be troubled beyond the sphere of matters
which they held to be indifferent. Still they gave heed to the just
prince in a fashion that would have outraged Andrew Melville.
Further the Erastian element in their thought was a link between
the older generation of Scottish bishops and their senior English

---

[1] The strength of the opposition may be indicated by the fact that, although
the articles were pressed on the King's instructions, thirty-nine out of eighty
ministers voted in the negative at the Assembly at Perth. In Parliament the
voting on the articles was fifty-nine and eighty-six in favour.

[2] Snow gives two examples from the session records of St. Nicholas',
Aberdeen, to show that Communion was administered in private houses in
1630 and 1633, *op. cit.*, p. 81.

[3] Calderwood, *op. cit.*, vii, p. 491.

colleagues who had come to their place in the old Queen's time. The majority of both groups would agree in viewing rochet[1] and surplice with profound detachment. They agreed in disliking everything that savoured of Roman practice. Strict Calvinism was a uniting[2] bond. This relation was, however, complicated by the antipathy between the sister kingdoms. The Scottish bishops had no desire for any English customs or English manners. At a later stage they would view the proposal to introduce the Anglican Prayer Book with dislike; they knew their countrymen. Still, the bishops of King James's creation were old men in his son's reign. Except for Spottiswoode, they were not masterful. It was not for them to pit their preference against their sovereign's orders.

They were clearly loth to separate themselves from the body of the Scottish ministers. Thus Bishop Patrick Forbes, who died before the coming of the troubles,[3] showed no sympathy with the theory of the divine right of episcopacy and held[4] that churches "agreeing soundly in all the essential points of faith" may differ in church government. Similarly the elder bishops were most unwilling to separate themselves from the peers, who were their kinsmen and protectors. Whatever their ecclesiastical powers, prestige in the civil state was not denied them. In the Parliament of 1606, for instance, they had their precedence between the earls and barons. There is a record of Bishop Graeme of Dunblane and his friend Lindsay of Dunkeld riding to the Parliament together, both dressed in silk and velvet with their "foote mentles".[5] The Jacobean bishops in Scotland had a position in the country which was in some ways more solid and certainly more closely integrated with the lay peerage than that enjoyed by their English colleagues. Bishop Forbes had held Corse Castle and its estate for ten years before entering the ministry; Archbishop Spottiswoode purchased the lairdship of Dairsie in 1616. The latter's second son Sir Robert Spottiswoode was president of the

[1] There is no doubt as to Andrew Melville's attitude to this question when cited before the privy council in November 1606 he approached Archbishop Bancroft "and taking him by the quhyt sleives of his rochet, and schalking them, in his manner, frielie and roundlie, callit them 'Romishe ragis, and a pairt of the Beastes mark'," James Melville, *op. cit.*, p. 679.

[2] In the case of Archbishop Abbot personal liking for the Scots seems to have been added to doctrinal sympathy.

[3] He had a stroke which paralysed his right side in 1632 and died on 28 March 1635. Snow, *op. cit.*, pp. 98-101 modifies the judgment on Bishop Forbes's theological position reached in the article in the *D.N.B.*, xix, p. 408.

[4] Patrick Forbes, *A Defence of the Lawful Calling*, p. 5.

[5] *Letters and Correspondence of Bishop Graeme*, p. 235.

Court of Session.[1] In happier times this family might have ended as a stock of landed and political significance in Scotland like that which Archbishop Loftus founded in the kindlier climate of the Church of Ireland. William Law Mathieson has observed[2] that the restored episcopate was an experiment in compromise, but it was a thoroughly Scottish compromise. It was Laud who bedevilled it.

If this was the standpoint of the older Scottish bishops the question arises as to the nature and extent of episcopalian opinion among the clergy and laity. There was present among the leadership a small group of what may be called Anglicans in Scotland. These were divided into the clergy headed by Bishop Wedderburn and those without theological training like the fourth Duke of Lennox[3] and other courtiers. Separate from these were the Episcopalians of a specifically Scottish tradition. Bishop Maxwell represented this line of thought as will become clear when the Prayer Book of 1637 is examined.

When considering the roots of a more popular Scottish episcopal tradition it is natural to turn to the North-East and primarily to the diocese of Aberdeen. The character of the religious feeling in that region arose in part from the standpoint of the teaching staff of King's College, Aberdeen, and in part from the practical success with which the episcopal system had been administered in that diocese. There had always been a conservative element in Aberdonian Protestantism. In this region the feeling for an episcopate had been strengthened through a quasi-alliance between successive bishops and the local Presbyterians. They were united against the strong surviving Catholic body whom they both looked on as the true enemy. The sympathetic relations which later developed between the Catholics and Episcopalians in Aberdeenshire belong to the period of the Jacobite risings and especially to the time of the '15; they did not ante-date the fall of the House of Stuart.

Bishop Forbes was fortunate in having within his jurisdiction a

---

[1] Sir Robert Spottiswoode was called to the Court of Session in 1622 by the title of Lord Newabbey, a monastic estate purchased for him by his father. The Archbishop was a brother-in-law of Sir Jerome Lindsay of Annatland, Lyon king-at-arms and son-in-law to David Lindsay, Bishop of Ross.

[2] "As an experiment in compromise, the new order was mainly the work of Spottiswoode, who presided over it with more or less of authority from its beginning to its close", W. L. Mathieson *Politics and Religion. A Study in Scottish history from the Reformation to the Revolution.*

[3] The Duke of Lennox was educated at Trinity College, Cambridge. Bishop Wedderburn went to an English university at the age of twenty-three and much of his religious life was formed in England.

college which could supply him with ministerial candidates and this factor had some influence on the marked development of the organisation of the diocese during his rule. He filled pastorates which had long been vacant[1] and erected new parishes by sub-division.[2] In other cases he repaired pre-Reformation churches.[3] It was a notable record of development and reconstruction.[4]

At King's College, where he held the post of chancellor *ex officio*, he was primarily responsible for the establishment of the chair of divinity to which his son Dr. John Forbes was appointed in 1620. The practice of the French Reformed Church was reflected in some of the regulations for this new chair;[5] the bishop and the ministers alike viewed French Calvinists with a warm sympathy. At the same period the title of doctor of divinity was revived. The six divines, known at the time of the conflict as the Aberdeen doctors, all belonged to King's College and held this degree.

Naturally the mere fact of an episcopate, with whatever moderation its powers were exercised, aroused some difficulties. Thus one of the elements in the coldness between the professors at King's College and the ministerial leaders of the Kirk arose from the opposition to the conferring of this doctorate on the part of those determined to maintain the parity of ministers.

At the same time both the bishops of the older generation and the Aberdeen doctors looked with favour upon all Reformers. Some at any rate appear to have considered that a synthesis might be achieved acceptable to the various Reformed Churches. Thus Dr John Forbes in the *Irenicum* maintained the view that a disparity of ministers was sanctioned by the New Testament, but he also held that presbyters had by divine law the power of ordination. As a consequence ordination of ministers in the Presbyterian form remained in force throughout the reign of Charles I. In 1627 Samuel Rutherford was ordained to the parish of Anwoth by the laying-on of hands of the Presbytery. There was a wide-

[1] For instance the cures of Glenbuchat, Tarland and Midmar, *Fasti Ecclesiae Scoticanae*, xvi, pp. 126, 114 and 107.

[2] He divided Auchreddy from Old Deer and built the church in 1622; New Peter Church was built in 1620 when Peterhead and Crimond were divided to form that new parish; Strichen Church was built in 1627 and Pitsligo Church in 1630; the new parishes of Ordiquhill and Inverboynie were erected in 1622 and 1624, *Fasti Ecclesiae Scoticanae, passim*.

[3] For instance Greyfriars Church in Aberdeen and St. Clement's, Footdee. The new churches at Banchory-Devenick and Fraserburgh date from Bishop Forbes's time.

[4] For a recent assessment of the work of Bishop Forbes in Aberdeen cf. Snow, *op. cit.*, pp. 107-41.

[5] Cf. Campbell, *The Discipline or Book of Order in the Reformed Churches of France*, pp. 2, 3.

spread tendency to look to Geneva. Yet, as far as the bishops
were concerned, this implied no lack of kindly feeling towards the
Lutherans. There was at King's College, Aberdeen, a warmth
towards all those who had consummated the breach with Rome.
Every one of such bodies was looked on as "a part of the holy
kirk universall". This, however, was the more natural in view
of the acerbity with which the controversy with Rome was conducted by both sides. The priests coming from the Netherlands
to Aberdeenshire did not fail in their turn to scourge the "pseudo-
prelates".

There is in Bishop Patrick Forbes's teaching on this subject
phrases which recall the contemporary Anglican scene. Amid so
much bitterness they arouse sympathy. "The true Church," he
wrote,[1] "is in some sort ever visible, though not in herself, yet in
her infallible ensigns, as one who seeth the city and court, seeth
in a sort the Temple, for though he may not see it distinctly, he
is certain it is there". Surely there is a reminiscence here of George
Herbert and Bemerton.

The Scottish bishops appointed in the second part of the reign
of James I were for the most part his own contemporaries.[2] They
were dominated by a sense of liberation from Rome which had
been at the core of their teaching in childhood. They were all
sons of those who had themselves adopted Calvinism. Bishop
Forbes, to quote one example, had been educated at Stirling
Grammar School under Thomas Buchanan and then at Glasgow
under his relative[3] Andrew Melville. He had accompanied the
latter when he went in 1580 as principal to St. Mary's College at
St Andrews. Never forgetful of the Roman enemy, the Scottish
bishops had for the most part entered on their episcopate with
some reluctance. In general they were much concerned to keep
on good terms with those ministers who would accept them. They
were easy with one another and some of the prelates were bound
together by the ties of genuine friendship.[4] It was in part their

---

[1] *A learned Commentarie*, p. 133.
[2] James I was born on 19 June 1566, Archbishop Spottiswoode in 1565,
Bishop Patrick Forbes on 24 August 1564. Archbishop Patrick Lindsay in
1566, Bishop Andrew Lamb in 1565 or 1566, Bishop Couper in 1568.
[3] Andrew Melville was, through his mother, a nephew of Patrick Forbes of
Corse, the bishop's grandfather.
[4] These points are illustrated by a letter written in 1619 by Bishop Graeme
of Orkney to his son-in-law Patrick Smyth of Braco on the death of his
friend Bishop Couper of Galloway. "Lett me have ane it were bot a
scholatchet of his for my rememberance; quhile I lieve I will never see, no
nor heir of his mack. I hier how Breichane sal be Galloway, Dunblain
Brachene, and Lyndsay Dunblane . . . Son do what ye will I must go to
Galloway, good Galloway, who will be to me as was Galloway", Letter
printed in the introduction to *Correspondence of George Graeme*, p. 238.

assured position in the world which made them so accommodating. A Scottish bishop of that period could very easily regard himself as a co-presbyter governing in conjunction with the parish ministers. This was the old world of the sixteenth century, it was very far from the thought of Dr Laud.

There was a marked contrast between these older men and the younger prelates. The bishops consecrated in King Charles's reign were to be protagonists in a fierce struggle. The order and the seemliness of the Church of England called to them. In this new generation the churchmen of sacramental views would see the office of a bishop as Laud and Andrewes saw it. It is difficult to estimate how far this view can be said to have been reflected among the laity. There was a body of generally-speaking conservative opinion which, welcoming the episcopal framework in its moderate phase, might well have been brought to value a more developed doctrine and ceremonial. This matter was never put to the test for the doctrinal question could not be isolated from its unwelcome political setting.

In the whole picture there is one churchman of the younger generation who stands out beyond the rest, William Forbes, first Bishop of Edinburgh. He died in 1634 before the conflict opened. He was a preacher and a man of the study, publishing little. His important and unfinished work, *Considerationes Modestæ Pacificæ* remained in manuscript until 1658.[1] The treatise consists of two parts, the first dealing with Justifying Faith and the second with Purgatory, the invocation of saints and angels and the sacrament of the Eucharist.

Throughout Forbes shows himself a reconciler, a searcher after the moderate Romanist and an opponent both of Bellarmine and of those whom he would call the rigid Protestants. The book has a profoundly eirenical spirit; it is instinct with charity. It bears little relation to the seventeenth century debates as most men experienced them. Bishop William Forbes invariably speaks of Calvin with respect[2] and often quotes his words. At the same time

---

[1] The original edition was printed in Latin with a brief life, likewise in Latin, by Bishop Sydserff. An edition in two volumes was published in the library of Anglo-Catholic Theology in 1856. This contains an English translation. A slightly abridged version of the part of the treatise was made by Dr. Cosin in Paris in 1646 and is now in Bishop Cosin's Library at Durham. This manuscript contains a heading *De privatis et solitariis Missis*, which is not found in the printed versions.

[2] A rare example of a critical approach occurs in reference to his Eucharistic doctrine. "But—may I say it with the good leave of Calvin and his followers?—to many very learned men the opinion and teaching of Calvin upon this matter has always appeared exceedingly uncertain, and doubtful, and slippery", *Considerationes*, ii, p. 386.

there is another aspect to these writings. There is little doubt that had they been available for study by the public the writer would have been held to have betrayed the principles of the Reformation.

A comment[1] on the reception of the Eucharist will indicate the tenor of his approach. "Yet I would not that on account of this opinion as to the oral manducation of the Body of Christ even by the unworthy, when soberly and modestly maintained, as is done by very many both of Romanists and Lutherans, that they be railed at and condemned as Capernaites. . . . For these revilings are as devoid of truth as they are alien from all Christian charity; and therefore we must abstain from them, if we love God, or truth and the peace of the Church".

Bishop Forbes's general standpoint on this subject was that adopted by Melancthon whom he quotes[2] with marked approval. "Assuredly, it is a wonderful and great pledge of His exceeding love and mercy towards us, which he wishes to be testified in this Supper, in that He imparts Himself to us, in that he joins us to Himself as members, that we may know that we are loved, looked to and saved by Him." His own statement[3] relating to this controversy has its own appeal. "May the merciful God grant in Christ with the Holy Ghost, that, all contention being done away, all Christians may again, on this matter as in all others, return to unity with concord in their hearts."

The bishop was influenced by Marco Antonio de Dominis and quotes from him frequently. In dealing with most questions his elaborate approach led to a *via media*. His discussion of the Mass is temperate. "For very different ends," he writes,[4] "was prayer and offering made for the dead in the ancient Church, as we have shown at length against Romanists when treating of purgatory and prayers for the dead. Consult the treatise itself. Not lightly do many, both Romanists and Protestants, sin in this matter. Extremes are to be avoided, and the truth which lies in the middle is to be embraced."

In earlier sections of his book Bishop Forbes maintains that the practice of prayers for the dead must be detached from the doctrine of the "Romish Purgatory".[5] He believed that guardian angels were set to watch over countries.[6] His discussion of other aspects of this subject would certainly be looked on in an un-friendly fashion by those who were attached to the Reformed

---

[1] Bishop Forbes's *Considerationes Modestae et Pacificae Controversiarum*, ii, p. 505.   [2] *Ibid.*, ii, p. 391.
[3] *Ibid.*, ii, p. 381.   [4] *Ibid.*, ii, p. 611.
[5] The subject of Purgatory is discussed in detail, *ibid.*, ii, pp. 1-138.
[6] *Ibid.*, ii, p. 153.

Faith in its purity. "It is,"[1] wrote Bishop Forbes, "a matter beyond controversy that whatever things are done and said by those to whose keeping they are appointed, are seen and observed by the Guardian Angels when they are present; and that they are always present is probable, though not of faith." The bishop continued to write until he died, for he is found quoting Peter Heylyn whose history of St George of Cappadocia was printed in 1631. He did not treat of General Councils and there are only occasional references to the papal power. A comment[2] will reveal the authority which he accepted. "The Christian commonwealth stands altogether by holy antiquity, nor will it be more properly repaired when waste than if it be re-modelled by its original." The next sentence[3] provides the gist of his ideas. "Let them," the bishop is speaking of Protestant dislike for prayers for the dead, "reverence the judgment of the Ancient Church, and recognise a practice confirmed by the unbroken series of so many centuries."

This was in effect an appeal to history. Scotland, with the doubtful exception of Aberdeen, contained no group which was prepared to receive eirenic teachings. It was at St John's College, Oxford, and even more in the Cosin circle that the constant references to Chrysostom and Peter Martyr and Isaac Casaubon and Picherellus would find some understanding. To the great Scots lords such names were meaningless. The families of the Edinburgh lawyers were likewise of a very different temper. Wariston had his own view of what had happened in the "unbroken series of so many centuries". He saw the Reformation in its purity as a God-sent Apocalypse.

[1] *Ibid.*, ii, p. 155.   [2] *Ibid.*, ii, p. 141.
[3] *Ibid.*, ii, p. 139.

CHAPTER VI

THE ECONOMIC BACKGROUND

THE dominant religious traditions, those that is to say which were associated with the ruling power, have been discussed as a prelude to the consideration of the economic background and social structure of contemporary Scotland. In any consideration of this period in Scottish history the question arises as to how far the country had emerged from the chronic poverty which had afflicted both the Crown and the great landowners throughout the first half of the sixteenth century. As far as a proportion of the chief families was concerned, this condition had been alleviated by the traffic in church lands, but the evidences of relative prosperity are fairly widespread. Thus the extensive foreign travel involved the capacity to meet the expenses of life in France and Holland. In earlier times the student and the priest and to some extent the merchant had gained his living on foreign soil by the services that he rendered there, but in the reigns of James VI and Charles I the moneys needed by those going abroad to complete their education had to be sent to them from Scotland, and this applied both to the sons of the Scots lords and to those who belonged, like Wariston or Alexander Jaffray, to the new legal and merchant groupings. A marked contributory factor was certainly the ending of external wars which can be dated from the Treaty of Edinburgh between Elizabeth I and the Scottish Regent. Just as the wars with England had proved disastrous so nothing did more to nourish trade than the establishment of peace between the sister kingdoms.

This went side by side with the slow but steady development of the royal burghs and especially of those lying on the coast line between Dundee and Stirling. There was a string of such towns along the north shore of the Firth of Forth.[1] The importance of such burghs was enhanced by their capacity for co-operation in defence of their own privileges. As an example, until 1517 not a

[1] Some figures given in Scots money for the custom on imports for 1599 are interesting. At Dundee £2,579 for one year and four months; at Crail, Anstruther and Pittenweem £409 5s. 1d. for two years and a half; at St. Andrews £342 for one year and four months; at Dysart £315 2s. for one year and four months; at Stirling £94 15s. 9d. for one year and six months, *Exchequer Rolls*, vol. xxii, p. 315.

single legal fair or market was held outside a royal burgh.[1] Each such town exercised a trade and craft monopoly over a large rural area. In consequence there was a lack of villages in Scotland until a much later period, nor could domestic cottage industry develop. On the other hand the position was mitigated as far as the town as opposed to the village was concerned by the erection of burghs of barony depending on a mesne lord and possessing the right to buy and sell certain articles and to have bakers, brewers, butchers and other craftsmen.

Naturally it was in the royal burghs themselves that the restricted middle class developed. This was nowhere numerous and the scale of the townships in question was for the most part very modest. "The merchants," writes[2] I. F. Grant in her study of *The Social and Economic Development of Scotland before 1603,* "were not a small rich oligarchy in the burghs, but in relation to the small size of these towns themselves, a fairly large proportion of the citizens. In 1558 the contingent that the merchants undertook to raise in defence of Edinburgh outnumbered those of all the crafts put together". A further consequence followed from this situation. "The quarrels[3] between the craftsmen and the burghal authorities were often not class conflicts between craftsmen and merchants, but struggles against the small clique of the most influential merchants who had monopolized the Burghal offices."

The monopoly did not only extend to such appointments; the merchants alone had the right to trade in the more valuable commodities, hides, skins, wool, and also all foreign imports. The Edinburgh burgesses especially valued their right to bring in wine. The wholesale trade was within their absolute control. The merchants, however, only received their privileges because they met a heavy obligation. They dealt for the most part with the customs-paying commodities which the Crown desired should pass through few hands and enter the kingdom at those points where the tax could be most easily collected.

A certain status was involved in membership of the Gild Merchant. Gild brethren were obliged to keep a horse and craftsmen working with their hands were to be excluded. The hereditary element was long apparent. An act of the Edinburgh town

[1] Cf. A. Keith "Trading privileges of the Royal Burghs of Scotland", *E.H.R.,* vol. xxviii, p. 456. The position of the five church burghs of St. Andrews, Brechin, Dunfermline, Arbroath and Glasgow was assimilated to that of those of royal foundations.

[2] *Op. cit.,* p. 382.

[3] *Ibid.,* p. 383.

council ordered all sons of Gild brethren trading on their own account to join the Gild Merchant. So far as a barrier existed in the towns it was placed between the merchants and the craftsmen. This is clear from an instruction[1] given in 1587 to Robert Vernour, skinner, on his admission as a Gild brother. "To desist and cease from all trade and occupation in his own person that is not comely and decent for the rank and honesty of a Gild brother; and that his wife and servants shall use and exercise no point of common cookery outwith his own home, and namely, that they shall not sell nor carry meat dishes or courses through the town to private chambers, hostilare houses, or any other parts outwith his own house under whatsoever colour or pretence, nor pass to bridals nor banquets within or without this burgh to the occupation of common cookery, or yet to be seen in the streets with their aprons and serviettes as common cooks and their servants uses to do."

This discrimination was made very clear because in addition to administering the burghs the merchants entertained the nobles[2] when they came into the town or city. They had something of the prestige of the later wholesale houses, concerning themselves with imports and exports between Scotland and foreign countries. The craftsmen on the other hand did their own selling at booths and stances round the market cross. Figures relating to Glasgow in 1604 give the proportion between the two bodies, two hundred and thirteen merchants and three hundred and sixty-one craftsmen. The most numerous groups were the sixty-five tailors and fifty-five maltsters. Among the craftsmen were two surgeons.[3] In any calculation allowance must be made not only for apprentices but also for the many servants in the merchants' houses and also for the servants of the craftsmen. There was also the urban population which had grown up in the vicinity of the greater burghs like the dwellers in the Canongate, the West Port and Leith, who troubled the craftsmen by their competition. It should, however,

[1] Cf. J. D. Marwick, *Edinburgh Gilds and Crafts*, p. 151. For a discussion of the whole question of the Gild Merchant, cf. I. F. Grant, *op. cit.*, pp. 382-93.

[2] Thus Sir John Seton directed a letter from London on 10 January 1642 to the Earl of Eglinton "att Eglinton, or Edinburgh at Henry Setons house besyd the Weyhowse". The Earl superscribed letters on 5 July and 16 October of the same year to "our gude friend Henry Seaton, merchand burges of Edinburgh", Fraser *Memorials*, pp. 249 and 256-7.

[3] In addition to these three avocations the crafts were represented as follows: cordiners 50, weavers 30, hammermen 27, bakers 27, coopers 23, skinners 21, wrights 21, fleshers 17, masons 11, bonnet-makers 7, dyers 5. Cf. I. F. Grant, *op. cit.*, p. 413.

be mentioned that the shipowners of Leith were normally burgesses[1] of the capital city.

One consequence of the strict organisation of both gilds and crafts was the relative stability of the families concerned. Aberdeen provides some well-known examples. Alexander Jaffray the diarist born in 1614 was a great grandson of Alexander Jaffray, baker, who was admitted a burgess of that craft[2] in 1534. George Jameson, the portrait painter, was the son and grandson of masons, his grandfather being[3] deacon in 1554. Andrew Jameson had built for his own occupation in 1586 the turreted house in the Schoolhill of Aberdeen which ultimately passed to his son. Three documents belonging to the Dallmahoy MSS. reflect the life of a lower economic level. They are concerned with the Earl of Morton's property at Aberdour[4] and the most interesting deals with the passing of a tenement and half a rood of land by Francis Stevinsone, a cordiner, as part of his son's marriage portion.

There is a sense in which the South of Scotland appears to present the picture of a relatively egalitarian society or at any rate a scene in which no rigid barriers existed between the literate sections of the population. This is seen, as far as the shipping interests are concerned, in an account of a proposal made in 1635 to erect a light or lights upon May Island.[5] A visiting commission, with David Anderson, sheriff-clerk of Fife, as secretary, was named by the Privy Council to take evidence on this matter from shipmasters working out of the Firth of Forth. The first session, attended by shipmasters from Leith, was held at the Tolbooth in Edinburgh. Later sessions were held at Dysart, Anstruther Easter and St Andrews. A material factor was the cost of the lights and the profit that would accrue to the undertakers, John Cunningham the younger, of Barnes, and Charles Geddes.

---

[1] Cf. A charter party dated at Leith on 24 August 1626 between Colonel Sir Donald Macky of Strathnaver and William Robertsone, skipper, burgess of Edinburgh, master of the ship called the *Archangell* of Leith, Reay Papers, no. 134, General Register House.

[2] Cf. *Miscellany of the Third Spalding Club* (1935), vol. i, pp. 133-8.

[3] Cf. *Miscellany of the Third Spalding Club* (1940), vol. ii, p. 169.

[4] There is a charter dated 14-15 February 1615 granted by William Earl of Morton to Richard Wilsone, smith in Aberdour, of a tenement there resigned by Janet and Christina Wilson, daughter of George Wilsone, tailor. A charter dated 24 July 1630 granted by Francis Stevinsone to his son David conveying land and at the Greinheid of Aberdour Easter. On 28 September 1647 there is a note that Isobel Thomson received a cottage on the south side of the street of Aberdour as heir to her deceased father John Thomson, mason, Inventory of Morton Papers, Box 34, General Register House.

[5] *Register of the Privy Council of Scotland*, vol. vi, second series, pp. 59, 562-79.

The Leith shipmasters[1] were divided, seven favouring the erection and five considering this unnecessary. Thomas Lyndesay, one of the supporters of the proposal, claimed that six hundred thousand pounds of ships and goods had been lost for the want of such a light and declared that in the previous winter he had been forced to bear north since he durst not enter the Firth at night in certain weather. This was supported by a shipmaster of Leven giving evidence at Dysart to the effect that many ships were cast away on Inchcape and the neighbouring coasts. Discussion turned on the distance that the light would be visible on a calm clear evening and opinions varied[2] between eight miles and twenty. It was pointed out that it would be useless in a snowy night.

The shipmasters from Burntisland, seven in number, considered the light unnecessary, a merchant suggesting that it would only be useful for ships waiting to go into their own harbours on the Fife shore of the Firth. At St Andrews the evidence seems to have been confined to merchants, who perhaps owned the ships sailing from the harbours between Anstruther and Kirkcaldy. It was this more influential grouping which reinforced the opinion sent from Dysart that the costs should be kept low. It was proposed that the burghs should have the right to modify the charges made. Some of the evidence was sent in letter form. Twelve shipmasters from Crail wrote favouring the proposal.[3] It is interesting that seven of these signed and five "signed with their hand led by the undersigned notary public".

It seems likely that the capacity to read sufficiently to grasp a bill of lading and the ability to sign commercial and official documents was fairly widespread. A certain interchange of opinion can be traced between the different classes. Thus, although the personnel of the commission of enquiry varied, Alexander Gibson of Durie was present at all meetings and the Earl of Southesk attended at Edinburgh, Anstruther and St Andrews. There was by this time a conscious desire on the part of the landed interest to win the sympathy of the burghs and the town representatives.

These were the established authorities against whom the law-breakers would operate. As an example,[4] in the winter of 1627 the customer of Burntisland sought to impound the ship *Daniell,*

---

[1] Thomas Heriot, skipper in Queensferry, gave evidence with the Leith shipmasters, *ibid.,* p. 563.
[2] Witnesses from Kirkcaldy, Largo and Dysart gave the distance of visibility as eight, fourteen and twenty miles respectively, *ibid.,* pp. 564-5 and 579.
[3] *Ibid.,* p. 573.
[4] *Ibid.,* vol. viii, p. 439.

John Balconquhaill master, which had lately reached that harbour coming from the Low Countries. The customer alleged that after darkness on 9 November between six and seven in the evening, when patrolling the sands of Kirkcaldy to make sure that no goods were embarked without paying duty, he arrested a woman having on her back a great burden of small cloth which she was going to put into a boat at low water at a quiet place. He accused David Spens, mariner, of taking the cloth away and rowing with it to the *Daniell*. We receive the impression of life on both sides of the Forth going forward, purposeful and orderly. A commission of the Privy Council making a regular survey[1] found a fresh silting just south of Clackmannan, a bank "in the middle part of the river that was dry at the low water and at a spring stream tyde."

Detailed information in regard to middle class Scottish life is still fragmentary, but some light is thrown on customary expenses by the accounts of the executor of George Forrest, postmaster of Haddington,[2] who died in 1637 leaving a considerable personalty. His assets included a debt of £2,000 Scots due to him from the Exchequer for his fees as postmaster. In 1645 the plague broke out at Haddington and the executor sent the two surviving children to a lodge for safety with a maid to look after them. All clothing was discarded for fear of plague infection. Details are given of the cost[3] of feeding three persons week by week and of the expenses[4] of a new outfit. The same documents include a note on inexpensive student life in Edinburgh. The son George Forrest went there to study[5] law, but later decided to become a miller.

It is particularly difficult to envisage the accommodation of the poorer classes in Edinburgh for the development of the great house used as a tenement for many families has not yet been studied. Certainly the high stone buildings with wooden galleries reached from the street by forestairs were already old-fashioned and new houses with their fronts carried on stone arcades were by now

[1] Report dated 21 July 1635, *ibid.*, vil. vi, p. 58.

[2] These documents were deposited in the General Register House by Messrs. Montgomerie and Co., of the Bermaline Mills, Haddington. "An East Lothian Executor's Accounts 1645-1650" by A. Montgomerie, *The Scottish Historical Review*, vol. xxx, p. 144.

[3] This includes, "Item, for fish 20s. It. for eggs, two disson 11s.", *ibid.*, vol. xxx, p. 147.

[4] Cf. "Imprimis, for ane clok, doublet, breikis, and ane four tail'd coat of Inglish cloath med and furnished to George (Forrest), and a pair of hose of Scots gray, 25 lib. 10s", *ibid.*, vol. xxx, p. 147.

[5] On arrival in the city he stayed with Jean Young, who charged £33 6s. 8d. for three months board and lodging, and in addition 13s. 4d. for his laundry. He paid £3 4s. for a "red frieze gown", *ibid.*, xxx, p. 153.

G

under construction.[1] The High Street was traditionally the area
of the merchants and tradesmen, perhaps the artisans were
already lodged in the great blocks that had risen in the wynds
and closes.

The Canongate was a burgh of barony formerly depending on
the Abbot of Holyroodhouse. In 1636 that part of the abbey
property was sold to Edinburgh by the Earl of Roxburgh, its
then possessor. There was here a subordinate corporation of
craftsmen, while earlier in the century the government of the
Canongate had been engrossed for twelve years by nine maltmen.
Along the Water of Leith[2] mills were established and at the port
there was a crowded area compressed between the Kirkgate and
the Shore. In 1645 two thousand four hundred and twenty-one
persons, reckoned as one-half of the population, died of the
plague in South Leith alone. Scattered throughout the suburbs
were the apprentices who had become journeymen and the great
mass of the "unfree". It is worth noting that these hardly make an
impact upon the political developments of the time. The women
of Edinburgh who assembled in crowds to prevent the use of the
new Prayer Book were probably the wives and daughters of master
craftsmen. Reading might be difficult for them, but in time they
could master the Old Testament and they had preaching to inflame
their hearts.

For the rest we obtain glimpses through legal proceedings and
expense sheets. Thus William Lamb, dwelling within the city, is
found going along the High Street on his way to Dalkeith to serve
as foreman under the master cook of the palace there.[3] Twelve
servants were engaged for the farm at Arniston:[4] one gains the
impression of Edinburgh as a pool of labour. There was increased
employment due to the opening up of salt pans and the beginning
of extensive coal workings in Fife and in the Lothians. The
description of Sir George Bruce's mine at Culross is familiar[5]

[1] For an account of contemporary buildings cf. *An Inventory of the
Ancient and Historical Monuments of the City of Edinburgh* (1951), introduction, pp xlv-xlviii. The stone front of Gladstone's Land in the Lawnmarket
was erected in 1631, *ibid.,* p. 75.

[2] Thus in 1659 a storm and deluge of water destroyed eleven mills belonging to Edinburgh and five belonging to Heriot's Hospital, all upon the Water
of Leith, with their dams, wheels, and other equipment, cf. *ibid.,* p. lxii.

[3] *Register of the Privy Council of Scotland,* second series, vol. viii, p. 349.
This entry relates to 22 November 1627. It is likely that employment at the
palace was seasonal.

[4] Cf. *The Arniston Memoirs* 1571-1838 by George W. T. Omond (1887),
p. 10. The wages of James Jackson described as "smith and servant"
amounted to £25 Scots.

[5] The description of the visit of John Taylor the water-poet to Scotland
in the summer of 1618 is printed in extenso by P. Hume Brown in *Early
Travellers in Scotland* (1891), pp. 111-30.

It stretched beneath the water from the north shore of the Forth. "They did dig," it is explained,[1] "forty foot downeright, into and through a rocke. At last they found that which they expected, which was sea-cole . . . in the space of eight and twenty, or nine and twenty yeeres, they have digged more than an English mile under the sea, that when men are at worke belowe, an hundred of the greatest shippes in Britaine may saile over their heads. Besides, the mine is most artificially cut like an arch or a vault, all that great length, with many nookes and by-wayes; and it is so made, that a man may walke uprighte in the most places, both in and out. Many people are there set on work, which otherwise through the want of employment would perish."

This mine was in the nature of a show-piece and it is important not to exaggerate the amount of external trade in which Scotland was involved. Salt, for instance, was not an export[2] as so much was used in salting various fish especially herring, a trade which had by this time suffered severely from Dutch competition. In the case of the rich corn lands of Fife and Lothian, England was the chief customer. Timber, mainly brought from Norway, was always a principal import. The trade of the East Scottish ports was concentrated on the Low Countries, although during the sixteenth century the traffic between Aberdeen and Dundee and Danzig and Königsberg almost rivalled in volume that sent to the Netherlands from these two ports. The body of Scottish merchants in Poland was considerable and the country was overrun by Scottish pedlars.

The bulk of the continental trade passed through Campvere in Zeeland, which was recognised in 1541 as the sole staple in the Netherlands for Scottish goods. Under James VI it was reaffirmed, in 1616, that all Scottish ships should sail to this one port. The list of goods[3] which were bound to pass through the staple provides an interesting commentary on the general nature of external trade. This includes wool, woollen and linen yarn, all woollen and linen manufactory, hides and skins of all sorts, plaids, carsays, Scots cloth, stockings, butter and every kind of barrel flesh and pork. By contrast the trade with France was less significant. The harbours most used were Rouen and Dieppe, and in later years Bordeaux and La Rochelle. The traffic had never proved

---

[1] *Ibid.*, pp. 116-7.
[2] For a general discussion of Scottish trade cf. *The Scottish Staple at Veere* by John Davidson and Alexander Gray (1909), pp. 86-113.
[3] *Records of Convention of Royal Burghs,* vol. iv, p. 217. Cf. Davidson and Gray, *op. cit.,* pp. 356-9. The list dates from 1697, but with the exception of the linen manufactory the other items had been articles of trade throughout the century.

sufficient to justify the establishment of a staple. Still, in France Scotsmen had one clear advantage. On the marriage of the Queen of Scots and the Dauphin in 1558 their respective subjects were naturalised in both their countries.

A list of Scottish exports in 1614 will indicate the value of each trade. The total amounted to £820,524 Scots, the most substantial items[1] being skins and hides, fisheries and woollen cloth. These figures do not amount to an impressive total. Apart from the trade with England, the bulk of the traffic was dealt with through the East Coast ports. There was also a good deal of coast-wise shipping. Sea transport was favoured for the movement of goods between Edinburgh and the northern counties. The general situation is well described[2] by Miss I. F. Grant. "Scotland was a land mainly devoted to supporting a struggling population, the small surplus of produce being employed in supplying the luxuries of life to those who could afford them. The Gordon rent roll of 1600 shows how small were the contributions of wool and hides from individual holding—the land was evidently primarily devoted to subsistence farming."

Communications have a bearing on this question. There was considerable traffic on the coast road up from England which ran through Cockburnspath,[3] and coaches were sent from Eglinton to Edinburgh.[4] Roads ran through the Lothians and Fife and up to Dundee and Aberdeen. They stretched northward to the lowlands in the "planure" of Moray.[5] Still, over great areas there was nothing except tracks, including the ancient drove ways along which the cattle[6] passed.

The urban centres, the trade and the still nascent industry were of small significance in the Scottish economy. The crucial factor was the possession of land. The purpose of successive generations was to obtain or to augment a solid rural property; this was only

[1] The hides and skins were valued at £238,712, the fisheries at £153,354 and the woollen and linen cloth at £115,365. It is interesting that victuals including beer, malt, oats, flour, bread, beef and aquavitae only amounted to £37,653, small salt to £39,780, coal to £25,232 and lead ore to £20,000. Cf. I. F. Grant *Social and Economic Development of Scotland before 1603*, pp. 309-11.

[2] *Ibid.*, p. 311.

[3] Cf. Request for a coachman and coach horses along that road, Fraser *Memorials of Eglinton*, p. 213.

[4] Taylor the Water-Poet has an account of the inn at this place, P. Hume Brown, *Early Travellers in Scotland*, p. 127.

[5] "The third, and beautiful soil, is the delectable planure of Murray thirty miles long, and six in breadth; whose comely grounds, enriched with corns, plantings, pasturage, may be called a second Lombardy, or pleasant meadow of the north." William Lithgow writing in 1628, P. Hume Brown, *Scotland before 1700*, p. 298.

[6] Cf. A. R. B. Haldane, *The Drove Roads of Scotland*.

alienated in extreme necessity. The richer sections of the community were marked by a tenacious respect for landed property. The marriage of heiresses, even in the case of a heritrix of a small holding, was kept carefully within a family grouping and that of its immediate associates. Lands were often parcelled out to cadets in wadset,[1] a Scots form of mortgage by which the occupant or wadsetter was given the usufruct of a certain acreage in return for the loan of a sum of money. The wadset would continue until the original capital was repaid.

The most characteristic Scottish tenure was the feu-farm holding which had been developing in the two previous centuries. This was an heritable tenure[2] granted in return for a fixed and single rent, the superior exacting no services but having the right to certain "casualties" less onerous than the dues payable on ward, relief and marriage, which characterised late mediæval systems of tenure. The early feuars were for the most part men of property. In certain cases, as for instance in the crown lands of the Stewartry of Fife, there had been a change-over from the granting of three-year leases to the practice of feu-farming. In the generation immediately prior to the Reformation there had been extensive feuing of church lands.

Various motives led to the undertaking of a feu-farm. In rare cases land was acquired by a burgess[3] as an investment. It was common for the feu-farmers to acquire large holdings, but when the feu area was very small it seems usually to have been acquired for the purpose of making an estate compact. The initiative was normally taken by the Crown when it was a question of major transactions. There was naturally a tendency towards the dispossession of smaller tenants in favour of those who could pay more. The Crown obtained considerable benefit from the feuing of secularised church lands.

This tenure was in contrast with the old rights of "kindly tenants", a system which could with difficulty maintain itself in modern times. This is evident from Spalding's account of the situation of Clan Chattan which refers to a traditional claim that could hardly continue in the Covenanting period. The tenants "began," it is explained,[4] "to call to mind how James, Earl of Moray, their master, had casten them out of their kindly possessions whilke past memory of man their predecessors and they had kept for small duty, but for their faithful service, and

[1] Cf. I. F. Graham, op. cit., p. 178.
[2] For a discussion of feuing cf. ibid., pp. 265-87.
[3] Thus George Forrest the postmaster of Haddington was feuar of Gimmersmills, Scottish Historical Review, vol. xxx, p. 144.
[4] John Spalding, History of the Troubles, p. i.

planted in their places, for payment of a greater duty, a number of strangers and feeble persons, unable to serve the earl, their master, as they could have done, by which means these gentlemen were brought through necessity to great misery." The question of kindly tenancies was bound up with the right of a son to occupy the position of his father in respect to his lord. It lost its meaning as landed property began to pass by purchase.

There was great variation in the size of holdings and the tenants normally employed sub-tenants or cottars. The numerous servants who held the lowest rank and passed from household to household, usually within a fairly restricted area, were for the most part children of cottars who had been sent in the hope that they might make good and secure a permanent post. Such contact between the classes was rendered easier because a great proportion of the rents were still paid in kind, the proprietor being kept supplied with grain, meal, meat and other produce. A rather surprising feature of Scottish rural life was the prevalence of a meat diet. Whatever view was taken of the nature of the area under cultivation, all travellers were impressed by the masses of sheep and cattle.[1] There were large quantities of hides and woolfells. The country people were preoccupied by the problem of providing winter fodder, for there was a lack of natural hay. Broom was sown extensively[2] to feed the cattle. Peas and beans were grown between Forth and Tay, but apparently not to any great extent in other districts.

The greater part of Scotland must be conceived as a country very bare of standing timber.[3] Thus on the lands of Cupar Abbey before the Reformation tenants were only allowed to take wood for building purposes under certain safeguards. Leases contained provision for the planting of osiers and ash trees. It was forbidden to strip bark.[4] Such agricultural enactments suggest a rural society which was closely integrated and endowed with a marked sense of mutual obligation. The reciprocal duties were very many. These last characteristics were modified by the fact that they

---

[1] Thus Estienne Perlin writing in 1551-2 stated that "the arable lands of that country are but indifferent, and the greatest part of the country is a desert. They (the Scots) have plenty of cows and calves, on which account their flesh is cheap", printed by P. Hume Brown, *Early Travellers in Scotland*, pp. 73, 74.

[2] I. F. Graham, *op. cit.*, p. 291.

[3] "In the southern parts of Scotland forests are few", John Major's description printed by P. Hume Brown, *Scotland before 1700*, p. 51. William Lithgow refers to "the Highland mountains overclad with fir trees, infinite deer, and all other sorts of bestial" printed *ibid.*, p. 299.

[4] For these and similar enactments cf. *The Register of Cupar Abbey*. They are discussed in I. F. Graham *op. cit.*, pp. 288-303.

existed, at least in Scotland beyond Forth, within the frontiers of a series of large units. A latent antagonism was normally present in the relationship between the dependents of neighbouring superiors. In the case of substantial landowners the position was complicated by an elaborate system of mutual indebtedness.

Light is thrown on this situation by the Book of the Annualrentars and Wadsetters in the sheriffdom of Aberdeen, which was compiled in 1633. In this survey the miller emerges as an important factor. Nineteen mills are mentioned, each with a separate owner. In several cases landowners appear as indebted to these millers, although it is not clear whether these are normal payments or perhaps the result of some form of loan. In any event the miller had his special place in the rural economy.

Certain points should be noted relating to the northern and western parts of the country. Although the dislocation due to raids into the more settled lands has been exaggerated, it cannot be wholly ignored as a feature of the economic situation. This was a matter that affected various limited districts, and perhaps most of all the rich fields in Moray. A letter explaining the actions of the Camerons will make this clear. "Praised be God," wrote Lochiel in reply to a complaint, "I am innocent of the same, and my friends, both in respect that they were not in your bounds, but in Murray lands where all men take their prey." The position could not be set out more succinctly.

The great factor in the northern regions was the seasonal movement of cattle coming from the Out Isles and throughout the hills bound for Stirling and the lowland cattle markets. By comparison the export of wool was not significant; a certain amount of plaiding was sent southwards, mainly to Glasgow.

One error in regard to the North had its effects. James VI was persuaded of the riches of the country. He had ideas, which were never to be realised, as to the value of the northern fisheries and the presence of mines of precious metals. These were notions which his subjects hardly shared with him. In economic matters their ideas were lucid, short-ranged and unhopeful. The correspondence of the lords suggests that they left such detailed questions to their factors. The magnates had their own yardstick. They saw the situation in terms of land and the men that that land carried.

CHAPTER VII

THE LIFE OF THE MAGNATES

I N any survey of Scotland in the first half of the seventeenth century it is essential to include an examination of the status and way of life of the magnates and then to consider how far these standards were reflected among other strata of the Scottish people. This approach is the more natural in dealing with a nation which was always singularly free from the forms of class consciousness then existing in England or in Germany.

It would perhaps be useful to attempt to determine in a rough fashion the series of families which would be considered as magnates, a term denoting a man of noble rank with a great position in the kingdom or having the command of a wide affinity. This would not be co-terminous with the Scottish peerage for men such as Lord Borthwick with his strong rather antiquated castle on the road south from Edinburgh would not fall within this category. In addition to the heads of great families in the north of Scotland the group would include nearly all the holders of earldoms which had been created before James VI ascended the English throne as well as some of more recent date. These grants of honour were often a tribute paid by the sovereign to the position of his greater subjects. Thus the earldoms created in the century and a half prior to 1603 were for the most part exacted by the peers as a tribute to the antiquity of their lineage and to their standing. From the purely technical point of view their precedence was determined by the Decreet of Ranking issued in 1606.

At the same time any assessment must be provisional. Apart from the four leading families, which had a clear political ascendancy, it is difficult to arrange the great stocks in any order which can indicate the extent or nature of their influence. Much more work has to be done on the strength of their economic position and the sources and extent of their real wealth.

Leaving aside the House of Stuart in its various branches, the Scottish scene was dominated by the four great houses whose heads bore the titles of Hamilton, Angus, Argyll and Huntly. After these leaders, but associated with them in the public mind, there came the holders of those earldoms which seem to have derived an element of prestige from the fact of regency. These were the representatives of the Regent Moray, the Regent Mar and the Regent Morton, who had governed Scotland when James VI was a small child. Four other families held a special position. The Earls Marischal and the Earls of Erroll, the latter as High Constables of Scotland, had a standing derived from their hereditary offices about the person of the sovereign. The Earls of Caithness and Sutherland, the former stock sharply declining and the latter coming into the ascendant, ruled these two northern counties. Their influence was, however, localised and did not extend as far south as Inverness.

Further, the small number of great lords mentioned did not all belong to distinct families, for Sutherland was a cadet of Huntly and Morton and Angus were of the same stock. There were also two frequently opposed conceptions, that of prestige and that of actual power. At the time of the accession of Charles I neither Caithness nor Erroll had the financial stability to make good the former influence that their house had wielded. This factor of impoverishment operated still more in the case of the "broken" Earls of Crawford, who had been accorded the third place in the Decreet of Ranking of 1606 immediately after Angus and Argyll. This document reflects the traditional precedence granted by virtue of privilege or office,[1] but it is important not to place emphasis on a distinction in the cases where this was not supported by reasonable wealth.[2]

Still, it seems exact to state that unless the actual holders were impeded by poverty a special weight attached to those great stocks whose earldoms went back at least as far as the reign[3] of James II. The four chief houses held their unique place; Hamilton supported by Abercorn; Angus linked by certain bonds to the other Douglas earldoms of Queensberry and Morton; Argyll with his great cadets; Huntly supported by Sutherland. Differences within each family group will be considered later, but there certainly

[1] Thus Angus claimed the right of the first seat and the first voting and the privilege of leading the van of the army and of bearing the Crown at coronations. Similarly Argyll's precedence derived from his office as justice general. Since Hamilton and Huntly were already marquises, the list ran Angus, Argyll, Crawford, Erroll and Marischal all of whom owed their place to office, although the justification for including Crawford is not easy to formulate. After them came the earldoms of Sutherland and Mar. Cf. *Complete Peerage*, vol i, p. 160 note.

[2] After Mar the decree, as amended on 8 July 1628 by the Court of Session, ran Rothes, Morton, Menteith, Buchan. Among these Rothes was generally regarded as financially embarrassed and Mentieth had little solid backing. The heiress of Buchan was married to Mar's second son and the lands of Buchan had vanished in Scotstarvet's phrase "like snow off a dyke".

[3] Apart from the earldom of Moray whose Stewart line derived from James V, the most recent earldom under discussion, that of Morton, was created in 1485.

existed in these stocks a striking combination of ancestral rank with widespread alliances and actual wealth. They had their own internecine feuds and naturally aroused much jealousy. It is hardly fanciful to imagine that their leaders shared a capacity for understanding one another. One man alone would seek to dominate or challenge them, the Marquis of Montrose.

After these four houses it is difficult to suggest an order of political significance. Their long and close connection with government gave a special influence to the Earls of Mar, while it was the policy of Charles I to strengthen the position of the House of Moray. At this point with the Leslies of Rothes we reach the second rank of the old peerage which may be held to centre on a group of earldoms erected before Flodden and possessed of solid wealth but carrying for the most part a strictly local influence;[1] Eglinton; Montrose; Cassilis; Glencairn.[2] All these four lent their weight to aid the Covenant. Marischal was their counterpart in Aberdeenshire.

At the same time the position of the Keiths in the north-east and that of the Montgomeries, Kennedys and Cunninghams in the West Country was paralleled by that of other families differentiated from them only by the fact that they had risen more recently from the old-established baronage. The Murrays of Tullibardine, who had taken over the inheritance of the Stewart earldom of Atholl, were in a class apart;[3] but the Earls of Perth, Kinghorn, Dumfries, Nithsdale and Wigton represented in the male line the ancient baronies[4] of Drummond, Glamis, Crichton, Maxwell and Fleming. All this grouping shared the same background of territorial influence, local in character, and a contact with the Scottish Court lasting over two centuries. Except for Nithsdale, the only avowed Catholic, they were none of them closely linked with the modern Court and had owed little to their sovereign's complaisant generosity. As an example only two of the Scottish abbeys and priories had been absorbed by these ten

[1] The Graham influence was, however, more scattered, partly in Perthshire and partly around Montrose.

[2] This is the order given in the Decreet of Ranking, but by a private contract between the parties dated 7 June 1617 and 27 November 1620 Eglinton ceded his place to Montrose. From 1606 until 1649 the Earls of Glencairn lodged complaints with the Court of Session claiming to rank above both these peers.

[3] The earldom of Atholl was held to have become extinct in 1592 and that created in 1629 for John Murray Earl of Tullibardine was accepted as a new peerage.

[4] The five earldoms had however all been created between 1606 and 1623 after the accession of James VI to the English throne.

families,[1] Kilwinning which had gone to Eglinton and Deer which had passed to the Earls Marischal. No gratitude bound them to the royal cause and individually they had small hope of favour. In regard to their relations with Charles I it may be said that they viewed with detachment a King who did not know them. Their financial situation varied from the accumulated wealth of the builders of Glamis Castle to the relative penury of the Earls of Perth.

The standard of living among these families had considerable local variations, but they and the stocks allied to them in different fashions were all dominated by the concept of shared noble blood and by the obligations of hospitality. Again, Scotland was singularly free from the noisy but obsequious respect extant in England. This was due to the much greater inherent stability of the social structure in the northern kingdom which was linked with the restricted and comparatively static character of its middle class.

A multitude of Scottish officers on foreign service considered that they should be recognised as noble.[2] The idea of kindred was conceived on a wide basis and not only in the Highland districts. Among the clans legitimate and left-handed descents were hardly to be distinguished from one another and with both groups were mingled those who had some wholly indefinite claim of descent or adoption. It was a society deeply coloured by the concept of visits of courtesy and honour. Except in the towns there was very little privacy in the lives of men of position. The marks of civilisation were manifest; each object of luxury was for display.

In its external aspects this situation had been modified by changes whose development was very gradual. Thus, although their use had become much more widespread during the years of peace which James VI gave to Scotland, ornamental furnishings were found in the North as early as the middle of the sixteenth century. As an example, among the goods brought to Holyrood from Strathbogie Castle[3] on the forfeiture of the Earl of Huntly in 1562 there were elaborate tapestries, beds covered with velvet and hung with fringes of gold and silver-work, vessels of gilded and coloured

---

[1] A list of the principal abbeys and priories with the names of their owners in 1625 is given in the introduction to the *Register of the Privy Council of Scotland* 1625-1627, p. cxlvi.

[2] Cf. A letter from George Ogilvy dated at Spielberg on 27 August 1649 to the Earl of Airlie in which he states that he has been admitted to the title of Earl in Germany as a cadet of the house of Airlie, Cortachy MSS., no. 1624, H.M.C., Appendix to second report, p. 187.

[3] Inventory among the Gordon Castle MSS., H.M.C., Appendix to first report, p. 114.

glass, figures of animals, the marble bust of a man and a wooden carving of the Samaritan woman at the Well. These may be compared with the standing beds of carved work and fir which formed part of the furnishing[1] of a modest house in Moray in 1517.

The Earl of Huntly's plenishing may be compared with that of the Earl of Mar, later the Regent Moray, which was likewise noted down[2] in 1562. These were paralleled by the furnishings recorded as then placed in the private chapel in the Place of Inchinnan. These included Mass books, an image of the babe Jesus, statues of Our Lady and of St Anne and a small image of carved ivory.[3] With the coming in of the Reformed Faith the emphasis on the position of the head of the family did not diminish. Among the household fittings of the Campbells of Glenorchy were great cramoisy velvet cushions for the Kirk. Such insignia of rank were found in the wild hills wherever there was a great house of sufficient consequence. Display was satisfactory to the rich Scots lords.

The point is made that a magnificent way of life had been established for several generations. The setting which the Campbells of Glenorchy had built up in their various castles can be examined in a certain detail. In one respect this account has an especial interest for there were no houses of quite this quality to the westward of Glenorchy. Going north from Inverary along all that indented coast there was no great house, except Dunvegan, which resembled the Breadalbane castles with their self-conscious civility. Allowance must be made for the note of panegyric which recurs throughout the *Black Book of Taymouth*,[4] which was apparently composed shortly before the Restoration of Charles II. Among other points it throws an interesting light on the background of the first Earl of Breadalbane. The connection with the Argyll family was of course close, and a crucial factor in the developing power of this family had been Duncan Campbell's

[1] Descent of Spuilzie in the House of Petty, *Miscellany of the Spalding Club,* vol. ii, p. 78.

[2] Inventory among the Donibristle MSS., H.M.C., report vi, part i and appendix. The catalogue included six pieces of tapestrie then hanging in my Lord of Coldingham's chamber, p. 647.

[3] This inventory was taken about 1570 and is no. 168 among the documents printed by Sir William Fraser in *The Lennox,* vol. ii, muniments, p. 276. It was noted that there was a stand bed in the chapel chamber, presumably for the chaplain's use. The paper is inscribed "Inventur of the graithe in Inchinane withe the auld rotten papistrie thairin", *ibid.,* p. 277.

[4] *The Black Book of Taymouth* with other papers from the Breadalbane Charter Room, ed. Cosmo Innes, Bannatyne Club, 1855. The various sums mentioned in this volume are all Scots money.

conversion into a secure free tenure of the "tack"[1] of many lands in Breadalbane held of the Charterhouse of Perth or of the Crown. The position had been further consolidated by the seventh and eighth lairds of Glenorchy, who between them led this branch of the Campbells from 1583 until 1640.

Sir Duncan Campbell was a great builder. He is credited with constructing[2] the tower of Achalladour, the house of Lochdochart and the great house at Barcaldine in Benderloch. In his last years he rebuilt the castle of Finlarg, ornamenting the chapel with "pavement and painture". These works, which occupied him between 1621 and 1629, synchronised with the erection of a baronetcy of Nova Scotia in Sir Duncan's favour. Fallow deer had been introduced[3] into his lands as early as 1611 and the park of Finlarg was begun ten years later. He is said to have planted[4] chestnut and walnut trees around his dwellings. In 1628 Sir Duncan erected a building upon the west side of the close at Finlarg "of tua house height,[5] conteining four fair chalmers". In the following year another house of similar proportions was built on the north-west side of the same close. This new building was intended to take the place of his old headquarters, the house of Balloch.

There are inventories of the plenishing of Balloch made in 1598 and 1600. These two castles lay far inland at either end of Loch Tay on the eastern borders of the Campbell country. The details of their furnishing may serve to indicate that overt glory by means of which the heads of the great stocks in Northern Scotland sought to impress their rivals and their kinsmen and all their followers. At Balloch, as also at the McLean stronghold of Dunvegan, there is emphasis on the taking of wine as a sign of almost ostentatious "civility". Parallels can be worked out with the manner of life of the contemporary O'Neills and O'Donnells. In the inventory from Finlarg there is classification into claret, white and Spanish wines, which would have reached the west of Scotland from the Biscay ports or from Bordeaux. In this connection the Tutor of Inveraw undertook, among other obligations, "to help the said Duncan (Campbell of Glenorchy) home with wine every summer as the rest of his lands did".

The impression conveyed was that of calculated splendour with a military background. At Balloch in the chamber of dais there were stands of corselets with collars and murrions and suits of armour for horsemen made in Leith. The inventory taken in 1600

---

[1] *Black Book of Taymouth,* p. 21. [2] *Ibid.,* pp. 35-6.
[3] *Ibid.,* introduction, p. iv.   [4] *Ibid.,* p. iv.
[5] *Ibid.,* p. 68.

also mentions the two-handed swords "that came out of Men-teith" and the gilt piece with the laird's arms that had been worked in Dundee. Above the long tables in the hall were ranged the Arras hangings and the curtains of red and green "say". There was purple plaiding "pasmentit with orange", apparently in use as a wall covering. Sewn cushions, either red or orange, were provided for the guests of greatest quality. Great carved beds with silken coverings to do honour to the laird and his lady were brought up from the Lowlands. All men would be impressed who came for the great feastings.

The household accounts for 1590 mention[1] the salmon and trout from Loch Tay, the herring from Loch Fyne, the dried fish of several kinds, fresh and salt beef, the mutton from the Braes of Balquhidder, the capon, venison and partridges. Men were constantly coming to the house of Balloch. To give one example of the transactions. When the McGillekeyrs chose John Campbell of Glenorchy to be their chief and protector[2] in all just actions they agreed that when any of them died he was to have the "best four-footed beast in possession at the time of death". They undertook the obligation of "ryding and ganging on horss and on futt in Heland and Lowland". It was the general practice "to visit[3] the chief's house with suitable presents twice in the year".

Apart from a disagreement[4] with Campbell of Loudoun there seems to have been an easy relation with the other members of the Clan Campbell. Both Glenorchy and his eldest son had been put out in fosterage[5] with Campbell of Duntrune and his wife and this stock had received an undertaking that Glenorchy would espouse their just quarrels, those with the Earl of Argyll always excepted.

At Balloch there were many chambers each with its special name[6] and these included one known as Duntrune's chamber. The house contained two studies, a term which seems almost anachronistic, one of them being described as situated at the door

[1] Breadalbane MSS., H.M.C., Appendix to fourth report, p. 512.
[2] Bond entered into on 2 June 1548, *Ibid.*, p. 512.
[3] *Ibid.*, p. 512.
[4] In 1629 twenty thousand marks was given by Sir Duncan Campbell to John Lord Loudoun, heir to Campbell of Lawers, who had married the heritrix of Loudoun in return for the renunciation of claims to Glenorchy's lands in Benderaloch. It was asserted that these lands had been given by an old charter by King Robert Bruce to Lady Loudoun's predecessor Sir Duncan Campbell, *Black Book of Taymouth*, p. 69.
[5] *Ibid.*, p. 511.
[6] The names are recorded in the appendix to the *Black Book of Taymouth*, pp. 342-3. These give little indication of their place within the structure except that there is reference to the "Over-chalmer of the Wester Tower" and to the "studie in the Wester Tower".

of the King's chamber. There was also a room known as my Lord of Lorne's chamber. These were perhaps merely ceremonial appellations. In Sir Duncan's time the visitors would seem for the most part to have been confined to persons of standing living on the marches of his own country. A list of those present at a week's feasting in September 1590 includes Murray of Tulli-bardine; the laird of Inchbrakie who was a cadet of Montrose; the Tutor of Duncrub; the Bishop of Dunkeld; the Prior of the Charterhouse. All those of lesser rank who came to Balloch would be affected by the power displayed there. The inventory does not omit to mention great iron fetters to bind men's hands and feet and a beheading axe.

The death of Sir Duncan Campbell in 1631 and the succession of his son and heir Sir Colin marked another stage. It is now for the first time that portraits appear at Balloch, which was clearly the dwelling that the new laird preferred. He began by entertain-ing a German painter in his house during eight months and gave him the sum of one thousand pounds Scots for his work. This included thirty "broads" of the Kings of Scotland and two of the recent Kings of Great Britain, besides portraits of Sir Colin Campbell and his predecessors. All were set up in the hall and chamber of dais at Balloch. This series also contained likenesses of two "Queines of gude memorie",[1] probably Anne of Denmark and the Queen of Scots. An interesting development occurred in 1633 when Sir Colin gave[2] George Jameson, painter in Edinburgh, two hundred and three score pounds for portraits of King Robert and King David Bruce, and nine more portraits of the Queens of Scotland. These, together with new portraits of Charles I and Henrietta Maria, he set up in the hall at Balloch. Later, a further commission was given to Jameson[3] "for the knight of Lochow's lady, and the first Countes of Argyle, and six of the ladys of Glenurquhay, thair portraits, and the said Sir Colin his awin portrait". These were placed in the chamber of dais. A man would have to walk many miles across the hills before he came on such another gallery.

It is in keeping that considerable sums were expended on "dames napery" which was ordered[4] from West Flanders. Two house clocks were installed and a chamber clock. A pair of little organs were placed in the chapel of Finlarg and a pair of harpsichords[5] secured for Balloch. In 1632 Sir Colin spent[6] three

[1] Ibid., p. 75. [2] Ibid., p. 77.
[3] Ibid., pp. 78-9. [4] Ibid., p. 76.
[5] For these details, appendix, ibid., p. 350.
[6] Ibid., p. 73.

thousand marks on hangings, silk beds and other furniture for Balloch and Finlarg. He rebuilt[1] the chapel and chapel yard at the latter castle. He spent[2] two thousand marks on a dyke of stone and lime about the close of Balloch and on an outer gate and a gate between the close and garden. Two points are worth noting to complete the general impression. All these expenditures are recorded by the compiler of the *Black Book of Taymouth;* they were therefore considered worthy of panegyric. It is mentioned[3] that the two western chambers at Finlarg were now roofed with slates; hitherto these had presumably been thatched.

There were constant reminders of the great stocks with whom Glenorchy had contracted marriage. Sir Duncan was a son-in-law of Atholl and was Gowrie's[4] cousin. At a great bridal held the year before he died he had wedded his youngest daughter to the Earl of Atholl giving a dowry of forty thousand[5] marks and spending six thousand marks upon her espousals and the bridal clothes. In general the tastes of the southern lords were followed in some detail. Almost within the space of a generation the lairds of Glenorchy had moved from assembling the wooden panels of the Kings of Scotland and the equally imaginary representations of their Campbell ancestors to the collection of portraits of their distinguished acquaintance. Among the pictures at Taymouth Castle noted by Cosmo Innes in 1855 were portraits of the Marquis of Hamilton and his mother, the Earls of Kinghorn, Mar and Marischal, Lords Leslie, Binning, Napier and Loudoun. They are attributed to Jameson and dates are assigned[6] to them. They give an interesting impression of Sir Colin Campbell's politico-social affiliations provided that the series is complete and that they were in fact brought to Balloch when they were finished.

---

[1] *Ibid.,* pp. 73-4.   [2] *Ibid.,* p. 79.
[3] *Ibid.,* p. 76.

[4] In this connection Hume of Godscroft describes William Earl of Gowrie as "looking very pitifully upon his gallerie where we were walking at the time which he had but newly built and decorated with pictures", *History of the House of Douglas,* ed. 1644, p. 177. The example of the Ruthvens of Gowrie may have influenced Glenorchy's furnishing.

[5] *Black Book of Taymouth,* p. 70. The great dowry was due to the husband's rank. Another sister brought only ten thousand five hundred marks to Alexander McDougall, Fiar of Dunoulich, *ibid.,* p. 68. The dowries of Sir Robert Campbell's daughters, given in the reign of Charles I, were less considerable, five thousand marks to Margaret on her marriage with John Cameron of Lochiel, three thousand to Marjorie on her marriage with Archibald Stirling of Coldach and two thousand to Anne on her marriage with Dougall Campbell of Inneraw, *ibid.,* pp. 90-91.

[6] *Black Book of Taymouth,* introduction, p. viii. Binning and Leslie were the heirs to the Earls of Haddington and Rothes. The portrait of Lord Leslie is dated 1633, the three Hamilton portraits 1636, the remainder are dated 1637.

Countess of Dunfermline.

THE COUNTESS OF DUNFERMLINE

By the middle of the seventeenth century a library had been created. Certain books had been at Balloch for some generations. On the flyleaf of a copy of Sleidan's *Chronicle,* printed at London in 1560 and probably brought to Scotland about that time, there is written,[1] "This buke pertaines to Catherine Ruthven, Lady of Clenurquhay". The manuscript of a romance, "The Buike of King Alexander the Conquerour," belonged to her son Sir Duncan Campbell. It is stated that this laird copied Italian and Latin apophthegms[2] into his volumes.

The house of Balloch was rich in heirlooms;[3] the "stone of the quantity of half a hen's egg" set in silver which Sir Colin Campbell the first Laird of Glenorchy wore when he fought at Rhodes against the Turks; the target of gold set with diamonds and enamelled jewellery given to Sir John Campbell by James V; the round golden jewel given by Queen Anne[4] to the Baronet of Nova Scotia. On the tables were set out the silver cups. In this careful furnishing Balloch Castle was assimilated to all the great houses throughout Scotland. In one respect it differed from the houses in Angus and Fife and south of the Forth. The Campbells of Glenorchy lived in public. The glories of the mansion were displayed for all soldierly men of their allegiance who journeyed there.

Details of the life of a great house in the south of Scotland will mark the contrast between relative privacy within a narrow neighbourhood and a restricted circle and that easy relationship which the magnates in the northern part of the country maintained with their clansmen and their sworn adherents. The first example chosen is in some ways not typical, for the Setons, whose successive chiefs built both Seton Palace and Winton House situated close to one another on the coast lands in East Lothian, were essentially a Court family devoted to and wholly dependent upon the Stuart dynasty. It is also true that Alexander Seton Earl of

[1] *Ibid.,* introduction, p. vi.

[2] This is stated by Cosmo Innes, who considers that the Italian texts were for the most part copies from *Oracoli politici cioe sentenze e documenti nobili ed illustre,* printed in 1590. A copy of this work was in the library at Taymouth and marked with Sir Duncan Campbell's initials, *ibid.,* p. vii.

[3] These are described in an inventory of gear left Sir Colin Campbell in 1640, *ibid.,* appendix, pp. 346-51.

[4] This golden jewel was in a setting containing twenty-nine diamonds and four great rubies, *ibid.,* p. 346. It resembled contemporary jewellery in the possession of the Montgomeries of Eglinton. These latter heirlooms included a little jewel in the form of an anchor, a chain of pearls and a gold jewel set with diamonds and blue sapphires. An inventory of Lord Eglinton's own jewellery taken on 20 February 1632 included two music boxes, a pair of spectacles bounded with silver and a very fine enamelled striking clock, *Memorials of the Montgomeries,* ii, pp. 290-1 and 317-9.

H

Dunfermline, who was Lord Chancellor until his death in 1622 and built Pinkie House, had a very clear preference for English models in constructing his suburban palace. On the other hand Tyninghame, which became the principal residence of the first Earl of Haddington and is the second house to be considered, appears to be purely Scottish in character.

It was likewise an accidental factor that the Setons had no series of cadet branches whose interest lay in following their leadership. It is perhaps hardly a tribute to their independence that they were never out of favour with any Stuart sovereign. At this stage, however, it is only their domestic setting which is in question. The heads of the family were essentially conservative, noted for their consistency and for a rather unexpected business acumen. They hardly stand out as distinct characters. They were wealthy landowners with compact properties, managing farm land and salt pans and coal mines.[1] Their history was set down[2] by Lord Kingston, who was born in 1621. His account of his grandfather's funeral[3] suggests that withdrawn pride which was the note of all the Seton stock. In their personal affairs they moved with energy, developing their own port at Cockenzie,[4] a few miles east of Leith. Winton, of their two great houses, alone survives. Seton Palace was eventually demolished after the family fortunes had been wrecked[5] through adherence to the House of Stuart. Sir William Brereton, later the Parliamentarian commander in Cheshire, gives an impression of this house in his account of his travels in Scotland in 1636. James VI and Charles I both stayed

[1] The dedication of *Satan's invisible world discovered*, printed in 1685, praises the fourth Earl of Winton for the management of his coal mines, "the meanders and boutgates, the levels, airshafts, pumping therein".

[2] *Continuation of the History of the House of Seytoun* by Alexander Viscount of Kingston second lawfull son of the same house, Bannatyne Club, 1829.

[3] "He (the first Earl of Winton) was buried that day King James the Sixth took his journey from Holyroodhous to England, to take possession of that Crown. His Majestie was graciously pleased to rest himself att the southwest round of the orch-yard of Seton, in the highway, till the funeral was over, that he might not withdraw the noble company", *ibid*.

[4] "The said Robert Earle of Winton . . . built the old harbour of Cockainie, for which King James the Sixth granted him a large chartour, a free conquest; with the gift and privilidge of custome and anchorage of all ships and goods imported and exported, with all other privilidges which burgh royalls have", *ibid*., p. 75. His son "built in Cockainie twelve saltpans, where never any formerly wes. He built, to his great charge, ane harbour in the west end of Cockaineie, which was destroyed by a storme in January, *anno* 1635", *ibid*., p. 75.

[5] The Earls of Winton and Dunfermline and Viscount Kingston were all forfeited after 1715 and these titles extinguished.

at Seton Palace. "From Dunbarr to Edinburgh," wrote[1] Brereton, "we came this day (26 June) in the afternoon. By the way we observed very many stately seats of the nobles, one we passed near unto, which is the Earl of Winton's, a dainty seat placed upon the sea. Here also are apple-trees, walnut-trees, syca-more, and other fruit-trees, and other kinds of wood which prosper well."

Seton Palace had only recently been completed. "He built," wrote[2] the family historian in regard to his father the third Earl of Winton, "in anno 1630 two quarters of the house of Seton, beginning at Wallace's Tower att the east end . . . and continued the building till Jacob's Tower on the north side of the house." The roof of the great hall had been constructed[3] by the first Earl of Winton, but much of the palace[4] dated back to Queen Mary's time. The judgment of McGibbon and Ross[5] on this vanished house appears convincing. "Seton Palace, near Tranent, was probably the most sumptuous example of the Domestic style of the period 1542–1700, both as regards its arrangements and design." It was the representative great country house lying in a peaceful neighbourhood; stone tracery around the window shafts; ceilings with fine plasterwork; wide staircases.[6]

In 1620 the third Earl of Winton planned a new building[7] on the site of the old Place of Winton. This was at first conceived as a dower house,[8] but the project was enlarged before completion. Lord Winton's account books begin[9] in January 1627 when the house was finished. They give a remarkable impression of the nature of his expenditure. The sums mentioned are in Scots

[1] *Journal*, p. 98.   [2] Kingston, *op. cit.*, p. 75.
[3] *Ibid.*, p. 59.

[4] "In the year 1561, the great dungeon of Seton fell to the ground, without hurt of any. From the south side of which, the said Lord George (Seton) built the great quarter of the hall, and he built all the dykes from the old entry down to the links, over the banks", *ibid.*, p. 57. It seems likely that "dungeon" is a transliteration of *donjon*.

[5] *The Castellated and Domestic Architecture of Scotland* by David McGibbon and Thomas Ross, vol. iii, p. 32.

[6] This fashion was only just developing. At Lethington Tower, now Lennoxlove, the "easier staire" has a panel dated 1632.

[7] "He founded and built the great house from the foundation, with all the lairge stone dykes about the precinct, park, orchard and gardens thereof", Kingston, *op. cit.*, p. 74.

[8] Cf. article in *Country Life*, vol. xxx, p. 260 seq.

[9] These were preserved among the Forbes Leith MSS. at Whitehaugh. in Garioch. They consist of fairly detailed accounts for three years made out in Lord Winton's handwriting and a more cursory series of notes made by Robert Setoun, but checked by Lord Winton until the latter's death in 1650.

money and include £40 given to a mason in part payment for "winning and working"[1] the hearth stones and kitchen pavement, a similar sum for timber work, and £100 in part payment for the plaster ceilings. The glass was put in for £200. An interesting item indicates the trade by sea between Scottish ports. Nine thousand slates were ordered from Caithness.[2] Other disbursements relate to the old house in the Canongate[3] in Edinburgh, which he was pulling down. One entry gives the bill for dressing the leather[4] of Lord Winton's little country coach.

He gave £40 to "Adame the painter" for his portrait to be sent to his sister Lady Perth.[5] Moneys were set aside to cover losses at bowls and for the purpose of constructing a bowling alley. There was payment to a doctor who had cured his daughter's[6] leg and to another who had attended his young son Lord Seton,[7] when he was sick of the pox in London. There were disbursements for his son's "gentleman" and for his friends' attendants. The largest item was two thousand pounds given to Sir George Hamilton in repayment of moneys lent and for gold provided when he was in London. The world here envisaged could be paralleled among English families of the same standing.

Winton and Seton Palace, as reconstructed, were wholly without that defensive element which still continued to condition so much of the building of the lairds' castles especially those beyond the Forth. From Edinburgh through Berwick-on-Tweed and thence to wherever the Court might be residing communications were fast and posts were regular. The introduction of plaster[8] work and the attention paid to the construction and decoration of

---

[1] This entry suggests that the mason, William Pedenn, was also a quarryman, Forbes Leith MSS., H.M.C., Appendix to second report, p. 199.

[2] They cost £22 *per* thousand, *ibid.*, p. 199.

[3] A sum of £100 was given to William Wallace, the architect of Heriot's Hospital, in part payment for this work and putting up a new entrance there. Other similar payments include £300 towards furnishing Winton and £302 19s. 2d. for furnishing the house in the Canongate, then re-built, for occupation during the Convention of 1630, *ibid.*, p. 199.

[4] A sum of £72 was paid to "ane inglische fallow", *ibid.*, p. 199. English tanners were brought into Scotland about 1620, cf. *Domestic Life in Scotland,* Rhind Lectures in Archaeology (1920), by John Warrack, p. 144.

[5] In 1627 Lord Winton was forty-three and this gift seems to mark the beginning of the convention of giving portraits to one's relatives.

[6] Lady Anna Seton, who was then aged sixteen and died unmarried.

[7] Payment was made on 24 January 1629; Lord Seton was then fifteen.

[8] The plaster work at Winton is identical with that at Moray House in Edinburgh. The arms and monograms of the third Earl and his first wife are on the drawing room ceiling at Winton.

bedrooms[1] were both quite novel, but, these points apart, there was at first little explicit evidence of English influence.[2] Although the accession of James VI to the English throne was long fore-seen, it may be said that wars and forays had both ended un-expectedly. In the Border country, houses such as Ferniehurst and the older and rival Kerr stronghold at Cessford were over-taken by the sudden peace.

Change filtered through very slowly. Until the nineteenth century there was much less rebuilding in Scotland than in England due in part to the poverty of the Scots landowners in terms of ready money. Emulation did not take the form of rivalry in new constructions. A house like Winton presupposed that the owner would have no followers in the traditional sense, but what was still normally required was sleeping quarters for many men and stabling for their horses. Thus side by side with Winton stood an old and unchanged house such as Traquair, and the latter was much more characteristic. The special features of Winton were not copied; the tall chimney stacks alternately wrought[3] in convolutions and in flutes; the friezes with their heavy mouldings; the two great freestone fireplaces; the balustrading which defined the terrace;[4] the broad steps leading down to the lower walk.[5]

Such importations from south of the Border had little effect upon current design. Thus the Place of Ochiltree in West Lothian, a tall block with high crowstepped gables and wing turrets, a narrow entrance and a vaulted kitchen, appears to have been built[6] in 1610. It dominated the open lands which shelved north-ward to the Forth near Abercorn. Lethington Tower, even when

[1] Thus the plaster work in a bedroom at Lethington Tower is dated 1618 and decorations were renewed by John Earl of Lauderdale and Isabel Seton his wife in 1626. In the absence of other records these dated monograms are an essential indication.
[2] Pinkie House, built by the first Earl of Dunfermline and begun in 1613, is an exception. The long gallery, apart from the carved wooden ceiling, and the wellhead in the forecourt with its stone corona top, might have found a place in any Jacobean lay-out.
[3] "This manner of decorating stalks, while familiar in the Jacobean archi-tecture of England, is unknown elsewhere in Scotland", *Inventory of Monu-ments in East Lothian* (1924), p. 85.
[4] Cf. for a detailed account of Winton House, *ibid.*, pp. 84-6.
[5] In this connection a MS. diary written by David second Earl of Wemyss and begun in 1634 gives an account of a contemporary garden. It contains a detailed plan of the garden at the Chapel of Wemyss with notes on the trees and the flower and herb plots, *Memorials of the family of Wemyss* by Sir William Fraser (1888), vol. i, p. 41.
[6] This house also known as Ochiltre Castle and not to be confused with Ochiltree in Ayrshire is described as dating from the early seventeenth century. One of the dormer pediments bore the date 1610. *Inventory of Monuments in Mid-Lothian and West Lothian* (1929), pp. 218-9.

modified, remained essentially a defended mansion. Putting aside
the fact that accommodation for retainers was not needed, this
likewise applied but on a smaller scale to the high lairds' houses
around Edinburgh whose estates gave their titles to the lords of
session.

Away in the lands towards England the change from the old
Border hold had come abruptly. Not only did the foreign enemy
disappear but the jealousies between the leading stocks were
uprooted once the great posts which involved the guardianship
of the frontier had become obsolete. The rivalry of the principal
branches of the Kerrs is a case in point. "There had been," wrote[1]
Spottiswoode, " a long and old emulation betwixt the two families
of Cessford and Farniherst for the wardenry of the Middle
Marches and the provostry of Jedburgh." An account of the
transformation of Ancram House and the plans for laying out
the policies gives a sharp impression of this new peace. It has the
additional interest that it was the work of a Scot long resident
in England and writing from the Court, a man who recalled each
detail of his Scottish house and his own country.

Sir Robert Kerr, who was to receive the earldom of Ancram
in 1633, was a cousin of the old King's favourite, the Earl of
Somerset, who acted as his protector. He was a steady courtier, loyal
and acquisitive,[2] easy of approach,[3] no cherisher of feuds. A
strong religious vein perhaps rendered him acceptable to Charles I.
He gave much time to a translation of the Psalms.[4] In his old age
he was benevolent and a little prosy. "If wyse and good be not
joyned together," he wrote[5] to his son in his last years, "they are

[1] *History*, Bannatyne Club edition, vol. ii, p. 411.

[2] Cf. a letter from the Earl of Ancram to Secretary Windebank dated 12
November 1636. "And for that reversion of Nicolsons, part of the preter-
mitted customs, I left you the coppye of his gift, and my desyr by petition,
and God forbid that the Kyng stick att so small a matter, so far off to cum
as fyve yeair hence, to a man he promiseth more pregnant satisfaction." Also
a letter to Sir Edward Nicholas dated at Whitehall 31 January 1637–8, "Sir,
I pray you do me the favour to ansuer for me to the Lords if I be cald on
for this Logwod busines to-day", State Papers Dom.

[3] In a letter to Sir Robert Kerr dated 1 February 1632 Sir Thomas Hope
described himself as "one quho long since hes takin yow for patron",
Correspondence of the Earl of Ancram, vol. i, p. 58.

[4] Sir Patrick Hume of Polwarth wrote to his cousin Sir Robert Kerr on 7
December 1625: "Thare is not a craftisman to make a steal bonett in al the
land lyk as quhen thyr was no smyth in Israel, The God of Hosts must be
our scheild. I redd your translationes of these Psalmes you left with Mr.
David (Hume) of Godscroft, and wes bold to put to my hand *ad limam*." In
the foreword to the translation addressed to his son William Kerr and dated
24 April 1624 Sir Robert wrote: "I haue sent you, according to your desire,
some of the Psalmes which I told you I had put in this forme upon the
occasion of hearing in the Low Countryes the Dutch men and French sing
in their severall languages to one tune", *ibid.*, pp. 482, 488.

[5] *Ibid.*, p. 382.

neyther of them wyse nor good. This my philosophy I haue learned in this my solitude, out of better books than Cicero or Seneca." With this preamble we can consider the letters about Ancram House. They begin in December 1632 when Sir Robert Kerr was fifty-six years of age and are addressed to his son who had lately been created Earl of Lothian.

In the first place he explains[1] the renovation of the Tower where his heir proposed to live in the next summer. The room below the hall should be Lord Lothian's ordinary eating chamber. The walls were not to be weakened by striking out new windows, but partitions were to be removed and the lights glazed. The apertures were to be kept as they were "strong in the out syde because the world may change agayn". A pantry was to be constructed for pots and glasses or cups or for the plate "with a strong doore". The actual dining room was to be made into a fair chamber and the old long tables taken out. "Put a round table only in it," he suggests,[2] "which is to be used square most tymes; but may be lett out round when yow please to eate there with some extraordinar frend. Yow have hangings enow, and stooles and chayres for it." A deep iron fireplace was to be constructed and fed with Lothian coals. The main bedchamber was to contain a single bed, but the old partition was to be kept standing. A servant could be lodged behind it and the master's "trash" placed there. At the top of the stairs a fine cabinet was to be arranged for books and papers. New constructions were to include a gallery[3] with a gate beneath it and a set of dining rooms and lodgings and a paved court. There were to be "accesses[4] in the fashion of this country or France".

It was not, however, the house that was remarkable for this was secondary to Lord Lothian's greater mansion the Place of Newbattle. The unusual feature is the exact description of the

[1] *Correspondence of the first Earl of Ancram and his son the third Earl of Lothian*, ed. David Laing, Roxburgh Club, 1875, vol. i, pp. 62-3.

[2] *Ibid.*, pp. 63-4.

[3] Sir Robert Kerr intended "to lett the fore gate be built upp as ones (once) it was, and to make a gallery with some lodgings on the other syde, because all the bewty of the garden must be cast that waye, and it lyes to the sunne, which in Scotland is a main consideration; and therfor I would build on that side the principall fyre roomes of my house, with a low hall . . . and that to be kept sweet for interteyning my frendes at solemn tymes, a whole bodye of a lodging with back stairs and easy lodgings to lodge a great man, and this to be joyn'd to the tower by a balcon or ship-gallery going about the tower to the entry above stayres", *ibid.*, pp. 65-6.

[4] *Ibid.*, p. 66. One comment has a special interest. "By any meanes do not take away the battelement, as some gave me counsale to do, as Dalhoussy your nyghtbour did, for that is the grace of the house, and makes it looke lyk a castle, and hence so nobleste, as the other would make it looke lyke a peele", *ibid.*, p. 64.

policies and gardens. The wall was to be completed with three gates.[1] There was to be an outer field for football[2] and "on the burne under Gawne Trumbull's house a low bridge to be made for a coach or cartes to passe". Sir Robert recommended his son to leave that part of the killing brae that is right under the entry where the thorns are for the women to dry the clothes and bleach. The wells and water lay beside this slope.[3]

On the ground between the Thomas thorn and the dovecots an orchard was to be planted containing the best fruits that could be got in the neighbouring abbey land for that place was the most suitable in the lands about Ancram since it lay well to the sun and under the north wind. Sir Robert added[4] that he would keep the hazels along the little bank for they bear the best and earliest nuts in all that country. He then suggested perch for the great deep lake at Ancram townfoot. The high trees should be cut down that grew up to the Tower by the women's house, and apples, plums and choice pears[5] laid out along the walks between the women's house and the "doucat" alley. Plane trees should be planted next to the dyke within the orchard. Arbours were to be formed and the gardener's house placed high up towards the byre and all that part planted with cherry trees.[6]

Sir Robert took thought for the placing of sheep on the two windy edges and on all the Woodheid bounds beyond the burn

[1] "The one gate to goe furth to the park, and the other to goe furth to the toun that those that cum or goe from Edinburgh, or to Langnewton or to Tweedside may cum in that way. And forgaynst the gate of your house, the third gate for your selfe to go to Jedburgh or eastward, or to Nether Ancrame and that way", ibid., pp. 67-68.

[2] Arrangements for this purpose are described in detail. "In this outer green I would have George Karrs house tane quyte away, and Pate Wrights and Ninian Rutherfords and Mitchells, and all that side, that this may be converted in a grate warde for horses to goe in that cum loads or erands from any place, or strangers' common horses whom yow would not admitt to your parke or stables, and may not stay . . . and heir (here) to run at ring and glove, and play at football and these exercises which young men must have a place for", ibid., pp. 67-8.

[3] He also suggested the making of "a slop passage to goe along from the park gate doun vnder the place where the old Schoole was", ibid., p. 69.

[4] Ibid., p. 70. One English preference is worth recording: "I would have noe trees nor bushes within the park. . . . Iff yow agree with Mr. David Symmer, and so put his kirkland into your parke, with a high wall round about it, it would compare then with an Englishe parke", ibid., p. 70.

[5] He noted that where the old ball green was "peare trees will grow wele, whereoff seek put the best within Newbatle and Jedburgh", ibid., p. 73. These were both monastic orchards.

[6] "For I have seen excellent cherryes grow there with little caire, so as I know it will be an excellent cherry garden, which in Scotland is one of your best fruits where they are choysed, and plant abundance of grosers and risors and strauberryes, and roses and all flowers all over your orchard, for they will grow wele in Ancram", ibid., p. 74.

that runs from the mosse to the broomebank and Gersetlaw. He
discussed the good corn land on Pallace Hill and about the Sandy
stanes. Each comment was the fruit of deep affection.[1] After
some other details[2] he concluded with the project for an avenue.
"You should do wele," he wrote,[3] "also to make your owne way
to Edinburgh . . . so mending the wayes in these hollow pathes
beyond the burne to goe upp Lilliarts Cross, and so be (by) Melrose
or Dryburgh, which yow will." The description of these lands
supposed a state of peace. This was a well-managed example of
a great man's property; the avenue introduced a note of
grandeur. The wild country to the south seemed far away.
Ancram House looked towards Edinburgh.

Thus there was for a time a certain contrast between on the
one hand the policy of the sober accretion of property and the
purchase of adjacent land as an endowment for a younger[4] son
and on the other the old-style buildings which still continued to
be erected. An example from the same East Lothian countryside
is the mansion house of Tyninghame, whose outlines are now
only known to us through a print made in 1829 before it was
re-faced and transformed and wholly incorporated in a later
building. This house has an especial interest since the inventory
of each room with its contents made on behalf of the first Earl
of Haddington in 1635 is probably the most complete that has
survived from this period.

Tyninghame had an eastern and a western great hall and the
old arrangement of the chamber of dais, which however seems

[1] Cf. this comment: "Sir I would have you labour nothing of the Woodheid with plewces, but on this syde the burn and the scauroods; for the rest
is barren ground not worth the ploweing, and excellent for sheepe, or rather
(will?) yeeld nowt about the mosse; for there abouts, and all the moor vp
towards the Morhous-law, grows a rott gerse, which I know full wele, for I
have not forgotten a footstep, nor a know, nor a bushe of that bounds, and
could wink and goe to it", *ibid.*, p. 71.

[2] "And at the toun foote, by Will Ayres house and towards the burne, I
would have yow make your balt barnes and steeps, both because it would
save yow bringing of watter so far vpp on weemens heads or in barrells on
sladds", *ibid.*, p. 75. Sir Robert noted that the men displaced by these
arrangements were to be placed either at Hobbs Houds or the town head or
in houses "where other decaying men be", *ibid.*, p. 75. He urged his son to
raise the sides of the kirk bridge, to pave it and to make steps at the end so
that horsemen may not pass "for it was only ordayned for foote folk",
ibid., p. 75.

[3] *Ibid.*, p. 75.

[4] Thus the third Earl of Winton in 1643 bought from Sir Alexander Towers
for 95,000 marks the lands of Garmilton-Noble, Garmilton-Alexander and
others as an endowment for his son Christopher, *Scots Peerage*, vol. viii,
p. 594. Detailed notes on *The House of Seton* by Sir Bruce Gordon Seton,
Bt., were printed privately and posthumously in 1939.

to have been used as a store room.¹ Twenty-five rooms are catalogued² not including the store place known as the wardrobe.³ There were not many chairs,⁴ but the furniture of state was listed separately. This included great velvet chairs⁵ and a set of twenty red leather ones; new tapestries depicting David and Abraham; rich hangings⁶ showing forth the theme of Jacob; state beds with their embellishments.⁷ There were three and a half dozen silver plates.⁸ The house was arranged for entertaining thirty persons of the first quality.

The inventory does not mention the books which we know to have been at that date in Haddington's possession; they may

---

¹ It contained four beds, a wainscot table, a blue rug, a stand of blue taffeta curtains complete with valances, and two sponges, Inventory of the plenishings in the dwelling house of Tyninghame, *Memorials of the Earls of Haddington*, vol. ii, Correspondence and Charters, by Sir William Fraser (1889), pp. 300-4.

² These include the western and eastern chambers both in the outer close. In the eastern work were the high south and north chambers and the low south and north chambers. These six rooms contained between them fourteen standing and "draw" beds and fourteen feather beds. In the north chamber above the chamber of dais and in the little room beyond were an oak and a wainscot bedstead and three feather beds, also a stand of sad green curtains with broad lace, a green table cloth and a yellow rug.
There were three rooms over the western greathall. One of them contained a marble table and a mirror and another a table with drawers, two short wainscot tables and a clock. The room above the pantry, the outer chamber above the "lettermeit" house and the small back room adjoining all contained beds as did the outer and inner high chambers situated in the old tower.
In the "lettermeit" house was an oak table and eight muskets with bandoliers to match. In the pantry and cellar were twenty-seven bottles, thirty cups and seventy-four drinking glasses; in the kitchen were seven-and-a-half dozen puther (pewter?) plates, a toasting iron, a dripping pan and a frying pan, *ibid.*, pp. 300-4.

³ This contained in addition to six feather beds and twenty-five chamber pots, a black velvet "paill" (pall?), and a large supply of curtains, red flowered durata and green durata, red "steining" and "sprainged" silk with velvet valances.

⁴ Two rooms had a chair of oak, one had two leather chairs and another four folding chairs with lace and a "greene cloth stule conforme". In the low north chamber in the eastern work were two stamped leather chairs, *ibid.*, pp. 300-4.

⁵ Besides the three great velvet chairs there were six smaller chairs covered with the same material.

⁶ In addition to these three series there were eighteen less valuable pieces of tapestry.

⁷ As an example, "ane grein French cloath bed, with rich lace and fringe, with chairis, stoolis covering and table cloath", *ibid.*, ii, pp. 297-300.

⁸ The list also mentions three dozen silver spoons, a sugar box with spoon, a vinegar stoup double gilt and fourteen dessert dishes. It is stated that the word "dessert" was introduced direct from France not later than 1594, Warrack, *op. cit.*, p. 116.

have been in Edinburgh. It would seem that the Jameson portraits[1] had not yet been introduced. The tall bare house[2] stood in the open fields looking southwards across the tidal water and exposed to the east winds from the sea. There was, perhaps, a rather grim splendour at Tyninghame.

Certain heirlooms have been mentioned in considering the Campbells of Glenorchy, but the taste for personal display characterised the heads of all the leading Scottish families. There were various reasons for this ostentation. Among these may be numbered that desire for portable wealth represented by the chests of jewellery which on some occasions formed a bridal gift. In an era when banking was still undeveloped these sets of jewels were kept in the castles behind strong doors.[3] The great ladies of the Protestant tradition were not behindhand in building up such great collections. There was no Puritan prejudice against adornment.[4]

Attention was concentrated on the public life of the chief's family on its great occasions. This in part explains the elaborate funerals and sumptuous marriage feasts which were an enduring feature in the circle of the Scottish magnates. In a sense this society was united and even relatively harmonious and no equals absented themselves on such occasions from purposes of policy. The chief would be surrounded by the gentlemen of his name each in their place. At funerals especially the heads of each cadet branch would have an office to perform in the high ceremony. An excellent example of the custom can be seen in the arrangements made for

[1] It would seem that the portrait of Lord Binning later second Earl of Haddington as well as that of Lady Binning and the Haddington family group were painted in 1637 and the following years, cf. *George Jameson* by John Bulloch (1885) *passim*.

[2] Tyninghame resembled the central block of Traquair before that house was modified and the pavilion wings constructed. It had an outside stair which led to part of the first storey and a single semi-circular turret "the old tower".

[3] A volume of Inventories of Plenishing preserved in the General Register House contains a memorandum, no. 9, of some jewels and other things belonging to the Earl of Roxburgh on 16 May 1644. These include a round jewel for the breast containing thirty-nine diamonds, eight "collett" diamonds set in gold, a ring with six turquoises, an emerald ring, two little pendants of rubies and diamonds, twelve pendant pearls and thirty small loose diamonds.

[4] One of the most elaborate inventories of jewellery is that taken on the death of Lady Anne Hamilton first wife of Hugh Lord Montgomerie and is dated 24 October 1632. The Marchioness of Hamilton who gave a great jewel in the form of a feather set with diamonds was a Cunningham of Glencairn and a strict Presbyterian, *Memorials of the Montgomeries,* ii, pp. 290-1.

the burial of the first Earl of Buccleuch.[1] This practice also masked the difference of belief or religious preference. The heirs of no rich lord would forgo the obsequies to which his rank entitled him and in such a ceremony the ministers of the Kirk had their due place.

The appeal of such functions was very real in a country that was without a yeoman class and where the claim to gentle blood was so often linked with association with some great house. In Scotland there was not found that agricultural prosperity and independence of all ties which led to the building up of the innumerable small manors in the English counties.

As a consequence ceremonial dress occupied a considerable place in the inventory of the goods of any man with pretensions to rank. As an example the list of the plenishings[2] of Captain John Sempill taken after his death in 1647 is for the most part an account of clothes and the material for clothing[3] whose value far outstrips that of the blue and yellow curtains, the dornik cloths and kitchen gear which are also set out. He appears to have been a bachelor or widower. The greater part of his real estate consisted of the gold buttons and gold lace[4] and the crimson satin in which he would wait upon Lord Sempill.

Inevitably it is much more difficult to reconstruct the material background of the lairds of middle rank. In the north and west the evidence is very scanty in regard to the actual furnishing of the houses occupied, for instance, by the cadet branches of the Macdonalds. Our knowledge is for the most part confined to the

[1] The Earl's body was interred at St Mary's Hawick on 11 June 1634. The procession was headed by Robert Scot of Houschaw armed at all points and carrying on a lance a banner of the defunct's colours, azure and or. After the led horses came three trumpets on foot sounding sadly. Then the "grate gumpheon" of black taffeta borne by Mr. James Scott. Walter Scot of Lauchope carried the spurs, Andrew Scot of Brandmedowes the sword, Francis Scot of Castlesyde the gauntlets and Mr. Lawrence Scot the coat of honour. After the bearers of the arms of the Earl's eight grand-parents came Walter Scot of Goldielands with the great "pincell", Sir James Scot of Rossie with the motto and Sir William Scot of Harden with the defunct's arms in metal and colour carried aloft. Sir John Scot of Scotstarvet carried the coronet "overlaid with cypres" and borne upon a velvet cushion. Account printed in *The Scotts of Buccleugh* by Sir W. Fraser, vol. i, pp. 264-5.

[2] It is preserved at the General Register House and forms no. 10 in a volume of Inventories of Plenishing.

[3] The total value of these goods amounted to £585 13s. 10d. Scots money. The most substantial item was a crimson satin doublet and scarlet breeches both with gold lace valued at £66 13s. 4d. and seven ells of crimson velvet and two-and-a-half ells of scarlet cloth which were together valued at £86. The more considerable items of a general character were three silver goblets marked at £64 13s. 4d., and a piece of hangings at £36.

[4] He had four dozen gold breast buttons and a dozen old great gold buttons. The material of red flowered taffeta with a blue flower design was perhaps for a waistcoat.

great houses like Dunvegan.[1] Detail relating to the southern counties is more plentiful. An interesting inventory has survived dealing with a country house of modest size in Berwickshire. It was taken[2] in 1631 and describes all the moveables in the house of Tofts which at that date belonged to Alexander Belshes. Curtains are mentioned[3] for the principal rooms, but there appear to have been no tapestried hangings. The house contained about a dozen beds[4] and there were arm chairs[5] for the head of the family and his chief guests. The inventory lists a fair amount of brass and pewter,[6] including two pewter basins and a laver; there was no silver. Four muskets and six lances were kept for defence. There were two books, a Bible and a Titus Livius. Among houses still surviving and radically unaltered Pilmuir in East Lothian perhaps gives the clearest impression[7] of the life of a family of comparable standing.

It is natural that it was at the apex of the social structure that resemblances in Scottish life appear most marked. There were great variations in the different regions quite apart from those resulting from the predominance of Gaelic speech. Thus the development of a merchant class which established itself among the landed gentry or alternatively the emergence of a group of landowners with some mercantile interests can be traced in the

---

[1] Glasgow played a chief part in providing for the needs of the richer families in the north west. The muniment room of the MacLeods contains a tailor's bill "Att Glasgow ye 16 of August 1633, McCloyd's accompt". On this occasion grey English cloth and green worsted stockings had been ordered. On 2 April 1653 the sum of £405 13s. 8d. Scots was owed by the Laird of MacLeod to Peter Pattoune, draper of Glasgow, *The Book of Dunvegan* ed. Rev. R. C. MacLeod, Third Spalding Club (1938), vol. i, pp. 206, 186.

[2] It is dated 26 September 1631 and is preserved at the General Register House in a volume of Inventories of Plenishing, no. 7.

[3] There were two pairs of scarlet grogram curtains, two stands of blue "bumbesie" curtains and one stand of green and another of yellow.

[4] There were eleven feather beds, fourteen bolsters and fifteen timber bedsteads. There were two canopies one yellow and the other orange.

[5] Four red arm chairs and four red chairs without arms. Among oddments were six turkey work cushions, one dozen and a half of damask "serviets" and three dozen linen "serviets".

[6] There were a dozen pewter trenchers and nine brass candlesticks. Two red rugs are mentioned, but no personal clothing except one felt coat and hood.

[7] Pilmuir House had a basement kitchen, living rooms on the first floor and bedrooms at the attic level. There was a turret with a spiral staircase. The house was built by William Cairns and Agnes Broun his wife. The wide outside stairway leading to the first floor would seem to be a later feature, *Inventory of Monuments in East Lothian*, pp. 11-13. A simpler house, now in a ruined state, is Kipps near Bathgate, built in 1625-6 by Robert Boyd, advocate. The structure was just under sixty feet long by twenty-five broad, *Inventory of Monuments in West Lothian*, pp. 237-8 containing also an excellent plan.

neighbourhood of Aberdeen and dependent upon the trade of that city. The string of royal burghs along the northern shores of the Firth of Forth also tended to create a special outlook both in politics and religion among the gentry and burgesses of Fife. It was in that county that the Earl of Leven proposed to establish himself on his return from Germany; here also was the home of the Earl of Rothes and his affinity.

Under another aspect Fife and the neighbouring counties came within the sphere of influence of the University of St Andrews. Mark Napier in his study of Montrose's youth has collected a great body of material reflecting the privileged life of the noble students of St Andrews, who came from large properties in Fife and from the quiet estates beyond the Tay. Glamis and the home of Montrose's father-in-law Southesk were near the northern limit of this area whose peaceful character was emphasized by the elaborate Renaissance garden at Edzell Castle. It is desirable not to overstress the surface courtesy and quiet which marked the social contacts in these rich lands. Northwards lay the Gordon country with its great open feuds where men still took a pride in rivalry.

CHAPTER VIII

THE NORTH EAST

THE traveller going north across the Mearns found in Aberdeenshire and in the neighbouring counties of Banff and Moray a region which was radically different from the rest of Scotland. This was due both to the support and opposition engendered by what was almost the viceroyalty of the Gordons of Huntly and to the especial character of Aberdeen. That town had a confident and self-sufficient corporate life and drew strength from its two colleges. It was the scene of more Catholic activity than any other Scottish city, while the ruling class was Protestant and Episcopal. Rutherford, a hostile witness, adverts[1] to this aspect. "This town (Aberdeen) hath been advised upon of purpose for me; it consisteth either of Papists, or men of Gallio's naughty faith." Certainly the power of the Presbytery diminished when a man left Dunnottar[2] behind him and rode up past Stonehaven towards the Dee.

An account of the lay-out of Aberdeen is given in Gordon of Rothiemay's description written about 1661. The town clustered round the Castle Hill and St Katherine's[3] Hill; it stretched from Woolmanhill to the Dee Loch. The houses are described as built of stone gathered from the sea shore. They were roofed with slates and were mostly three or four storeys in height, some of them higher. "The streets," it is explained,[4] "are all neatlie paved with flint stones, or a gray kinde of harde stone not unlike to flint. The dwelling houses are cleanlie and bewtifull and neate both within

[1] *Letters of Samuel Rutherford,* no. lxxvii, to Lady Boyd, undated, p. 163.
[2] Dunnottar Castle, belonging to the Earls Marischal, was the northern stronghold of the lords who would support the Covenant.
[3] On 9 August 1626 a licence was granted to enclose a portion of St. Katherine's Hill on an undertaking being given that the bounds would be planted with trees and that it would be made a common walking place. Reference was made to the "back dyke" of Lord Forbes's yard and it was stated that "pairt of the said hill betwixt the auld chappell and the lard Forbes yaird is made ane filthie vennell", *Extracts from the Records of the Council Register of the Burgh of Aberdeen,* Scottish Burgh Records Society, ed. John Stuart (1871), p. 7. A few years earlier Lord Forbes's winter lodging at Aberdeen was situated in Shiprow, *Powis Papers,* Third Spalding Club, ed. John George Burnett (1951), p. 27.
[4] *Description of Bothe Touns of Aberdeen,* p. 9, also quoted in *Aberdeen Council Letters,* vol. i, 1552-1633, ed. Louise B. Taylor (1942), introduction, p. xvii.

and without and the syde that looks to the street is mostly
adorned with galleries of timber, which they call forestairs. Many
houses have their gardens and orchards adjoining; every garden
has its posterne and these are planted with all sorts of trees which
the climat will suffer to grow; so that the whole toune, to such as
draw neere it upon some sydes of it, looks as if it stood in a
garden[1] or little wood."

The six gates of Aberdeen included the Upperkirkgate Port,
the Netherkirkgate Port at the east end of the road to the "Flor"
Mill, and the Trinity or Quay Head Port at the south end of the
Shiprow. The principal church within the town was dedicated to
St Nicholas; it was built mainly of ashlar with a leaden[2] roof and
a high steeple. The harbour was guarded by a Block House to
give protection against pirates and the mouth of the Dee was
"locked[3] with chains of iron and masts of ships crossing the river
not to be opened but at the citizens pleasure".

It is not difficult to reconstruct the details of the tenements in
the Shiprow area. In 1608 the accommodation in one such building
consisted[4] of a hall with a chamber above it, a gallery hall, "Jack
chalmer" and kitchen loft. The furnishing was meagre. Citizens
of the middle rank had much more space;[5] the burgesses were
noted for their hospitality. There was constant contact with the
outer world,[6] although regular inns seem hardly as yet to have
been established.[7] The population of the town was rising steadily
and has been estimated[8] as 7,031 in 1592 as against 8,750 half a
century later.

[1] In the original text the words "garding" for garden and "quholle" for
whole are both used.
[2] The lead had been stripped from the roof after the victory of the
Reformers, but it was replaced about 1614 when the Master of Kirkwood
received authority to import from Danzig lead worth £105 for this purpose,
Aberdeen Charter Room, vol. xlii, p. 734 quoted in Taylor, op. cit., note
p. xxi.
[3] Taylor, op. cit., p. xxii.
[4] Powis Papers, p. 27.
[5] Among the inhabitants of the Spital in 1636 were John Anderson, tailor,
and his wife, who had with them four children and Andrew Duthie, Arthur
Anderson and Agnes Walker, their servants. In March 1638 Andrew Gray,
son of Laurence Gray, cooper and burgess of Aberdeen and himself resident
at the Mill of Mondurno, sold the Twelve Roads to John Anderson, tailor, of
Old Aberdeen, ibid., pp. 4-5.
[6] On 9 August 1635 a licence was granted by the Council to Alexander
Rolland to teach a French school within the burgh and to put up a board or
sign before his school door to give notice of the said licence to all who were
desirous to learn the French tongue, Records of the Burgh of Aberdeen, ed.
Stuart, p. 80.
[7] In January 1632 the Earl of Sutherland "lodges in Andrew Haddingtoun's
at the yett cheik, who was ane ostler", John Spalding, Memorials of the
Troubles (1828), i, p. 13.
[8] Kennedy Annals of Aberdeen, i, p. 186.

Aberdeen was very consciously the north-eastern capital. In this connection the Burgh Accounts indicate both the courtesies shown[1] to persons of distinction and payments which reflect[2] the details of the civic life. The neighbouring lairds show a close concern for the town's welfare.[3] The register of burgesses throws light not only on the *ex gratia* admissions with the record of the lords and their attendant gentlemen and "servants" who received[4] this privilege, but also on the matter of the admittance of foreigners. This latter question would only concern students, usually Dutch or French, who proposed to settle[5] in Aberdeen and those who came to exercise a trade or craft. There seems reason to suppose that these latter would normally require some powerful protection[6] before being admitted. In regard to Scots a sidelight on the state of retail trade is sometimes given. Thus in 1641 a glover and perfumer was accepted[7] as a burgess because there was at that time no one else of this calling within the town.

A curiously modern note is struck in the regulations regarding the nomination of a librarian for the town library "within the

[1] As examples £12 Scots was expended "for the tounis courtasie to the Ladie Errol" and on 20 May 1631 £11 4s. was spent on wine and sugar to entertain the Earl of Perth in Gilbert Anderson's house on his coming to the town, *Accounts of the Burgh of Aberdeen*, Miscellany of the Spalding Club, vol. v, pp. 104 and 148.

[2] E.g. "To John Duff, skipper, for shooting the tounes ordinances at the Lady Marqueis (of Huntly's) buriall, 1 lib. To George Jaffray, for hame bringing of Dr. Reid's buiks from London to the college of New Aberdeen, 20 lib. For a barrow to carie the cripell witches, 6s." The discharges for these payments are under 1637-8, 1641-2 and 1626-7 respectively, *ibid.*, pp. 105, 106 and 102.

[3] Cf. The detailed correspondence of Marion Douglas, Lady Drum, carried on during 1630 with the provost, baillies and council of Aberdeen on the subject of her late husband's benefactions, *Aberdeen Council Letters*, vol. i, pp. 312 and 317-29 *passim*.

[4] On March 1630 Lord John Gordon, Viscount Melgum, brought with him two "servants" and James Gordon, page to my Lady Marquis of Huntly, On 30 August 1631 Thomas Herries, John Ker (servitors to my Lady Lothian) *ex gratia* were admitted burgesses, *Burgesses, of Guild and Trade of the Burgh of Aberdeen 1399-1631*, Miscellany of the New Spalding Club, vol. i, pp. 154-160.

[5] Thus in 1630 three students of philosophy were admitted burgesses, John Legeai, Maximillian de Berendrecht and Rochus Bastardus, the two last-named being natives of Zeeland. On 23 May 1630 Mr John Maill, an advocate before the senate of Rouen, was admitted, but he may have been a Scotsman practising abroad. Mr Alexander Donaldson, who was admitted as a burgess on 24 September 1642, is described as eldest son of the late Mr Walter Donaldson LLD, Professor of Philosophy in the Academy of Caen, *Register of Burgesses of the Burgh of Aberdeen 1631-1700*, Miscellany of the New Spalding Club, vol. ii, pp. 15, 32.

[6] On 22 June 1637 Emmanuel de Blais, frenchman, chirurgeon to my Lord Marquis of Huntly and George Gordon, browdinstair, servant to my Lord Gordon were admitted with free liberty to exercise their craft at the request of the said Lord Marquis, *ibid.*, p. 24.

[7] Admission on 27 April 1641 of Ochtrie Fairindaill, *ibid.*, p. 31.

I

colledge of the said burgh". In February 1632 Robert Douny was appointed[1] for life subject to the conditions laid down in the founder's will. In accordance with the terms of this instrument the librarian was to "hold the doore of the librarie patent and opin" four days each week both in term time and during the vacations. On Mondays, Wednesdays, Fridays and Saturdays the library was to be open in summer from seven till eleven in the morning and again from two until five in the afternoon. In winter the morning hours were to be nine till twelve and the library was to close at four o'clock.

This suggests an immutable calm which is reflected in the orderly management of the great houses, the Marquis of Huntly's in Old Aberdeen and the Earl Marischal's in the new town. Even in the laird of Pitfoddel's lodging in New Aberdeen twenty-four gentlemen could sit down at table besides the family.[2] External precautions had mainly involved a system of warning against a singularly improbable invasion by the Spaniards. The treacherous rocks around the coast had made it necessary to maintain a fire beacon on the Castle Hill; there was a "great bowet[3] with three flameing lichts" to warn off shipping. For a different purpose but on a similar model "beall fires" were organised in the summer of 1627 by the landward lairds so that any danger could be quickly known across the length and breadth of the sheriffdom.[4] The list of the chief landowners and the detail of the beacons in the charge of each leaves the impression of an ordered countryside.[5] "Upward on the hills of Fair," runs[6] one such entry, "at sic places as the laird of Drum sall think expedient. At Craigymill by the laird of Drum and as many as the lairds of Drum and Culter judge convenient between that point and the Stockett heid of Aberdene."

[1] Robert Douny was son of Wiliam Douny in Banchory and sister's son to Dr Thomas Reid, the founder. "Contract betwixt the Towne and *Bibliothecar*" dated 8 February 1632, *Records of the Burgh of Aberdeen,* pp. 40-5.
[2] Cf. John Spalding *History of the Troubles,* Bannatyne Club, 1828, i, p. 91.
[3] Aberdeen Charter Room, vol. xxxvi, pp. 139-40, cf. *Aberdeen Council Letters,* introduction, p. xxii.
[4] *Ibid.,* p. xxix. It is estimated that the last fire would be lit within two hours.
[5] Beacon fires were established on the Hill of Thaynestoun and the Hill of Monymusk by the lairds bearing these names and at the Hill of Dunecht by the laird of Echt. The lairds of Foveran, Frendraught and Meldrum were responsible for the beacons on the hills of Southfardine, Fuddes and Barra and the laird of Udnie for that at the Cowhill of Manry. The Marquis of Huntly had charge of the area stretching beyond the Hill of Gartlie. One beacon was in charge of a man who was not a laird, the "beall fire" at the Ruiff of Kincoussie which was in the care of the "gudeman" of that place. At the hill above the Blak Dog a beacon was set up by the Chamberlain of Balhevie in the name of the Earl of Kinghorn, *Aberdeen Council Letters,* vol. i, no. 242, pp. 264–5.
[6] *Ibid.,* p. 265.

The Earl of Erroll was responsible from Stirling Hill to New-burgh and Forbes of Pitsligo for the country between Mormound and the Glens of Troup.

John Spalding, in his *Memorials of the Troubles*,[1] has passages which recall the peaceful setting. It is in this case the nostalgic memory of the late clerk to the Consistorial Court of the Diocese writing after the episcopal and royal disaster. The particular refer-ences are those to the Marquis of Huntly with his "lady and[2] virgine daughter" at harvest time in the Plewlands and to the autumn days "matchless[3] fair in Murray", without winds or any storm, the corn well in, the garden herbs revived, July flowers and roses springing at Martinmas.

A similar impression is conveyed in the account of the town houses in Banff, the Palace and the Earl of Airlie's lodging. An orchard separated these two headquarters of the Ogilvies. "Adjacent to that garden," writes[4] the author of the *History of Scots Affairs*, "in the very heart of that town stood Banfess pallace, high built and qwarterly; the structure magnificent, with two base courts; and few houses in these places of Scotland comparable to it."

Viewed from the angle of sea communications, Banff was a port which fell within the orbit of Aberdeen. None of the ports along that shore were satisfactory,[5] but the burgess roll of Banff at this date includes[6] the names of skippers from Leith and Kirkcaldy. On the other hand the commercial life of Aberdeen was domi-nated by the trade that came in from the sea. Leaving aside the coastwise traffic between the harbours strung out from Wick to the Firth of Forth, the sea-borne commerce concentrated on Aberdeen. Here was established the customs house for north-

---

[1] There are two editions of this work which was written between 1650 and 1660. The first edited by William Forbes Skene for the Bannatyne Club and the second by John Stuart for the Spalding Club.

[2] *Memorials of the Troubles*, Bannatyne Club, p. 12.

[3] *Ibid.*, p. 26.

[4] *The Annals of Banff* compiled by William Cramond, New Spalding Club (1891), vol. i, p. 94, cf. Gordon's *History of Scots Affairs*. There is a refer-ence in the *Annals* to Lord Banff's garden "inclosed with excellent stone-walls, and planted with the best fruit-trees there could be had", i, p. 21.

[5] Alexander Garden of Troup has a comment on this point which is quoted from *Sibbald's Collections*. "There are none of our sea harbours (on the north side of the Coast of Buchan) that, except at stream tide, can receive above ten foot vessels. Banf, which stands at the infall of Divern (Deveron), is so subject to banks of pebbles that sometimes at full sea four feet is enough and too much; at other times it can receive nine or ten foot," *Annals of Banff*, vol. ii, p. 214.

[6] The burgess roll of Banff under 18 July 1642 includes the following names, "William and Alexander Broune, skipperis in Kirkadie, James Stainehouse skipper in Leyth, Alexander Robertsone and David Williamsone mariners in Kirkadie", *ibid.*, p. 418.

eastern Scotland. In this connection a customs book, whose entries extend[1] from mid-April until the end of May 1614, indicates a fairly flourishing general trade including luxury articles. In addition to the silks, taffetas, calicoes and cloths of various kinds,[2] there was a large quantity of sword blades.[3] It may be noted that there was already a steady demand for looking-glasses.[4] Such imports were required to stock and furnish the new large houses. In the Aberdeenshire countryside these were still built to withstand armed attacks which were envisaged as coming from the clans in the high country.

The Midmar group of castles were already completed about this time. They are of exceptional interest on various counts; they were the achievement of certain private families who combined a landed origin with, in most cases, a commercial fortune built up in Aberdeen. They seem specifically Scottish in character unlike such great houses as Huntly Castle or Fyvie. This is perhaps because their builders lacked those Court contacts which would have brought them into touch with England and the Continent. The most perfect example, because the least modified by later changes, is Craigievar, which lies between Alford and Aboyne, about twenty-five miles almost due west of Aberdeen on the farthest borders of Midmar towards the hills.

Craigievar was erected on an isolated site in the midst of an estate purchased by William Forbes in 1610; the date of the completion of the house[5] was 1626. Although the building was in fact L-shaped,[6] it suggested a single tower as the walls with their

[1] King's College Library, Aberdeen, MS.M.70 has on the *recto* of each leaf a catalogue of the library of Marischal College dated 1624. On the *verso* is this customs book.

[2] These included "Gentische" (Ghent) cloth, narrow Germanic cloths, "broad Harfords" and calico, the latter sometimes wrought with gold and silver. There were 7,244 yards of taffetas, both broad and narrow, and 3,314 yards of satin, *Aberdeen Council Letters,* vol. i, introduction, p. xxii.

[3] Ninety-four dozen sword blades were imported during this period of six weeks, *ibid.,* p. xxii.

[4] Other luxury goods brought into Scotland included small ebony cabinets and glass bottles. There were French and Italian tapestries. Foodstuffs included brown and white sugar, raisins and 3,200 lb. of ginger, *ibid.,* pp. xxii–xxiii.

[5] McGibbon and Ross, *op. cit.,* vol. ii, p. 104. Crathes Castle has the date 1553 over a doorway and a monogram of Alexander Burnett and Jean Gordon dated 1596. Tolquhan Castle, near Udny, has a panel on the outer wall to the west of the entrance gateway which reads, "Al this worke excep the Auld Towr, was begun be William Forbes 15 April 1584 and endit be him 20 October 1589". Muchalls Castle has a wall tablet which reads, "This work on the east and north be Ar. Burnet of Leys 1619, ended be Sir Thomas Burnet of Leys his sonne, 1627", *ibid.,* ii, pp. 110, 295, 369–70.

[6] According to the categories suggested by McGibbon and Ross, *op. cit.,* Craigievar and Crathie are castles built upon an L-shaped plan, and Tolquhan and Midmar are castles with courtyards.

harled surface rose to the full height of the seven storeys. The
castle was entered by a doorway at the ground level. A straight
staircase, then a novel feature in a northern stronghold, led to a
landing on the first floor which contained a withdrawing room
panelled in Scotch pine and a small private chamber. The great
hall was on this floor and had small galleries for musicians over
the oak screens.[1] Craigievar was built for defence, to enable the
laird to oversee the Forbes estate and only to a very limited extent
for hospitality.

It was in an area studded with castles; Midmar lay on the road
to Aberdeen; Crathes rather to the south; Cluny a little to the
north; Drum on the way into the city. There was much that was
prosperous in the peaceful scene, although the strength of the
houses still recalled the sudden feuds like that connected with the
Frendraught tragedy, which will be studied in a later chapter.
Spalding saw portents of calamity. He speaks of the monster
that was sighted off Aberdeen in July 1635. "It never shrinked[2]
nor feared, but would dowk under the water, snorting and
bullering, terrible to the hearers and beholders. It remained two
dayes, and was sein no more. But it appears this monster came
for no good token to noble Aberdein, for sore was the seamen
oppressed be great troubles that fell in the land, and great skaith
they sustained be shipwrack as in thir (these) notes doe plainly
appear."

Aberdeen played a part in the politics of the surrounding
countryside which was not paralleled by that of any other Scottish city with the sole exception of the capital. Much was due to
the local patriotism which had already come to surround the two
colleges in Aberdeen. The bishops of that see had an enduring
influence and received a solid measure of support from the landowners of Aberdeenshire. As far as the city and county were
concerned the Marquis of Huntly, the Earl Marischal and the
Bishop of Aberdeen possessed a large measure of power; respectful to one another, each suspicious in regard to the ultimate
intentions of his great neighbour; successful in avoiding the
appearances of enmity.

In terms of political authority there was, however, no real
parity between these rivals. The Keith influence was localised as
was that of the diocese which became closely linked with the lairds
and merchants of the Forbes affinity. On the other hand it may

---

[1] In addition to a state bed with hangings, Craigiever was provided with
box beds of Scotch pine, one of them being double-tiered. Feathers for beds
were among the imports listed in the 1614 customs book.
[2] Spalding *Memorials of the Troubles,* i, p. 37.

be said that the politics of the northern and north-eastern counties were in great measure dominated by the House of Gordon and the attraction and repulsion which their power evoked. The fear of their expansion was ever-present and the key to their almost royal authority lay in the commission of successive Earls of Huntly as royal lieutenants north of Esk. This made the Gordons the principal political factor in that part of Scotland.

CHAPTER IX

THE GORDONS

I T is worth making a careful examination of the roots and consequences of the Gordon power; the background of the chief's high family; the long ascendancy of the first Marquis; the brief vacillating rule of his son Enzie. This may be seen as a prelude to and explanation of the "apartness" of the Gordon country. In the crucial years that great house had everything save leadership. There is a sense that this might have been provided by old Huntly's son Melgum or in the next generation by his nephew Gordon, who was Montrose's friend. Melgum's death in the burning of the Tower of Frendraught is the essential tragedy of the Gordon country. It is sketched here in some detail since the reports incidentally describe so many rural practices and customs. In reading through the different allegations it seems almost impossible to believe that the signing of the National Covenant was only eight years away.

To the long memory of the North the Gordons seemed almost newcomers. The Huntly line would never lose an air of the capital, a sense of France. Unlike the rest of the Gordons they were never truly acclimatised in the North East. The post of royal lieutenant had in the first place been granted to the second Earl, who became the son-in-law of King James I; it remained in the hands of the family for one hundred and sixty years. The Earls of Huntly were a southern stock, belonging .to the Setons in the male line and coming northwards early in the fifteenth century through marriage with the Gordon heiress. Cadet branches mingled with their neighbours, but it would seem that the heads of the house never lost a certain alien quality. The Earls and Marquises of Huntly maintained a fairly close contact with the Court of France and, above all, a sense of calculation. It was, perhaps, the distance from the seat of royal authority as well as their actual power which gave to these and other northern stocks a semi-regal quality. At Strathbogie, as with the Earls of Tyrone, there would be advisers whose *rôle* it would be to remind their master of Europe and of his own quasi-independence. In considering the power and ancestry of the Guises the Earls of Huntly would not be allowed to forget the "Dukes Gordonii" at the Court of Charlemagne.

135

The heads of the house, although reasonably courteous to all the gentlemen of their name, were distant towards the members of the various clans who were brought transiently or sometimes in a fairly permanent fashion to their alliance. Relations with their cousins the Earls of Sutherland, who had obtained that earldom by marriage and then combat, were very close and a comment by Sir Robert Gordon of Gordonstoun sets out the true opinion of both earls upon their private attitude to northern customs. "Use your diligence," writes[1] Sir Robert to his nephew on laying down office as Tutor of Sutherland, "to take away the reliques of the Irishe Barbaritie which as yet remains in your countrey, to wit, the Irishe langage and the habit." Such a standpoint was one of the factors which forced them to become "politicians" as the sixteenth century understood that term.[2] The policies of the Earls of Huntly were inevitably polarised towards the Scottish Crown, whose holder they tended to look on with a certain jealous intimacy. Their history suggests a desire, which was inevitably ineffectual, to act on Scottish policy. They had not sufficient power to make themselves a force in Scotland's capital. A feeling for Machiavellian principles went very easily with a position of inherent weakness. The possession of almost viceregal power upon the northern borderlands did not provide a sufficient leverage for action upon a national scale.

This was the cardinal factor in the situation, but other elements contributed towards the same result. The history of the political intervention of the Gordons down to the death of the second Marquis of Huntly on the scaffold in the year of the execution of Charles I took place against a background of steadily diminishing power, heavily embarrassed finances and finally a curious quality of personal indecisiveness.

Something, too, must be set down to their Seton blood. They were the hereditary intimates of kings and in time their victims. And this quality kept them very far away from their northern neighbours. Their court-life, which the second Marquis pursued in France as well as in England, was inexplicable. They had many adherents but few relatives. Apart from those who came from the four lines of Cluny, Gight, Letterfourie and Abergeldie in that order,[3] there were very few families of Gordon who had any

[1] Sir Robert Gordon, *op. cit.*, ii, 359.
[2] Cf. a comment made by Patrick Gordon of Ruthven writing under the Commonwealth, "Hamiltoune, who was thought to be one of the greatest politicianes in the Christian world", *A short abridgement of Britane's Distemper*, Spalding Club, 1844, p. 15.
[3] In the middle of the seventeenth century there were no immediate cadets of Huntly. The four families named came from younger sons of the third, second and first Earls of Huntly respectively.

discernible relationship to the holders of the marquisate and earldom.

The long rule of the sixth Earl and first Marquis of Huntly was in a sense an interim period. His family had all fought at Corrichie in conflict with Queen Mary's forces, but he himself received nothing but kindness from King James VI. It seems that they both held the same concept of monarchy, while the sovereign loved a noble subject to be large-minded and extravagant. In this cordial relationship there lay, however, the seeds of future misfortune since Huntly came to rely on a friendship with his master which would prove neither hereditary nor enduring.

Charles I would be cold both to the first Marquis and to his successor. He would remove from Huntly the royal lieutenantship in the North and the sheriffdoms that went with it. He was inaccessible where his father had proved accommodating. King James never made his son's mistake of considering that because he was their anointed king his subjects would accept without resentment the curtailment of their power by him. At the same time the ill-husbandry of half a century and the accumulated indebtedness of both Huntly and his eldest son had crippled the Gordon independence; they were left with an impotent resentment and only a weak power to manifest the loyalty that remained to them.

In regard to the relationship of James VI and Charles I with the House of Huntly two points suggest themselves. Would it have been possible for both sovereigns to have given full support to that great family and if such support had been accorded could the Gordons have notably assisted the Royal Cause? It seems likely that the answer to the second question would be in the negative. The Huntly's form of semi-feudal conservatism and their religious preference which varied from Catholicism to pure indifference both set them apart from the majority of their own class. Argyll was to prove for a time successful, but he had harnessed the powerful support of the Presbyterian ministry. The second Marquis of Huntly had no such engine, nor had he a single-minded purpose. The French Court taught many lessons but certainly not constancy. With these preliminary comments we can consider the position of the Gordons at the beginning of King Charles's reign.

The old Marquis of Huntly was a survivor from the days of King James's boyhood. Head of his house for a period of sixty years, he had in consequence become a legendary figure. Courageous and marked by a relentless energy, he leaves in some respects an imprecise image. It appears that those who for the sake of his family offered praise, like John Spalding the author of *The History of the Troubles,* did not really grasp his character or at least have not set down the truth about him.

Huntly's father had been Bothwell's ally and had died in 1576 when the young Lord Gordon was about fourteen. On his mother's side he was a grandson of the Duke of Chatelherault, and he was in fact the fruit of the third of the three alliances which his grandfathers had arranged[1] during the regency of Queen Mary of Guise. All the same he never had any kindness for the Hamiltons. In any case he was distant with his few equals. It was perhaps a reinforcement to his pride to be generous to the burgesses of Aberdeen and cordial to the gentlemen of his name. It seems likely that he was essentially a politician as that term was then used in France in regard to men of his own rank. For his years of education in France at the Court of Henry III gave him a detachment in political and religious questions; he never allowed his preferences in such matters to involve him in any serious inconvenience. Thus he disliked the Kirk of Scotland, but he bowed to her requirements. He would never permit the Kirkmen, whom he despised, to triumph over him to his material disadvantage.

He had one close, and indeed hereditary, friendship which was left as a legacy to both the Huntly and Sutherland branches of the House of Gordon. It was characteristic that it was with a stock that lacked his own almost viceregal power, the Stuarts of Lennox. When he had returned from France as a youth, he had supported Esmé Duke of Lennox and later he married his eldest daughter. Henrietta Marchioness of Huntly had been brought up at Aubigny in Berry and only came to Scotland on her marriage. This alliance strengthened his French connections and perhaps also increased his sense of separateness. He had many qualities which attracted the King's sympathy. James VI was always taken by a man of rank who combined martial vigour with an experience of the manners of the Court of France. He gave Huntly a marquisate in 1599; the sovereign was always very faithful to his friendship for him.

For his part Huntly humoured his royal master. He gave his son to be educated in the King's religion since this was a matter which King James had at heart. He understood and shared the King's political antipathy towards the Kirk; he believed and rightly in the royal word; he was always deferential. This last point was important. There came a time when James VI grew weary of his own genial pleasantries about "Tam o' the Cowgate" and "Jock

---

[1] His uncle Alexander Lord Gordon married Lady Barbara Hamilton about 1546; his father the fifth Earl of Huntly was contracted in 1554 to Lady Jean Hamilton and married in 1559 her youngest sister Lady Anne.

o' the Sclaitts".[1] The longing that the King possessed for the
society of his royal equals, the impulse that drove him towards
the Spanish Marriage, had been seeded many years before in his
northern kingdom.

There is, however, one problem in the personal relationship
between James VI and his great subject. It is raised by the
correspondence which Huntly maintained with Spain and included
the episode of the Spanish Blanks.[2] The explanation would seem
to lie in the fact that the King was at no time unaware of these
manœuvres in which it was vital that he should not be implicated
on account of the war in progress between Philip II and the Queen
of England. At the same time both the King and Huntly appreciated a well-worded piece of dissimulation; this was an attribute
of statecraft as then conceived.

The King had no great wish to interfere with the Marquis of
Huntly's extensive and inherited jurisdictions. The desire to retain
church lands within the control of a great family was very comprehensible to the sovereign. King James, who among his other
pleasing traits loved giving, had made Huntly Commendator of
the monastery of Dunfermline. Spalding in a moment of truth,
when he had for once subdued his flattery, has this comment[3] on
the Marquis. "In his youth a prodigall spender; in his elder aige
moir wyss and worldlie." This was what the royal wisdom appreciated, this and his great building. Considering the same subject
Sir Robert Gordon[4] gives a princely catalogue. "He (the Marquis
of Huntly) gave himself whollie to policie, planting, and building.
He repaired the house of Strathbogie, to his great cost and charges,
after it had been demolished and throwen down. He built a hous
at Kean-Kaill upon Hunthill on Dee, called the Newhous, which
standeth in the midst of thrie hunting forests of his own." These
were the buildings of his middle years. As a young man he had
built Ruthven Castle[5] in Badenoch close to his other hunting
forests away on the edge of the Mackintosh country. "The house
of Riffen . . . tuyse," so the catalogue continues, "being burnt by
adventure and negligence of his servants, after he had once
furnished the same. He (the Marquis) built a new house in Aboyn;
he repayred his house in Elgin; he hath built a house in the
Plewlands in Murray; he hath enlarged and decored the house

[1] Names given by their royal master to Lord Binning and the Earl of Mar.
[2] These were blank papers signed in 1592 by Huntly and others apparently
intended to be filled up with letters inviting the assistance of the King of
Spain.
[3] *History of the Troubles and Memorable Transactions in Scotland,* by
John Spalding, ed. John Stuart, Spalding Club, 1850, p. 73.
[4] Sir Robert Gordon, *op. cit.,* p. 231.
[5] *Ibid.,* p. 215.

of Boig-Gight, which he hath parked about; he repaired his house in the old town of Aberdeen." The policy thus described was one of ordered reconstruction. It may be noted that attention was paid to the town houses so that the Gordon influence could be exerted more effectively on the burgesses of Aberdeen and Elgin.

The King had some sympathy with the almost viceregal style of Huntly's life. He was wary and, unlike his son, was not tempted to break the ancient system of delegated authority in the North of Scotland. Huntly had several times submitted to an honourable confinement when his difficulties with the Kirk were most acute. It was sweet to the King to receive such submission from one who was the ruler of what was very nearly an independent principate.

In this connection a bond between the then Earl of Huntly and Lord Spynie throws light upon the nature of this relationship. The latter, who was an intimate of the royal circle and vice chamberlain, had received from Huntly all his rights in the lands of the bishopric of Moray. In return Lord Spynie had undertaken an obligation for himself and his heirs "to serve[1] and be partaker in quhatsumevir querrellis or actionis the said noble lord (of Huntly) or his successoris either hes or sall happin to have." This reads like an alliance, all the more significant because of Spynie's standing.[2] Both lords added the usual reservation to the agreement. "The quhilk bond onlie reservis theire faithfull and obedient deutie to the kingis majestie, their souerane lord and maister." The King savoured the tribute paid to the royal authority; he did not seek to interfere with the great satrapies.

The outlook of the principal lords resembled that of independent princes in their system of alliances; the bitterness of rivalry was not diminished by the arranged marriages.[3] Child-betrothal was

[1] Bond signed at Edinburgh on 18 December 1590 and printed in *Spalding Club Miscellany*, vol. iv, p. 244.

[2] Alexander Lindsay first Lord Spynie, a brother to the eleventh Earl of Crawford and grandson of Cardinal Beaton, was married to Jean widow of Sir Robert Douglas and of Archibald eighth Earl of Angus. He was guardian to his stepson William later eighth Earl of Morton. John Row, who was summoned by Lord Spynie to act as tutor to the boy has this comment. "Wearied of that attendance, and of the court there, for indeed that familie at Aberdour, all that Earle of Morton's tyme, even from his infancie, wes rather lyke a court than a nobleman's familie", a short narrative of the life of John Row written by himself and printed in *The History of the Kirk of Scotland*, Wodrow Society, 1842, p. 470.

[3] There was something "quasi-royal" in the custom by which the greatest families married their heirs within a very restricted circle. Thus in this and the immediately preceding generations the marriages are repetitive. *Douglas of Angus*: Oliphant, Hamilton, Gordon, Stuart of Lennox. *Argyll*: Cunningham of Glencairn, Douglas of Morton, Douglas of Morton. *Huntly*: Hamilton, Stuart of Lennox, Campbell. *Hamilton*: Douglas of Morton, Keith, Cunningham of Glencairn.

an accustomed practice.[1] There was a constant care for spheres of influence. Dominating every line of action was the determination to retain land and to increase it, to gain vassals and subordinate allies and to dispossess those who supported a rival family.

Spalding has a comment in his eulogy on the Marquis of Huntly. "A weill set nichtbour in his merchis, disposit rather to give nor tak one foot of ground wrangouslie. He was hard say he neuer drew suord in his awin querrell." This may perhaps be accepted if it allows for Huntly espousing the quarrels of the Gordon lairds and of their neighbours who held by them. At the same time it was worth considering a statement made in a memorial prepared by Lord Forbes. He was a Presbyterian and now in straitened circumstances,[2] a man who had suffered much from his hereditary enemies. "Lord Forbes," he wrote,[3] "is na ways Marquis, Viscount nor Erle, but only ane nacked (naked) lyfrenter of ane small part and portion of his old estaits and liveing of Forbes." At the moment he was being pressed by Gordon of Tulloch, but behind Tulloch stood Huntly.

One range of the Gordon interests and one aspect of the Marquis of Huntly's power and policy is illuminated by the tragedy of the Tower of Frendraught. This was considered at the time to be a mystery and still remains unsolved. It is very doubtful whether there is sufficient data available to enable a solution to be reached. A detailed account of the whole matter will provide a number of vivid sidelights on the life of the countryside in Aberdeenshire.

In essence it is the story of the burning of a free-standing tower in the courtyard at Frendraught, which was occupied only by distinguished visitors and their servants. It is not certain whether the destruction was the result of an accident or of design, and in the latter case there is a difficulty concerning motives. Those brought forward are confused or insufficient; perhaps they are

[1] For various reasons children were often brought up by their grandmothers. Jean Countess of Sutherland brought up her granddaughter and the Marchioness of Huntly her younger grandchildren. Fostering was common. Sir Robert Gordon makes this comment on Alexander Earl of Sutherland. "He was in his infancie noorished and brought up in Grangehill, in Murray, among the Dunbars", op. cit., p. 149.

[2] Lord Forbes left a memorandum dated 1 August 1620 relating to a journey in Mar and Buchan ending at Aberdeen. "Item, my horse in Drumminor schod in tyme, and a pockmantel nag (pack horse) brocht in Pitachy." A similar note was made before a journey to Edinburgh and dated 29 October 1633. "Item, ane buik callit 'ye sanctuary off a trubli soul' and sum uther guid littel buik and sum tobacco", The House of Forbes, ed. Alistair and Henrietta Tayler, Third Spalding Club, 1937, pp. 163 and 166.

[3] Ibid., p. 167.

ultimately indecipherable. In view of the various interests and many personalities involved it is simplest to state at the beginning that if it was a crime it was probably directed against Gordon of Rothiemay by either Frendraught or his wife or by both acting together. Should this have been the case it is probable that the true motive will never be known. If on the other hand the fire was accidental there was at any rate present a sufficient weight of suspicion to prevent Frendraught and his wife from persuading the relatives of the dead gentlemen of their own innocence.

Certain facts are not in dispute. James Crichton of Frendraught was a considerable landowner of ancient stock with a relationship with the Earls Marischal; he was likewise a cousin of the Arbuthnotts. He had been married for ten years to Lady Elizabeth Gordon, the Earl of Sutherland's sister. Both Crichtons and Arbuthnotts belonged at that time to the Protestant tradition and were to receive viscounties[1] from Charles I. At the beginning of October 1630 Frendraught was called by the old Marquis of Huntly to Strathbogie to explain an attack made upon John Leslie younger of Pitcaple, who had been shot through the arm a short time previously. Huntly had in the house with him Gordon of Rothiemay, whose father had been killed by Frendraught in the course of an affray arising out of a dispute as to the rights of salmon fishing in the Deveron.

At this point there emerges the name of John Meldrum of Reidshill. He was a brother-in-law of Pitcaple and in the earlier dispute had supported Frendraught against Rothiemay. Later he had changed sides and was accused of stealing two of Frendraught's horses. In an attempt to regain the horses Frendraught's men attacked Meldrum and John Leslie of Pitcaple, who was with him, and the latter received a wound. Pitcaple had recently visited Huntly with complaints against Frendraught in this matter, but he had been compelled to leave the castle without receiving any satisfaction. The comment on the opening phase by Sir Robert Gordon of Gordonstoun, the historian, is restrained and may be taken within limits as objective. "Upon the accident," he writes[2] in regard to the killing of William Gordon of Rothiemay, "the Marquis of Huntly was much incensed against Frendret, becaus that for so small matters, and for civill actions, he had proceeded so far against his kinsman, and a chieff barron of his surname, as to take his lyff." However, a fine had been paid and the feud at least temporarily healed. "All parties having shaken

---

[1] In 1641 and 1642 respectively.
[2] *The genealogical History of the Earldom of Sutherland* by Sir Robert Gordon of Gordonstoun, ed. Edinburgh, 1813, p. 147.

hands in the orchard of Strathbogie, they were hartilie reconciled."[1] This reconciliation did not include Pitcaple.

On 7th October Frendraught and Rothiemay set off home together and were accompanied by Huntly's youngest son Lord Melgum, who acted for his father since his elder brother the Earl of Enzie was in France. Lord John Gordon, who had been raised to the peerage three years earlier under the titles of Melgum and Aboyne, was about twenty-four[2] years of age. He seems to have remained in Scotland for his education; he was an energetic and an ardent Catholic. "The Marquis," explains[3] Sir Robert Gordon, "hearing that the Leslies had assembled, and did lie in wait for Frendret on his return home, he sent his son, the Viscount of Melgum, and the Laird of Rothimay to defend him, and to conduct him saiff to the house of Frendreth." From this it would appear that an attack by Pitcaple was apprehended.

The distance to Frendraught was some seven miles; the stronghold lay in rising wooded country to the south of the Deveron. Lord Melgum and his followers were lodged in an isolated tower standing at a little distance from the main building of the castle. It is a relevant point that the vaults of the tower contained Frendraught's charter chest and a store of money. From subsequent evidence it appears that Melgum and Rothiemay slept on different floors, Melgum in the principal guest chamber and Rothiemay above him. Six other gentlemen of their name were in other rooms. During the night a fire broke out in the lower part of the tower and at about four o'clock in the morning Melgum and his seven companions were burned to death. "The stairs," according to Blakhal,[4] "being in fire, and the windowes grated with strong barres of yron, ther was no moyen to escape." The first warning seems to have been heard by George Spens, one of Frendraught's household. Later he testified[5] that, awakened by a cry of fire he went to the door of the vault and saw all on fire there. Penetrating to Lord Melgum's chamber he could not find him for he had gone upstairs obviously to arouse Rothiemay. It is a curious comment on the many contending perils that upon

[1] *Ibid.*, p. 149.
[2] *The Scots Peerage* describes Melgum as the Marquis of Huntley's fifth son and in that case he was preferred before his brothers Lord Adam and Lord Laurence Gordon, who were both living at this date. The two youngest daughters Mary Marchioness of Douglas and Jean Lady Strabane were born in 1611 and about 1612 respectively. It is unlikely that Melgum was made a peer before he came of age. This would place his birth in about 1606.
[3] Sir Robert Gordon, *op. cit.*, p. 240.
[4] *Brief Narrative*, p. 125.
[5] Examination on 1 February 1631, *Register of the Privy Council of Scotland 1630-2*, second series, vol. iv, p. 610.

hearing the outcry the Laird rose[1] and put on his doublet and breeches and the Lady went down to the close with her night-gown in her hand, fearing that the barn yards had been fired by James Grant. One of the servants Thomas Jose admitted[2] that he had been in the Tower removing meal from the vault but claimed that he had left by six o'clock the previous evening.

From the outset it was clear that a feud of the most serious dimensions had been started. The Crichtons at first contended that the fire was accidental and this possibility cannot be excluded. An impartial investigation of the site led only to the statement that the fire must have originated[3] within the Tower. Very soon the Crichtons were pursuing John Meldrum, while the Gordons were concentrating on the examination of John Tosche or Toschach, who was Frendraught's master of the house-hold. The Gordons, supported by Melgum's brother-in-law the Earl of Erroll, insisted[4] on the pursuit of both these men. The inconclusive examinations are of much interest.

John Cruickshanke, who was under sentence to be hanged for theft, stated[5] that he and Isabella Cruickshanke, a cripple, were "shearing upon a rig" late in the evening before the tragedy when they saw John Meldrum upon horseback and Robert Ridfurde upon foot with a number of horse come riding by them in that part of the bounds of Tillimorgun that leads towards Frendraught. We can reconstruct the household there; Thomas Jose, the steward, John Gibb, the gardiner; Robert Bewlie, the cook. There was Marie Bothwick, who was John Tosche's leman. A crucial figure was John Meldrum's houseman Robert Wilson, who lived in Dykeside of Auchterless. He was alleged[6] to have said the day before the burning that Frendraught and his master "wer not aggreid and that within twentie four houres the heighest stane of Frendraught wald be the laighest".

The hours were given during which the servants were seen standing in the hall at Pitcaple. There is a reference[7] to Robert Fraser "alias callit Domingo". An impression of the times is well conveyed by the names[8] of two of Pitcaple's servants John Leslie

---

[1] Examination of Magdalen Innes who lay in the chamber where the laird lay, *ibid.*, p. 611.   [2] *Ibid.*, p. 610.   [3] Findings printed, *ibid.*
[4] *Ibid.*, p. 502. Sir George Ogilvie of Banff deposed that "he is informed that in all places quhair Johne Toshe hes dwelt he hes ever kythed to be evil conditioned and a slyme youth, and that if the hous wes brunt by these that wes within he wald suspect Johne Toshe to be the actor rather then ony other", *ibid.*, p. 609.   [5] *Ibid.*, p. 2206.
[6] Statement by Robert Spens on the evidence of Patrick Barclay, *ibid.*, p. 609. This was denied by Robert Wilson who however admitted meeting Patrick Barclay, who had his wife riding behind him, at Cowan fair on the Thursday before the burning, *ibid.*, p. 610.
[7] *Ibid.*, p. 186.   [8] *Ibid.*, p. 112.

"callit the Sojour" and Irish Donnald. Perhaps the most striking episode refers to a clue which either was not followed up or proved abortive. Captain George Ogilvie reported[1] a conversation at Elsinore with Major Francis Sinclair. The latter stated that he had with him a recruit taken up by his sergeant who one night when in liquor said that he had a hundred gold pieces in his pocket and that he might serve the King of Sweden all his days before he gained as much money as he got by helping in a piece of service in Scotland when he was a cook serving in the house of Frendraught the night that the same was burned.

In the upshot Meldrum was executed still protesting his innocence. Gilbert Blakhal, through his association with Lord Melgum's widow, represents the extreme Gordon standpoint and charges Frendraught with the murder. He mentions[2] that the Laird had "prepared and laide in that tower a great quantity of combustible mater before he did implore his (Lord Melgum's) protection, which he needed not". According to this account John Toschach kindled the fire at two o'clock after midnight as his master had commanded him. The traitor with his men-at-arms walked all night in the court to kill Melgum and Rothiemay in case they should escape the fire.

These last details recall earlier scenes in Scottish history such as that of Darnley's murderers patrolling the grounds of Kirk o' Fields and also the burning of Donibristle. There are elements in this second tragedy which bear an odd resemblance to the Frendraught setting. The "Bonnie" Earl of Moray escaped alive from his mother's house, which had been set on fire, but was traced through the night by the flames which had caught the silk plumes of his helmet; he was despatched on the rocky northern shore of the Firth of Forth. The resemblance, which is indeed most probably accidental, may have fostered the rumours that linked the burning of Frendraught with the earlier killing. A letter written from Ireland within about a fortnight of Lord Melgum's death bears on this point. "The general comment," wrote[3] George Rawdon to Lord Conway, "is that the said Marquis birnt the Earl of Murray's father's house upon him, and Rothiemay's father was a chief actor in the business." There were, however, two theories as to the murder and two as to the intended victim. It may be mentioned in passing that one of the difficulties

[1] Report received on 7 June 1632, *ibid.*, p. 634. Cf. a letter from the Council to Major Stewart dated 14 June 1632, *ibid.*, p. 497.

[2] *Brief Narrative*, p. 125. Blakhal also refers to the execution of John Tosche or Toschach, but it is not clear that it was in connection with this matter.

[3] Letter dated 24 October 1630, Cal. S. P. Ireland 1625-32, p. 592.

K

in regard to Meldrum's guilt is that he is alleged to have burned the Tower when his enemy Frendraught was not inside.

Some held, with Rawdon, that Frendraught had deliberately planned the murder of both Melgum and Rothiemay, possibly in the interests of the Earl of Moray. The arguments in favour of this theory are not plausible. It is true that the houses were traditionally at enmity[1] in spite of a formal reconciliation when the third Earl of Moray married Huntly's eldest daughter. The Gordons had for eighty years encroached upon the Moray country. A contemporary ballad[2] sets out this feeling.

> The gool, the Gordon, and the hoodie craw
> Are the three worst faes that Moray ever saw.

Still Moray was not a fighter. He was suave in his methods preferring to discomfort his rivals through diplomacy. In addition he was already middle-aged and it appears most improbable that he should suddenly have embarked on this revenge nearly forty years after his father's death, nor did the Marquis of Huntly seem to suspect him.

According to another theory the murder had been planned by Lady Frendraught and on this basis Rothiemay was the intended victim. On such a reading it was the wife rather than the husband who watched in their courtyard through the last hours of that October night. This point of view is set out[3] very clearly in the last stanza of the well-known ballad. Melgum at the wire window is described as looking down on his hostess on the green below.

> O, then out spake the Lady Frendraught,
> And loudly did she cry.
> "It were great pity for good Lord John,
> But none for Rothiemay.
> The keys are casten, in the deep draw-well,
> Ye cannot win away."

So little is known of Lady Frendraught[4] that one cannot pass

---

[1] Thus in 1549 the fourth Earl of Huntly received a grant of the earldom of Moray, which had been held by his maternal uncle from 1501 until 1545. In 1562 after the Gordon disaster at Corrichie this earldom was bestowed on Lord James Stewart.

[2] Printed among the Gordon ballads collected by the Rev. Stephen Kee in *The House of Gordon,* ed. J. M. Bulloch, New Spalding Club, 1907, vol. ii, p. 7.

[3] *Ibid.,* ii, pp. 70-1.

[4] A reference to Lady Frendraught in the accounts for 1619 kept by Sir Robert Gordon, when Tutor of Sutherland, indicates a fairly close association with Lady Huntly. "Item, 266 lib. 13s. 4d. for two rooms to Lady Elizabeth Gordoun and other necessaryes at hir marriage by my lady Marquise of Huntlyes adwyse," *Cal. Sutherland MSS.,* Appendix to the second Report of the Royal Commission on Historical Manuscripts, p. 179.

beyond surmise. The position of the Crichtons was difficult[1] in the heart of the Gordon country. Huntly's own attitude was clear. He harried or permitted the harrying of the Crichtons throughout the last years of his life. "The Marquis of Huntly," wrote[2] Sir Robert Gordon, "still prosecuted the Laird of Frendret for the burning of the haus, and was cold in any other pursute." He made no accusation against Lady Frendraught, who was his own cousin; still less did he in any sense interrupt his relations with the Earl of Moray. All the same the landless men ravaged the Crichton lands till Huntly died. Lady Rothiemay stirred them up to the same work.[3]

There was also another aspect of the affair. Lord Melgum was said to have declared his Catholic faith as the flames took hold and Rothiemay is supposed to have joined him[4] in the same profession. The tragedy was held by all conservative opinion to have been a great misfortune for the cause of the Old Religion and the ancient stocks.[5]

This detailed examination of a single episode gives rise to various general considerations. On the assumption that it was not an accident, the burning of the Tower of Frendraught was one of the last of the man-made catastrophes which pursued high Scottish families. The motives and indeed the actions of the principals have that quality of incompleteness and inscrutability that we associate with the account of the deaths of the last Earl of Gowrie and his brother. From such a background the soldiers of fortune went out to the German wars. These were also the years of the murder of Wallenstein by his Scots and Irish officers.

Already an era was drawing to a close. In 1630 the new King had

[1] Until the next generation the Crichtons were Protestants. Thus Blakhal refers to the "castle of Frendret belonging to a heretick," *op. cit.*, p. 124. Gordon of Rothiemay was likewise a Protestant, his mother being Katharine Forbes.

[2] Sir Robert Gordon, *op. cit.*, p. 467.

[3] For these troubles cf. *Registers of the Privy Council of Scotland*, vols.

[4] Cf. Blakhal's *Brief Narrative*.

[5] Among the Parerga of 1637 collected by Arthur Johnston are two elegies, LXIX, Lament of Sophia Hay on the Fire of Frendraught and L, On the deaths by fire at Frendraught of Viscount Melgum and Gordon of Rothiemay. The following passage occurs in the argument for the Dirge of the Two Victims. "Bright youths they were: one was of the gentry. the other of the nobility; the latter by his ancestral line touching the royal race—both cut off in their prime." The Lament concentrates suspicion on Lady Frendraught. The argument runs as follows: "Tis known what guilty one fired Troy towers or Delphi's shrine, who burned Cycliades and Creusa. . . . Combustion broke out with all sulphurous elements, and there followed the crash and roar of burning beams and stones dissolved. . . . The rest God only knows, or Night, or the guilty Tower with its surviving stones", *Musa Latina Aberdonensis,* ed. Sir William Duguid Geddes, New Spalding Club, 1892, vol. i, pp. 292–9.

taken away from Huntly the posts of hereditary sheriff in Aberdeen and Inverness. The organisation of the National Covenant would give an opportunity to all his enemies. On 13 June 1636 the Marquis of Huntly died. He had been warded in Edinburgh Castle and was journeying northwards in a "wand bed within his chariot"[1] towards Strathbogie. He reached Dundee and could go no farther. On his deathbed he declared his attachment to the Catholic Faith.

George Earl of Enzie succeeded his father as the chief of the Gordons. Throughout life he was hampered by circumstances and by his own nature and training. In the first place his resources were not equal to those of the Campbells of Argyll, who were always present in his calculations. Then he was himself the very type of the disobliged Royalist for the King had deprived his father of the two sheriffships. Yet there was no place for Huntly in the Opposition ranks. This is evident in a comment made by the Earl of Rothes, who did not care for him. The Earl of Roxburgh had asked whether Huntly might not prove a source of embarrassment. "Whereto Rothes replied[2] he would not give a salt citron for him; for two Fife lairds could keep him from crossing the Cairn o' Month; that three parts of his name is decayed, and he wants the two sheriffships." This weakness in actual strength runs through the whole of his public career. His situation invited discourtesies from his rivals and he was not a man who could forgive a slight to his own dignity.

The second Marquis of Huntly had been brought up at the English Court, and had been created a Knight of the Bath in 1610 and a privy councillor some six years later. He was of pleasing appearance and had been in a mild way favoured in the old King's time. Certain charcteristics impressed the observer. It may, however, be noted that the severe comments[3] about to be mentioned were made by a gentleman of the Gordon name, perhaps unduly sensitive to the way in which Huntly had treated his well-born followers. "With a certain kynde of reserved inclinations," it is explained, "he seemed desyrous to keip a distance with his inferiours, without distintione of qualitie; for frinds and followers were equalled with domestickes and common observance onless his affaires required it, and then could he be both familiare and obsequious." Gordon gives a reason for this defect, "his breiding in England, the habit and longe custom he gott there.

---

[1] Spalding, *op. cit.*, p. 74.

[2] Rothes's *Relation,* Bannatyne Club, pp. 62, 63.

[3] *A Short Abridgement of Britain's Distemper* by Patrick Gordon of Ruthven, Spalding Club, 1844, pp. 229, 230.

. . . And for his excuse, I darre avowe, that this his reseruedness, his keiping of distance, and the proud show of affecting steat (state), was no part of his naturall inclinatione; he was knowen to be both affable, courteous and sociable befor he was called to court."

The date of Huntly's birth does not seem to be known, but it may probably be placed about 1592.[1] His marriage had taken place in 1607 as part of a series of reconciliations by which James VI proposed to bring to an end the feuds which had divided the houses of Huntly, Moray and Argyll. His bride Lady Anne Campbell was thirteen at the time of the wedding. Later they went to France together; she did not check his extravagance; she played little part. This computation of his age makes Huntly half a generation older than Hamilton and Argyll; he was by twenty years Montrose's senior. The memory of his ancestors' power was galling to him as he dealt with those so much his juniors whom his sovereign had preferred before him. Gordon of Ruthven puts it succinctly.[2] "His predecessoris had euer beene mightie in former ages, of greatest powers of all be north the Graingebean mountanes, for they had often augmented there greatnesse be taimeing the greatest insurrectiones in this kingdome; such was euer there faith and loyaltie to their prince." Bearing in mind the history of his house and the Catholicism of so many of his followers it would seem reasonable to suggest that the only way open to the Marquis was the path of loyalty.

He made an impressive figure, marred a little by what John Buchan has called his "peacock head". As Earl of Enzie he had held an ornate position in the Court at Paris in the days before the rise of the Cardinal de Richelieu. He shared his mother's feeling for all things French, but was immune to her Catholicism. In religious matters it would seem that he was sceptical; like Wallenstein, he was addicted to astrology. He cast about to meet his great expenditures and was deeply in debt in Paris[3] when his father died. As a young man he had given some time to reviving

---

[1] His parents were married in 1588 and his mother was born in 1573; he was the eldest son of the marriage.

[2] Gordon of Ruthven, op. cit., p. 14.

[3] Cf. A letter from Henrietta Marchioness of Huntly to Sir Robert Gordon dated from the Canongate, Edinburgh on 12 February 1636. The bearer has received a letter of exchange of twenty thousand pounds to bring home my son to Court, yet I know it will not be enough to defray his other debts in France. I ask you to solicit our noble friends, especially the Duke of Lennox and the Duchess of Richmond, to intercede that speedy payment may be made of moneys due to him from His Majesty. Sutherland Book, vol. ii, pp. 162–3.

under his command the company of Scots men-at-arms[1] in the French service; in his case this meant soldiering at the royal court.

In certain respects his nearest counterparts were the great nobles, themselves subdued uninterested Calvinists, who lent support to the policies of the French Crown. He was no innovator. In some ways he was bound to the House of Stuart which had made him what he was and separated him from his own family. In this matter he resembled the Marquis of Ormonde who, like himself, had been brought up by the King's order away from his own relatives. All Huntly's brothers and sisters were Catholics, nor for the most part did they share his foreign travels. It is not surprising that his thought had a lack of contact with that of other Gordons.

Various factors served to increase this isolation. His wife died in 1638 and thenceforward he remained a widower. His four younger daughters and his two youngest sons were brought up by their grandmother the Dowager Lady Huntly.[2] There is reason to suppose that the Marquis was attached to his eldest son Lord Gordon, to whom he had given a French upbringing. In Scotland Lord Huntly was without friendship in the very small circle of his equals and it seems that he saw from the beginning that he would not have the power to do those things to which he had a mind. "His greatest falt," wrote[3] Gordon of Ruthven, "was a self will and obstinate opinione, which made him cairlesse of counsell, so had he such a nimble and apprehensive witt, as he could find reasons for whatsoever he did, evin to convince reasone itself. And from his abstinancie, or self willed opinion, proceided all his mallours." This is certainly the portrait of an isolated character.

The second Marquis of Huntly was notable for his loyalty to his advisers, like Gordon of Straloch, and to the hereditary clients of his house. "He was," it is explained,[4] "both constant and reall in his friendship to whom he professed it, nor could anie

[1] In 1624 Lord Gordon, Earl of Enzie, came to France to solicit the re-establishment of the company of Scots men-at-arms under his uncle the Duke of Lennox. This was granted, and on the death of the Duke, the Earl of Enzie succeeded him as captain leaving the lieutenantcy to Lord Gray. Cf. *The Scots Men-at-Arms and Lifeguards in France* by William Forbes Leith S.J., 1882, pp. 11–5.

[2] It appears that the eldest daughter Lady Anne, who was married to the Earl of Perth in 1639, was probably brought up in her mother's Faith. She was certainly a Presbyterian from her marriage. Similarly there is no reason to suppose that George Lord Gordon was ever a Catholic. The younger children were all educated as Catholics.

[3] Gordon of Ruthven, *op. cit.*, p. 229.

[4] *Ibid.*, p. 229.

threatenings or fair persuasions be able to alter or change[1] him."
This was important in view of his wide lands.[2] Their possession
was the enduring factor. In the restricted circle of the magnates
Huntly would recognise his only equals, Hamilton, Lennox,
Douglas and Argyll, the heads of the first houses in Scotland. The
Earl of Montrose was not among that number and there were
many reasons why Huntly would not forgive any favour which
his master might in the future show James Graham. Thus many
factors came to reinforce his native indecision. He would not
or perhaps he could not lead, but no one else could claim the
leadership. A study of the Catholic life in the countries within
the sphere of influence of Strathbogie will stress the severance of
outlook between Huntly and his younger brother Melgum, who
was at one with all the other home-keeping Gordons.

[1] The following account by Gordon of Ruthven may perhaps have been
influenced by some personal grudge. "Service done and not to doe, was forgotten, and some old seruants for whom thire was no use, must be brusht
of or rubt off as spots from cloathese", *ibid.*, p. 229.

[2] Thus in an account of the free rents of the whole shire of Aberdeen
begun on 1 January 1667 the following properties are given as part of the
Huntly estates with which those of Aboyne may be included. The Marquis
of Huntly held lands whose annual value amounted (in Scots money) to
£1,100 in Dumbenan, £959 10s. in Ruthven and Botarie; £775 18s. 4d. in
Rhynie and Essie; £620 in Gartley; £500 in Kinnoir; £425 in Drumgeldie.
These estates lay within the presbytery of Strathbogie and represented only
a fragment of the family property. The Earl of Aboyne held £1,030 in
Aboyne; £345 6s. 8d. in Coull; £160 2s. 7d. in the Cabroach; £153 6s. 8d.
in Glenmuir; £150 in Glentanar. The other principal landowners at that date
were the Earl of Erroll and the Earl and Dowager Countess Marischal,
Valuation Roll of the County of Aberdeen 1667, edited from an MS. preserved at Fettercairn House by Alistair and Henrietta Tayler, Third Spalding Club, 1933, pp. 3–33 *passim*.

CHAPTER X

CATHOLICISM IN THE NORTH EAST

AN attachment to Rome was common among those who had some form of dependence on or connection with the House of Huntly. As far as the men of the Gordon main line are concerned it is difficult to disentangle religious interests from a general preference for the old traditions. It was rather the women who were fervent. A desire for sacramental practice was a note of the life of the old Marchioness of Huntly with her rooted French Catholicism. Around her are seen grouped her daughter Lady Moray and her daughter-in-law Sophia Lady Aboyne. Compared to the determination they displayed the men appear hesitant, all except Lord John Gordon who perished in the Frendraught tragedy.

In this context the Gordon chroniclers consider that the Hamilton and Campbell strains were in their different ways prejudicial to the chieftain's family. The account of Lord Adam Gordon bears on this point. "His brains being cracked," wrote Patrick Gordon of one of old Lord Huntly's younger sons, "either through some distemper, or rather through a malignant temper of melancholic blood, which ran in his veins through his grandmother Duke Hamilton's daughter." There is perhaps not much substance in this comment. It is, however, clear that the Campbell influence led those who yielded to it away from the normal Gordon interests; it was likewise manifestly the solvent of Catholicism. It may be said of many of the great Scots families which adhered to the old religious tradition that they were brought away from their ancestral allegiance through marriages made from policy.

The most intimate account of Scottish Catholic life during this period that has survived is concerned with the Huntly Gordons and those who depended on them. The narrative of Gilbert Blakhal deals with the missionary work that he carried out from his headquarters at Aboyne Castle. This description is incomparably spontaneous and fresh. The manuscript has throughout a note of self-justification for the writer in addition to his work as chaplain acted as comptroller of the household to his protectress. The account opens in 1637 and at that date the congregations in

Aberdeenshire were still benefiting from the easing[1] of the position
of Catholics which had taken place in the summer and autumn of
1633. These comments may serve as an introduction to a closer study
of the survival of Catholic influence in the north-east of Scotland.

As an autobiographical fragment the *Brief Narrative*[2] is in
some respects difficult to assess. Gilbert Blakhal, who had been
ordained as a secular priest in 1630, had made his studies at
Rome in the new Scots College in the Via Quattro Fontane. He
came of a family of standing[3] in Aberdeenshire and was related
to the Leslies.[4] The document that he has left is an account of the
services that he had rendered to three ladies, Lady Isabella Hay,
her sister Lady Aboyne and the latter's only child Henrietta
Gordon. From internal evidence the manuscript would appear to
have been composed about 1648 and it has real value as a
description of the life of a noble family of the second rank between
1637 and 1642. It is in the main a recital of the help given by
Blakhal to Lady Aboyne and of his ungrateful treatment by her
daughter whom he had taken after her mother's death to the
Court of France.

One of the more sympathetic passages deals with Blakhal's
pastoral work and visits. He describes[5] the circuit of his missionary
journeys as "not very great, but only from the house of Aboyne
to Aberdein, two and twenty miles, where I did confesse and
communicat all the Catholics that were their; and from Aberdein
to Buchan, a matter of nyntein or twenty miles, where I had but
five Catholic houses to go to; Blairs, twelve miles from Aberdein; and Shivas, five or six miles from Blaire; and Gight, as
far as Shivas, and Artachy, nynne or ten miles from Gight; and
Cruden, six miles from Artachy." The tour being set out, he makes
some points. "The distance betwixt these houses obliged me to
stay a night in each of them to say masse, confesse, communicat

---

[1] This was a result of the King's visit to Edinburgh for his coronation,
although Fr. John Leslie S.J. in his annual letter sent to Rome ascribes it to
the marriage celebrated in the previous year between the Earl of Angus and
Lady Mary Gordon. Cf. *Memoirs of Scottish Catholics,* ii, p. 133.

[2] *A breiffe narrative of the services done to three noble ladyes by Gilbert
Blakhal,* edited by John Stuart, Spalding Club, 1844.

[3] He appears to have been related to Mr. William Blakhal, a Regent in
Marischal College. The latter is described in the *History of the Troubles,*
ii, pp. 10–1, as "a prompt scoller, bred, borne and brocht up in Aberdeine,
and never yeit out of the countrie, refuisit to subscrive the countrie Covenant
. . . and at last he planelie and avouitlie declared he was ane Roman Catholik". Gilbert Blakhal stayed regularly with Robert Blakhal "at the Little
Milne of Crudarne (Cruden)", *Brief Narrative,* p. 54.

[4] Blakhal described Fr. Andrew Leslie S.J. as his cousin. In reference to
Henrietta Gordon, a waiting woman at Aboyne, he wrote "Henrietta called
me her cousin because we were both come of the name of Lesly, but of
divers houses, she of Wardes and I of Balwheine", *ibid.,* pp. 62 and 98.

[5] *Ibid.,* p. 68.

and exhort the Catholics by way of a short preaching." He then describes his journey from Buchan to Strathbogie, "where I used to stay but three or four nights, the first in the village, they cal it the raws, in robert Rinne his house, an hostellerie wher the poor Catholics convened". The last point, as so often in Blakhal's descriptions, is made deliberately. The Dowager Marchioness of Huntly would not grant him admission to Strathbogie Castle.

In resuming his account Blakhal explains that it was his custom to go for the second night to "Carneborrow, wher Neulesly[1] and his daughter did come to me, and sometimes I did go to Neulesly his house; the third night to Craigge, six miles from Carneborrow, and Carneborrow is four miles from Strathbogie". This was the final stage of the journey. "And last," he writes, "to Aboyne back again, through the Arishney hills, as wyld a part as in al Scotland, which I have crossed many times at midnight al alone, when I could not see whether I was in the way or out of it, but trusted my hors, who never failed nor fanted in the way."

The *Brief Narrative* is a unique document and worth a careful study. In spite of hardships these long journeys give a certain impression of security. It seems that priests had some freedom of movement wherever the House of Huntly and their friends had influence. Indeed, Blakhal insists[2] upon this point. "The ministers . . . never troubled me as long as she (Lady Aboyne) livd, although they knew wel aneugh, and did know when I did go away to mak my visites."

These north-eastern counties were the only parts of Scotland beneath the Highland line in which complaints were made that permanent buildings were used for Catholic worship. "They repaire," so began an accusation[3] made in 1588 against the Jesuits, "commonly with Airth, Laird of Leslie elder . . . and to young Glenbervie, excommunicat, where they have their mass house at their pleasure, and their publick mass creatit in the Laird of Leslie's chapell, with 'twa idols above the altar'." Six years later there was another complaint[4] to the General Assembly of "the erection of the idolatrie of the Masse, in diverse quarters of the land . . . in the Earl of Huntly's house of Strabogy and Auld Aberdeene, in the Earl of Errol's houses of Logyamont (Logy Almond) and Slaines." Admittedly this was past history, but the Gordon memory was tenacious as was Huntly's loyalty to the cadets of his house.

The measure of freedom was also in large part due to the

---

[1] The Laird of New Leslie.   [2] *Brief Narrative*, p. 75.
[3] Printed in introduction to *Brief Narrative*, p. xvi.
[4] Printed *ibid.*, p. xvii.

rights of jurisdiction enjoyed by successive heads of the Gordon family. The leaders of this great stock varied in their attitude towards the religious issue, but it is safe to affirm that no head of the House of Huntly ever truly loved the Presbytery. Many were Catholics, one had Anglican leanings and one was so indifferent as to be said to be "atheist". No Earl or Marquis of Huntly of the elder line was ever Calvinist.

The cadet branches among the Gordons had indeed in many instances a violent attachment to the Auld Kirk which it was not in the interest of their chief to curb. In 1608 it had been requested[1] "that His Majestie give order for the downcasting of Gight's Chappell," while a letter of the previous year refers[2] to the burials and funeral services for Lord Ogilvy of Airlie and the Laird of Gight "quhairin ther was sum superstitiouse ceremonies and rittes used as gif the profession of papistrie had bene specialie licenced and tolerated". Even as late as 1648 the commission of the General Assembly stated[3] in reference to Gordon of Gight and Gordon of Ardlogie that the presbyteries where they lived were overawed.

This family, to whose house Blakhal went regularly, was one of the most turbulent and also cosmopolitan of the Gordon cadets. For several generations they had had French connections. George Gordon of Gight had accompanied Adam Gordon of Auchindoun to the Court of Charles IX. In the first year of the reign of Charles I Gight's nephew Ardlogie had joined the Scottish Men-at-Arms in the French service. In 1624 George Gordon the younger of Gight was described[4] as an "apostat" and his wife Elizabeth Ogilvy, sister to the first Earl of Airlie,[5] as a

[1] Printed *ibid.*, p. xviii.

[2] Documents in *The House of Gordon* by I. A. Bulloch, vol. i, p. 47. At Gight's funeral George Crawford "bore a crucifix on a speare immediately before the corps the whole way in the place of burial". On 13 May 1604 John Melville, painter in Aberdeen, was summoned by the Presbytery for painting this cruicfix, *ibid.*, pp. 47, 48. The elder George Gordon of Gight was excommunicated at Aberdeen Kirk Session on 20 September 1601. He is quoted as saying "Giff if sall pleiss Majestie and your wisdomes of the Kirke of Scotland so to tak (take) my bluid for my profession quhilk is Catholick romane, I will maist willingly offer it for the same," *ibid.*, p. 73.

[3] For an account of the difficulties of this family with the Kirk cf. Mair, *Presbytery of Ellan.*

[4] Mair, *Presbytery of Ellan,* p. 67. In 1597 the presbytery had learned that the Laird of Gight and his wife "had caused a popish priest to baptise ane bairne to them", *ibid.*, pp. 72–3.

[5] In regard to the religious affiliation of the Ogilvies, the fifth Lord Ogilvy had been a Catholic, but his son made Presbyterian marriages with the Ruthvens of Gowrie and Napiers of Merchistoun. Lord Ogilvy's grandson the first Earl of Airlie was a Royalist and opponent of the Covenant. The second Earl was excommunicated as a Catholic in 1650 but subsequently gave satisfaction to the Kirk.

"recusant". Enquiries made by the presbytery of Ellan elicited the curious fact that they kept a French governess for their daughter at this time. It is probable that she had been brought to Scotland in the household of the Marchioness of Huntly.

The Gordons of Gight always remained the wildest among the cadets of Huntly. Successive lairds were embroiled with the Keiths and also maintained a blood feud with the Hays. A younger son of Gight was executed for the killing of the "Bonnie" Earl of Moray; a cadet of the family, Colonel George Gordon, was one of the conspirators who assassinated Wallenstein. Catherine Gordon, the last of the line,[1] was Byron's mother.

A whole network of Catholics in the Aberdeenshire countryside is revealed by the occasional prosecutions. The ministers appear to have been in some doubt as to who were priests.[2] A list compiled about 1630 mentions the names[3] of those held to be "resetters" of seminary priests and Jesuits, but who were not as yet excommunicated. These include[4] Lords Erroll and Aboyne, the Lairds of Dalgettie and Gight, Patrick Gordon the younger of Kincraigie, George Gordon of Letterfourie and George Gordon of Drumgask. These last may be regarded as the Catholic leaders among the Gordon lairds. A more significant register[4] is that of those who were excommunicate. These were the key men, not so well protected as the gentry; the men who suffered most directly. Their names and occupations give an impression of the way in which the Catholic Faith survived among all groups and at all levels in Aberdeenshire. They included two burgesses of Aberdeen and a notary public,[5] Robert Bisset of Lessendrum, bailiff to the Marquis of Huntly, Adam Strachan master of the household to Lord Aboyne, and Thomas Layng a goldsmith. Layng and John Gordon of Bounty were described as responsible for arranging the

---

[1] An entry in the Diary of George Turnbull, when he was a member of the committee of the General Assembly for the North, indicates that this branch of the Gordons had become Presbyterian before 1694, "Moonday 16th we dined at Gicht", *Miscellany of the Scottish History Society,* vol. i, p. 360.

[2] This seems indicated by the following list. "Faither Steven a most busie and dangerous traffequer, Mr John Ogilvie, Faither Stitchell, Faither Higgetts, Mr William Leslie commonly called the Capitain, Mr Andro Leslie, Mr John Leslie, Faither Scott, One Faither Mortimer laitlie come in his place quho died in Aberdene. Faither Tyrie, Thrie Father Robertsouns, Doctor William Leslie doctor of physick a seditious traffequer and reasoner who under pretence of administratioun of physick is a most dangerous seducer and is suspect to have receavit orders, Faither Broun son to umquhile James Broun at the Netherbow", Documents in *Spalding Club Miscellany,* vol.   p. liv.

[3] *Ibid.,* p. lvi.

[4] *Ibid.,* pp. liv–vi.

[5] The burgesses were Alexander and Robert Irving and the notary public John Spencer in Peiresmill.

journeys of priests. Among others who were accused of co-operating with them were John Urquhart a surgeon, the miller of Craigtoun,[1] Robert Abercrombie in Homecrook of Birnes, John Rinne a messenger-at-arms and William Anderson, sheriff clerk of Aberdeen.

Gilbert Blakhal's narrative must therefore be considered against a background of more or less constant Catholic life and practice. The laws stood against the Old Religion, but it was appreciated that their strict enforcement would not be palatable to the great families. Blakhal's own life was sheltered by the protection of Huntly's name. The chief of the Gordons had an important part in the general political movement of his time and his relations with the Catholics only form one facet of a complex life. Besides, Blakhal's account has an especial interest as revealing the structure of the household of the widow of a cadet of a great family.

Lady Aboyne, who received Blakhal into her service in July 1638, had been married to the first Marquis of Huntly's younger son Lord John Gordon,[2] who had perished in the burning of the Tower of Frendraught. She came from a family divided in religion[3] and was the sixth of the nine children of Francis ninth Earl of Erroll, who had been Huntly's associate as a Catholic leader.[4] She was at this time about thirty years of age. It is Blakhal's contention that, since the death of her brother the Constable of Scotland, Lady Aboyne had no further support from the Hays who had moved out of the North, while her friendship with the Gordons ceased on her father-in-law's death.[5] It seems

[1] The miller's name is given as John Alshenden.
[2] He had been created Viscount Melgum and Lord Aboyne in 1627 and died in 1630. His widow was always known by his second title.
[3] William tenth Earl of Erroll had been educated as a Presbyterian. The Ladies Margaret and Isabella Hay were Catholics. Besides these, Sophia Lady Aboyne had "two other sisters in the south, the one a Catholick, to wit my Ldye Semple, and the other, a heretick, my Lady Marre. My Ladyes Winton and Buccleugh were dead long before", *Brief Narrative*, p. 56.
[4] Blakhal told Lady Aboyne, "Your father and mother of happye memory and yourself, ever since you have keped houses, have served yourself of these (Jesuit) Fathers", *ibid.*, p. 64.
[5] Both Erroll and Huntly died in 1636. "After the death of her brother William, Earle of Erroll, she (Lady Aboyne) found no more frindship in her owen kinred; and after the death of her father-in-law, the first Marquis of Huntley, she had no more frindship in her allayes", *ibid.*, p. 94. "Lady Isabel, her sister, did wreat ane letter to her from Mons (where she was a nun), in nynne yeares, praying her to send tokens to the ladyes of Mons, as if Cromar had bein more aboundant of such things than Haynault. Lady Margaret did wreat another to her from Edinbrough to show her that she was to marie Sir John Seatoun of the Barnes. Theise two were al that she receaved al the tyme of her widowhead, which lasted eleven years and a halfe. I may bauldly say, that in al the worlde ther was not a ladye of her condition so desolat as she wes", *Ibid.*, p. 94.

that her relations were not close with her sister-in-law Lady Moray, who was accustomed to maintain a Jesuit chaplain[1] in her house in Elgin. Lady Aboyne was very devout[2] and Blakhal witnesses[3] to her charity. "Although my Ladye of Aboyne had but a smal rent, in comparison of my Ladye Marquise of Huntley, or my Ladye Murray, yet she had a more noble and generous hart than any of them."

An account of a pilgrimage made annually from Aboyne recalls the survival of ancient Catholic practices. "Shortly heirafter," wrote[4] Blakhal, "in the octave of the Assumption of Our Lady, she did go to the Bogge of Gight to see her mother-in-law my Lady Marqueis of Huntley, and to go from thence a pillgrimage, two milles, to Our Lady of Grace, in Murray land. It had bein of old a very devote place, and many pillgrimages had bein made to it, from al the partes in the Northe of Scotland; but then there was nothing standing of it but some brocken walles." Later Blakhal reverts[5] to this subject. "She used to make that pillgrimage every year so long as she had health to do it, a mater of threttie miles from her own house, whereof she made two of them afoot, and barefooted, next to the chappel."

In tune with such a character went a marked unworldliness. This last quality is indicated in the account of the household at Aboyne. In this connection it is interesting to observe the recognition of the claims of kindred and also that note of equality which existed side by side with the right to offer service. On Blakhal's arrival Lady Aboyne's property was controlled by Mr Adam Strachan, who has already been mentioned as a leading Catholic. He was a brother of the Laird of Glenkindie and had "governed[6] her house in quality master household many years". Although he was married to her gentlewoman Barbara Hay, he had originally served the other side of the family and had been her late husband's "praeceptor". The butler was Patrick Kinman, a young man of twenty-four who "spent what he pleased in the pantrie which was open to all that would keep him company till midnight. The pantrie," Blakhal explains,[7] "was right under my chamber".

---

[1] Blakhal has a note on the Jesuit chaplain with the Countess of Moray. "Father Grant was very soon therafter put to that ladye, who died within that yeare (1638)", ibid., p. 59.

[2] "Once every month she did confesse and receave forby all the great feastes of the yeare," ibid., p. 67.

[3] Ibid., p. 62.

[4] Ibid., p. 71.

[5] Ibid., p. 71.

[6] Ibid., p. 66.

[7] Ibid., p. 70.

The priest then goes on to give a convincing[1] account of the mistress's attachment to her servants. She favoured the butler on account of her affection for his family. "And this Kinman, because he was something in kindred to the Laird of Hill, in the Carse of Gowrie, a vassal of her father's, wher she had bein weined and brought up in his house until she was six years old, and therfor loved al that perteanes any way to that family. And for David Maxwel, she would not consent to put him away becaus he was the first footman that ever served her, and was become old and could not earne his living. Her compassion of the miserie he would fal into made her kepe him considering that his owne drinking wold not be considerable, if she gette an honest pantryman." Between them her servants had wasted her property.

It is clear that Blakhal took charge of this situation and his influence over Lady Aboyne may have accounted for the coldness of her husband's family towards him. Among other matters he provided double muskets, light guns and other weapons for the defence of her castle. "When I did enter her service," he wrote,[2] "thir was put only two pistolets in al the house, and they belonged to Allexander Davidson, a man who keeped ever a pair of pistolets, but never in all his lyf did fire one: so they served to him only for a parade as he avouched to me. Al her servants had swords, but theise armes al alone are too short to defend houses." The muskets proved useful for the house of Aboyne was twice attacked, first by men from Badenoch and then by Cameron clansmen from Lochaber, "a wylde kinde of[3] people, to mak their pray in the lawland, betwixt fourtie and fiftie men. They did come to Aboyne, thinking to mak their fortune their". Both attacks were repulsed.

A picture of life at Aboyne emerges. The priest at first ate in his chamber "as they[4] who wer before me used to doe". Later he was invited to take his meals in the parlour where Lady Aboyne and her child dined alone. There were his journeys. "The snow[5] before the thaw did go to the midst of a man's thigh." Once he was nearly drowned in the Water of Hay and saw[6] his hat and a little valise of red Spanish leather, containing his Mass vestments, carried away towards the river. There is an account[7] of the Lenten observances. "I made exhortations every Sunday, Tuisday, and Fredday, upon the Passion of our Saviour, which did please her (Lady Aboyne) and her domesticks, especially her maister cook, Alexander Lambe, who thereafter abjured his heresie before me, and dyed some two yeares therafter a devote Catholick."

[1] *Ibid.*, pp. 70-1.   [2] *Ibid.*, p. 77.
[3] *Ibid.*, p. 80.   [4] *Ibid.*, p. 64.
[5] *Ibid.*, p. 60.   [6] *Ibid.*, p. 39.
[7] *Ibid.*, p. 60.

The background is filled in with other figures: John Thomson who had been Lord Aboyne's man and had then returned to Lady Huntly's service; the priest's personal servant Thome Blakhal;[1] the principal tenants of Aboyne who were all millers,[2] Robert Coutts at the Mill of Gellen, Malcolm Durward at the Mill of Bounty, James Gordon at the Mill of Desse. These tenants are seen discussing a loan requested from them and dissatisfied at the security.[3]

It is clear that Catholics and Protestants lived at close quarters, and within certain groups of families, whose branches were divided in religion, there was an over-riding sense of Leslie or Gordon loyalty. In so far as the Douai Register is an indication,[4] the number of students sent abroad to seminaries in these years seems very small. There was probably a certain amount of secret Catholicism, although it is possible to exaggerate this factor. Blakhal has a note[5] in regard to the General Assembly of the Kirk which met in Aberdeen. "I learned (that I was believed to be in the town) from Mr Patrick Chambers, who was clerk of their Assembly and Catholick in his hart." It seems more likely that Chambers was merely a friend. Until the death of the second Duke of Gordon in 1728 the influence of the House of Huntly should never be undervalued when it was a question of making life more tolerable for Catholics in Aberdeenshire.[6]

Early in March 1642 Lady Aboyne fell ill of a "languishing fever" and died. Blakhal[7] refers to the great regret of all the

[1] He appears to have been identical with Blakhal's servant described earlier as being the son of the porter at the Earl of Moray's house in Elgin, *ibid.*, p. 58.

[2] *Ibid.*, p. 73.

[3] In this connection a network of indebtedness is revealed in the Book of the "Annualrentaris" and "Wedsettaris" within the schirrefdome of Abirdein, 1633, printed in the *Miscellany of the Spalding Club*, 1846, vol. iii, pp. 71–137. There are details of the indebtedness of Sir James Gordon of Lesmoir and of the Gight family. One entry relates to Aboyne. "Mr William Doglas, minister at Aboyn, declarit that he haid restared to him be the airis and executouris of umquhill John Viscount of Melgome vc.l.merkis," *ibid.*, p. 135.

[4] According to the Douai Register Robert Francis Irvine of Aberdeen entered on 6 January 1633 aged 19. He died in 1671 at Somerset House as a Capuchin. The two sons of James Forbes of Blacktown by his wife Magdalen daughter of Sir Alexander Fraser of Philorth entered on 10 September 1643, Walter aged eighteen and Arthur aged twelve. James Forbes a son of John Forbes of Corsindae and a relative of William Forbes, Bishop of Edinburgh, entered Douai on 25 March 1644, *Cal. Maxwell Witham MSS*, Appendix to the fifth report, pp. 653–4.

[5] *Brief Narrative*, p. 112.

[6] The first and second Dukes of Gordon, although Catholics, had much local influence and were never wholly disavowed by the Governments which ruled Scotland after 1688.

[7] *Brief Narrative*, p. 69.

Catholics of that countryside and "especially the pouer, who she did protect by her authority and succour by her meanes". He concludes on a religious note. "I . . . preveinning her publick burial, did bury her privately in her chest, with Catholic cere-monyes, and so did finish the services that I was able to do her in the quality of a priest."

It was an old-fashioned way of life that has been described and one ruled by a sense of mutual obligation. Poor kinsmen and younger sons of cadet branches would give their lives to managing property ready to undertake all tasks that were not menial. Clients of the family lived in the house upon this basis. The case of Agnes Gordon may be noted. Blakhal sets out[1] the position. "Duncan Gordon, a gentleman of the house of Lesmore, and his wyffe, Agnes Barclay of the house of Gartley, souffered great persecu-tion for their constancie in the Catholick religion. Having loosed their whole meanes they were reducted to great necessity. My lady (Aboyne) did keep the wyffe with her as a servande, being aaged, and would have extended her charity to the husband also." This was a type of order that was passing away; its feuds and loyalties belonged to an age that was about to vanish. There was little to link Aboyne with the seventeenth century. It belonged to the old Scotland as did its central tragedy the burning of the Tower of Frendraught.

Nevertheless the position was extremely complicated. This re-sulted from the feuds within the Catholic grouping like that which separated the Gordons from the Hays of Erroll throughout the last twenty years of the reign of James VI. Again, Moray and Frendraught, who may be regarded as the protagonists in the feuds arising from the tragedy at the latter place, were both on the Protestant side, while their wives had been brought up as Cath-olics and Lady Moray was ardent in that Faith. One factor they had in common; it can be said that all the Catholics in the Gordon sphere of influence had some protector.

A wholly new picture is presented when the complex Leslie affiliations are considered. Here was a stock whose branches were autonomus and often Catholic; in this matter they had no help from any chief. The situation of this kindred is on several counts difficult to disentangle. They were divided in their area of in-fluence between Fife and the north eastern counties; they were sharply separated in religious allegiance; the details of their blood relationship are open to question. In regard to this last point it seems to be the best opinion that the senior line, Leslie of that

[1] *Ibid.*, p. 101.

L

ilk, descended from the eldest son of Sir Andrew Leslie, who died in the last years of King Robert Bruce. The Earls of Rothes perhaps derive from Sir Andrew's second son, while the fourth is the reputed ancestor of the house of Balquhain which can be regarded as the central Catholic stem. One characteristic was shared by them all, a chronic and adventurous poverty. It seems natural that in their various branches they should have proved themselves to be born soldiers of fortune.

The Leslies were without a recognized head and their senior branch was in decline. The barony of Leslie in Aberdeenshire had been alienated.[1] If one can trace a family character in the stock it is a readiness to accept risks and, in the Presbyterian branches, a vaulting material ambition. To make good in such a sense was impracticable in Scotland at that time for the Catholics. As far as the earls were concerned, it was a race between ambition and insolvency. Their hold on the Rothes lands on Speyside was very loose;[2] it was in the kingdom of Fife that they built up their affinity. This dated back to the time when the Master of Rothes had organized the murder of Cardinal Beaton at St Andrews.

These tendencies were reflected in the sixth Earl of Rothes, remembered as the working mind among the Covenanting lords, and in Alexander Leslie, who combined his soldiering with an effort to build up an estate which could maintain the Earls of Leven. The dukedom of Rothes would be short-lived; Leslie House remains their monument. That, however, was the achievement of the Fife side of the family. In the north-east the barons or lairds of Balquhain remained predominant.

John Leslie of Balquhain, who died in 1622, had been the leader of the northern families of his own name. In addition to his paternal lands he held the barony of Fetternear, which had been leased[3] from the diocese of Aberdeen in his grandfather's time.

---

[1] This question is discussed in *The Scots Peerage*, under Rothes.

[1] In 1618 John Forbes of Enzean obtained a decree apprizing the barony of Leslie then held by George Leslie, *Historical Records of the family of Leslie* by Colonel Charles Leslie of Balquhain (1869), vol. i, p. 61.

[2] On 28 June and 4 July 1627 the Earl of Rothes sold to John Grant of Carron and his heirs, the mains and mill of Rothes for £10,180 Scots reserving to himself the castle tower with the castle bank and the green under the walls thereof. John Grant and his heirs were established as constables and heretable keepers of the tower, fortalice and castle on condition of removing when the Earl of Rothes gave fourteen days notice of his intention to reside, *ibid.*, ii, pp. 99, 100.

[3] In 1550, Patrick Forbes, Bishop of Aberdeen, with the consent of the Dean and Chapter, granted a *novo damus* on 13 November 1621, Balquhain Charters no. 467 summarised *ibid.*, iii, pp. 84–5. Until 1621 Balquhain held the office of constable of the Bishop's Palace in Aberdeen, *ibid.*, iii, p. 73.

He also owned house property[1] in the city and lodgings[2] for his own use there in the Castlegate. Lands were constantly exchanged among members of the stock and Balquhain was among those who benefited[3] from the embarrassments of the Laird of Leslie. Behind them all lay the memory of the Queen of Scots' ambassador John Leslie Bishop of Ross.

This prelate had been the natural son of a member of a cadet branch of Leslie of Cults.[4] During his brief episcopate in Scotland he had made provisions[5] for his family out of church lands. His own closest link was with Andrew Leslie of New Leslie,[6] who was married to his daughter Janet. The bishop's grandsons were sent to France for their education. In a stock, whose northern grouping was in general conservative, the families of New Leslie, Wardis[7] and Conrack adhered most firmly to Catholicism, while the coming of the Jesuits brought about a revival of that ancestral attachment among the Leslies of Balquhain and Pitcaple. The difficulty of the position of all these families lay in the absence of a leader since John Leslie's successor at Balquhain followed the lairds of Leslie into a mortgaged penury.[8]

The remedy lay in military service overseas and the Jesuit tradition, now beginning to affect Catholics in Aberdeenshire, encouraged enlistment under the Emperor's standard. Here lies the explanation of the career of the most successful of these Scottish soldiers of fortune who supported the Catholic side in the Thirty Years War, Walter Count Leslie. This officer, who was

[1] For the reversion of a house in the Netherkirkgate cf. *ibid.*, iii, p. 58.

[2] Obtained from Andrew Lawson, burgess of Aberdeen, in 1595, *ibid.*, iii, p. 66.

[3] On 24 March 1610 George Leslie of that ilk granted to John Leslie, fiar of Balquhain, a charter of the sunny half of the farm and lands of Aquhorties, Owertoun and Nethertoun thereof, with the half of the mill and mill lands thereof, and half of the lands of Blairdaff and half of those of Woodhill, Balquhain Charters no. 280, *ibid.*, iii, p. 81.

[4] The Bishop was a grandson of Alexander Leslie of Auching a cadet of the Cults family.

[5] John Leslie, Bishop of Ross (1527-1596) granted in 1567 to William Leslie of Balquhain his right to the castle and castle lands of the Channonrie of Ross and the lands of Learney and Craighead and the Mill of Avach all in that diocese, *ibid.*, iii, pp. 45 and 50.

[6] It would be convenient to set out the relationship of the various families. Kincraigie, Wardis, New Leslie and Pitcaple were descended in that order from the four younger sons of Sir William Leslie of Balquhain (d. 1470). Kinninvie, from whom the Earl of Leven claimed descent, was a cadet branch of New Leslie and Conrack a cadet of Kinninvie. Crichie came from a natural son of Sir William Leslie and Cults from a natural son of Andrew Leslie of Balquhain (d. 1420).

[7] Sir John Leslie of Wardis and Elspet Gordon his wife were excommunicated by the Presbytery of Aberdeen in April 1601, cf. *ibid.*, iii, pp. 285–287.

[8] Thus much of the property including the lands and barony of Fetternear were wadsetted (mortgaged) to John Leslie's son-in-law Sir Alexander Hay of Dalgety, *ibid.*, iii, p. 79.

among those responsible for Wallenstein's assassination and was
subsequently an Imperial field marshal and privy councillor and
ambassador to Constantinople, was born at Balquhain in 1606. He
was to represent a link with the Schotten Kloster at Vienna.
Characteristically he had honoured the ancestral alliance with the
Gordons by beginning his military service in Germany under
Colonel John Gordon then commanding a regiment of musketeers.
In the sequel it was Count Leslie's fortune that restored Balquhain
and left this house and its successor Fetternear[1] as a main support
of Catholicism in Aberdeenshire.

The links between Balquhain and Pitcaple were very strong
and the leaders of these stocks travelled in company sometimes as
far afield as Edinburgh. This appears from one of the charges
arising out of the long Frendraught stirs. Thus in the last days of
July 1635 charges were preferred[2] against John Leslie of Pitcaple,
James Leslie of Aquhorties[3] and his brother Alexander, John
Leslie of Balquhain and Hector Abercrombie of Fetternear on
account of an alleged attempt to murder David Seaton near the
head of the Canongate at six o'clock at night on the twenty-
second of that month "out of a deadly hatred to the Laird of
Frendraught and his servants". There was no reasoned outcome to
this proud poverty and the pursuance of the blood feud except
the setting out to serve in foreign wars.

Another aspect of this trend is revealed in the Diary of General
Patrick Gordon of Auchleuchries,[4] a distinguished officer in the
Russian[5] service. His great-grandfather had been a younger son
of Gordon of Haddo, but the small lands of Easter Auchleuchries
had belonged to Mary Ogilvy[6] the general's mother. It should be
mentioned that both parents were Catholics. After describing his
four years of schooling at the Kirk of Crochdan and his subsequent educational experiences Patrick Gordon explains how he
went overseas. "Haveing thus," he writes,[7] "by the most loveing
care of my dear parents, atteined to as much learning as the

---

[1] Fetternear was re-purchased from the Abercrombies by Patrick Count
Leslie in 1690. It is a curious point that in 1670 Alexander Abercromby
obtained from Pope Clement X a confirmation of his right to hold Fetternear, which was alienated church property, cf. *ibid.*, iii, p. 79.

[2] *Register of the Privy Council of Scotland* 1635–6, vol. vi, p. 74.

[3] Aquhorties was to become the seminary from which Blairs sprang.

[4] Patrick Gordon (1635-1699) died in Moscow having visited Scotland in
later life. His grandson of the same name and likewise a Catholic, sold
Auchleuchries in 1726, *Passages from the Diary of General Patrick Gordon*,
ed. Joseph Robertson, Spalding Club, 1859, introduction p. xxi.

[5] Count Leslie's nephew, John Leslie of Balquhain, was killed as a colonel
of cavalry in the Russian service at the storming of Igolwitz in 1655.

[6] Patrick Gordon's *Diary*, introduction p. xix.

[7] *Ibid.*, p. 5.

ordinary country schools affoord, and being unwilling, because of my dissenting in religion, to go to the University in Scotland, I resolved . . . my patrimony being small, as being the younger son of a younger brother of a younger house; I resolved, I say, to go to some foreigne country, not careing much on what pretence or to what country I should go."

In examining the question of the survival of Catholicism in the North East of Scotland an inadequate impression will result from an exclusive reliance on official records. It is necessary to attempt to reconstruct what lies behind the formal phrasing. There were, for instance, great variations of practice among the Catholic branches of the Leslies. Thus Balquhain exercised certain rights within his parish kirk,[1] and two of the same laird's marriages were dissolved by the commissaries in Edinburgh. It was said that his three wives were on one occasion all seen together[2] in the kirk or Chapel of Garioch.

On the other hand the Leslies of Conrack were always strict. For a long time they were protected by Lord Lovat who had been fostered as a child by the laird's grandparents. In the end Alexander Leslie of Conrack was charged[3] with harbouring Jesuits, with being married without the assistance of a minister and with having his children christened by popish priests. It seems likely that these last practices were more common among Catholics in the remote parts of Scotland than any existing records indicate.

A curious light is thrown on the outlook of certain families by a complaint made by Sir George Ogilvie of Banff. He stated[4] that "in the tyme of poperie and blindnesse" his predecessors had at their own charges caused vestments to be made for the priests

[1] According to Balquhain Charter, no. 909, which is undated, John Leslie in Meikle Durnes and Walter Farquhar made a declaration that they had no right, but leave and tolerance from John Leslie of Balquhain and John Leslie, younger, thereof, to place their desks in the east gable of the kirk of Chapel of Garioch, Leslie, *op. cit.*, iii, p. 90.

[2] John Leslie married first Elizabeth Grant and secondly Lady Elizabeth Hay. His third wife, Jean Erskine sister of the first Earl of Kellie, was the mother of Count Walter Leslie, *ibid.*, iii, p. 75. The *D.N.B.*, vol. xi, p. 988, describes Count Leslie's upbringing as Calvinist, but the *Laurus Lesleana* published at Gratz in 1692 by the Rev. William Leslie states that John Leslie, who inherited the lairdship in 1638, was the first Protestant member of the Balquhain family.

[3] This matter was discussed in the Annual Letter sent to the General of the Society of Jesus by Fr. John Leslie in 1629. It is preserved among the Stonyhurst MSS and was printed in *Memoirs of the Scottish Catholics* by Rev. William Forbes Leith S.J., vol. i, pp. 46–7. In this connection a Latin Bible, which was preserved at Fetternear gives details of two marriages and three christenings of members of the Balquhain family performed by their Catholic chaplain between 1661 and 1682, cf. Leslie, *op. cit.*, iii, p. 127.

[4] *Register of the Privy Council of Scotland* 1630-32, vol. iv, p. 247.

who served in their chapels and at their altars. These vestments
had been carefully preserved by his grandfather and father. The
matter became public when the gear in question was seized
by the customs after Ogilvie had attempted to find a purchaser for
the articles abroad. It seems likely that these vestments were kept
lest one day the Mass might be restored. Another aspect of
religious practice which awaits investigation is the extent
to which old private chapels and their grounds were used as
burial places as in the cases of Fetternear and St. Ninian's ceme-
tery near Letterfourie. There is a tendency to underestimate
the freedom with which the Catholic life went forward in
Aberdeenshire.

During these years it was a main purpose of the Bishops of
Aberdeen to reduce if not to exterminate this attachment to the
Roman See. Such sympathies, whether active or latent, constituted
a threat to the Episcopalian position. A bitter mood characterised
both sides and was equally reflected in the attitude of the missionary priests towards the "pseudo-ministers". It would need a shared
misfortune brought about by the Revolution Settlement and a
common attachment to the failing cause of the House of Stuart to
bring about a kindlier feeling between the Episcopalians and the
adherents of the Old Faith in North East Scotland.

It should, however, be noted that the official position of the
Bishop of Aberdeen would never be attacked except by the Presbyterians. On his journeys he was accustomed to be offered
hospitality by those lairds who were themselves attached to the
Holy See. In so far as such landowners occupied Kirk lands,
these were often held by leasehold from the diocese. No secular
magnate would be received with more respect.

In certain instances it is difficult to disentangle the position of
a particular family and decide whether its members possessed
Episcopalian preferences or perhaps a more or less secret link
with Rome. The situation of the Grants of Freuchie is a case in
point. The only explicit Catholic appears to have been Lady Mary
Grant, who was the Countess of Moray's daughter. At the same
time in 1616 Archbishop Spottiswoode in the course of a rather
severe letter[1] on the subject of the "desolation of the kirks of
Strathspey" refers to John Grant of Freuchie as "not a professor with
us." It seems doubtful whether at that date such an expression would
have been used except of one who was a Papist. His granddaughter
Lilias Grant, wife of Sir Walter Innes of Balvenie, compiled[2]

[1] Letter dated at Dairsie and printed in *The Chiefs of Grant* by Sir William
Fraser, 1883, vol. ii, Correspondence, p. 41.
[2] Letter written to Lilias Murray, Lady Grant, who belonged to the House
of Tullibardine, printed *ibid.*, ii, p. 54.

about 1630 a list of books for her mother's use. The following titles are included:

The Marrov of the Orrekallis of God,
Of Prayer and Medetasioun set furthe be Granada fra Collen,
Sant Augustyn,
The Prakteis of Peyattiey,
Of the Imitatioun of Chryst.

It would be interesting to speculate what light the nature of this small collection throws on Lady Innes's theological preoccupations.

Until the traveller reached as far north as the Episcopalian outpost of Fortrose the three religious traditions intermingled. Beyond that point and especially in the low country towards the eastern seaboard there was an episcopal framework and a line of well-planted Presbyterian kirks. Before considering the pattern of life in these northern parts it is worth examining the political significance of the Catholic elements which have been described and at this time played no *rôle* in Caithness or Sutherland.

There seems little doubt that the active attachment to the ancestral faith was strongest in those regions which lay within reach of Aberdeen as a result of the work of the missionary priests. It was likewise in this part of Scotland that the opposition to the General Assembly would crystallise under the leadership of the Aberdeen doctors. The fact that Catholic and Episcopalian opposition to the dominant Presbyterianism was concentrated in Aberdeenshire does not, however, suggest that there was serious contact between these two groups. Their aims were very different. The Episcopalians were concerned to defend an actual situation in which the Bishop was an important factor in the prestige and influence of Aberdeen. The Catholics on the other hand looked back to an old order which no element among the country's leadership was concerned to restore. Thus they supported a King who was equally cold towards both Rome and Geneva. Moreover their natural spokesmen the second Marquis of Huntly and his son did not share their religion. Montrose in time would show that he was in a measure their friend at least to the extent of welcoming them to the fellowship of his armies. Still, here again, the ties of kinship and clan support which bound so many Catholics to the Marquis of Huntly prevented the exercise of a free choice. Even before the conflict few avocations were open to them. The only way for one of their persuasion to build up a fortune was through military service with some foreign power. Within Scotland no leader would offer them assurances. Ahead they could see no outcome save the hope to preserve their own religion by a private fidelity.

CHAPTER XI

THE NORTHERN EARLDOMS

BEFORE considering the life in the islands and the Western Highlands it is worth examining the situation in the northern counties of Sutherland and Caithness and in the lands on the western shore of the Moray Firth. In this connection it is difficult to exaggerate the value of the work of Sir Robert Gordon of Gordonstoun, a minor figure of the period who had contacts with Edinburgh and London as well as the position of Tutor of Sutherland. His writings are informed with the desire to spread "civility"; he is always the protagonist of a southern victory. At the same time his account of the life of these counties is incomparable. Rural prosperity is equated with beauty in his pages, and the countryside is seen beneath the light of a northern summer. On questions of history and genealogy he was near enough to the feuds between the great houses to be unsurprised by any detail, however mediæval-seeming. The worldly-wise seventeenth century is summed up in the advice that he gave to his young nephew. Only fairly extensive quotation can give the feeling and the content of these two documents. The very long manuscript history was compiled between 1615 and 1630.[1] It was printed in 1813 as an act of family piety by the Countess-Duchess of Sutherland. The work is spontaneous and wonderfully fresh, somewhat partisan and idealistic; the set-pieces on the countryside are quite enchanting. "The cuntry or province of Southerland," he begins,[2] "doth abound in corns, grasse, woods, froots, bestiall, all kynde of wilde foull, deir and roe; all sorts of fishes, especially salmond; and all other commodities, which are usuall in this kingdom of Scotland or necessarie for men." Sir Robert then describes its situation. "It hath Catteynes (Caithness) toward the east and northeast; it hath the great ocean toward the north, northwest and westnorthwest. . . . It hath the cuntrey of Assint towards the

---

[1] The oldest manuscript of *The Genealogical History of the Earldom of Sutherland,* a work of 228 pages, is preserved at Dunrobin. A continuation, 68 pages in length, and dealing with the years between 1630 and 1651 was added by Gilbert Gordon of Sallachy. For one hundred and fifty years the MSS. remained a private heirloom and was bequeathed as such by the Countess of Sutherland to her eldest son in 1705. Cf. *The Sutherland Book* by Sir Wiliam Fraser, 1892, vol. i, introd., p. xiii.

[2] Sir Robert Gordon, *op. cit.,* p. 1.

west; it hath Rosse towards the south and southwest." The book is filled with the rivalry between the Earls of Sutherland and Caithness seen always from the standpoint of Dunrobin. "Souther-land," we read, "is separated and divyded from Catteynes by the brook or strype called Alditaver, and by the hill called Ord with a range of other hills which doe streatch from the south sea to the north ocean." It is interesting to note the place which the northern ocean holds in Sir Robert Gordon's memory.

"Durines[1] is eighteen mylls in lenth from the south towards the north, and tuelve mylls in bredth from the montanes to the west and northwest ocean. . . . The dayes are of great lenth in Durines in summer, and thereis no dark night at all; the dayes in winter be verie short, and the night exceeding longe. I do verilie think that there is no land directlie north from the point of Durines, called Ardurines; at least there is none found out as yit." Again, "in Durines,[2] west and northwest from the Diri-More, ther is ane excellent and delectable place for hunting, called the Parwe, wher they hunt the reid deir in abondance; and sometymes they dryve them into the ocean sea[3] at the Pharo-Head,[4] wher they doe tak them in boats as they list".

Sir Robert Gordon then sets out[5] the advantages. "Ther are hills of Marble[6] in divers pairts of this province. Their is good sea coale some half myle be-west of the mouth of the river of Broray. . . . Ther is a fyne and excellent quarrie of frie-stone a little be-west that coale-hugh, besyd Ald-Sputy, which is careid from thence into other pairts of the kingdome. . . . Ther is a quarrie of sleat hard by the town of Dornoch. . . . The corns and grain of Southerland are excellent and chieflie the barley is so good, that it giveth greater pryces, in other pairts of the kingdome, then the barley of Orkney, Cattenes, Murray, or any of the rest of the provinces of the north, excepting Rosse, the barley whereof is almost of the like goodnes with Southerland."

The history, as described, is a constant struggle to protect this Eden. The figure of the enemy does not emerge with clarity. It is a difficulty in assessing the situation that the archives of the Earls of Caithness seem to have perished. The House of Sinclair

---

[1] *Ibid.,* p. 10.

[2] *Ibid.,* pp. 4-5.

[3] In contrast to the ocean sea it is noted that "Southerland . . . hath the German sea toward the south, southeast and eist", *ibid.,* p. 1.

[4] Gordon returns later to the same subject. "I have spoke alreadie of a place in Durines called Parwe, or Pharo-Head, which is ane exceeding delect-able pairt for hunting of reid deir", *ibid.,* p. 10.

[5] *Ibid.,* pp. 6, 8.

[6] "It is thought that in Durines ther are mynes of gold", *ibid.,* p. 10.

did not recover from the troubles[1] which came upon her in the seventeenth century. Very little can now be ascertained about the personal character of the Sinclair Earls. The remains of their castles mostly date from an earlier period.[2] Their physical likenesses cannot be recaptured; they had fallen into poverty before the age of portraiture.

The account given by Sir Robert Gordon has curious affinities with that provided by Sir John Wynn in his *History of the Gwydir Family*. Both of them write of a recent past in which attacks made by the enemies of their house seem barely credible. An old disordered world keeps breaking in on their careful newfound "civility". The following passage from Sir Robert Gordon's work shows the resemblance clearly. "This George Earle of Catteynes," it is explained,[3] "at his verie first entrie to his lands and earldom, killed, with his owne hands, two of his kinsmen, David and Ingrahm Sinclairs, brethren, which wes thus done; One of these tuo gentlemen had invyted Earle George to the brydell-feast of one of his daughters. The Earle went cheirfullie, and after denner, playing at foot-ball (which wes ane exercise much on request then among the Scots, but decayed of late), the Earle himselff, without any other preamble, came to Ingrahm Sinclair, who suspected no such matter, and shott him in the head with a pistoll, whereof he died instantlie at that place. David Sinclair wes immediately thereafter slaine by the earle with a suord." The cause of this slaughter is then given. "The reasone that moved Earle George to kill them, wes, because they favored the Earle of Southerland."

During a period of one hundred and fourteen years, from 1529 until 1643, there were only two holders of the earldom of Caithness, both named George Sinclair. The estimate of the elder is set down[4] plainly. "Earle George was a worldlie-wise man, politique, craftie and provident; whereby he heaped together a great quantitie of treasure, all of which he left unto his sone George Sincklair of May."[5] The intentions are set out[6] no less distinctly. "These tuo cuntries, Southerland and Strathnaver, he

[1] Throughout the first half of the seventeenth century the Earls of Caithness were heavily in debt and in 1672 the whole of the remaining lands were disposed of by the sixth Earl to Sir John Campbell of Glenorchy.
[2] Keiss Castle, an old-fashioned four-storied house with an attic, was characteristic. Castle Sinclair was built at this period and seems to date from 1616.
[3] Sir Robert Gordon, *op. cit.*, p. 180.
[4] *Ibid.*, p. 178.
[5] George Sinclair of Mey founded the most substantial cadet branch of the family.
[6] *Ibid.*, p. 179.

(George Earl of Caithness) intended to reduce under the obedience of Catteynes, by vertue of his pretended justiciary of the whole dyacie (diocese)." There are accounts of the Sutherland archers[1] and the "running guard"[2]; detailed numbers[3] are provided. It is clear that the enemy was pertinacious. "This George (now Earle of Catteynes) hath alwyse followed the steps of his grandfather, as in other things, so in this also, that he still continues his malice and hatred towards the house of Southerland." A note[4] under 1616 maintains the theme. "Since the slaughter of John Sinclair in Thurso, the Earle of Catteynes never desisted to entyse his cuntriemen, sometymes one, sometymes another, by all the fair allurements he could, to effectuat some stratagem, either in Southerland or Strathnaver."

Over against this there is described[5] the just authority of the head of the northern Gordons. "The Erle of Southerland is at this day verie strong, and of great power. He holdeth his earldome and lands in regalitie and blench; he is hereditarie shireff of that whole province, and of Strathnaver also; the deputie whereof he hath given of late to Macky. The gentlemen of that earldome doe hold there lands of the erle; most pairt warrd and relieff. He hath power to exercise justice within all the territories of his province, both in criminall and civill causes; and to keep and appoynt courts to that effect, and also for the manadgeing of his owne revenues."[6]

The other permanent element in the situation was the place held by Mackay. His clan occupied Strathnaver and he was courted[7] by both his greater neighbours. "Yea, Earle George

---

[1] "The Southerland archers so galled the Catteynes armie, that they forced them to remove their camp from the river syd wher they did ly and to encamp among the rockes above the village of Easter Helmisdale", *ibid.*, p. 194.

[2] After an attack on the Sutherland watch in the village of Liribell in June 1589, "Earle Alexander, to prevent such suddent incursions thereffter, did alwayes mantyen a cursarie and runing guard, to preserve the cuntry from such vnlooked-for invasions", *ibid.*, p. 198.

[3] The archers of the Earl of Caithness were said to number "weill neare 1500" at the skirmish of Clyne. "The inhabitants of Southerland, with resolute valor, took the booty of cattle with them, and so retired themselves to a bush of wood in Strathbroray, tuo myles from the place wher they had so long foughten with vncertain victory", *ibid.*, p. 203.

[4] *Ibid.*, p. 327.

[5] *Ibid.*, p. 12.

[6] In addition he held from the Duke of Lennox the "heretable gift" of the Admiralty of the whole diocese of Caithness, *ibid.*, p. 12.

[7] "The eleventh day of September 1614 yeirs, Houcheon Macky of Far died of a bloody flux and issue, at Toung in Strathnaver, the 53 yeir of his aige. His vertures were accompanied by a vice that overruled him, which was his extraordinary lust. . . . He left behind him alyve tuo sons and tuo daughters, by Lady Jean Gordoun, the sister of this John Earle of Southerland. . . . He had also a daughter called Cristian Macky, by the Earle of Catteynes his daugher", *ibid.*, p. 302.

thought," wrote[1] Sir Robert Gordon of the younger Earl of Caithness of that name, "that he had played the pairt of a good and wyse politician, if he could have maid them (Mackay and the Earl of Sutherland) to rwyn one another, thereby to be revenged of both".

The notes on Strathnaver[2] have their own interest. "In Strathnaver there are two castles, Borwe and Toung; Mackay his special residence is at Toung, one myle from the place where the castle doth stand. Macky his buriall place is at the chapell of Kirkboll, which is one myle distant from Toung, and is latelie repaired. The cuntry of Strathnaver is full of red deir and roes, pleasant for hunting in the summer season. . . . Macky hath also a summer dwelling in ane land within Loch-Stalk, in the Diri-More. In divers of these lochs, or lakes, ther is pearle found." There are now two passages which suggest Sir Robert's interest in the promotion of "civility". "It is full of great mountanes and wildirnes, yit verie good for pasture. . . . Ther is no doubt bot that cuntry might be much bettered by laborious and painfull inhabitants." Sir Robert was guardian of the earldom; he was travelled and knew the Courts. Like the second Marquis of Huntly he, too, looked southward. His upbringing and experience had brought with them a Lowland mentality.[3] The thought of lands not yet reduced to order was displeasing. There came before the Tutor of Sutherland the many advantages of "planting" and "plantation".

Sir Robert Gordon was a man of forty-five at the accession[4] of Charles I; he appreciated all that had been done to bring the land to peacefulness and order. "In the days[5] of Earl Alexander there came into Southerland out of Rosse one Mr. William Pape, who was admitted schoolmaster in the town of Dornoch. He was appointed resident minister of that place and later Chanter of Caithness." His brother Charles became public notary and then sheriff clerk of Sutherland. It was from William Pape that Sir Robert and his brother received their first schooling.[6]

Memories of feuds and the sense of family allegiance were both more real than the as yet uncompleted religious changes. "The yeir[7] of God one thousand fyve hundred and fourtie-fyve William

---

[1] *Ibid.*, p. 355.   [2] *Ibid.*, pp. 10, 11.

[3] His father had been compelled when a boy to marry Lady Barbara Sinclair who was Mackay's mistress. Cf. "Barbara Sincklair . . . hir licentious life with Y-Macky", *ibid.*, p. 307 and p. 169. Sir Robert was the son of a second marriage.

[4] Sir Robert Gordon was born at Dunrobin Castle on 14 May 1580.

[5] Sir Robert Gordon, *op. cit.*, p. 256.

[6] "After his infancie and chyldhood, he wes sent to the school, together with his eldest brother John (then Master of Sutherland) to be bred in the town of Dornogh with Mr William Pape, schoolmaster of that place wher he stayed untill the yeir of God 1596", *ibid.*, p. 314.

[7] *Ibid.*, p. 112.

Gordon, chancelar of Moray, a good and learned man, was made Bishop of Aberdeen by Cardinall Beton his suite, greatlie to the displeasure of the Earl of Angus, and the whole surname of Douglas." This note of patriarchal loyalty recurs. "In this earle his tyme," we read[1] in connection with the mid-sixteenth century, "John Gordon of Drummy settled himselff in Southerland; of whom are descended divers of the surname of Gordon, dwelling in that cuntry. He wes a faithfull and diligent servant to his master Earle John (the grandchyld of this Earle Adam) who gave him the lands of Balldon in fue. He mareid a gentlewoman called Margaret Mackreth, who was then in service with the Countess of Southerland. This Margaret Mackreth long afterward, in the tyme of her widowhead, did foster and bring up Sir Robert Gordoun, now tutor of Southerland, and knight-baronet." Each semi-feudal relationship is set out very exactly.[2]

Sir Robert, who lost his father when he was fourteen, was much influenced by his mother, Jean Countess of Sutherland, who had been Bothwell's first wife before his marriage to the Queen of Scots. A Gordon of Huntly and a woman of firm character, she began the salt works at Broray and dug the "colehugh" there until this latter enterprise was stopped through a difference of opinion with her daughter-in-law. Sir Robert himself opened a quarry in 1619 from which he brought the slate roofs of the church at Bornoch and those of Skibo Castle, "the first[3] buildings covered with this new sleat". There was also a careful repair of the highways and bridges.[4] The account of the setting of the family life[5] has that note of elegance which Sir Robert Gordon prized. "Dunrobin (the Erle of Southerland his special residence), a house weill seated upon a mote hard by the sea, with fair orchards, wher ther be pleasant gardens, planted with all kynds of froots, hearbs and floers, used in this kingdome, and abundance of good saphron, tobacco and rosemarie. The froot heir is excellent,[6] and cheeflie the pears and cherries." It was at Dunrobin that the Countess of

---

[1] Ibid., p. 104.

[2] "Earle John wes a great manteyner of the family of Mackeinze (now Earle of Seaforth) and wes the cheiff instrument of the advancement of that house; haveing maid Mackenzie his chamberlain and baillie in Rosse", ibid., p. 146.

[3] Ibid., p. 346.

[4] "This year of God 1619 the Bridge of Broray (being altogether decayed) was re-edified and repaired by Sir Robert Gordoun and his brother Sir Alexr, with the rest of the gentlemen of the countrey of Southerland; and upon the north syd of the bridge the Erle of Southerland his armes wer carved in a fyn stone", ibid., p. 8.

[5] Ibid., p. 8.

[6] There was also a reference to the excellent cherries in the orchard at Skibo Castle, ibid., p. 8.

Sutherland died in 1629 in her eighty-fourth year. "Shee[1] left her son, Sir Robert Gordoun, her onlie and sole executor of her will and testament, though he was of a contrarie opinion with her in religion."

The fact of Lady Sutherland's attachment to Catholicism is clear.[2] It is said that her eldest son, who died in 1615, followed her preferences, but what did this amount to in actual practice? There seems very little evidence of the activity of surviving priests in the northern parts. Perhaps the King's Government was fearful of "Jesuits and seminaries," who did not come. There is no monograph dealing with the survival of the Old Religion from Inverness northwards.

Sir Alexander Gordon and his wife are mentioned as Catholics in proceedings taken by the Privy Council.[3] A little earlier Sir Robert Gordon went surety that his mother would not receive priests.[4] At the same time the old Countess interested herself actively in a project for naming the Bishop of Caithness. The project came to nothing, but she was determined that no "unfriend" to her house should reach that country. In one whole department of life the unit was the diocese and the parish, filled or unfilled. It had been so for two centuries in the struggle between the Houses of Caithness and Sutherland. The phrases recur[5] in Sir Robert's writing. "The parish of Kildonnand (which doth march with Catteynes)." And again, "Let ws begin the yeir of God 1618 with a sudden and strange alteration in this dyocie". The Gordons of Sutherland would support the Bishop of Caithness since he and his officers were the victims of their enemies. Sir Robert has a curious account[6] of the Earl of Caithness in his

[1] *Ibid.*, p. 409.

[2] "About the beginning of July 1648 Lady Anne Gordon, Lady Pitfodels perished by storme of weather, upon the coast of Holland, as shoe intended to goe into France, being bred in the Romish religion under her grandmother Jean Countess of Southerland", *ibid.*, p. 542. A letter from Lady Sutherland to Sir Robert Gordon dated at Dunrobin 25 May 1623 refers to the return of Lady Anne from Strathbogie and then continues "Gif he (presumably the second Marquis of Huntly) vill lat his eldest sonne cum vith hir I vald be glaid of it, that I micht shaw thankfulness to him. He nedis not feir materis of religioun, quhairof he hes evir maid his excuis to me, for the bairn is not capable of that," document no. 142 printed in *The Sutherland Book,* Correspondence (1892), vol. ii, p. 142.

[3] Sir Alexander Gordon and his wife excommunicated on 4th September 1627. *Register of the Acts of the Privy Council of Scotland,* vol. x, p. 75.

[4] Letter dated at Rubron on 24 September 1616 printed as document no. 133 in *The Sutherland Book,* vol. ii, p. 123.

[5] Gordon, *op. cit.,* pp. 9 and 368.

[6] "After that the Earl of Catteynes had caused burn the cornes in Sanset, and was urged, for this cryme, to resigne a pairt of his fue-lands of the bishoprick of Catteynes to the bishop of that dyocie. . . . The Earle still grudged thereat, and continuallie molested the bishop's servants and tennants: and in speciall, he moste hated and always vexed Robert Monroe of Aldie, commissar of Catteynes", *ibid.,* p. 366.

lodgings in the town of Thurso molesting Monroe of Aldie, "who was alwayes[1] the bishop's chamberlain and factor in that dyocie". It was essential to the well being of Dunrobin that the Earl and Bishop of Caithness should not make common cause against the Gordons.

There 'was a certain amount of church building[2] which was linked with the concept of bringing in "civility". And from the beginning of the seventeenth century Presbyterianism, as we know it, was gaining ground. The fourteenth Earl of Sutherland had his first book-learning from the minister at Dornoch.[3] Still it is very doubtful how far the Presbyterian system had penetrated at this date in the northern counties, always excepting the coastal towns. For a period a lingering attachment to Catholicism, which nothing had come to uproot, seems to have existed side by side with the new religion of the ministers, which few men sought to propagate. The ministers themselves had to tread warily for they were working under powerful lords who had little wish to touch upon doctrinal questions. The fifth Earl of Caithness was excommunicated by the Kirk[4] in 1627 and was reconciled with the ministers two years later. This was when the Sinclair power was failing. Still it is interesting to find action so positive. The old ways were changing at Dunrobin. Only a long lifetime had passed since the head of Alexander the Bastard of Sutherland had been placed on the parapet of the castle tower. He had believed the prophecy which the witches made to him that his head would be raised higher than all his stock.

The Norse element in Caithness was now diminishing. Some of the phases of the struggle between the rival houses, and in particular the claim[5] that the servants of Sir Alexander Gordon of Navidale had built their summer sheilings beyond the accustomed limits, recall the world that Sigrid Undset described in *Kristin Lavransdatter*. The new factor in these northern counties was the rather gradual establishment of the Reformed Kirk and the Genevan outlook.

Presbyterianism had been introduced into the Orkneys at an early date. There was good communication by sea between

[1] *Ibid.*, p. 366.
[2] "The parish churches of Southerland were repaired beginning with Golspikirktoun near the house of Dunrobin", *ibid.*, p. 361.
[3] *Ibid.*, p. 361.
[4] The fourth Earl of Caithness, who died in 1582, was regarded as an open Catholic. In 1606 the Earls of Caithness and Sutherland were ordered to confine themselves within the bounds of certain towns on suspicion of Popery. But on 22 July 1614 Caithness was placed on a commission for the apprehension of Jesuit priests in his county. Cf. *Register of the Acts of the Privy Council of Scotland*, vol. x, p. 251.
[5] *Ibid.*, vol. 1629-30, pp. 480-1.

Kirkwall and Leith. The Earls of Orkney, Lord Robert Stewart and his son,[1] supported the Reformation. The architecture of the great houses was elaborate,[2] resembling in many ways the building carried out in the southern Scottish counties. On the easy slopes and good land of Pomona there was no ground where the Old Faith might linger. A small but integrated society centred upon Kirkwall[3] and was spread among the farmsteads within reach of Scapa Flow and its empty waters.

By the beginning of the reign of Charles I Presbyterianism had gained control of all the coastal lands between Wisk Water and the Moray Firth. It was a form of religious observance which young men of standing would find proposed to them. The Calvinist doctrine had been for the most part accepted tranquilly. The fourteenth Earl of Sutherland and his contemporary[4] the Master of Caithness were both brought up from childhood as Protestants. Their friends and relatives served with Gustavus Adolphus and his allies. The climate of the Reformed Faith was congenial to them. They accepted the new tradition in its entirety.

These observations may serve to introduce another document left by Sir Robert Gordon, the letter of advice which he composed c. 1620 for the young head of his House. It is preserved among the Dunrobin Castle MSS. and bears the following circumstantial title. "Sir Robert Gordon his Fearweall, conteyning certane precepts and advertisements to his nepheu Jhon, Earle of Southerland."

As is common form, the letter[5] contains moral aphorisms all placed within that cultivated setting which the author valued. "Few noble men in Scotland," we read, "can frie themselfs from robbing of the church in some degrie, which resembleth Seianus, his horse, still procuring a cure to the possessours". The next two comments[6] are in the tradition of selfconsciously worldly advice at that place and period. "Be courteous towards all men, and chieflie towards your inferiours, who ar not bound by dewtie

---

[1] Lord Robert Stewart, Commendator of Holyrood, and one of the Lords of the Congregation was a step-brother of the Regent Moray. He was also able to secure the priory of Whithorn in commendam for his son Patrick second and last Earl of Orkney, who was executed in 1615.

[2] Birsay Palace was a relatively modest structure consisting of buildings two storeys in height surrounding a courtyard. The surviving chimneys up the outer wall resemble those in the later courtyard at Dunnottar. In Earl Patrick's Palace at Kirkwall the dtae 1607 is found on a doorway. The great hall had two private rooms adjoining. The Palace was furnished with oriel windows and corbelled turrets, cf. McGibbon & Ross. Domestic and Castellated Architecture of Scotland.

[3] Cf. Records of the Earldom of Orkney, ed. J. Storer Clouston passim.

[4] The fourteenth Earl of Sutherland was born in 1609.

[5] Printed as document no. 347 in The Sutherland Book, vol. ii, pp. 337–68.

[6] Ibid., ii, p. 356.

1621
Ætatis suæ · 41 ·

SIR ROBERT GORDON

to follow yow, whereby yow shall insinuat yourself into their affections. . . . Be never so intire or familiar with any man, but if it happen that you discord, yow may retire with safetie, without disclosing your most inward secrets to any flesh breathing, yea, not to the wyffe of your bossome. For it is a meir follie for a man to inthrall himself farther to his freind then that he needs not fear him being his enemie."

The advice on marriage[1] reveals the sense of dynasty which was so strong among the great Scots families. "I do not lyke the humour of our noble men in Scotland, who do scorne to match with the barones and gentilitie, and do marie their own equalls for the most parts. I confess it is best to march with the nobilitie, if you can find contentment and riches correspondent thereunto. Yet do not you spair (fear) to marie a laird or barrone his doughter, of a good stock and well descended, prowyding shee lyke you well, and that shee be wealthie."

This dynastic sense is again reflected in references[2] to the head of the young Earl's House and to his enemies. "Acknowledge the Marquis of Huntley as your cheif, but if he do not respect yow as your place and qualitie deserweth, then desist to follow him." The next comment turns upon the main preoccupation of Sir Robert's policy. "Be ever circumspect and attentive to hearken what courses the hous of Cathnesse taketh. . . . The place in Parliament (which hitherto seemed to breid all jarres among yow) is now out of question, yow being so many degries ranked before him."

The points[3] that follow are strictly practical. "Hawe ever some trustie secret freind both in Cathnesse and Strathnaver, who yow shall enterteyne as your secrit pensioner, that he may still adwerteis yow of all things either spoken or dewysed against yow and yours. . . . Do yow endewoir to be ewer suir of the Clan Gun, for since memorie of man they never harmed the hous of Sutherland, but have alwayes folowed the same whersoever they did dwell." And again, "Do your best to get all the coast syde of Southerland into your owne hands from the Craigbeg to the Ord, and plant it all with tennents fitt for service."

It was clear that Sir Robert Gordon's thought turned often to the capital. "Retain[4] still the best men of lawe and advocats in Edinburgh for your counsell. Hawe a good, diligent, skillfull and

---

[1] *Ibid.,* ii, p. 343. Marriages between the eldest son of a great family and a laird's daughter were rare in the extreme. Lord Lewis Gordon, later third Marquis of Huntly was a younger son at the time of his marriage in 1644 with the daughter of Sir John Grant of Freuchy.

[2] *Ibid.,* ii, pp. 358 and 348.   [3] *Ibid.,* ii, pp. 349 and 354.

[4] *Ibid.,* ii, p. 355.

M

faithfull agent still resident at Edinburgh, who shall be your pensioner, and shall advertise yow from tyme to tyme of all occurrences there. If at any tyme yow be able to buy any lands out of Southerland for your eldest sone,[1] then buy some resting place to him about Edinburgh, wher he may dwell and remain when any occasion drawes him south, either for himselfe or his freinds."

An attitude to dependents is then prescribed.[2] "Do few business with your countreymen by the intercession of others, or by the mediation of these that ar in greatest credite with yow; for they will suck the margh and substance of your tennents, and your own reputation shall be thereby diminished. It is also requisite that yow learne to speak the vulgar langage of the countrey that yow may trulie understand and uprightlie judge the complaints of the poor ons. . . . Cherish your countreymen and train them up in all kynd of honest exercise, such as hunting, ryding, archerie, shooting with the gun, gofing, jumping, running, swimming and suck lyk. Eschew the footeball as a dangerous and unprofitable exercise."

Sir Robert's view about the Gaelic customs and language is made clear.[3] "Purge your countrey peice and peice from that uncivill kynd of cloithes, such as plaids, mantels, truses and blew bonnets. Make sewere acts against those that shall weare them. . . . The Ireishe langage cannot so soone be extinguished. To help this plant schooles in ewerie corner in the countrey to instruct the youth to speak Inglishe. Let your cheif scooles for learning be at Dornoche."

"Be careful," the admonition continues,[4] "(as I said) to enlarge and to mentayne the liberties of the town of Dornoch, because it holds of yourself. . . . Perswade the inhabitants of that towne to build wessels and shippes of ther owne to transport from thence such commodities as the countrey yeelds, and to bring thither from other parts such merchandise as is requisite for the weill of the countrey. Suffer as litle wyne and spyce to be brought hither as yow can, for that serwes lytle purpois, but to give occasion of drunknes and gluttonie. Erect it a brough (burgh) royall if yow can."

It is plain that Sir Robert envisaged a speedy victory for southern customs. "The first thing[5] I would wish yow to interpryse, when yow arr out of debt and your wedsetts reliwed, is to build a house in Dunrobin, for that is the werrie heart and centre

---

[1] Ibid., ii, p. 347. Cf. "Whatsoever yow purchase in Southerland or Strathnaver, let it still be for your eldest sone, because that Southerland is lytle anugh to mayntene his qualitie of ane earle", ibid., ii, p. 346.
[2] Ibid., ii, pp. 257 and 359.   [3] Ibid., ii, p. 359.
[4] Ibid., ii, p. 361.   [5] Ibid., ii, p. 363.

of your countrey, and the most plesant habitation yow hawe. Ther yow may easilie mak a fyne delicat park." It is explained that this feature should be laid out in the lands around the house of Dunrobin and should include the Gallowhill and both sides of Golspie burn. The building of a library at Dornoch is recommended[1] "boith for your credit and the weel of this countrey, to amend ther ignorance which increases through laik of bookes." The Earls of Sutherland must not break the links that had been forged with Edinburgh.[2] They should also travel through their outer lands to preserve the power of their House upon the borders.[3]

These lessons were absorbed with marked fidelity. The pull of the capital was henceforth strong. Political principles of a Protestant character, the standpoint which would later become Whig, were henceforth the hall-mark of Dunrobin. In 1639 the Earl of Sutherland rode to Beauly, which lay some fifty miles to the southward. He was about to embark upon a second marriage[4] with Lord Lovat's daughter. Here was another family which had come by different paths to the same cast of political conduct.

Just as their history was distinct, so, too, the Lords Lovat found a different sort of commentator. *The Chronicles of the Frasers* are written from a standpoint which has little in common with that of the author of *The Genealogy of the Earldom of Sutherland*. On the other hand Sir Robert Gordon's work is paralleled by Viscount Kingston's *Continuation of the History of the House of Seytoun*. These two writers have the pride of a cadet in the achievements of their family and also a pleasant carefulness wherever the honour

[1] *Ibid.*, ii, p. 365. The phrase used by Sir Robert Gordon "Cause erect a biblioteck in Dornoch" is an example of the French expressions which came to interlard his English writings.

[2] Cf. A letter from Sir Alexander Gordon of Navidale to Sir Robert Gordon dated at Dunrobin on 8 July 1636. The Earl, their nephew, is now in the hills hunting, Sir Alexander requires a suit of black figured silk and a taffeta cloak and as much scarlet or fine grey London cloth as is required to line it, and silver lace and buttons and material for a riding suit. The black figured silk is required for the wedding of the Master of Reay and was left with John Turour, tailor in Edinburgh and son-in-law to George Ker "who was our old man", document no. 166 printed in *The Sutherland Book*, vol. ii, pp. 168-9.

[3] Cf. A comment by Sir Robert Gordon in his letter of advice "Hunt oft in the Diriemoir and Durines, therby to keip yow in possession of hunting in these bounds seeing it is holden of yow, howsoever it is Macky his heritage", *ibid.*, ii, p. 364.

[4] In his youth the Earl of Sutherland had built up southern contacts. In 1624, by the advice of friends, he had settled at Leith "until he was acquainted with the air of Edinburgh where he remained two years". In February 1632 he married Lady Jean Drummond then living at Seton Palace, "the best marriage in Scotland then, either for meanes or friendship, or the person of the woman", Gordon, *op. cit.*, pp. 389 and 459. Jean (Drummond) Countess of Sutherland died at Edinburgh on 29 December 1639.

of their stock is concerned and an open dislike for their families'
enemies. Both men were educated in France and, although it is
difficult to be certain on this point, seem to have shared a religious
approach which was slightly ambiguous: they were probably political conformists to the King's religion.

Now that the consideration of his work has been completed, it
is worth attempting an impression of Sir Robert Gordon. In the
first place he was something of a courtier and rather more of a
placeman. He had held the post of gentleman of the privy chamber
to James I and had a reversion to the office of protonotary of the
common pleas. He interested himself in properties in Ireland and
later in Nova Scotia, while his marriage with a Gordon heiress
brought him estates in Scotland and in France. He became and
remained closely associated with the interests of the Dukes of
Lennox in both countries.[1] It was a great satisfaction for him
to be called to be Tutor of Sutherland. His writings evidence his
feelings for the wide sweep and far horizons of his ancestral
lands. Except where the Sinclairs were concerned, he had many
of the instincts of a mediator. He had deep admiration[2] for
Duplessis Mornay. The catalogue of his library[3] reveals his tastes.
In his later years he would sit in the parlour at Gordonstoun with
his "sasaphas" cup edged about the mouth with silver and his
tablemen of whalebone.[4] James Fraser of Phopachy was altogether
a simpler proposition.

[1] For references to this subject cf. Gordon, *op. cit.*, pp. 126, 128 and
The Sutherland Book, vol. ii, pp. 162–3.
[2] Sir Robert Gordon thus describes his visit to France in 1603. "He remained at Saumur fyve moneths, often frequenting the company of Philip
de Mornay, Lord of Plessis, Governor of that place, a learned and wyse
gentleman", *op. cit.*, p. 215. Sir Robert's connection with France ceased in
1620 when he sold his estate at Longmore to Walter Stewart "sone of
Antonie Stuart of Clerie", *ibid.*, p. 363.
[3] In 1816 a Catalogue was printed of the Library then at Gordonstoun
which had originally been formed between 1610 and 1650 by Sir Robert
Gordon. Making allowance for the possibility that certain early seventeenth
century books were added to the Library at a later date there is a considerable indication of Sir Robert's interests. The works listed include Arminius
de Predestinatione, Lugd. Bat. 1613, *Anatomie of Pope Joan*, London 1624,
Antonie de Guevara, *The Golden Book of Marcus Aurelius or Diall of
Princes*, translated by Sir Thomas North, London 1619, Jean Bodin *De la
République*, Paris 1583, Bishop Patrick Forbes *Eubulus or a Dialogue*,
Aberdeen 1627. Some books were printed in Edinburgh by J. Wrettoun.
These include James Acheson, *The Militarie Garden*, or *Instructions for all
Young Soldiers*, 1629, and Gordon of Lochinvar, *Encouragements for such
as have intention to be undertakes in the new plantation of Cape Briton,
now New Galloway in America*, 1625. The library also contained Sir W.
Alexander's *An Encouragement to Colonies*, London 1624, Robert Har-
court's *Relation of a Voyage to Guiane*, London 1609, and Higgersons'
New England's Plantation, London 1630.
[4] These objects are mentioned in Sir Robert Gordon's will dated 1 March
1656, and printed in *The Sutherland Book*, Charters, vol. iii, p. 200.

The history of the Frasers was composed by Master James Fraser, minister of the parish of Wardlaw, now Kirkhill, some ten miles to the west of Inverness on the southern shore of Beauly Firth. It is for this reason that the book is usually known as the Wardlaw manuscript. The author was born on 1 January 1634 at Phopachy while his father William Fraser was minister at Kilmorach. He had an intimate knowledge of the private background of the heads of the clan for his grandfather was major-domo[1] to successive Lords Lovat, and had acquired from his first master the lands of Phopachy in wadset[2] in 1599. James Fraser was educated at the grammar school at Inverness with the chief's son whose names he shared. Both boys boarded with the schoolmaster[3] James Robertson.

The book is marked by a veneration for the chief as such, and by a sense of Fraser solidarity. The fact that the author combined deep respect with dependent status is perhaps responsible for the lack of candour in his comment. A sub acid note is occasionally apparent. The description of Lord Lovat's various houses are marked by a lavish insistence on their grandeur. In this connection the *Chronicles of the Frasers* contains a recital of the gradual development of the great seats on the Lovat property. Beauly had been taken over at the Reformation and for the most part the castles were reconstructed in the later portion of the sixteenth century. An account[4] may be quoted of the situation at the time of the marriage of Lord Simon Fraser of Lovat with Kintail's daughter, Dame Katharin. "The wedding feast was held at Brean House. . . . In January (1590) he brought his lady home, a great infarr in the house of Beauly, where for building there was great accommodation, the forecourt surrounded with all needfull office houses, and the back court, with several "leach"[5] lodgings, especial the painted chamber called Shamerbrea, which was the priors prime lodging, a strong, curious, well contrived building with lofts and parlours." These were the traditional appurtenances of entertainment in the remoter parts of Scotland and of Ireland

This former monastic house was the centre of the family life, "the painted chamber" was the birthplace of the heirs.[6] Beauly had been the accustomed residence of their friend and adviser

[1] "The man of the house" equivalent to the master of the household.
[2] His grandson held this farm. He was wadsetter of Phopachy in 1660. the year before his call to Wardlaw and survived until 1709.
[3] *Chronicles of the Frasers* edited from the Wardlaw Manuscript by William Mackay, Scottish History Society, 1905, p. 258.
[4] *Ibid.*, p. 201.
[5] "laich", low.
[6] Thus Katharin Lady Lovat died in child bed in the "painted chamber" in the old Priory of Beauly called Chamber brea, *ibid.*, p. 219.

Bishop Reid. . . . James Fraser has a pleasant panel[1] of the ancient days. "Lord Alexander," he is here writing of Lord Simon's grandfather, "was a religious, pious youth. Robert Reid, Bishop of Orkney, was his great patron and tutor, they being related; the Bishop's mother being Rosse, and was commendatory of Kinlosse and Beauly, and tooke the whole guiding of Lord Alexander. . . . *Anno* 1550, the Bishop built the great house of Beuly and the new work at Kinloss, called the Queenes Lodging. His name and arms upon both, but no date. The Bishop had not his paralell amongst all churchmen for generosity and hospitality; he kept noblemens children with him for table and lodging, and, which was best, his conference and advice. The Lord Lovat, his brother William, Mackenzie (of Kintail), Foules, Ballnigown, Cromarty and the Shirref of Murray were all with him at once. He had his barge or pleasure boat to transport him twixt Beuly and Kinlosse". It is worth considering these passages for they throw a light on the background of the Lovat family. Bishop Reid created one aspect of their life. He was the last ecclesiastic to die in possession[2] of the priory of Beaulieu or Beauly.

The Frasers of Lovat were sufficiently remote to give a tranquil loyalty to the Crown of Scotland. Under James V they had been exemplary Catholics;[3] under James VI they gave a quiet adherence to the Reformation. They accepted the properties of Beauly without bitterness. They had no internal feuds; the headship passed from father to son without a break until the close of the seventeenth century.

When Katharin Lady Lovat[4] died, James VI offered to the widower the hand of his cousin Lady Jean Stewart.[5] The mention of this second marriage, which took place in 1596, is the occasion

---

[1] *Ibid.,* p. 141.

[2] The Bishop died in 1558 at Dieppe when returning from an embassy. Sir Robert Gordon has this comment on him. "Bishop Reid was a great favorer of Macky his house and familie", Gordon, *op. cit.,* p. 137.

[3] "The Lady Dowager, Janet Ross, lived in Kirktown of Farnuay, with her children, quher Lord Alexander had built her a good lodging, and settled her there near the Church of St. Corridon, and Father Thomson her priest and chaplin", *Chronicles of the Frasers,* p. 146. When Alexander Lord Lovat died in 1558, his son was at first brought up a Catholic. "Beuly, where he (the Tutor) had left young Lord Hugh, his brother's son with the monks, who had taught him his catechism, as well as his constructions and grammar," *ibid.,* p. 147.

[4] There is a comment on Lady Lovat's attitude to the Fraser country. "She (Lady Kathryn M'Kenzie) had so much respect to this country that she kept no servants about her but Frasers; she brought none home with her but a single maid, her own foster sister, Agnes Dinguall," *ibid.,* p. 217.

[5] In this connection James Fraser recounts a variant of the old story. "She (Lady Jean) said 'Sir, he is not bonny'. The King laughs heartily and told her, 'Jean, though Lord Simon be not bonny, yet Lovat and Beuly are bonny' ", *ibid.,* p. 223.

for a new account of the Fraser establishments.[1] Simon sixth Lord
Lovat survived through the reign of the old King and at the
accession of Charles I was a widower for the second time and
in treaty for a third alliance.[2] Politically his links were with the
former reign and his association with the House of Huntly; his
family were sent to Aberdeen for their education. Now he was
ageing, over-kind to both his later wives,[3] perhaps he was
uxorious. Among his sons his affections were concentrated on
Inveralochy. "Sir Simon of Inveralochy,"[4] writes James Fraser,
"came north with his lady and family in the close of 1619, and
lived with his father in Lovat, sometime at Beuly and for their
greater convenience and satisfaction all the three families lived
together, my Lord Lovat, the Master, and Inveralochy. . . . They
kept a happy harmony, especially the good ladyes among themselves with their sweet, pleasant children, and servants—Mr
John Spence, chaplain, David Carr, musician, James Fraser of
Phopachy, chief master household; John Burt, butler, Agnes
Ferguson, his wife, chief wardrop woman; all the servants,
Frasers." The last four words well indicate the point of loyalty.

A very pleasing touch describes Lord Lovat's preference for
his younger son. The chronicler mentions[5] "Lord Simon's extravagant provision for the heiress of his second marriage, with
Dame Jean Steward, giving Inveralochy an estate of eight or nine
thousand a yeare, which was more than the Earles of Caithness,
Sutherland or Seaforth benorth us ever did, nor the Earles of
Murray, Huntly or Marr besouth us reacht in the best of
times".

This list of the great lords in the north and north east of Scotland indicates the balance that was attributed to the Fraser
power, while another comment suggests their position on the very
edge of the settled lands. James Fraser is describing[6] the ill
results of old Lord Lovat's final marriage. "After his death a
burden of thirty yeares great jointur upon his estate, which to my

[1] "And the house of Beuly then was singular in the North for accommodation and stowing in its two courts, and indeed this Lord Simon was but too
prodigall in his expense over buildings; for he repared Beaufort and the
palace of Lovat, built a good stone house in Bunchrive, had a great manure
(manor) house at Inverness, and also built the Castell of Dalcross from the
foundation", *ibid.*, p. 245.
[2] "Lord Simon, *anno* 1624, about 54 years of his age, married Dame
Katherin Ross, Lady Moynes", *ibid.*, p. 248. *The Complete Peerage*, vol. viii.
states that he married probably in March 1627/8 Catherine widow of James
Grant of Logie and daughter of William Rose of Kilravock.
[3] The sixth Lord Lovat had likewise completed his education at King's
College, Aberdeen. He was head of his family from 1576 until 1633.
[4] *Chronicles of the Frasers*, p. 245.
[5] *Ibid.*, p. 253.
[6] *Ibid.*, p. 248.

certain knowledge was the marrow of his Low Country rent, the
barrony of Farnuay and Goine and Dinask."

In his account James Fraser shows a manifest prejudice in his
references to Jean Lady Lovat. It was, perhaps, an example of
jealousy arising between a steward and his employer's wife.[1] Should
that have been the case it would be a reflection of the grandfather's opinions. Sir Simon Fraser of Inveralochy died[2] before
his father, who was gradually failing through the early years of
the new King's reign. In the spring of 1632 he was confined to
the "stone house of Bunchrive". "At the same time," writes[3] the
chronicler, "Earl Collin of Seaforth lay under a consumption and
had ane doctor, John Philip of Dundee, attending him, whom
because of his singular love to Lord Simon he sent over to him,
being at Bunchrive, the onely dwelling and aire he loved best."
This help, however, was unavailing.[4]

His successor makes a faint impression.[5] One entry[6] strikes
a note characteristic of this period. "There is here one Thomas
Fraser, one of the house of Belladrum, gathering voluntyres up and
down this country (for the German wars)". A single personal
trait of Hugh Lord Lovat is recalled.[7] "So exact in genealogy
that he could give an account of the meanest tennants origin and
parentage once hearing his name, whether stranger or native, in
all his country." It is natural that throughout the Wardlaw manuscript wherever the Lovat chiefs are concerned the author is
critical only obliquely or by implication.[8]

[1] An example of the same process is the account in the *Lives of the
Berkeleys* by John Smyth of Nibley when he comes to his own times. In the
Chronicles of the Frasers Lady Katharine is described as "a woman of grace
and virtue, a woman of piety, humanity and affability". Lovat's second wife
is referred to as follows: "Dame Jean Stuart (had) six children. . . . There
were two abortions, for this lady turning gross and too fat (kindly to the
house of Doune) left off bearing too soon", *ibid.*, p. 225.

[2] "There was one doctor Lovell out of Perth attending him, who had his
feares of spells . . . this brave spirit was in and given over, put under a
milk dyet", *ibid.*, p. 246.

[3] *Ibid.*, pp. 251-2.

[4] At his burial there were present "six hundred Mackintosh, eight hundred
Grants, nine hundred Mackenzies, one thousand Rosses of Balnigown, one
thousand and more Frasers, Camerons, Macdonnels, Monros not under one
thousand".

[5] Hugh seventh Lord Lovat (died 1646) was the only son of Simon Lord
Lovat by his first wife Katharin McKenzie. "In 1615 the Master brought
home his lady Isabell Weemes", *ibid.*, p. 242. Their nine children included
Simon Master of Lovat born 1621, Anne Countess of Sutherland born 1619
and James born 1634, who was the chronicler's schoolfellow.

[6] *Ibid.*, pp. 255-6. Cf. Gordon, *op. cit., passim*.

[7] *Ibid.*, p. 309.

[8] Cf. "Lord Alexander Fraser of Lovat was a bookish man, and his seden-
tary life did him prejudice, nor would he willingly travel abroad, but when
great affairs oblidged him", *ibid.*, p. 143.

In effect the principal figure during these years[1] was the new chief's son the Master. He was sent to King's College Aberdeen and gained the silver arrow there in 1636. "He had one thousand[2] gentlemen of his name out of Marr and Buchan present." This youth had the power to arouse enthusiasm. "He (the Master) had a wonderfull fancy for musick. . . . The trumpet and great pipe, both most martiall, he would have a mornings, and vocal musick was his delight[3] of which he had enugh." It is interesting to note the contacts with the South as evidenced by the doctors summoned from Dundee and Perth.[4] There is an account of Bishop Guthrie's visitation.[5] In this connection the chronicler writing in the years after the Restoration shows a suitable respect for prelates of either Faith so long as they found favour with the House of Lovat. A period of study was prescribed for the young heir at St Andrews. "This winter," writes[6] James Fraser in regard to the events of 1637, "the Master of Lovat tooke another tour and progress south, stayed a quarter of a yeare in the University of St Andrews, in the Leonardin College, to try the different methods of learning there from Aberdeen, where he had spent his former course. In the spring he returned north, and passed another quarter at King's College, wuher, as he said, there was more profit to be hade, where he best liked the grain of the students and genuine temper of the masters".

The scene was now set for the opening of the conflict. A certain unity was given to all the country whose great figures have been discussed by the fact of the long spine of Gordon influence and in another sphere by the power of attraction which the Aberdeen colleges exercised. The matter of language, also, had its importance. The organisation of the whole region depended on the gradual extinction of the Gaelic. At the same time the wars on the Continent provided another unifying factor. The ports of the eastern seaboard facing towards Denmark and Germany were the clearing centres for those levies who passed across to

[1] Quite soon the seventh Lord Lovat is described as "tender and valetudinarian", *ibid.*, p. 304.

[2] *Ibid.*, p. 258.

[3] *Ibid.*, p. 265. There is also mention of the harp and virginals.

[4] This practice was an innovation. When the fourth Lord was dying in 1558 "that summer by the direction of his doctor, Tully Mullach (the Mull doctor of the Beaton family), he was transported to Isle of Agis, to a milk dyet and for a frye aire", *ibid.*, p. 146.

[5] "Anno 1634. . . . At this time the Bishop of Murray, Mr John Guthrey, kept on his circular visitations of every church within the diocese, came up al through all Strathspey, Badenoch, Stratharrick, to Cilchummen in Abertarfe through Glenmoriston in to Kilman St. Drostan in Urquhart and to Kiltarlety", *ibid.*, p. 256.

[6] *Ibid.*, p. 260.

serve the Swedish King. Thus another link was forged between
the eastern Lowland shires and the northern section of the East
coast. The use of Scots and English rather than Gaelic characterised the great body of the soldiers of fortune. There was a
tendency to separate from those who held to Gaelic customs and
to what most Scotsmen thought of as the "Irish" language.

In a different connection the advice given by the Tutor of
Sutherland to his young ward could have been reproduced by
many a prudent courtier in the south of Scotland who could call
on memories of France and England. It was for such reasons
that the great lords in the northern parts were unlikely to differ
from the men of their own rank in the Lowland counties. This
would become clear at the time when the question of the
National Covenant was first mooted. Apart from Huntly and Airlie
and his supporters whose views were formed after another
pattern, the same arguments would appeal in most of the chief
houses whose lands lay between Dunrobin and the Carse of
Gowrie. The two stocks which we have considered in some detail
were now allied and the reactions of the Earl of Sutherland and
those of his brother-in-law the Master of Lovat would prove
very similar when the Covenant was presented to them. Both these
young peers agreed to subscribe without hesitation. The Master
of Berriedale, who represented the aged Earl of Caithness, seems
to have held much the same opinions. Their grasp of their own
interests was unimpeded; the standpoint in religion not extreme;
their outlook on their sovereign very calm. These three lords,
and they were typical of many of their class, appear to have
regarded Charles I with an absence of either friendliness or hostility which was in itself somewhat remarkable. They carried few
prejudices into their examination of the political situation as that
developed. It was very different in that tangled country of
North West Scotland which was known to the privy council as
the Highlands and Islands.

CHAPTER XII

THE ISLANDS AND THE WEST

ANY detailed consideration of the Gaelic-speaking parts of north west Scotland should emphasise that this was a separate world which only emerged into the political developments of the time in so far as it acted on or was acted on by the forces connected with the Government at Edinburgh. James VI had indeed worked out at different times a fluctuating policy in regard to this whole region, but his son throughout the years of peace never seems to have given any serious thought to a country whose lords had never penetrated to his presence.

This was accounted for by the fact that in the country north of Argyll's castle at Inverary there was no peer[1] of parliament. Lovat had no counterpart on the western seaboard. No single house had risen to inherit the power of the Macdonalds, Lords of the Isles, which had foundered in the fifteenth century. Viewed from the angle of the sovereign there was no one with whom the royal power could negotiate. The sheriffdoms of Argyll and Inverness met on the shores of Loch Shiel between Moydart and Ardnamurchan. King Charles saw no counterpoise, and perhaps no true counterpoise existed, to the rival ambitions of Huntly and Argyll. North of Moydart with their power centering on Kintail the Mackenzies[2] looked eastwards and southwards. They were linked with Grants and Frasers; the mother of the second Earl of Seaforth was a daughter of Sir Gilbert Ogilvie of Powrie in Forfarshire. At their own level they had Court connections which became apparent when Kintail obtained the island of Lewis from the McLeods after the brief episode of the "undertakers"

---

[1] The only exception was the holder of the new earldom of Seaforth at Brahan Castle.
[2] Sir Robert Gordon gives his version of their history. "From the ruines of the family of Clandonald, and some of the neighbouring Hylanders, and also by ther owne vertue, the surname of the Clankeinzies, from small beginnings, began to floorish in these bounds; and by the friendship and favor of the House of Sutherland . . . ther estate afterwards came to great height, yea above divers of ther more auncient nighbours. The cheiff and head of the familie at this day is Colin Mackinzie, Lord of Kintayle, now created Earle of Seaforth. He hath mareid Lady Margaret Seaton, daughter to Alexander Earle of Dunfermling, lord chancellor of Scotland; a wyse and verteous lady", Gordon, *op. cit.,* pp. 175-6.

from Fife, who had been encouraged in a project of colonisation.[1]

It is worth dwelling for a moment on this matter because it throws a light on the attitude of the Stuart Kings towards these regions. James VI had a didactic imagination which could not mask a lack of concern for those whose values did not include the royal conceptions of order, peace and industry. He was very consciously a modern prince as that term was understood in the great Courts on the Continent. The same mind lay behind the abortive plantation of Lewis and the singularly enduring plantation of Ulster.

The Lewis project dated back to 1597 and the second and final attempt was only liquidated in 1609. The second Duke of Lennox was the nominal leader of the enterprise which was carried out by a group of lairds from Fife. Lennox was given the title of lieutenant and to that extent the new stewartry derogated from the powers already possessed by Huntly. The foundation of Royal burghs not only at Stornoway but also in Lochaber was authorised by Parliament. All the privileges of a free baronry were conferred upon the settlers.[2] The King agreed to erect six parish, churches whose patronage would belong to the adventurers.

A significant aspect of the matter is the King's readiness to regard the outer parts of his own realms as suitable for colonization from Southern Scotland. He had no sympathy for old-fashioned systems. In consequence he was hardly more concerned to preserve McLeod of Lewis than he was to rebuild the shattered power of O'Donnell or O'Neill. In both cases he desired to rebuild the social fabric on new foundations. Here, too, there emerges the King's attitude towards the religious factor. In each instance James VI was ready to assist a Presbyterian development among a population which had been rooted in the Ancient Faith. It is reasonable to suppose that he considered that it was healthy that the leaders of the Kirk should concentrate attention on missionary enterprise rather than on problems at the seat of Government.

Thus, in spite of the failure of the Fife undertakers, James VI

---

[1] Cf. Sir Robert Gordon's account of this episode. "In this mean tyme, the barrons and gentlemen of Fyff . . . were intysed, by the persuasion of some that had been ther, and by report of the fertilitie of the island (of Lewis), to undertak a difficile and hard interpryse; and vnder pretence of civilizing the inhabitants of the yle, they goe about to plant a colonie ther, and to dryve away the auncient inhabitants", *ibid.*, p. 270.

[2] These included rights of pit and gallows, powers to erect burghs of barony, appoint ballies, hold markets and fairs and establish free ports and havens. There is an interesting discussion of this subject in *The Loyal Clans* by Audrey Cunningham, pp. 171-80.

was in part responsible for the tendency which would in time result in a Presbyterian hegemony in the Northern Hebrides. As a result in the years to come the large islands under Mackenzie domination[1] were immune from the Catholic and indeed "Irish" sympathies which survived among those who had inherited the fragments of Macdonald power.

Farther south there had been the perennial conflict between Macdonald and McLean. One passage from *The Genealogy of the Earls of Sutherland* gives an accurate impression of the nature and the scope of such a struggle. "This yeir of God 1598," writes[2] Sir Robert Gordon, "Sir Laghlane Macklain wes slain in the ile of Ila (Islay) by his owne sister-sone, Sir James Mackdonald, the eldest sone of Angus Mackdonald of Kintyre; all of which proceeded from ambition and revenge . . . In end Sir James, haveing gottin first the possession of that hill (of Gruinart), he repulsed the enemies vanguard, and forceing their main battell, he quyte overthrew them. Macklain was their slain, with fourscore of the cheiff men of his kin, and tuo hundred commoun souldiers lying deid about him." These actual figures are derived from hearsay, but they serve to suggest the degree to which these conflicts were maintained by those who were akin to the leading family, eighty men of the stock of McLean of Duart. They also indicate a state of internecine feud which would enable the enemies of the Clan Gregor to compass their destruction and likewise make practicable the frontal attack that the Campbells launched against the Macdonalds in Kintyre.

At the Privy Council in Edinburgh and at the English Court only one group could give expression to coherent policy. The King might in some respects be unfavourable to aspects of that pressure for expansion which lay behind each movement of the Campbells and which was also the intermittent policy of the sated Gordons. The point made is that their action, together with that of the Mackenzies, was entirely comprehensible. They, and

[1] Sir Robert Gordon has a comment on this matter. "The Lord Kintayle (yit hunting after the Lewes) did privatlie and vnderhand assist Neill Macloyd, and sent his brother Rorie Mackenzie, oppinlie with some men to aid the vndertakers by vertue of the king's commission. He promised great friendship to the adventurers, and sent vnto them a supplie of victualls in a ship from Rosse. . . . In the mean tyme he sendeth quietlie to Neill Macloyd, desireing him to take the ship by the way, that the adventurers trusting to these victualls and being disappoynted, might therby be constrained to abandin the iland, which fell out accordinglie. . . . Then did the Lord of Balmerinoch, Sir George Hay and Sir James Spence (the Fife undertakers) begin to weary of the Lewes, and sold their right and title to the Lord of Kintayle, for a sum of money. . . . The Lord of Kintayle was exceeding glaid that he had now at last catched his long-wished and expected prey", *op. cit.,* pp. 274-5.
[2] *Ibid.,* pp. 237-8.

in particular the Campbells and Mackenzies, employed Edinburgh lawyers. Alone of the great chiefs in the North West the Earls of Argyll could support an array of massive precedent by lucid modern argument. Under James VI, in particular, capacity to employ the contemporary idiom was vital. It is not surprising that they were feared.

Amid the confused efforts of impoverished clans which marked the later part of the reign of James VI and the first years of his son the single constant factor was the Campbell policy. The House of Argyll caused the union of their opponents by their own resolute aggression; thus they would provide Montrose with his support[1] in the Western Highlands.

In the Macdonald country we can discern a way of life which would remain unchanged till after the tragic days of the Massacre of Glencoe. An account[2] of a feud between McLean of Duart and the Macdonalds has just this quality; the arrival of McLean at Mullintrea in Islay with "four score and six of his kinsfolk and servants"; the whole day passed in sumptuous banqueting; McLean lodged "in a long house that was somewhat distant from the other houses" with his nephew and pledge James Macdonald in bed with him from "whome he never pairted"; the three hundred Macdonalds around the house in the silence of night; Angus Macdonald coming and calling upon "Macklain at the dore, offering him his reposing drink". In London this familiar pattern meant nothing.

It is not surprising that the weakened hold of the Macdonalds in Islay and Kintyre could not be maintained against a calculating adversary. Still, the position should not be over-simplified. King James had no desire for the extension of the Campbell power, but he could not provide a practicable alternative which would at once satisfy his own notions and be capable of adoption by the clans in their actual situation. Argyll had an understanding of the Gaelic world, to which he in part belonged, that was denied to any Lowland Scot. He thus emerged in time as the inevitable intermediary.

The terms "feudal" and "patriarchal" when used in relation to the Highlands are neither entirely satisfactory, nor was the position in any way static. New forms were gradually developing although they could not focus in a single great authority as a result of the vacuum created by the fragmentation of the Macdonald

---

[1] Lord Tweedsmuir puts this accurately. "The middle Highlands, for the first time since Harlaw, were united, but it was not in the king's cause. The hatred of every clansman was directed . . . at the house of Diarmaid", *Montrose*, p. 211.

[2] Gordon, *op. cit.*, p. 189.

power. The principle of individual ownership was growing steadily and was coming to replace the practice of common rights in the use of land, although the latter survived in the persistent claim to "kindness", a term which implied security of tenure. Under the old Gaelic system rights to land depended upon personal status and in consequence unchallenged descent carried with it a title to property. Such a system was compromised by the introduction of "superiorities" which were jurisdictions on a feudal pattern. The practical consequences of this change cut deep into the social structure. The marriage of an heiress belonged to the superior as did the right to take possession of an estate held by a minor. Further, both rights could be granted by the superior to a third party if he did not choose to exercise them in person.

Relationships were frequently involved as in the case of the clan Cameron who held certain lands from Huntly and others from Argyll. The note of many tenures was their precarious character. Thus the Macdonalds of Kuppoch held land as the "kindly tenants" of Mackintosh. Behind most situations there lay very complex financial transactions. Dr Cunningham has analysed[1] the position with clarity. "Debts or financial difficulties of any kind were peculiarly dangerous, since capital could not be realised easily or credit obtained upon any reasonable terms. Recourse was had to a ruinous system of wadsetting lands, by which they were mortgaged to the lender, who received the rents paid in kind as interest." At such transactions the Campbells were past masters. "It was[2] by taking advantage of private feudal and financial rights, combined with a public judicial position, that Argyll ruined the Macleans and Glenorchy the Macgregors."

Mention should here be made of the Statutes of Icolmkill. These were the outcome of a project formed by James VI in 1608 for a new pacification of the Western Isles to be carried out jointly by Lord Ochiltree and Andrew Knox, who had been appointed to the revived bishopric[3] of the Isles in 1606. Ochiltree opened a court at Aros in Mull and Bishop Knox summoned a meeting at Iona in the following year where nine considerable

[1] Cunnningham, *op. cit.,* p. 21.
[2] *Ibid.,* p. 21.
[3] In 1573 John Campbell, Prior of Ardchatton, had been provided to this diocese becoming administrator of the temporalities in the same year. Andrew Knox, the son of John Knox of Ranfurly, was a man of position who had become minister of the Abbey Church of Paisley in 1585 at the age of twenty-six. He became constant moderator of the presbytery of the Isles in 1607. In 1619 he resigned the bishopric of the Isles to his eldest son Thomas Knox, then minister of Sorabie in Tiree and Dean of the Isles, who died in possession of the see in 1628.

chiefs gave their consent to the statutes. The original project combined the idea of settlement with the maintenance of existing rights of possession and a reduction of the area of land held by the clans in order to make room for the settlers. The actual statutes, which to a great extent remained a dead letter, were mainly of interest in that they did nothing to undermine the authority of the chiefs over their people.

A band was annexed to the statutes and contained an interesting declaration of political faith. "We and everie ane of us," it runs,[1] "protestis in the sicht of the evirliving God that we acknowledge and reverence our soverane Lord his sacred Majestie allanerlie supreame judge under the Eternall God in all causis and above all personis, both spirituall and temporall, avowing our loyaltie and obedience to his Heynes onlie." The declaration then concludes with a passage which suggests certain reflections on the position of the bishop and on the religious temper of the period. The signatories declare that they make this protest "conforme to his Majestis most lovable Act of Supremacie, quhilk we imbrace and subscryves unto in our hairtis". The chiefs who included three Macdonalds, Angus of Dunyveg, Sleat and Clanranald, and three Macleans, Duart, Coll and Lochbuy, agreed to submit themselves to the discipline of the Church of Scotland.

As far as the King was concerned these measures reflect the policy of his later years when the resources of the English Crown were at his disposal and he had come to use bishops as administrative officers, as had been for so long the custom on the Continent. It seems probable that the bishop enjoyed a certain inherent authority provided always that he was not himself a Campbell.[2] There was, perhaps, a certain vagueness as to the prelate's standing. The Scottish had never suffered from that excommunication which had made the attitude of the Papacy towards Elizabeth I so plain to every Catholic. It is, however, worth noting that the further islands were not represented. McNeill of Barra, who was a tenant of McLean of Duart, was absent.

Conservative by instinct and attached to their own traditions the Band of Icolmkill was a statement of fidelity. It was an assurance of loyalty to the sovereign in whom they placed such hopes as they could muster. It did not mean that the Macdonalds were

---

[1] *Register of the Privy Council of Scotland*, vol. ix, p. 25.
[2] Thus Neil Campbell had been provided to the bishopric of the Isles in 1580 when minister of Kilmartin. On his resignation in 1608 he was succeeded by his son John who died in January 1613. His younger son Neil Campbell became Bishop of the Isles in 1634 when minister of Glassary. He was deposed in 1638, *Handbook of British Chronology*, pp. 216, 229. The brief notice of the elder Bishop Neil Campbell in the *D.N.B.*, viii, p. 389 contains inaccuracies.

unwilling to receive emissaries from their kinsmen when these should come. This introduces another consideration. Opposition to the Macdonalds was one among several reasons which would lead the Campbells to foster a Protestant development. As the Minutes of the Synod of Argyll make very plain it was in their interest to plan new kirks. They must endeavour to thwart communications between the two branches of the rival house.

It is interesting to note that the area in western Scotland where the latent Catholicism was revived lay precisely in the lands of the northern Macdonalds and of those clans who were their friends. The new missionaries came north by the outer passage, Islay, Colonsay, Barra, South Uist.

It is very difficult to form an exact estimate of the situation at the time of their arrival and it is probable that materials do not now exist for the reconstruction of the religious life of north western Scotland during the two generations that followed the breach with Rome. It seems likely that burials were conducted where possible by the surviving priests and according to the Catholic rites, but very little evidence has so far come to light to prove or to disprove this contention. The matter could only be examined in the light of an exhaustive study of the religious facilities provided for the people of the Highlands and Islands at the eve of the Reformation.

Valuable fresh detail in regard to the actual coming of the missionaries is provided in the notes and comments published recently[1] by Fr Cathaldus Gibbin, O.F.M. The material used consists of documents preserved in the archives of the Sacred Congregation *de Propaganda Fide*. The reports appear balanced and worthy of credit. It is explained that after protracted negotiations it had been decided to send four Irish Franciscans into Scotland and that the Nuncio in the Spanish Netherlands had been instructed to treat of this affair[2] with the General of the Observants. It would seem that the area to which they would be sent was defined by the fact that they were Gaelic-speaking.

The first reports were those from Fr Cornelius Ward who described his cordial reception by Iain Muidertach the young

[1] *The Franciscan College Annual,* 1952, pp. 7-24.
[2] On 29 November Fr Patrick Anderson had written to Pope Paul V that the northern part of Scotland and those islands adjacent to Ireland had hardly ever seen a priest since the beginning of the so-called Reformation, Vat. Lib., *Barb. lat.* 6805, f. 153 v. He favoured sending Irish Franciscans as did the successive nuncios at Brussels, Guido Bentivoglio, Ascanio Gesualdo, and Lucio Morra. The last-named obtained a favourable response from St. Anthony's College, Louvain and two Irish priests Fr Edmund Cana and Patrick Brady and one Scottish lay-brother John Stuart set out from Louvain on 4 January 1619. Florence Conry, Archbishop of Tuam and at that time in the Netherlands gave his support to the project, *ibid.,* pp. 9-11.

chief of the Clanranald branch of the Macdonalds. He arrived in
1624[1] and some of his actions throw light on the situation at the
time of his coming. Thus Fr Ward asked for faculties[2] to regularise
the marriage of Clanranald's uncle Ranald Macdonald of Benbecula since the parties were within the prohibited degrees. He
likewise sought for permission to re-consecrate the church in
Benbecula which was then roofless. In the following year he reconciled the whole population of Colonsay[3] and it is noted that
the laird, Coll Ciotach Macdonald, was a Catholic before his
arrival. At about the same time the people of North Uist were
reconciled with the exception of fourteen persons who are
described as being for the most part members of the minister's
household.

In all these cases the term "reconciliation" seems to cover the
awakening of early teaching or ancestral training. Sir John Campbell of Calder was in a different situation for he had been Argyll's
agent in his long and successful struggle to obtain Islay for his
house. Perhaps he was influenced in making the change[4] by his
Macdonald wife or by the step that the seventh Earl of Argyll
had taken.

Fr Ward paid two visits to Barra, in 1625 and 1626, and is said
to have reconciled two hundred and eighteen persons. It is significant that the statue of St Barr was still in its place in the roofless chapel dedicated to that saint at the north end of the island.
The fact that as late as 1593 Barramen were in the habit of going
on pilgrimage to Cruach Phadruig[5] in Mayo suggests the con-
tinuity of the Catholic life on the island.

Taking a general view of the facts, Clanranald appears as the
principal friend of successive Irish Franciscans. His men were
responsible for the rescue of Fr Hegarty when he was captured[6]

---

[1] Fr Cornelius Ward, Fr Patrick Hegarty, Fr Edmund Cana and Fr Paul
O'Neill reached Scotland in the same year.

[2] These matters are discussed in *The Innes Review,* vol. iv, pp. 43-8.

[3] The report for 1625 referring to work in Islay and Colonsay forms part
of *Scritture Riferite nei Congressi dal 1623 al 1700 Scozia,* I, ff. 1r-23v.,
printed by Fr Cathaldus Giblin, O.F.M. in *The Innes Review,* vol. v,
pp. 39-73.

[4] It is stated that Fr Ward obtained access to Sir John Campbell in 1624
presenting himself as an Irish poet. On 17 February 1631 a charge was preferred against Sir John Campbell of Calder, knight, and others, all Papists,
of breaking up the drawbridge of the place or fortalice of Caddell, making
new locks and keys and keeping the house to resettle Jesuits, seminaries and
"mass priests". Sir John had made "shamefull apostacie and defectioun from
the trew religioun", *Register of the Privy Council of Scotland,* iv, p. 147.

[5] For a discussion of this matter and of disputed points in the McNeill
genealogy cf. "The McNeils of Barra and the Irish Franciscans" by John L.
Campbell, *The Innes Review,* vol. v, pp. 33-8.

[6] *Register of the Privy Council of Scotland.*

in 1631. Naturally the use of the convent of Bunamargy[1] as the house from which priests were despatched would emphasize the links that bound together both branches of the Macdonalds. At a later date the Catholic sympathies of the stock played a part in the projects which the Marquis of Antrim pressed on his sovereign.

In one respect the Catholic life in the Isles and in Knoydart and Morar was different from that in the rest of the country; while the congregations in the Lowlands were declining and those in Banff and Aberdeenshire at best static those in the West were tending to strengthen and consolidate. In this first generation of the missionaries only the foundations were being laid. It was, perhaps, an evidence of the interest shown by Propaganda that the first figures produced from western Scotland should have been queried.[2]

The reports to Rome show signs of tension[3] between the Capuchins and Jesuits. A curious episode in these years was the project for the restoration of the bishopric of the Isles. Bonaventure Magennis, Bishop of Down and Connor and a Franciscan appears to have been the driving force on the ecclesiastical side. Fr Ward had brought up this matter[4] in 1634, and Fr Patrick Hegarty seems to have been the candidate principally favoured. It is interesting to note that both Lord Antrim and Fr Hugh Sempill, S.J., Rector of the Scots College at Madrid supported[5]

[1] This house had been founded about 1500 as a friary for members of the Third Order of St Francis. It was given to the Franciscan missionaries by Propaganda on 1 June 1626, *Annales Minorum*, xxvi, p. 450. It is described as being four or five hours rowing from the shelter of the Scottish islands. In a report from Patrick Hegarty dated December 1640 it was stated that during each of the eight previous years five hundred from the Isles of Scotland had presented themselves at Bunamargy seeking spiritual assistance, Propaganda Archives, *Scritture Rif. nell Congreg. Generali*, vol. 285, f. 88v. For the history of this house cf. "The Ancient Franciscan Friary of Bin-na-Margie, Ballycastle" by F. J. Biggar printed as a supplement to *The Ulster Journal of Archaeology*, vol. ii, 1896-7.
[2] The difficulty probably arose as a result of the confusion between actual conversions and the large mass ready to acknowledge that they were Catholics at the bidding of their chiefs. A letter sent to Fr Hugh McCaughwell on 1 July 1626 stated that the first four missionaries had received six thousand persons into the Catholic Church and that three times that number could have been converted if it had been possible to attend to all those who presented themselves for instruction, *Archivium Hibernicum*, xii (1946), pp. 115-21. On 16 April 1627 the Congregation was informed that the converts made by the Irish Franciscans on the Scottish mission numbered ten thousand. The accuracy of this statement was queried at Propaganda, cf. notes and documents printed by Fr Cathaldus Giblin, O.F.M., in *The Innes Review*, vol. v, p. 46.
[3] Cf. reports of Fr Richard and Fr Anselm dated 1636 and mentioned *ibid.*, p. 52.
[4] *Annales Minorum*, xxviii, p. 174.
[5] Cf. documentation in *The Franciscan College Annual*, 1952, p. 21.

this choice. It is possible that the Irish exiles in Spain may have made some move[1] in this question. The project was discussed at Propaganda late in 1640, but Bishop Magennis had died in the previous April. Political developments in Ireland and Scotland rendered any such move impracticable. This plan has not yet been set in a political framework. It may well have been bound up with the recovery of Macdonald power as envisaged by the Marquis of Antrim and his supporters. In the years under consideration the work of the priests centred on Bunamargy was essentially a mission from Ireland to the Gaelic-speaking islands and the adjacent shore.

A certain weakness of character and uncertainty in action masked the dynastic element which seems to have lain behind Antrim's ambitions. His life is poorly documented and his political action is often considered in the light of King Charles's friendship for his wife Katherine Duchess of Buckingham. There is no doubt that the King was very ready to grant courtesies and favours to his friend's widow and that Wentworth, as lord deputy, was often exacerbated by the use that Antrim made of this approach. The Duchess, who had conformed to the Church of England during the period of her first marriage, had later returned to Catholicism and this factor made both husband and wife objects of suspicion to the House of Commons. At the same time behind the jealousy of Wentworth and a certain desire to gain influence with the sovereign it is possible to detect an intention to rebuild once more the ancient power of the Macdonalds. The plantation of Ulster was seen as inimical to such development on both political and economic grounds and this applied to every other cause which Argyll sponsored. Ineffective as their action would prove in fact, it is easy to understand the fear that the McDonnells at Dunluce would inspire when the scene in the north west of Scotland was examined by the leading ministers of the Kirk.

The regional survey of Scotland has now been completed and we turn to two elements in the general scene which had a bearing on the development of events, the effect of contact with France and the degree to which Catholicism survived as a force in the Lowlands.

[1] In this connection two of the Irish Franciscans from St Anthony's at Louvain served as chaplains to the Irish soldiers embodied in the Spanish forces in the Netherlands, *ibid.*, p. 11.

CHAPTER XIII

THE FRENCH INFLUENCE

ALTHOUGH the intimate links and constant contact between France and Scotland had never been interrupted, it is evident that they had been greatly strengthened by the bond of the Reformed Religion. For centuries Scotland had never been attacked except by England and in consequence France was always looked on as friendly soil. Before the Reformation the contacts had been made with the general currents of French life and then for a time, when opinion had not yet crystallised, it was rather a question of association with the universities and with the *politiques*. Finally there had developed an earnest and brotherly relationship with the men of substance and position who adhered to the *Eglise Reformée*. The plea that the Kings of Scotland and Navarre were at one in their religious outlook could be phrased acceptably by the princes of the House of Bourbon. Two letters addressed to James VI, the first by the Prince of Condé and the second by Henry IV bring this out clearly. "A quoy je me sents," wrote[1] Condé, "d'autant plus obligé quant plus je recognois outre vostre dignité royalle et les rares et heroiques vertuz qui si clairement reluisent en vous, la piété et la réligion, dont par la grace de Dieu nous faisons une mesme profession." The young King was only twenty-one and such praise meant much to him. All his life he was rather pathetically to over-value praise from an equal; he had so few. "Combien il importe," wrote[2] the King of Navarre at about the same period, "que les princes de la Chrestienté soient unis ensemble, et qu'ils cognoissent les artifices de noz auversaires."

The Scots understood exactly what was implied by "L'auance-ment de la vraye religion".[3] In fact the expression "the religion"[4] was accepted at once in Scotland. It may seem strange that the sympathy for France does not appear to have been diminished

[1] Letter from Henri Prince de Condé dated 28 June 1587 and printed in Fraser *Memorials of the Earls of Haddington,* ii, p. 41.
[2] This forms the final section of a letter praising Sir James Colville of Easter Wemyss and apparently dated about 1588, ii, pp. 42-3.
[3] This phrase occurs in a letter from Henry IV to James dated 3 January. It probably belongs to the year 1587 and is printed, *ibid.,* ii, p. 39.
[4] A letter from Archbishop Spottiswoode to the Earl of Haddington dated 7 October 1629 relates to measures to be taken against the Marquis of Huntly. "Another (letter) wes to myself, for enjoyning him to retain none in his family but those of the religion", *ibid.,* ii, p. 162.

when the King of Navarre submitted to the Church of Rome. Two factors may serve as an explanation. In the first place the principal personal influence on the Scottish travellers was that exercised by Duplessis-Mornay, who was at the same time a patron of the Scottish ministers and a guide to the Scotsmen of fashion. At Saumur, established in his own governorship, he could explain the necessity for tolerating the line of action which his sovereign had felt bound to follow to unite the nation. At the same time the stream of Scottish travellers was henceforward canalised on Paris and on those towns where the Huguenots had secured for themselves a solidly entrenched position.

The long association of Scottish scholars with the French universities and the teaching posts that they were accustomed to hold made it natural to introduce them into the new Calvinist colleges. Robert Wodrow has a comment on this subject in his collections for the life of Robert Boyd of Trochrig.[1] "And I observe at this time that most of the professors, in the accademies at Saumure, Montalban, Sedan and Lescar, were Scotsmen, and I recon it was so in severall other Protestant academies . . . in France." The case of Robert Boyd provides an example of the influence of one Scottish teacher. Having held a pastorate at Verteuil he was elected to a chair at Saumur[2] in 1606 at the age of twenty-eight. He stayed there until 1614, when he left to return to Scotland as principal of Glasgow University. During these eight years Monsieur de Trochorige,[3] as Boyd was always described, was a pervasive personality in the life of Saumur. His Lamentation on the death of Mornay's son[4] had been much admired and he was

[1] *Collections upon the Lives of the Reformers and most eminent Ministers of the Church of Scotland* by the Rev. Robert Wodrow, Minister at Eastwood, Maitland Club, 1844, vol. ii, p. 27.

[2] His movements are interesting. Boyd arrived in Dieppe on 7 May 1597 after a voyage from Scotland lasting seven days. From Dieppe he went by way of Orleans and Chatellerault to Poitiers "wher I found Messrs Dunbar and Legat". At Thouars he worked under Dr Rivet instructing "certain noble youths in a school lately founded at the charge of the noble Duke De Tremouille". He was five years in the "town and Accademy of Montauben". *Memoyers et Observations Journalières* by Robert Boyd quoted in Wodrow, *op. cit.,* ii, pp. 12, 13, 16.

[3] Trochorige or Trocherige. Scotsmen in France wisely used the *particule nobiliaire* when they were entitled to it.

[4] The Lamentation on the death "before Guelders of Monsieur de Bauves, the only son of Monsieur Du Plessis" was composed about the time of Boyd's arrival. "I see," writes Wodrow, "the designe of bringing Mr Boyd to be minister and professor of divinity at Saumur was laid summer or harvest 1605—that Monsieur Du Plessis has been very earnest in this matter, and Monsieur Montmartin (Minister at La Rochelle) very active. He argues the long desolation of Saumur, the great confluence of students that would come, Sedan being on the matter blocked up", Wodrow, *op. cit.,* ii, p. 39. In Boyd's Journal, "Memorandum that I came to Saumure, Aprile 19, 1606, with Monsr. Pinald", printed, *ibid.,* p. 39.

asked to compose the Latin address of welcome for the Prince
of Anhalt's visit[1] in 1609. Two notes, both dating from the latter
part of that same year,[2] indicate how closely Boyd and other
Scotsmen were concerned in each detail of the management of
the college. "Upon October 14 (1609), present in the council of
the Academy conveened in the consistory chamber, Monsieurs
Bouchereau, Du Gautmont, Craig, Duncan, Du Bignon and
Trochorige, Monsieur Benoist, Professor of Greek, was received
as a member of our body and society after he had solemnly declared his readynes willingly to subscribe the Confession of Faith
and discipline of the churches of France." The second reference
is to a reunion some two months later. "Upon Monday, December
7 1609 the councill meet in the high cabinet of the Governour,
Monsieur du Plessis, who was present with them . . . to make up
the difference betwixt Monsieur Benoist and Duncan about their
precedency."

During his stay in Saumur Boyd married Anne Maliverne and
there is an exact account[3] of his expenditure on this occasion and
also an interesting list of the books that he bought as a wedding
gift[4] for his young wife. In 1612 he invited to Saumur his cousin
Zachary Boyd, who remained in France until 1623 when he
returned home to become minister of the barony parish in
Glasgow. In 1623 Duplessis Mornay died and the Scottish connections with Saumur tended to languish, but throughout the reign
of James I it was a stage on the journey of most young Scotsmen
going to France for their education. At Saumur they were assured
of a welcome from their own countrymen.

An impression of such a journey having Saumur among its
objectives can be gained from the account of the travels of Henry
and Alexander Erskine the third and fourth sons of the seventh
Earl of Mar. They were children of that Countess of Mar who
became Sir Thomas Hope's supporter. For an understanding of
certain aspects of the journey it should be explained that the
family had a tangled religious history. The grandmother Anna-
bella Countess of Mar, the widow of the Regent, had been a

---

[1] *Ibid.*, p. 67. Boyd was in Scotland from August 1607 until June 1608,
ibid., p. 57.

[2] Printed *ibid.*, pp. 75, 76.

[3] The marriage took place in May 1611 and his wife's name is sometimes
given as Anne Maliverne a Vineola. His gifts included rings, rubies, diamonds
and a bracelet.

[4] "The Prayers of Merline: Questions for the Children of God by Tossin:
Monsr. du Plessis' Meditations: Monsr. Goulart Considerations. Two
volumes of the sermons of Beza, Sedan edition: on Christ's Passion: "His
Meditations on the seven Penitential Psalms." Also "The Funeralls of the
Daughters of Sodome", *ibid.*, p. 93.

determined Catholic,[1] but both her son and grandson were Presbyterians married to Catholic wives who had adopted the Reformed Faith after their marriage.[2] The mother of Henry and Alexander Erskine had been brought up at Aubigny in the strongly Catholic household of the old Duchess of Lennox; but Aubigny was also one of the six towns in Berri where a Calvinist place of worship was permitted under the general provisions of the Edict of Nantes.[3] With this inheritance the young men seem to have been brought up without fanaticism.

In the summer of 1617 Henry and Alexander Erskine, with their tutor John Schaw, had established themselves at Bourges, which apart from other advantages was convenient for visits of courtesy to their mother's family. Their grandmother the Duchess of Lennox was still alive. The correspondence with Lord Mar contains this note.[4] "On the 19 of June we took jurnay to Glatanny[5] to see our mother sister that is religiousse." Then they returned to Bourges and rejoined Lord Morton, who had been lodging in the same house as the Erskines throughout the summer. "We did feinde," explains[6] Henry Erskine, "the Leard of Pitmillie excidinge seik. . . . The xi of Julie Pitmillie randrit his spreit, quike wes no litle greife to us all. . . . My Lord Morton and all the rest of our contraymen convoied him to Santere,[7] ane toune of the religione, and ther interit his corpes."

A clear idea of the programme of Scottish travellers of standing is provided in a letter to Lord Mar from his son's tutor. The

[1] In an account of "certain greeves of the Generall Assemblie of Scotland assembled in Edinburgh, given in to His Majestie the 20th of February 1587" there occurs this passage. "The Ladie Mar interteaneth in the place of Areskin an excommunicated priest, called Sir Andrew Naismith, whose masse-cloths were once apprehended", Calderwood, *History*, vol. ii, p. 664. Lady Mar, who was described by Knox as "a verry Jesabell", died in 1603.

[2] The seventh Earl of Mar married Lady Marie Stuart as his second wife in 1592 and the eighth Earl married Lady Jean Hay in 1610. She was a Catholic and daughter of the Earl of Erroll. King James required before the marriage that "the young ladye do give full satisfactioun to the Churche therein, whatever can be of her justlye demandeit, for testimonye of her owne professioun", *Cal. Mar and Kellie MSS.*, p. 65.

[3] A Calvinist temple existed at Aubigny as early as 1552. The argument that Esmé Duke of Lennox was a strong supporter of Catholicism, who pretended to adopt Presbyterianism and maintained this fiction on his deathbed seems far-fetched. It appears more likely that he was a supporter of the Guise party for political reasons, but that as far as religion was concerned he was at heart indifferent or sceptical. He was brought up in a town and countryside with a mixed religious outlook.

[4] *Cal. Mar and Kellie MSS.*, Supplementary Report (1930), p. 78. In the same letter from Henry Erskine to his father there occurs this passage. "And out of that to Averry, quhar my goodame presently remeans", *ibid.*, p. 78. This presumably refers to a visit to the Duchess of Lennox at La Verrerie.

[5] Lady Gabrielle Stuart was at this time a nun at Glatigny in Berri.

[6] *Ibid.*, p. 78.

[7] Sancerre, one of the six Hugenot centres in Berri.

THE EARL OF DUNFERMLINE

first part relates to the journey of two lords who were half a generation older than the Erskines and were travelling for pleasure. Lord Angus belonged to the specifically Catholic grouping which will be considered later. "The Erle of Mortone," began[1] Schaw, "is still at Bourges, but he and the Erle of Angus hes concludit to begin their traveling upon the 4 of September. This is thair cours, from Burge to Lions, from that to Geneve, from Geneve back Lions, from thence to Marsail, from thence to Burdeas. Thairfra to the Rotchell, from that to the river of Loir till they cum to Orlians. Thairefter the Erle of Morton mynds to cum home be the Lou Countris, yea, it is in his mynd to go Count Pallatins court."

The programme contained the inevitable journey to Geneva which was included in the itinerary of nearly every Scottish traveller who penetrated as far as Eastern France. Apart from the natural appeal of this town to Presbyterians, it is likely that it was prudent for travellers who were suspected by the Kirk to make a visit there. It is possible that the tutor hoped that Lord Mar would include a visit to the King's daughter at Heidelberg in the Erskine itinerary. The passage along the "river of Loir" involved visits to Angers, Saumur, Tours and Blois on the way to Orleans. It will be seen that the Erskines proposed to make this journey in the reverse direction.

"As for your lordships sonnes," continued Schaw, "they mynd not to remove till after Mertimes (Martinmas), than they mynd to Orlians, whair haveing stayed ane month we mynd to go down Loir to Blois, to Tours, to Angers, and from thence to Somer (Saumur)." In December Henry Erskine wrote to his father from Saumur. The party had left Bourges without obtaining Lord Mar's permission and his son describes the disadvantages of remaining within a closed Scottish community.

"As conserning your Lordships direction," began[2] Henry Erskine, "quharby ye direke us not to remove from Bourges till your nixt advertisment, albeit that we had recevit it befor we came from Bourges, yit it wes ane thing that we could not have done, for if we had stayed still in Bourges we could not have lernit the Frence, in respek of the great number of Scotsmen that is there for the present, for we met every day together at our exercise, so that it was impossible for us not to speak Scotis. I confess that we have not the Laus teched us in this toune,[3] bot that is no great meater so that we be diligent uthervais."

[1] Letter dated 7 August 1617, *ibid.*, p. 79.
[2] Letter dated 22 December 1617, *ibid.*, pp. 81-2
[3] On the same day the tutor had written to Lord Mar that "they intended at Easter to go to Angers where Law was taught", *ibid.*, p. 82. The practice of

"I am persuadit," he goes on, "that your Lordship is resolvit to let us have ane seighte of France, so that the summer before we come home it vald be most convenient for us to traivell." He then explains the need for passing a winter in Paris so that the brothers could obtain that acquaintance with polite usage, and with the fashions in riding and in sword play, which was so essential. These matters came within the general term of "exercise". It was for these necessary "to come to Paris agene vinter (for your Lordship knaws we must be ane vinter seasone in Paris to steampe all our exercises), so your Lordship vald do weill to cast our daiet (diet) so that we be not in Paris in summer, for it is impossible to exercise, the weather is so heat".

The party remained at Saumur for rather over nine months. In April John Schaw wrote[1] to his employer describing the progress made by his charges. "Your Lordships sonnis had spend ane yeir in dansing, eight munths in fensing, that Allexander dansis verie properlie, he playis prettelie weill upon the lutt: Henrie gois farder beyond him in studie. As for the tennis, I did bargane with ane maister to lerne them so that they have also exercisit that pastym all this winter. Thair is verie litill tyme idillie spent." There is a special reference to Duplessis Mornay who furnished them with "letters of recommendation and address" when they left his town in September 1618. Henry Erskine wrote[2] to his father in regard to "Monsieur de Plessis Marlay, quha hes shawn us great courtessie heire, and I wald wise ane occasion quharby your Lordship micht give him thanks for his kindness".

An impression of a much longer course of education in France is provided by the memoirs of John second Earl of Perth, which were printed in the Spalding Club Miscellany. Internal evidence indicates that this account was composed after the destruction of the walls of La Rochelle as a result of the siege in 1628. It deals with the period between 1604 and 1610. John Drummond, who appears to have been travelling without either a guardian or a Scottish attendant, arrived in France when he was twenty years of age; the tone of the narrative is rather querulous.

visiting Saumur was of long standing. The papers of Sir Patrick Keith Murray at Ochtertyre included (in 1872) "The Compt off the Master of Marshallis (Marischal) expensis and his serwandis sen his arriving in Diep quhilk wes the xvi day off Junii till his arriving in Semour (Saumur) quhilk wes the vii day of Julii *anno* 1601 yearis". This account for travelling expenses on the journey from Dieppe to Saumur *via* Rouen, Paris, Orleans and Tours amounted to £216. A further sum of £404 was expended mainly on articles of dress for the Master and his servants, *H.M.C.*, Appendix to the third Report, p. 409.

[1] Letter dated 21 April 1618, *ibid.*, pp. 83-4.
[2] Letter dated 9 September 1618, *ibid.*, p. 87.

"Special care," the account begins,[1] "was taken of my elder brother James Master of Drummond his educatione, who proved thereafter a verie fine youth. He was sent to France in *anno* 1598, where hee was bred at schooles and learned his exercies. . . . Shortly after that he (now Earl of Perth) was married to Ladie Isabell Seaton, the Earl of Wintouns onlie daughter." After this excursus John Drummond turns to the description of his own upbringing.

"I was all this while but litle regarded, improvided by my father to anie considerable fortune, and sent to the school of Dunblain, wher I was but carelesslie looked to for the space of seven or eight years, my teachers being but ignorant persons, using their slavish discipline conforme to their own humors, teaching Ramus his grammar unprofitable. My second sister (Lady Fyvie) caused send for mee to Edinburgh, where I stayed almost the space of two years, and when King James was proclaimed King of England in the month of March 1603, the colledge was neglected. . . .

"At the end of this year I obtained leave to goe to France upon a verie meane allowance. My voiage by sea was both longsome and dangerous, being in the dead of winter. Our first landing from Leith was at Yarmouth, after five nights sailing. . . . Then after mooch labour and stormie agitations, wee arrived at the Isle of Rae, where I, with certain other passengers, quit our ship, and by boat came to Rochell, where, for the time they were building their onbrisst walls, which since have been ruined and the town sacked. From that place I went by water to a litle town called Royan, at the mouth of Garronne, and so up the river by boat to Bordeaux, where I rencontred with Monsieur Balfour, Principall of the Colledge, and a great mathematician, who used mee verie kindlie, and in many things, as it were, bare my charge. I remained with him three years and above."

Robert Balfour, whose life has not yet been studied in detail, had been a member of the teaching staff of the College de Guienne for more than twenty years.[2] Being a firm Catholic he was separated from the Scottish ministers at La Rochelle and St Jean d'Angély. It was probably his recommendation that led on to the next move. "Then," continues[3] Drummond, "I went to Toluse, a faire citie, and stayed in companie with Monsieur Cadan or

[1] A brief account of the life of John Earle of Perth, *Spalding Club Miscellany*, vol. ii, p. 393.
[2] Balfour had published his edition of Gelasius, the Greek text accompanied by a Latin translation, at Paris in 1599 and his *Cleomedis Meteora Graece et Latine* at Bordeaux in 1605.
[3] *Spalding Club Miscellany*, ii, pp. 394-5.

Kid, a learned doctor in the lawes, and with Monsieur Red,[1] a doctor in physics. At this time, almost for a year I frequented the publick lectures of the lawes, not understanding anie thing else, nor having anie friend who could informe me how the world went, so that I saw manie things, but observed litle, though I wes alwayes in good companie, though unfit for mannaging of affaires, as being meere schollers and careles of anie thing else. At lenth I went to Paris, where moir was to be seen than in all France else, by reason of the King and court abiding there, with all that great dependence."

It is evident that until he reached Paris Drummond had not followed the accustomed lines of foreign travel. However, immediately on arrival in the capital he made contact with his own countrymen. "Ravaillack," he remarks,[2] "killed his owne Soveraigne Prince in Paris the fourteenth May, 1610, where I was for the time with sundrie other gentlemen of our nation." He returned in the following August to England where his sister Lady Roxburghe was serving Queen Anne. In the winter of the next year his elder brother died of "a hecktick sicknes". Two notes[3] will conclude this brief impression. "The estate," wrote the new Earl of Perth in describing his inheritance, "was small, yet, by the help of friends and honest mannagerie, it proved better than was expected." He then describes his next experience in England. "Immediatelie after this, I went to court, and stayed ther seven or eight months, wher I encountred manie seeming friends. My sister was very kynde and beneficiall to me, so that my abode at Court cost mee litle or nothing to speak of." The next summer he married his sister's eldest step-daughter Lady Jean Kerr.

A postscript brings back Saumur. Lord Perth mentions[4] among the wedding guests his new brother-in-law "William Master of Roxburgh, a verie handsome and hopefull youth, who shortlie after went to France and died at Somer". The date of his death was early March 1617, the year before the Erskines reached Saumur. There was a constant stream of Scottish travellers.

In the provinces which stretched southwards from the Loire, where French Calvinism was still strong, there was a welcome not only for the traveller and for the minister in good standing, but also for those who had been compelled to leave Scotland

[1] James Kid, a native of Dundee, held the chair of Law at Toulouse where he died in 1612. The second reference is to Dr Reid.
[2] *Ibid.*, ii, p. 395.   [3] *Ibid.*, ii, pp. 395, 396.
[4] *Ibid.*, ii, p. 397. On the other hand it is stated that the Master of Roxburgh died at Bourges shortly before 9 March 1617 and was carried for burial to Saumur, *Cal. Mar and Kellie MSS.*, p. 76.

through the harshness of the times. Thus John Welch, minister at
Ayr and son-in-law to John Knox, was appointed as pastor of the
Protestant church at Nérac after his banishment in 1606. He
found a patron in Robert Boyd of Trochrig and soon there was
a question of his transfer either to Jonsac or to Châtellerault, the
fief owned by the House of Hamilton. "Thei," he wrote,[1] to
Monsieur de Trocherige of the Synod of Saintonge, "hes gevin me
purement et absolument to the Kirk of Jonsack, and wald nocht
geve aucht dayis to essay gif I culd get my contentment to remane
there. . . . Monsieur, gif these of Chattellerhaut demand me at the
General Assemble, and obtain my liberte for theme, assure theme,
gyf the Lord wil, that I sal nocht fail on my syde." Welch's
application for Châtellerault failed, but he soon transferred to
the pastorate of St Jean d'Angély, where he remained until 1621.
Young Scotsmen belonging to families of strict views were sent
out to complete their education under the exiled minister, the
Master of Ochiltree coming to him at Jonsac[2] and John Gordon
of Lochinvar staying for a considerable period in his house at
St Jean d'Angély.

In the Presbyterian world Duplessis-Mornay and the Duc de
Bouillon were regarded as the leading patrons. In Scotland these
were household names. They received a suitable recognition from
the ministers whom they protected.[3] Distinguished travellers sent
home news[4] of them. There was naturally a certain rivalry
between the colleges at Saumur and Sedan, but in Scottish Presbyterian circles the founders of both institutes were seen as bene-
factors. It was characteristic of this situation that when Andrew
Melville was banished from his own country he was offered a
chair of divinity at La Rochelle before he was invited by the
Duc de Bouillon.

There were concentrations of Scotsmen throughout the area
traditionally associated with the Huguenots. John Carnegie of
Ethie, later the first Earl of Northesk, wrote[5] from Paris to his
elder brother at Kinnaird that as soon as he could get company
he would take a journey to Poitiers "for be reason of the gryt
number of Scottis men I can do no guid here". The same young

[1] Letters of John Welch to Robert Boyd of Trochrig dated 1607-19, *Miscellany of the Wodrow Society*, ed. David Laing (1841), pp. 549-50.
[2] Cf. *ibid.*, p. 554.
[3] Letter from John Welch dated 9 June 1609, "Si vous plait de saluer Mr
de Plessis en mon nom, car je suis fort son serviteur", *ibid.*, p. 555.
[4] Letter from Henry Erskine to the Earl of Mar dated at Bourges 5 June
1617. "Al the Princes cam presentlij to Courte, excep Duke de Bullong
(Bouillon) for, as the bruitis he is exceedingly trublit with the goote in his
legs". *Cal. Mar and Kellie MSS.*, p. 77.
[5] Letter dated 3 January (1610) printed by William Fraser in *History of the
Carnegies Earls of Southesk*, 1867, vol. i, p. 342.

laird is found[1] consulting David Ramsay as to which clockmaker's
work was best worth the outlay of his silver. Just a quarter of a
century later David Lord Carnegie, who was Northesk's nephew,
was studying[2] in Paris in his turn.

The welcome accorded to Scotsmen of birth by their French
co-religionists is emphasized in a letter from Henry Montgomery
to his mother Lady Eglinton. "I have," he wrote[3] from Saumur in
the late autumn of 1632, "hade the fortoune heir wher I am to
falle in verei good companie, being heir tuo nepveuis of Monsieur
le Counte Montgomery, vith a grat maynei of other veil borin
genteilmen, all of them being of the religion." Two of Montgomery's brothers were travelling in France at this time and at
Caen there was the Master of Ross[4] and Alexander Jaffray the
diarist. The latter, who came of burgess stock from Aberdeen,
made the accustomed circuit,[5] Caen, Rouen, Paris and home by
Dieppe again. During the next year he returned and stayed for
more than five months in the Calvinist stronghold of Neuchâtel.[6]
These last journeys were characteristic of those made mainly
with a view to business. There were Catholic communities in
Paris and in the remoter provinces. The two Chisholms, uncle and
nephew, held for many years[7] the little diocese of Vaison near
Avignon in the Comtat Venaissin.

After Louis XIII reached his majority Scots ministers were no
longer welcome, but the French Court set a standard which most
young Scots lords would wish to emulate. France was a land of
promise to all Scotsmen who moved within the circle of government. Travel to Paris formed an almost essential element in the
training of a man of politeness and of affairs. There were very
few Scotsmen who did not look with friendship to one element or
other in the French economy. This applied equally to Calvinist
and to Catholic.

[1] *Ibid.,* i, p. 342.　　　　　　　　　　[2] *Ibid.,* i, p. 359.
[3] Letter dated 6 November 1632 printed by Fraser in *Memorials of the
Montgomeries,* i, p. 226.
[4] *Ibid.,* i, p. 229.
[5] *Diary of Alexander Jaffray,* ed. John Barclay, p. 44.
[6] *Ibid.,* p. 45.
[7] From 1570 until 1629.

CHAPTER XIV

LOWLAND CATHOLICISM

IT is unfortunate that apart from Bellesheim no historian has as
yet made a serious and constructive study of Catholicism in
Scotland in the two centuries that followed the Reformation. The
unbroken attachment to the Old Religion in the Gordon country
is copiously documented. On the other hand the situation in the
Western Highlands, as has been seen, is very hard to fathom in
the years between the proscription of the Catholic Faith and the
coming of the new missionaries in the middle years of the seventeenth century. In some ways it is surprising how Catholicism both
survived and re-emerged among the great families in the Lowlands whose estates were sometimes placed in the very heart of
the country most closely mastered by the Presbyterians. The
degree of their independent authority was often greater than that
of their English counterparts, but the final pressure brought to
bear on them was much more formidable. They had against them
the power of the Kirk and its unremitting hostility. Society in
Scotland was more egalitarian. The local Presbyterian minister
never showed that respectful kindness which at times could mark
the intercourse between the Anglican incumbent and the wealthy
Catholic squire. Naturally the heads of these Scottish stocks tended
to marry within their own politico-religious grouping and it was a
Maxwell marriage which strengthened the Catholicism of the
House of Winton. Yet the degree to which this same family was
harassed by the members of the Presbytery of Haddington had no
parallel in the southern kingdom. Deputations approached them
on many different aspects of their personal lives. In England
there was a privileged Catholic grouping which at least in the
reign of Charles I secured a measure of immunity. In Scotland
south of the Firth of Tay there was no such protection. The
families of the Auld Kirk were isolated in a world that was pre-
paring for the Solemn League and Covenant.

Besides, Scotland never passed through the experience of the
Henrican schism. After years of victorious Catholic government
the practice of that Faith was abolished suddenly. There was no
slow wearing away of men's allegiance. In cases like those of the

Maxwells[1] and the Setons, Catholic families who had always been attached to the Queen of Scots, the Old Religion was maintained from generation to generation. Similarly the "Church Papists" were a peculiarly English phenomenon. At the same time in Scotland the situation was confused by the presence of a defined adherence to Catholicism alongside what may be called a "Catholic interest" among the magnates; it is worth pausing to consider to what extent this latter attitude could be held to reflect a positive theological standpoint.

The religious history of the families of the Catholic lords can hardly be understood without a brief general survey of the "Catholic interest". It is worth noting that in its broadest sense, and for the two generations during which it lasted, this was a political approach. It was therefore independent of sacramental practice and could co-exist with a certain measure of attendance at the services of the Kirk when this was demanded. The life even of the more zealous members of a great Southern family of Catholic sympathies and attachments was often marked by long periods when the hearing of Mass had become impracticable. At the same time the stately funerals, where the display of heraldry was so important to the leading families, were conducted by the minister of the Kirk. It seems probable that the children were also christened by the local ministers. Among the lairds' families were those who were attached to the lords of the "Catholic interest" and shared their outlook and their general practice. Among the burgesses and the small landowners it is clear that there were instances of a simple and direct regret for Catholic times, but the whole subject awaits a detailed study. For various reasons we have more information about the peerage than about any other element of Scottish life.

During the reign of Elizabeth I lists had been compiled by that Queen's agents dividing the Scottish lords into groups described as Protestant, neutral or Catholic; but the last-named division, even if men were placed in it with accuracy, need not have implied more than a general conservative standpoint. Such an outlook often went with a desire for a Spanish alliance, but certain lords who had some contact with the "Catholic interest" were entirely French in their affiliations. All men with this cast of mind shared,

[1] Cf. A speech made to Hume of Godscroft by the ninth Earl of Angus in regard to his difficulties with the Master of Glamis. "Yes, what concurrence or assistance should I have? Or, of whose friendship could I assure myself? Maxwell, you know what his respects and what Religion he is of. I can never forget the Watch-word he gave at Fawkirk, whereby he did plainly professe his disposition to superstition, Saint Andrew was it", *A History of the Houses of Douglas and Angus* by Master David Hume of Godscroft, 1648, p. 424.

during the period before 1603, a distaste for any close contact with
the Queen of England or the policies which her supporters represented. The whole group adhered unquestioningly to James VI for
he was never harsh with them. In his eyes they had one clear
advantage; they were bound to be immune from any sympathy
with the Kirk leaders.

Various factors tended to reduce the possible significance of
this "Catholic interest". King James VI after attaining his
majority gradually formed a party or a group of his own supporters. He himself came to represent a general policy of authoritarian Conservatism, which chimed well with the conservative
aspirations of those who had once supported the Queen of Scots.
The King was himself concerned to protect his royal position
against the Kirk; he was very ready to convert the church and
abbey lands into hereditary baronies for those lay commendators
who had done him service. Towards the Scottish lords he was
always generous and unrevengeful.

It was a consequence of this policy that the "Catholic interest",
as such, was diminished and then finally eliminated. Thus the
first Earl of Dunfermline, who became lord chancellor, had been
brought up a Catholic and had studied[1] at Rome during the reign
of Gregory XIII. As a Seton he had been a traditional supporter
of the Queen of Scots; but, whatever his private attitude[2] on
religious questions, he did not belong to the "Catholic interest"
Dunfermline's policy seems to have been wholly identical[3] with
that of his sovereign.

[1] Cf. Lord Perth's comment. "Alexander Earl of Dunfermling . . . being
instructed with most vertuesm learned and heroick qualities, as having spent
a great part of his youth in the best tounes of Italie and France, where all
good literature was professed: A man most meek, just and wise, deserving
greater commendation than paper can containe", *A brief account of the life
of John Earle of Perth*, Spalding Club Miscellany, vol. ii, p. 396.

[2] Lord Dunfermline gave his brother's family the impression that he was
a secret Catholic, cf. Bellesheim *op. cit.*, His will contained a reference to a
portrait of the Virgin Mary in gold and among his books was a copy of
Discours Chretien de la Divinite by Pierre Charron printed at Paris in 1604.
In Fyvie church there is a communion cup inscribed "Deo Sacrisque in
Ecclesia Fyvaeana faciendis dicavit Alexander Setonius Fermelinoduni
Comes. An Salutis 1618". According to the minutes of the Synod of Fife the
Chancellor gave great offence to the whole country in 1612 having had a
crucifix painted upon his desk in the church of Dunfermline. There was little
trace of Catholicism in the families of his sons-in-law, the Earls of Lauderdale and Seaforth, Lords Fenton, Lindsay of Balcarres and Yester, cf.
Memoir of Alexander Seton earl of Dunfermline by George Seton, 1882,
passim. In 1649 Lord Dunfermline's widow, then Countess of Callendar,
incurred the displeasure of kirk sessions by placing "superstitious images in
glass windows" of Dalgety kirk and also by tarrying at home upon the Lord's
Day and not coming to the kirk, quoted *ibid.*, p. 161.

[3] Two comments on Dunfermline by rival historians have their interest.
According to Spottiswoode: "He was ever inclining to the Roman faith as

o

By the time of the accession of Charles I the "Catholic interest" had been extinguished. It was in any case a phrase which had belonged to the childhood and early maturity of James VI in Scotland with its reflection of the Duke of Guise, the League and Spain. Henceforward the Catholic lords were simply Royalists, but a new divergence of outlook was occasioned by King Charles's policy. In any matter that concerned the retention of former church lands by laymen or the political influence of the bishops the views of Catholic and Protestant magnates were identical. The effect of Archbishop Laud's work was to unite Scotsmen in opposition to his conception of a just relation between Church and State.

The liquidation of the "Catholic interest" had spelt the end of an independent foreign policy based on conservative and anti-Genevan sympathies. No longer separated from their equals, the Catholic lords found themselves aligned on politico-social questions with the rest of their class. They formed indeed the right-wing of the peerage. It is true that they were polarised in opposition to militant Presbyterianism; it is not surprising that in many cases their resistance crumbled when once the political power of the Kirk was broken.

Another factor was always present. There were very few examples of that reluctant conformity on the part of the husband coupled with recusancy on the part of the wife which had been the pattern of one section of English religious practice. In Scotland mixed marriages were not uncommon, but they generally resulted in the wife adopting her husband's faith. In the south of the country the Catholic minority was exposed to a militant evangelising Presbyterianism. In England a man of rank abandoning his Catholic upbringing would sometimes slip gently into the Anglican practice or give a purely formal acceptance. In Scotland it was more common to find a sharp repudiation of the Catholic past. The sixth Earl of Eglinton is a case in point, but the same tendency also applied to the women. Anna Countess of Eglinton and Jean Countess of Haddington after they had become Presbyterians appear to have had no more sympathy for the ideas of their own Catholic childhood than had Jeanne d'Albret or the Amirale de Coligny. The analogy in this case is with France and not with England.

On the other hand there were in the same rank during the reign of Charles I Catholic women of dominating character; Lady

being educated at Rome in his younger years". Calderwood states: "However he was popishly disposed in his religion, yet he condemned many abuses and corruptions in the Kirke of Rome . . . no good friend to the bishops".

Winton, Lady Herries and the English Lady Nithsdale are examples. The most remarkable was perhaps Marion Countess of Abercorn, who was almost certainly a convert to Catholicism since she belonged to the strongly Presbyterian family of the Boyds of Kilmarnock. It is however noticeable that in Scotland in the seventeenth century the literature of religious conversion came from the Presbyterian side.[1] The series of memoirs of devout women of rank, often written by their confessors, like those of the Countess of Arundel and Lady Falkland, appear to have had no counterpart north of the Border. They were the fruit of that close association which had developed between the English Catholic body and the religious houses in Northern France and the Low Countries.

At this time the four great families which still remained Catholic in the south of Scotland were the senior line of the House of Douglas, the Earls of Angus, the second branch of the House of Hamilton, the Earls of Abercorn, and the heads of the Setons and Maxwells, who now held the earldoms of Winton and Nithsdale. Only the last-named of these four stocks was to survive as Catholic. Although there was persistent opposition from the ministers, there was no social ostracism practised against upholders of the Old Faith, nor were the ties which bound the family unit together severed by any difference on religious questions. Thus the two brothers Eglinton and Winton remained in intimate and constant contact. The first and second Earls of Abercorn, although both Catholics, played their expected part in the Hamilton phalanx. It may in fact be said that one of the elements that led to the extinction of Catholicism in these rich families was the close friendship which their Protestant relatives continued to offer. As the years passed the heirs would yield to the desire for political advancement or give way to their Presbyterian brides.

The Abercorns had grown rich through the grant of Paisley Abbey and its properties; the Setons and Douglas's were established in the lands between Edinburgh and the sea at Tantallon; the Maxwells had a distant country and a strong affinity. They were alone among Lowland Catholics in possessing these advantages. There were two main lines holding the baronies of Maxwell and Herries; it was the heads of the senior line who were the consistent defenders of the Catholic Faith. The Herries branch had supported the Lords of the Congregation, but had returned

[1] An example of a tract of this character is *The confession and conversion of my Lady C. of L.*, printed by John Wreittoun in 1629 and edited with an introduction by George P. Johnston in 1929. This work clearly refers to Eleanor Countess of Linlithgow. It is possibly spurious.

to active Catholicism[1] in 1603. At the accession of Charles I the heads of the two branches were the first Earl of Nithsdale and his brother-in-law the sixth Lord Herries. Nithsdale was a younger son of the eighth Lord Maxwell, a turbulent character and leader of the "Spanish" faction, killed[2] at Dryfe Sands in a feud with the Johnstons. Nithsdale's elder brother had caused the priest Thomas Hamilton to preach[3] openly in his gallery; their father had had Mass celebrated[4] publicly at Christmas in Lincluden Kirk. There is a sense of enduring Catholic life around the Maxwells' burial place Lincluden and their chief houses Terregles and Carlaverock. They were not a wealthy stock, although Nithsdale was personally extravagant.[5] The impression is obtained that the Herries branch was relatively poor and that the inheritance of the senior line was wasted. Younger sons went with some regularity to the French[6] service.

Early in the new reign the Privy Council took action against the Catholics, in the first place issuing[7] a commission under the

[1] Sir John Maxwell, a younger son of the fifth Lord Maxwell, was educated at New Abbey as is stated in a bond dated 27 August 1577 and formerly at Terregles. He married Agnes eldest daughter and heiress of William third Lord Herries of Terregles in Dumfriesshire and was a Lord of the Congregation but a Marian. His son William fifth Lord Herries, who succeeded in 1582 and died in 1603, married Katharine Kerr and appears to have been a Protestant as were his daughters Lady Lochinvar and the Countess of Lothian. His son John sixth Lord Herries married his cousin Elizabeth daughter of John eighth Lord Maxwell. She was a Catholic and excommunicated as such, cf. documents printed by Sir William Fraser in the Book of Carlaverock, vol. i, p. 497 and pp. 371-2.

[2] John eighth Lord Maxwell was born in 1553 and succeeded his elder brother at the age of eighteen months. He was thus a minor throughout the religious changes and on coming of age was a supporter of the Queen of Scots. His mother was a daughter of the third Earl of Morton and sister to the wives of the Duke of Chatelherault and Morton the Regent. In 1581 he was created Earl of Morton, although he was usually still called Lord Maxwell. He was killed in December 1593. Spottiswoode has this comment on his death: "A tall man and heavy in armour (he) was in the chase overtaken and stricken from his horse. . . . His fall was pitied of many, for that he was not known to have done much wrong in his time, and was rather hurtful to himself than others", op. cit., ii, pp. 446-7.

[3] John ninth Lord Maxwell was imprisoned in Edinburgh Castle in 1601 aged fifteen for favouring Popery. "Mr Johne Hamiltoun the Apostat taught in Maxwell's galrie publictlie a little before, upon Luke ix, 8, 'The foxes have holes' ", Calderwood, op. cit., vi, p. 146.

[4] Cf. Calderwood, op. cit., iv, p. 489. Lord Maxwell did however subscribe the Confession of Faith before the Presbytery at Edinburgh in January 1593, Book of Carlaverock, i, p. 287.

[5] Lord Nithsdale had sought to borrow money from George Heriot. He wrote however on 29 September 1623 "I am sorie that George Hariot is put in such fear and distaste with me", ibid., i, p. 339.

[6] In addition to his successor, the sixth Lord Herries had seven sons. Two of them, Robert and William, were captains in France, Terregles MS. quoted ibid., i, p. 584.

[7] Register of the Privy Council of Scotland, 1625-1627, vol. ii, p. 211.

signet for the apprehension of some Jesuits and mass priests who haunt and frequent about Prestonpans and Acheson's Haven, and in especial the people attending the glass works there "unto whome they ofttymes say masse and uses otheris Popishe rites condemned be the lawis of this our kingdome". In September 1626 a missive was despatched[1] to the magistrates of Dumfries instructing them to take action against Elspeth Maxwell, innkeeper, whose house was the resort of all excommunicated persons and recusants "hanting that toun".

Parallel with this attack on the maintenance of Catholic life in town and country there went a process of excommunication launched[2] against the chief protectors of the poorer Catholics, Lady Nithsdale, Lady Herries and the wife of Maxwell of Kirkconnell. In 1634 five men and thirteen women, all actually or recently resident in Dumfries, were in prison there for hearing Mass or making their confessions. They included a fair cross-section[3] of the townsfolk, eight of the eighteen being Maxwells. There was one especially interesting case. Elspeth Maxwell, called of Conhaith, was also in prison at this time on a charge of having "made a pretendit mariage[4] by a popish priest with Robert Rig at the Brigend of Dumfries upon the fields under silence of night with candle light". Perhaps this marriage is mentioned because it was exceptional. The strongest complaint is that of conditions in the town of New Abbey where bonfires were lit "upon thair superstitious saints evenings" in the main street. It was no small grief, declared[5] the parish minister, "That seminarie preests suld be ordinarlie resitt within New Abbey, children baptised, persons maried by them, and be thair moyen (means) youth sent over sea to be brought up in Dowa and other Popish universities".

The practice of sending boys overseas for education in the Jesuit College at Douai developed gradually during the first half

[1] Letter dated 23 August 1626, *ibid.*, pp. 413-4.
[2] A letter dated 17 March 1629 sets out that Dame Elizabeth Beaumont Countess of Nithsdale and Dame Elizabeth Maxwell, Lady Herries, had been excommunicated in the Kirk of Teregles on 3 August 1628 and Elizabeth Maxwell Lady Kirkconnell excommunicated in the Kirk of Troqueir on the same day, *ibid.*, iii, pp. 96-7.
[3] The list included Jonnet McNacht, wife of James Andersone, flesher, John Maxwell "callit Captaine Jock", and Jonnet Redick, wife of John Maxwell, messenger, *ibid.*, v, p. 260. A month later on 3 July 1634 eight of the accused persons promised to conform, but seven women refused, *ibid.*, pp. 292-4. On 27 February 1634 the moderator and brethren of the presbytery of Dumfries gave a list of those already excommunicated for Popery in their own parishes. Among those named were John Broun, younger, of Lochhil, Grisel Geddes, goodwife of Drumcoltrum, and Robert Morisoun and Marjory Maxwell, servitors to the Earl of Nithsdale, *ibid.*, p. 606.
[4] *Ibid.*, v, p. 260.
[5] In this letter New Abbey is described as "my paroshin", *ibid.*, ii, p. 579.

of the seventeenth century and mainly among those families whose spiritual needs were served by the Scottish Jesuits. It was a custom already adopted by certain branches of the Maxwell[1] stock. Distance from the capital and the protection of the Nithsdales were the factors that favoured the survival of the Catholic Faith in Galloway. It was, however, a misfortune for the Catholics that in this generation they produced no leader. It is worth considering the impression made by the chief of the Maxwells on the Scotland of his time.

The character of Robert first Earl of Nithsdale,[2] who was the head of his family from 1613 until his death in 1646, hardly emerges with any distinctness; it is possible that his spirit had been broken by the execution of his young elder brother[3] for the killing of Sir James Johnston. That family maintained the ancient feud and Nithsdale always had the Annandale influence against him. He appears in his surviving correspondence as an uncertain man; gentle and rather querulous[4]; devoted to the Crown; a quiet persistent Catholic. He had had a brief apparent significance when he had become the husband of one of Buckingham's cousins,[5] but after the favourite's death he was seldom in England.[6] For the most part he lived retired at Carlaverock; remodelling the castle; constructing[7] the "dainty ffabrick of his new lodging"; accumulating[8] furniture. It seems likely that his only son was

[1] Among the MSS. in the possession in 1876 of R. Maxwell Witham at Kirkconnell there was the smaller Douay Register containing the following entries relating to the Maxwells. Robert Maxwell, known at Douai as Lindsay and his brother Edward known as Grahame, sons of the laird of Conhaeth entered the College in 1620 and 1621 respectively. Alexander Maxwell, son of Lady Gribton, entered in 1632 and Frederick son of Lord Herries in 1629. The last-named became a Jesuit and died as Rector of the Scots College at Madrid, H.M.C. Appendix to the fifth Report, pp. 653-4. Three generations of the Maxwell of Kirkconnell, whose male line became extinct in 1827, were educated at Douai, Book of Carlaverock, i, p. 601.

[2] In return for the surrender of the claim to the earldom of Morton he was created Earl of Nithsdale in 1620 with the precedence of 1581.

[3] At his execution the ninth Lord Maxwell stated that he died a "Catholic man".

[4] In August 1623 there was an altercation at Dumfries between Lord Nithsdale on the one side and Sir William Seton and the Master of Jedburgh on the other, Melrose Papers, vol. ii, p. 538.

[5] In 1619 he married Elizabeth daughter of Sir Francis Beaumont. She was the only one of Buckingham's kindred to marry in Scotland.

[6] He had however visited Rome in January 1625.

[7] Cf. Book of Carlaverock, ii pp. 136-7.

[8] An inventory of the contents of Carlaverock Castle in 1640 mention two silk beds with curtains, with chairs and stools answerable laid with lace. Each of the five principal beds with furniture was valued at £110 sterling. There were forty carpets with the furniture of a drawing room in silver cloth; two dozen chairs and stools covered with red velvet and garnished with fringes of cramosed silk and gilt nails; five dozen Turkey worked stools and chairs. A library of books was valued at £200 sterling, ibid., ii, pp. 503-4.

afflicted by some mental weakness.[1] When the conflict came the Earl of Nithsdale counted for very little.

Certainly he does not appear to have exercised influence over the turbulent Maxwells. It is for that reason that his kinsmen and followers gained no appreciable benefit from their very real isolation. This factor is brought into relief by an account of cannon being sent south from Edinburgh. "These late glustes of rain," it is explained[2] "have made both the wayes and waters in a manner unpassable. If they can bring iron peeces of battery betwixt Crawford John and the Sanker, and so to Drumlanrig, they must justlye brag off a greater master peece nor hath bin done in that country, and that kind of service these one hundred yeares bypast". At this time these Catholic Maxwells made little impact on the rest of Scotland living in their remote stone houses above Solway "in the glustes of rain".

It would be of interest to discover a detailed account of some Catholic family of the middle or lesser[3] gentry and perhaps the manuscripts inherited from the Maxwells of Kirkconnell may yet provide such material. It seems likely that relatively little correspondence has been preserved relating to the minor landed stocks; certainly only rare examples have been printed. As a consequence it is only the reactions of the leaders that are known to us, not those of their tenants or their followers. This should be borne in mind when we consider the other principal Catholic houses in the South of Scotland.

In the cat's cradle of relationship between the families which adhered to the Old Religion the influence of determined and devout women of rank is clearly visible. These are associated closely with the arrival of the Jesuit chaplains who came, mainly during the first years of Charles I, to take up their residence in the great houses.[4] Three successive generations of strong-minded

[1] Robert Lord Maxwell was born in 1620 and succeeded as second Earl of Nithsdale in 1646. He died unmarried in the Isle of Carlaverock in 1600 and is said to have been given to the study of astrology. On his death the earldom passed to John seventh Lord Herries. Cf. *Scots Peerage*.

[2] In an unsigned letter dated at Carlisle on 15 August 1640 and printed in *Book of Carlaverock*, ii, pp. 136-7.

[3] The valuable studies by Mr John Durkan printed in the *Innes Review* and relating to the case-histories of Fr. Hugh Sempill and Fr. John Chrysostom Campbell throw light on a rather earlier period. Hugh Sempill of Craigbet in Renfrewshire sailed from Irvine for France in September 1614 and entered the Jesuit noviciate at Toledo. He was among those who had attended the Masses said by Fr. John Ogilvie, S. J., whose stay in Scotland has been studied in detail. Barclay of Ladyland near Kilbirnie represents a Catholic family belonging to the middle gentry of that region.

[4] Thus a list of Jesuits living as chaplains in 1628 includes Fr James Macbrek at Seton with the Earl of Winton, Fr. Robert Valens in Edinburgh with the Earl of Abercorn and Fr. George Christie with the Countess of Linlithgow, W. Forbes Leith, *Memoirs of Scottish Catholics*, i.

wives had a profound effect on the Seton connection. They began with Nithsdale's sister Elizabeth Lady Herries, who strengthened the Catholicism of her husband's branch of the Maxwells. Their daughter Elizabeth Countess of Winton brought new force to the traditional religious convictions of the Setons. She was a matriarch, who lived to be praised for her charity to the Cromwellian soldiers.[1] At Traquair House there is a portrait of her, a Vandyck period figure, a light silver ruff on her black dress standing before a landscape set with pillars. Beside her are the young sons who died at sea. Their strawberry coloured suits set off with lace suggest the fashions of King Charles's court. The religion of the Stuarts of Traquair was, perhaps, the most abiding of her legacies. Lady Anne Seton stabilised in the Roman Obedience the wavering affiliations[2] of that careful stock. The Setons of Winton can, perhaps, be regarded as the central element[3] and almost as the fulcrum of the grouping. An examination of the history of the religious allegiance of this family will give a view of the nature of the pressure brought to bear on the leading Catholics.

George third Earl of Winton was the head of his house from 1607 until his death in 1650. He was twenty-three years of age when he inherited the estates and the harbour of Cockenzie and the great house of Seton Palace on the resignation of his elder brother, who had become insane on the night of his wedding[4] to Lord Thirlestane's daughter. Winton was a man of many projects and an "improver" in the eighteenth century sense of that term. Apart from his building plans and coal-mining operations already mentioned, he was deeply interested in his salt pans.[5] He was given

---

[1] This is paralleled by the kindness shown by Elizabeth Viscountess Thurles "although a Papist" to Cromwellian soldiers in Ireland.

[2] Lady Anne's sister-in-law, Margaret Countess of Queensberry, was accused as a suspected Papist. Cf. Andrew Hay's *Diary*, pp. 98, 132, 137, 155, 191.

[3] Thus by his first marriage with Lord Erroll's daughter Winton was linked with the northern Catholic stocks. He was a brother-in-law of Lord John Gordon Viscount Melgum. By his second marriage with Elizabeth Maxwell he became father-in-law to the sixth Lord Sempill and to the second Earl of Traquair. His aunt Margaret Seton was the wife of Lord Claud Hamilton and through this marriage he was a first cousin to James first Earl of Abercorn and to Margaret Hamilton who became the first wife of William Marquis of Douglas. The last-named married as his second wife Melgum's sister Lady Mary Gordon. By his first marriage Winton was brother-in-law to Lady Margaret Hay, who was married to his own first cousin Sir John Seton of Barns, and to Lady Elizabeth Hay the wife first of the fifth Lord Sempill and then of Lord Mordington, who was the Marquis of Douglas's younger brother. Sempill had been previously married to Abercorn's daughter.

[4] Robert second Earl of Winton was twenty-four at the time of his resignation. He was still alive in 1634.

[5] Cf. Sir William Brereton's account. "About six or seven miles from this city (Edinburgh) I saw and took notice of divers salt-works in poor houses erected upon the sea coast. I went into one of them and observed iron pans

to constructing herb gardens[1] as a recreation. He kept himself
aloof from political combinations, perhaps they did not interest
him. He attended the privy council with regularity and was, like
all his family, a resolute adherent of the House of Stuart. His two
wives bore him many children, ten daughters and eleven sons. In
the troubles of the time he remained passive. Since his property
lay within reach of Edinburgh such conduct was inevitable, but
it is probable that he shared the distaste of all his class for the
King's religious policy. His own attitude in the matter of religion
needs elucidation. This question is bound up with the existence of
Catholic schooling either at Seton Palace or in its neighbourhood.

Winton, known at that time as George Seton of St Germans,
was brought up a Catholic by his parents and when he was ten
years old his first teacher Stephen Ballantyne, described as a
"papist or atheist", was removed[2] by the orders of the Presbytery
of Haddington. Later a second schoolmaster was denounced[3] as
unsatisfactory, and finally a third tutor was dismissed[4] at the
request of the representatives of the Kirk. It was then the custom
to entrust youths of good blood to a noble family for education
and general training. It seems probable that there was a school
at Seton during this period.

eighteen foot long and nine foot broad; these larger pans and houses than
those at the Sheildes. An infinite, innumerable number of salt-works are here
erected upon this shore; all make salt out of sea water", Hume Brown, *Early
Travellers in Scotland,* p. 136.

[1] Cf. Letter from Robert Seton to the Earl of Eglinton dated at Tranent
9 April (1620), "My lord (Winton) your brother is bissie with hes new
Herberie, but sore against my will: I feare it prouffe ane inprofitable work,
and scars worthie hes paines; bot ther is no steying of him", Fraser *Memorials
of Eglinton,* i, p. 214.

[2] In 1593 Lord Seton was warned to come to the Presbytery meeting of
Tranent since he was "ane ill frequenter of ye Kirk". On this occasion it was
decided that "Steine Ballantyne scuill maister to me L. Setounes bairnes,
ane papist or athesit, is dischairged from teiching of anie youthe or scuil",
extract from Presbytery Records of Haddington printed in *A history of the
family of Seton* by George Seton, vol. i, p. 212.

[3] In 1596 Mr Thomas Segget "Lord Setouns bairns sculmaister" was
ordered to attend Presbytery exercises, extract printed *ibid.,* i, p. 213.

[4] In 1599 it was stated that Lord Setoun harboured Mr James Gordon a
papist, "but on ye Presbytery threatening public admonition his Lordship sent
him away"—extract printed *ibid.,* i, p. 214. Two years earlier it was stated
that Dame Margaret Montgomerie Lady Seton had never communicated
since she came within the bounds of the Presbytery. Bearing this in mind and
considering the state of the house into which she was married the Presbytery
declared that she "hes ever been suspectit of papistrie", *ibid.,* i, p. 214. As an
example of differences in other fields it was decided in 1588 that Lord Seton
was to be waited on by a deputation from the Presbytery asking him to
change the market held in Tranent parish from the Sunday to some other
day. Failure to comply would expose him to "ye hard measures of ye Kirk",
ibid., i, p. 212.

It was a consequence of the same vigilance that George Seton and his elder brother, then Master of Seton, were asked to subscribe[1] the Articles of Religion. Both young men stated that they had been in France and had had no opportunity to study theology. There are details coming from a rather later date of a school that was maintained at Prestonpans and apparently enjoyed Lord Winton's patronage. The bills for boarders amounted[2] to two hundred marks. Other expenses included clothes, laundry and candle silver at Candlemas. Each child was asked to bring two sets of bedding.

Some years went by without much interference, but in 1629 Winton received orders from the Privy Council that his eldest son, then aged sixteen, should be sent[3] either to Edinburgh or to St Andrews to be trained "in the knowledge of the truth". Nithsdale received a similar instruction, but both efforts in the event proved ineffectual. It was about the time of the Earl of Winton's second marriage that a Jesuit, Fr James Macbrek, came to reside[4] at Seton Palace. This move is reflected in the decision to send the younger sons of the Seton family overseas for their education. The first to go was Alexander, later the family historian, who sailed in 1636. According to his own rather curious description[5] "he, not acquainting his father, immediately went to the College of La Fleche, where he studied two years his philosophie". Meanwhile there are indications that a school may have been established or revived on Scottish soil. In 1640 David Abercromby of Petelpie, a former Douai student, was living[6] at Seton as tutor to the younger children. In all these matters the influence of the Countess of Winton[7] in regard to the upbringing of her own sons and daughters is very plain. An entry in the records of

---

[1] Decision of the Presbytery taken in June 1602, *ibid.*, i, p. 215.

[2] The annual figure, including apparently tuition, came to nine hundred marks. Cf. Letter from Robert Setoun, servant to Margaret Countess of Winton, to the Earl of Eglinton. It was dated 9 April (1629) and is printed in *Memorials of the Earls of Eglinton*, ii, p. 214.

[3] *Register of the Privy Council of Scotland* 1629-1630, vol. iii, pp. 30-21.

[4] Cf. *Memoirs of Scottish Catholics* i.

[5] *Continuation of the History of the House of Seytoun*, p. 81.

[6] According to the Smaller Douai Register among the Kirkconnell MSS. David Abercromby entered the College as a student of composition on 7 October 1627 and left for reasons of health in June 1631. He is stated to have become tutor to Lord Winton's second son, but this was probably Christopher Seton the second son by his second marriage.

[7] Three of her sons were sent overseas for their education. A sidelight on her character is provided in a letter written by an English soldier in Scotland, "And to my observation unlesse it were the Lady Winton, a papist who lives at Seaton, about seven miles from Edinburgh, there was not any of them that made officer or soldiour of this army eat or drink of their own accords", *Blairs Papers*, ed. M. V. Hay, p. 197.

the Presbytery of Haddington sets out[1] that it had been decided to purge the house of Seton of Popish servants and to proceed both against them and against the Earl of Winton should the latter protect or "reset" them. On the other hand Lord Winton was a member of the Privy Council and was present at meetings where steps were taken to repress[2] Catholicism. It is stated[3] that when he died of a palsy at Seton Palace "he was interrit with his ancestors in the churche ther without any funerall solemnity". This may indicate that he was buried privately with Catholic rites. As long as his widow and her children lived they remained faithful[4] to the Jesuit connection.

There was one other great house in the Lothians whose members shared something of the same approach, the close-knit group depending on the first Marquis of Douglas. Like Nithsdale and Winton he was long-lived and spanned this period. William Douglas succeeded his father as eleventh Earl of Angus in 1611 at the age of twenty-two and survived until 1660. He was raised to the marquisate when Charles I came to Scotland for his coronation. Until his father's time the Angus branch of the Douglas family had had a strictly Protestant tradition.[5] Their landed power was not considerable and they had no clients, nor any circle of political adherents. These last facts in part accounted for King Charles's favour. The position of the Marquis of Douglas was strictly comprehensible by English standards. In religion he can best be described as a pusillanimous Catholic. In this connection it may be mentioned that the members of these great households were often more fervent than their masters. An example may be seen in the case of Patrick Dickson, who had been excommunicated for his obstinate profession of Popery

---

[1] Extracts printed George Seton, *op. cit.*, i, p. 231. This decision was taken on 4 November 1647. It had been noted under 3 November 1645 that nothing had been done by Lord Winton "anent the receaveing of a chaplane in his familie", *ibid.*, p. 231.

[2] Cf. *Register of the Privy of Scotland* especially vol. iii. second series.

[3] Balfour's *Annals*.

[4] The Earl of Winton's elder son by his first marriage, Lord Seton, had predeceased him in 1648. On 30 May 1653 it was reported to the Presbytery that two young children of the late Lord Seton "were formerlie keeped at publict schoolis and now keeped at home, whairby it may be feared that they may be educat in poprie". The matter was closed in 1654 when a certificate was granted stating that "George, now Erle of Wintoun, is bred at his awin house att Seatoun with his oncle and tutor the Lord Kingstoune in the treu Protestant religioune", extracts from the records of the presbytery of Haddington printed in Seton *op. cit.*, i, pp. 232, 233. The Countess of Winton survived until 1671. Her sons Sir John Seton of Gairmiltoun and Sir Robert Seton of Windygoul were both educated at Douai.

[5] The eighth Earl of Angus (d. 1588) was devoted to the Kirk, "full of grace, a lover of justice, peaceable, sober and given to all goodness, and which crowned all his virtues, truly pious", Spottiswoode, *History*, p. 371.

when servitor to Douglas, then Earl of Angus. The complaint from the Lanark presbytery sets out[1] the matter. "He . . . being chamberlain to the said Earl, and having the greatest trust and credit of any about him, he corrupts the simple people of the country wherever he goes among them." Another servant in the household, Janet Brown, was under process[2] for Popery, and for some years the Old Faith had a strong support in one of the gentlewomen[3] in attendance. Such a position would be strengthened by the constant interchange of personal servants among the principal families so very closely related by marriage.

With the Marquis of Douglas went his only surviving brother James Lord Mordington, who acted as his adviser. Mordington was high-spirited and shrewd;[4] his original portion had included the kirklands of Abernethy; he was occupied in striving for the Oliphant peerage and estates whose heiress he had married. He appears in later life as a "quiet" Catholic. Both young men had for a time lived abroad with their father who was involved all his life in the political side of the "Catholic interest".

Douglas himself was an antiquary,[5] the patron of Hume of Godscroft's *History*; he had some knowledge of Italian[6] and a taste for travel; he was at first just a disciple of the Jesuits and then later a disappointment[7] to them; perhaps Lady Abercorn, the mother of his first wife, had an influence with him in a Catholic sense. As a widower he married Huntly's sister, but he was never associated with that family's fortunes. Three of his younger sons were brought up as Catholics, probably with a view to the colonelcy of the Scots Regiment in the French service which they held in turn. Angus, his heir, was a Protestant and in fact a moderate

---

[1] Complaint dated 17 March 1631 referring to Dickson's failure to obtain relaxation from his excommunication two years earlier. It is noted on 9 June 1631 that he had agreed to frequent the Kirk to have conference with the minister at Douglas, *Register of the Acts of the Privy Council* 1630-2, pp. 173 and 234.

[2] *Ibid.*, p. 174.

[3] Blakhal describes a visit in 1643. "When I arrived to Edenborough, I loged in the Cowgate, in the house of Jhon Crawford, an honest old gentleman, and a zealous Catholick, who suffered much persecution for his faith. This Crawford had a daughter serving my Ladye Marquis of Douglas", *Narrative*, p. 160.

[4] Cf. Blakhal's judgment, "Morningtoun (Mordington) was a very wyse nobleman", *ibid.*, p. 160.

[5] The Guthry Collection contained a series of letters from Douglas to Guthry dated 1643-50 with literary references, H.M.C., Appendix to second Report, 1871, pp. 197-8. They also give some indication of his character.

[6] For a letter in Italian from Marco Antonio d'Agazano dated 6 July 1620 proposing an exchange of family trees, cf. William Fraser *The Douglas Book*, vol. ii, p. 291. For further similar letters, *ibid.*, pp. 293, 298, 303-4.

[7] The annual Letters contain various references to Douglas. In 1632 it is stated that "Sir James Douglas, who is a very firm adherent of the Faith, has selected Berwick as his place of residence", Forbes Leith, *op. cit.*, p. 130.

Covenanter. The daughters, with one exception,[1] were prepared for marriage to the heirs of the wealthy Reformed stocks.[2] This matter has been treated in detail as an example of the liquidation of the Catholic life in one great house. A certain passivity seems to have served the Marquis of Douglas in the troubled times, this and his own good nature.

The Marquis has been described as an Episcopalian,[3] but this is a misconception. Bishop Burnet makes it clear that he counted as a Catholic and that historian would never have made such an adverse comment on one so closely related to the House of Hamilton if this course had been avoidable.[4] The question of alleged Episcopalian views having been raised, it is perhaps appropriate to consider here the outlook of those southern lords whose standpoint would fall under that term. The position is complicated by the fact that an episcopate endured until after the taking of the National Covenant. It is therefore not easy to separate a body of laymen into two groups. In general the term Episcopalian may be applied to those who appear to have regarded an episcopate as normal, however much they may have regretted the power in secular affairs which Charles I wished to attribute to members of the bench of bishops. In the case of the magnates a dividing line can be drawn between those who entered into the Kirk organisation and accepted the position of ruling elders and those who held aloof from the counsels of the ministers. On such a basis the Earls of Roxburgh and Traquair would come within an Episcopalian grouping, as also the secretary of state the Earl of Stirling, and the lord chancellor Kinnoull and his son. The outlook just described went with a distinctly conservative approach which was allied with a feeling for the maintenance of certain aspects of the royal power; it also involved some preparedness to support the sovereign in his efforts to preserve his authority from the encroachments of the Presbytery. Such a standpoint came easily to those lords, a diminishing body, whose lives were passed in the direct service[5] of the

[1] Lucy the youngest daughter married Robert fourth Earl of Nithsdale.
[2] His sons-in-law included the Duke of Queensberry, the Earls of Annandale and Perth, Lords Bargany and Alexander, Sir William Carmichael and Sir William Ruthven.
[3] Cf. *D.N.B.*, vol. xxv, p. 369.
[4] Burnet was a *protégé* of Douglas's son the third Duke of Hamilton. His evidence, which is supported by the Registers of the Privy Council and by Blakhal and other Catholic sources, runs as follows. "The marquis of Douglass was not able to do his majesty that service his illustrious ancestors had done the former kings; for himself was a papist, and so not followed by the friends and dependers of that noble family", Burnet, *Lives,* p. 147.
[5] Charles second Earl of Dunfermline and Thomas second Earl of Haddington may serve as examples of sons of officers of state who had gone out to serve the Covenant.

Crown. It was also shared by a majority of the chief families in Angus and by the senior representative of the Queensberry branch of the House of Douglas. In some respects the Earls and Dukes of Queensberry were to prove, both then and later, the prime example of a Royalist and Episcopalian family, ever ready to support the King's measures provided that no favour should be shown to Roman Catholics.

In the conflict that was approaching the Catholic lords were disqualified from any open action. It is worth noting that the three living in the South who were described as disaffected[1] were Douglas, Abercorn and Sempill. They were at certain points politically in sympathy with Royalists of an episcopalian colour, since both groups would dislike the National Covenant. Other objections apart, men of these ways of thought would regard the Covenant as derogatory to the royal dignity. In the lands south of the Tay these families constituted a support for the Crown that had no rallying point. It was a question of a threat to the Kirk leadership which was not and in fact could not be implemented. The more that the situation is studied the clearer does it become that there was no leader at this juncture who could compare in acumen with Argyll. The politico-religious history of the years from 1637 until 1640 may be read in terms of his slow entrance and final achievement of supremacy. His unalterable conviction soon inspired a tenacity that never faltered. Beside him most other men were cyphers for he knew and pursued his own high purpose.

[1] "Dowglas, Abercorne, and Semple are openly arming among us", Baillie's *Letters and Journals*, i, p. 65.

CHAPTER XV

ARGYLL

THE Campbells of Argyll had, beyond all other Scottish
houses, a dynamic quality that penetrated their whole policy.
In addition to their absorption in strengthening their own power,
they are remembered for their consistency. They had none of that
fickleness which seemed to beset the House of Hamilton. This was,
perhaps, because, to an extent to which their rivals did not attain,
they became in time freed from all attachment to the idea of
monarchy. The later Stuarts were to prove to them a disillusion-
ing series, exacting blood. For generations the Campbells of
Argyll were known both for their opposition and their loyalty;
opposition to the Stuart sovereigns; loyalty to the Elector of
Hanover and to his family. Eventually they gained a fixed position
among the shifting combinations of politics in Scotland. What may
be termed their Highland policy, the strengthening of McCailein
Mor, was ancestral; but their policy in relation to the kingship
was the creation of the first Marquis of Argyll.

The Campbells had in fact been notably Royalist and their
acquisitions, the most recent of which was Kintyre, had all been
gained as lieutenants for their sovereign who was often either
absent or else a minor. They had held for rather over a century
the great office of Justice General of Scotland. One characteristic
differentiated the Earls of Argyll from the heads of other stocks.
They were accustomed to resign their hereditary charges to their
eldest sons in their own lifetime.[1] And these offices were considerable comprising the combined posts of judiciary, sheriff,
coroner and chamberlain in Argyll, Lorne, Knapdale and
Kintyre. The effort of the Campbells to extend their authority,
while guarding against political disgrace, was prolonged and for
many years successful. They had, especially in their earlier period,
a well-developed sense of timing.

The religious history of the family had been chequered; they
were however bound up very closely with the triumph of the
Reformation. This is evidenced by the resignation of all offices
and lands made by the seventh Earl of Argyll in 1618 after he

[1] These offices were conveyed by the third Earl of Argyll to his son in
August 1529 and by the Earl to his son in 1552. The fifth Earl died childless
and the sixth while his son was still a minor.

223

had become a Catholic. There do not appear to have been any firm adherents of the Old Religion among the Campbell lairds. Queen Elizabeth I in her approaches[1] both to the seventh Earl and to his father assumed that the Argylls were linked with the Protestant and English interest. Henry IV had maintained contact[2] with the house when he was King of Navarre. The change of Faith of the seventh Earl of Argyll was not in character.

He remains a shadowy figure and difficult to place; perpetually embarrassed in his finances. He had succeeded to the earldom when he was eight years of age[3] in 1584; he had therefore been a factor in the life of James VI throughout that sovereign's manhood. The relation between them was always cold. The tone is set in a letter[4] written in 1588 and addressed to the Earl of Argyll and his tutors. The King makes it clear that in carrying out the royal commands "ye will do acceptable pleasour and gude seruice, and will give ws a pruiff of that affectioun ye beir to the furthering of our seruice, according to the lovable custome of your forbearis; Letting ws understand be your answer . . . quhat we sall certanelie lippin for (expect)". It is doubtful if James VI had a personal liking for any Campbell.[5]

During thirty years Argyll had followed the line of policy to which the heads of his house had grown accustomed. He was particularly active in harrying Clandonald. His relations were close with the great Reformation stocks; at seventeen he had married Lady Anne Douglas of Morton. A new factor had its importance for the family fortunes, the alliance that James VI had arranged between Huntly's heir the Earl of Enzie and the eldest of Argyll's six daughters by this marriage. It represented one of the King's attempts to reconcile the great houses that were at enmity. In his attitude towards Argyll the King had shown himself somewhat discontented; he was never inclined to give his trust to those of his Scottish subjects who had shown attachment to the Queen of England's policies.

[1] Cf. Letters written by the Queen on 20 January 1582 and 23 July 1595 and printed in *Letters to the Argyll Family*, Maitland Club, 1839, pp. 24-5, 31.

[2] Cf. Letters from Henry IV dated 28 May and from his French agents the Sieur de Mainville and M. de la Mothe Fénelon dated 9 April and 25 January 1583 printed *ibid.*, pp. 26-9. The first letter written from Paris and attributed to Henry IV should perhaps be ascribed to Henry III.

[3] His date of birth is given as 1575, *Complete Peerage*, and about 1576, *D.N.B.*

[4] Letter dated 21 September 1588 printed in *Letters to the Argyll Family*, pp. 29-30.

[5] There is a severe comment in a letter to Argyll dated from the Honour of Hampton on 8 February and suggested as belonging to 1604. "We haue thocht gude heirby to gif you warning, that in cais we heir any forder of thair oppressioun or truble, We will impute the blame to you, and provyde sic remeid as sall not stand with your contentment", *ibid.*, p. 33.

The Countess of Argyll died in 1607 soon after the birth of her only son, and three years later her widower married in London Anne Cornwallis. His English bride was an heiress on a minor scale for her mother had inherited Earl's Court in the borough of Kensington. She was also an ardent Catholic with the tastes of a bluestocking.[1] It is not easy to fit together the two portions of Argyll's life. The last twenty years, the military service in the Spanish Netherlands,[2] the life on a restricted income in Drury Lane, had certainly no relevance for Scotland. Even in early childhood his son Archibald Lord Lorne was in effect McCailein Mor. The boy hardly knew his father and distrusted[3] his step-mother. He was brought up under the supervision of his cousin the Earl of Morton, who was determined to secure him as a son-in-law. It is not surprising that no enduring friendship was formed with Morton.[4] There was always something solitary about the great Marquis of Argyll.

With his step-brother James, to whom his father wished to leave Kintyre, Lorne's relations were always difficult. Lorne's education, which was perhaps affected by the burden of family indebtedness, was exclusively Scottish, at first at Inverary under his pedagogue Robert Barclay and then at St Andrews. It was just the fact that he had never been subjected to any "foreign" influences that drew the ministers of the Church of Scotland to him.

During his childhood he had no close Campbell cousins, nor any contact with his step-brother. Robert Barclay had entered his household as a servitor. These factors were reflected both in his homeliness and in his native shrewdness. He was the only one among the greatest lords who was neither marred nor fashioned by continental travel or the English Court. The future Marquis of Argyll had a certain natural prudence, but in any case his position obliged him to show caution as long as his father was alive. From the beginning he was a great support to the ministers and was

[1] Lady Argyll collected and published in Spanish a set of sentences from the works of St Augustine. The second part of *Castara* contains verses dedicated to Archibald Earle of Ar. Cf. *The Poems of William Habington*, ed. Kenneth Allott, pp. 85-6.

[2] Cf. Letter from Giovanni Soranzo at the Hague to the Doge and Senate of Venice dated 31 July 1628, "Yesterday there arrived here on his way to England the Earl of Argyle, a Scot, after having been ten years at Brussels. . . . The return of a person known to be a Spanish partisan . . . seemed to me to justify the fear of evil practices", Cal. State Papers Venetian 1628-9.

[3] An undated letter from Lord Lorne to the Earl of Morton now among the MSS. at Dalmahoy states "Heaving some wrets to passe with my mother in law (step-mother) quhich I durst not trust to hir self, hes made me direct this bearer that at your Lo. sight all things may be ended", printed in *The Great Marquess* by the Rev. John Willcock, p. 362.

[4] Twenty-three letters to the Earl of Morton are printed by Willcock, *op. cit.*, pp. 354-366. Later events proved that the early cordiality was superficial.

P

probably their one true-hearted friend in all his circle. He had
none of that lurking sympathy with Erastian principles that
marked the great body of the peers. In later life he did not fear to
uphold the extreme Presbyterian position, but in the early stages
of the conflict he could not appear too openly as an opponent of
the King. There was always the chance that in such a case his
father might be permitted to recall the grant of the Argyll lands;
as it was he had secured Kintyre for his younger son, who took
that title until he was created Earl of Irvine. Until his father died
in the autumn[1] of 1638 Lord Lorne could not neglect the danger
from his step-brother,[2] who later entered the French military
service. It was said that his young step-sisters in their Belgian
convent hardly even knew English.[3] Such considerations would
only tend to increase the young Lord Lorne's distrust of foreigners.

In the matter of his education Lord Lorne shared the experience
of the leading Campbells.[4] By the seventeenth century they had
become a series of close-knit dynasties, self-absorbed, tenacious.
Their power of co-ordinated action was exemplary. Throughout
this period both Campbell of Lawers and Campbell of Glenorchy
maintained the closest contact with Inverary. Lord Lorne was
married shortly after leaving the university and before he came of
age[5] to his cousin Lady Margaret Douglas, a girl of sixteen. She

---

[1] The seventh Earl of Argyll died in London in October or November
1638. His second wife died in his house in Drury Lane on 12 January 1635.

[2] Lord Irvine was born in 1611. His religious affiliation, as also that of his
eldest sister Mary Lady Rollo, is uncertain. Lord Lorne's letters to the Earl
of Morton sent between 16 April and 29 September 1627 and dealing with
his difficulties with his step-brother are printed in Willcock, *op. cit.*, pp. 354-9.
The first and last are dated from Inverary.

[3] The Ladies Isabella, Victoria, Barbara and Anne Campbell all became
nuns either in the house of the English Benedictines at Brussels or with the
Augustinian Canonesses. A letter from the Duke of Perth to his sister Lady
Erroll dated August 1694 has an interesting comment. "We went to Bruxelles
the 16th July where we waited for the second time on our old great-aunt
Madlle d'Argile, who is near eighty years old. She was daughter to the old
Earl, the Marquises father, one of four *religieuses*. . . . She speaks no English,
is a good soul as lives, and in esteem with all the great folks at Bruxelles",
quoted in Willcock, *op. cit.*, p. 343.

[4] Apart from the children of the seventh Earl of Argyll's second marriage,
the first Earl of Loudoun appears to have been the only leading member of
the family in this generation who had travelled abroad. As a result the
Marquis of Argyll did not speak French. On 30 November 1647 Montereul
wrote from Edinburgh to Cardinal Mazarin: "The Marquis of Argyle having
come to see me on Wednesday last . . . to wish me to thank you on his part,
which his self-respect and his ignorance of our language prevented him from
doing himself", *The Diplomatic Correspondence of Jean de Montereul and
the brothers de Bellièvre, French Ambassadors in England and Scotland
1645-8*, ed. J. G. Fotheringham, Scottish History Society, 1899, vol. ii, p. 337.

[5] Lord Lorne matriculated at St Andrews on 15 January 1622 apparently,
then aged about fifteen. The *D.N.B.*, vol. viii, p. 319, incorrectly gives the date
of his birth as 1598.

was religious and devoted to him; politically she seems to have meant little. The chief consequence of the marriage was the double strain of Douglas blood that the House of Argyll inherited. Lorne was attached to his children and to his sisters' children and was very easy with them. His relations were particularly close with his brother-in-law Gordon of Lochinvar, who became Lord Kenmure; he exercised a definite attraction on the family of his sister Lady Huntly. He was a serious evangelising Presbyterian determined to secure the Gordons of Lochinvar from the ravages of Popery. In his correspondence with his nephew and nieces on the Huntly side it appears that he could not give his confidence except to those who were ready to adhere to the Kirk of Scotland.

He was, until the times became more troubled, very conscious of his own great power. Slender, with the reddish Campbell[1] hair and having grey-blue eyes with a slight cast in them, he yet possessed the gift of pleasing. He has suffered by the picture formed of his rival Montrose, whose great qualities were best seen in long perspective and by posterity. Patrick Gordon of Ruthven, an enemy of his house, has left a remarkable contemporary description[2] of the Marquis of Argyll. "For his externall and outward disposition, he was of a homely carriage, gentle, myld and affable, gratious and courteous to speake too. Naturallie, he had a large and understanding heart, a jealous and a far-reaching apprehension, and yet his presence did showe him of such plaine and homely aspect, as he seemed rather inclyned to simplicitie then any wayes tented with a loftie and unsatiable ambition."

Until he took his stand against his sovereign, Charles I had accorded to Argyll a certain negligent sympathy. The King often showed a degree of liking for those who held fast to Protestant convictions against the solicitations of a Catholic parent. The Queen had more persistence in her approach[3] to him. She was, perhaps, impressed by his great power and by his indubitable significance. His Presbyterianism was not a drawback in her eyes; she never ceased to think that he was purchasable and worth purchasing.[4]

[1] Scot of Scotstarvet has a comment. "The said Robert Earl of Lothian married the Marquis of Argyle's sister, a woman of a masculine spirit, but highland faced", *The Staggering State of Scottish Statesmen*, p. 91. The portraits at Newbattle Abbey reproduce the hair colouring and type of countenance of the Campbell wives of the first and second Marquises of Lothian.
[2] *A Short Abridgement of Britain's Distemper* by Patrick Gordon, Spalding Club, 1855, pp. 56-7. The manuscript which deals with the years 1639 to 1649 was composed during the Commonwealth.
[3] On 8 July 1644 Anne of Austria sent Argyll a warm letter of introduction in favour of Gray of Schivas, Cal. Argyll MSS., sixth Report, 1612.
[4] In contrast there is the King's comment to the Queen in his later years. He wrote from Newcastle on 17 June 1646 that "Argyle is very civil and cunning", *Charles I in 1646*, Camden Society, 1856, ed. John Bruce, p. 49.

It is difficult to decide when Argyll's preoccupation with religion, and with the State conceived as a religious entity, became predominant. There is some reason to suppose that he experienced "conversion" in the latter part of 1638. Certainly as a young man he had interests from which later he was to turn away as he sat at Inverary writing the sermons for his minister to preach and scanning the politico-religious horizon. An agreement preserved among the Duke of Argyll's manuscripts[1] is characteristic of the earlier period. In 1633 a contract was entered into with Captain David Alexander of Anstruther in Fife according to which the ship *Unitie* was to be taken into the main sea beyond the Hebrides "for the discovery of an island, which, Lord Lorne had been credibly informed, lay outside the *Hebrides Insulae,* had not yet been discovered, and could be found out only by navigation." Thus early his interests were concentrated on the affairs of Scotland and the neighbouring seas.

An examination of the position of the Campbells reveals differences which separated them from their great rivals. More than that of any other group the Campbell power partook of the characteristics of an independent principality with its own frontiers. The key to this influence lay in the hereditary judicatories and it was, perhaps, just the possession of these jurisdictions which in the end would prove fatal to the Marquis of Argyll and to his eldest son. They were the marks of an authority, in effect excluding the royal power, whose survival would hardly be permitted by a strong monarchy.

Besides, this geographical immunity, which was a consequence of their compact jurisdictions, gave a special value to the position of McCailein Mor as the leader of the party of the Presbyterian ministers. It was not only a question of the weakness of the Old Faith throughout all the Campbell lands, but rather the support that was derived from the positive strength of the Presbyterian position in Kintyre and in the traditional strongholds of Calvinism in the parishes to the east of the Firth of Clyde. Successive Campbell chiefs combined astuteness with a far-sighted political courage. Circumstances compelled them to a measure of flexibility, but they held to a core of principle when the Presbyterian hegemony was brought in question. In the matter of applying their religious convictions to the changing political situation their record was immaculate.

The excellent relations maintained between the leading branches of the stock was a tribute to the great authority that Inverary

---

[1] Contract dated at Holyrood House on 14 March 1633, Argyll MSS. in *H.M.C.,* sixth Report and Appendix, part i, p. 631.

possessed over all Campbells. Thus Glenorchy and Lawers, whose lands lay on the north and north-east frontiers of the clan territory, followed their chief with that self-interested exactness which was a Campbell characteristic. Such leaders were in no true sense cadets; they were rather the heads of separate branches[1] each with its subordinate affiliations. John Campbell, who was created Earl of Loudoun, inherited Lawers from his father and the Ayrshire properties through his wife. Throughout the years of conflict he was in effect the permanent representative of the policies of Inverary at the seat of government.[2] The actual Laird of Glenorchy was in no way notable, but there was growing up in the house of Balloch his young son John Campbell,[3] who later as Earl of Breadalbane would prove to be so celebrated a figure in Scottish history.

It was an element of strength in Argyll's position that his interest and experience were confined to his own country. These were assets when dealing with such rivals as Hamilton and Huntly, who could not easily rebut the accusation that they were cosmopolitan. This was borne out by a comment made later by the French envoy Monsieur de Boisivon. "The Marquis[4] of Argyle,—intelligent in the highest degree as to what concerns Scotland and nothing more." This concentration on Scottish questions, to which he brought an astute and lucid mind, was in fact the source of his great influence.

The Earls of Argyll had not only for long possessed the powers of a semi-independent principality, but they were also accustomed to employ the vocabulary appropriate to such a position in their formal documents. The will of the sixth Earl sets out[5] this plainly. "Item, becaus the burding (burden) wilbe havie (heavy) to my said spous to reull and governe the cuntrie of Argyll and Lorne &c induring the tyme of my sonis minoritie I will and ordane to be adjunit with hir in that behalfe . . . thir (these) persounes following conjunctlie, that is to say, Duncane Campbell of Glenvrquhy,

[1] In this connection it is easier to re-construct the material setting of life in Glenorchy's houses than at Inverary. No detailed memoranda have been calendared or printed in regard to the expenses and recreations of the Argyll family. Much may have been lost in the fire at Inverary Castle in 1878. An account of the Campbells of Glenorchy based on the Calendar of Breadalbane MSS. and on the *Black Book of Taymouth* has been given on pp. 108-13.

[2] He was appointed lord chancellor in 1641. There is an entry in Sir Thomas Hope's *Diary* under 28 January 1645. "Item, about this tyme Sir James Campbell of Laweris, father to John Erll of Lowdoun, Chancellar, deceissit at his awin place of Laweris", p. 212.

[3] He was born about 1635.

[4] Letter to Brienne dated from Edinburgh on 20 November 1643, *Montereul Correspondence*, vol. ii, appendix, p. 556.

[5] Will dated at Darneway on 5 September 1584 printed in *Letters to the Argyll Family*, Appendix, pp. 63-8.

Dougall Campbell of Auchinbrek, Johne Campbell of Calder, James Campbell of Arkinglass comptrollar, Archibald Campbell of Lochinzell, and Mr Neill Campbell Bischope of Argyll, qyhais counsall my said spous sall follow in all thingis concerning the weill of my sone and his cuntre."

On the other hand it was a power presented as a bastion of "civility" against the Islanders. This appears clearly in a memorandum[1] presented by the "Cadets, kinsmen and branches of the house of Argyle" to Charles II. "We shall not," they explain, "vex your Majesties patience by making mention of many horrid insurrections and rebellions of Islanders, and remote mountainous men that have been broken, destroyed and overthrowen by our Cheiffs and ther freinds, and how many notorious malefactors and cruell oppressors have been brought from ther strong holds and inaccessible places, otherwayes hardly to be overtaken without great blood shead and expence, and yet have been overcome and brought by our Cheifs to ther condigne punishment. . . . They (the House of Argyll) have alwayes been most willing, to sett themselves for bearing doun the insollencie of the remote rebellious lawless men, which is much occasioned by the remotenes and distance of these places quher we live, far from the lawes and Justice, the horror of rocks, woods and mountains contributing much unto this." The power of Argyll in the councils of the nation can never be divorced from the idea of the services that he was ready to perform on behalf of the safety of the Scottish Lowlands.

While he possessed the devoted support of his own clan, Argyll was very easily appreciated in the Lowlands where his shrewdness was never undervalued. His actual household was in some respects an outpost of the South. This is evidenced in a letter from Lady Argyll to Campbell of Glenorchy. "I heair," she wrote,[2] "my sone begines to wearye of the Irishe langwadge. I intreatt yow to cause hold hime to the speakeing of itt, for, since he hes bestowed so long tyme and paines in the getting of itt, I sould be sory he lost itt now with leasiness (laziness) in not speakeing of itt." This suggests that the Gaelic was a foreign tongue to Argyll's immediate family. The point is reinforced by the Marquis's connection with the English congregation at Inverary. He served among the elders[3] as did Archibald Campbell, his master of the household.

The account of the ordering of his day is very significant. The detail is given by Wodrow on the authority of Alexander Gordon,

[1] Memorandum from the friends of Lord Lorne, son to the Marquis of Argyll, dated 26 July 1661 and printed, *ibid.*, pp. 45-50.
[2] Cf. *Black Book of Taymouth*, quoted in Willcock, *op. cit.*, p. 26.
[3] Notes from the session book at Inverary quoted *ibid.*, p. 148.

minister of Inverary. "He told me," it is explained,[1] "that the Marquis of Argyle was very piouse. He rose at five and was still (always) in privat till eight. That besides family worship, and privat prayer morning and evening, he still prayed with his lady morning and evening, his gentleman and her gentlewoman being present; that he never went abroad, though but for one night, but he took his write-book, standish (ink-stand), and the English notes, Bible, and Neuman's Concordance with him." It is not surprising that Argyll's thoughtful modern biographer the Reverend John Willcock should have come to the conclusion[2] that from nature and from grace he had received the gifts which would have fitted him to be both an ecclesiastic and a leader in the General Assembly of a Presbyterian Church. In considering Argyll's position among the Presbyterian lay leaders it is important to stress how different he was from all the others.

Even his political objectives had little in common with those of his colleagues. Apart from the young Earl of Sutherland, he was the only one of the great Covenanting lords whose area of expansion lay in the Highlands. The particular interests and fears and hopes that moved the Lowland peers meant little to Argyll. He had his own duty, and meditation on the Old Testament would teach him how his Highland enemies should be treated. There is, however, a marked contrast in the impressions that he created. On the one hand Gordon of Ruthven had discerned his "homely carriage", while on the other a "close and false carriage" was attributed to him in *The Large Declaration*. As the position in time became clear the King had his reasons for disapproval and profound suspicion. The Marquis of Argyll was not accustomed to reveal the workings of his own mind to his enemies.

[1] *Analecta,* i, p. 22.   [2] Willcock, *op. cit.*, p. 149.

CHAPTER XVI

HAMILTON AND LENNOX

THERE was no strict parallel to the Campbell power, but at the opening of the conflict two further figures should be studied, the Marquis of Hamilton and the Duke of Lennox. Both these princes, for so they were in effect, held land in the South West, while the Lennox lay beside the southern frontier of Argyll's territory. Their significance thus depends in part on their immediate effect in Scotland but much more on account of their situation as filters through which the King could gain his very inadequate knowledge of his northern kingdom.

Certainly there were other influential Scotsmen about the royal person, the Earls of Ancram and Roxburgh, who were kinsmen heading two branches of the House of Kerr, and above all Will Murray. In different ways, however, these three courtiers all suffered from the same defect; they had not the rank, and Murray probably had not the desire to make an independent judgment known in that graded Court. Among secular lords only those who shared the Stuart blood could proffer advice on Scotland to their royal relative.

Roxburgh was an old man who had been close to King James and had in fact accompanied him to England. In 1637 he had become lord privy seal. Throughout he seems to have limited himself to a cautious following of his sovereign's wishes. Ancram was rather younger,[1] a true courtier who had progressed through each stage, gentleman-at-arms in ordinary to Henry Prince of Wales, gentleman of the bedchamber to Prince Charles and lord of the bedchamber on the King's accession. As master of the privy purse he had an apartment in Whitehall. His wife was governess to the three princesses. Ancram benefited by his court offices[2] and took pleasure in accommodating his royal master. Their own increasing years, gratitude for favours received and to

[1] Roxburgh was born about 1570 and Ancram in 1578.

[2] Thus Lord Ancram received on 7 January 1634-5 a grant for seven years of the impost of ten shillings levied on every cwt. of foreign starch imported and also the voluntary duty of four shillings a cwt. provided for the King by the Company of Starchmakers in respect to their own manufacture. This second imposé was charged with rent of £200 *per annum* in favour of the Crown. Cf. Cal.S.P.Dom., 1634-5, p. 454. Difficulties between Lord Ancram and the Company of Starchmakers continued for several years. On 23 June 1638 a grant was made to the Earl of Ancram of the right to find and retain ambergris in His Majesty's Dominions, Cal.S.P.Dom., 1637-8, p. 527. In

come, the custom of silent acceptance of the King's decisions alike combined to prevent both these lords from opening their sovereign's mind to the perils latent in the situation.

Will Murray had a very different background[1] and a character which is hard to decipher. Bishop Burnet has been successful in delivering a whole-hearted attack, but in this case it is worth remembering that the historian was moved by a profound dislike for the Duchess of Lauderdale, who was Murray's daughter. He had the nature of a royal page grown old in service and like all his kind would make his own opportunities. He was, within a year or two, the same age as Charles I and had been educated with him, brought south as a boy by his uncle Thomas Murray, the Prince's tutor, who was determined to push his nephew's fortunes. The elder Murray died shortly after receiving for no especial reason the provostship of Eton, but this did not prevent Will Murray's nomination as groom of the bedchamber. For the rest of his life he remained in his sovereign's intimate service.

He came from a clerical family in Fifeshire with certain landed contacts. His father had been minister of Dysart, which was to provide the title for the earldom which would prove his final and so unexpected recompense. An uncle was minister at Methven throughout the first part of the troubled years.[2] Will Murray was a man of modest origins and modest pickings; the King's domestic, very close in to him, warming his master's drink before the fire. It seems incongruous that such a man should have obtained Ham House. The grant of site and lands was, however, an intimate transaction by which the King and Queen both showed their friendship[3] for a trusted servant. The mansion was perhaps in

the same year he was involved in contentions with patentees for logwood, Cal.S.P.Dom., Charles I, vol. ccclxxviii, 62 and vol. ccclxxix, 15. In this connection Jane Countess of Roxburgh received on 13 July 1637 a grant of £300 *per annum* charged against the duties and profits payable to His Majesty by the gold wire drawers, *ibid.*, vol. ccclxiii, 10.

[1] Thus an undated letter written apparently in 1637 to the Earl of Ancram by the Countess of Carrick, formerly Lady Elizabeth Southwell *née* Howard, asked him to obtain for her from the King either the making of a baronet or a grant of £1,000 charged either against the Exchequer or against the Custom House, Court of Wards or Privy Purse, *ibid.*, vol. ccclxxvii, 131. On 28 March 1639 a pension of £2,000 *per annum* was granted to the Earl of Ancram and the Lady Anne, his wife, during their lives and to the survivor of them payable half yearly out of the Exchequer, *ibid.*, vol. ccccxv, 52. These details reveal perquisites on a lavish scale. Will Murray's grants were very much smaller. His most considerable windfall was a yearly grant of £240 out of the customs and subsidies of smalts, saffers and potashes with forfeitures of the same. Cf. *ibid.*, vol. cccxcvii. Docquet dated 6 August 1638.

[2] Robert Murray was minister there from 1615 until 1648.

[3] Thus a petition by William Murray dated 26 March 1639 states that he held certain lands in the manor of Petersham and Sheen, parcel of the Queen's jointure, for twenty-seven years at a rent of £16 9s., S.P.Dom. Charles I, vol. cccxv, 46.

poor condition and had been vacant since the death of the Earl of Holderness, who as Sir John Ramsay had played so fortunate a part in the Gowrie conspiracy.

Will Murray certainly understood much Scottish feeling. He was close in to the Kirkmen and trusted by them. There were Old Testament precedents for his faithful service. Besides, he always wished to stand well with both parties. It appears that at the least he tried to lull the King and not to warn him. This seems a very natural proceeding for there is no future for the page of the backstairs who warns his master.

By contrast this throws light upon the key position occupied by James Marquis of Hamilton. The viceregal power with which the King was to entrust Hamilton gave him a unique significance. He was in origin completely Scottish and had no English blood. He was never unconscious of his great position as the next heir to the throne of Scotland after the King and his sister and their families. Charles I gave him the affection of a friend and cousin, an attachment shot by a perennial jealousy. Close to the sovereign's person as Master of the Horse, it was inevitable that he should represent Scotland at the English Court. Hamilton had a quick and rather untutored intelligence. This combined with his youth and his high rank gave him a dislike for being used. His initial distaste for his marriage arose partly from the consciousness that Buckingham looked on him as a pawn. He was wary and suspicious like all the House of Hamilton.

The portrait in the National Gallery of Scotland conveys a clear impression. The Marquis is carrying a *bâton* for he stressed his military experience. He is wearing a court dress of cloth of silver; the face above is rather swarthy. His figure was a trifle cumbersome and almost stocky. He was very far in manner and in thought from everything that suggested the Vandyck epoch. He stood outside it, as did both Laud and Strafford. It is a measure of his influence that he was in some ways comparable with these two men, except that he had no policy and lacked tenacity. It was the King's misfortune that the absence of these two qualities was never a bar to his official favour. It seems, when all the evidence is considered, that Hamilton had a concept of loyalty to which he always adhered. In his manner and his correspondence he was very courtly. King Charles would always value a great subject's deference. His approach was contrasted with that of Strafford and Montrose; it was what the King approved of and expected. The key to Hamilton's concern would seem to have lain in his determination to preserve the great position that he held in Scotland. He knew much better than did the King when this was threatened.

This crucial concern perhaps explains his long association with Argyll. It is a possible reading of Hamilton's character that he alone foresaw certain elements in the catastrophe. No other magnate who shared his knowledge of the Scottish situation possessed his close experience of the King's character. It was not in his power or nature to constrain his sovereign as Montrose later wished to constrain him. He had also very limited security; he was dealing always with a King who gave him intimacy and affection, and, in the last analysis, did not trust him.

Hamilton's family feeling was, perhaps, centred on his younger brother whom their master created Earl of Lanark. He had a desire not to be separated from the lords of his family grouping, chief among whom were the Earls of Abercorn and Haddington. The former line was Catholic, but pledged to the head of their own stock. In this connection it may be noted that there was an equivocal element in the tradition of political and religious action followed by the Hamiltons. It was an erroneous but understandable notion that they were always waiting and that the successive heads of the family never gave a perfect loyalty to any sovereign, not to the Queen of Scots, nor in fact to her son, nor to her grandson. Their actions, or sometimes more especially their inaction, gave rise to the impression that they felt that circumstances might play into their hands.

For the rest their Scottish properties were great and well-administered; the rich lands in Clydesdale and about Hamilton; the great house at Kinneill to the west of Edinburgh which Chatelherault had left to them. The effect of these possessions was hardly understood at the English Court. There the Master of the Horse was accepted as just another great figure about the sovereign's person. Hamilton's service abroad emphasised his viceregal quality rather than his deep roots in the northern Kingdom. It is notable that he was not happy with his wife, perhaps he felt that Sir William Feilding's daughter was not fit to match with his high blood. Behind him lay the many generations of the great stocks[1]

[1] Scot of Scotstarvet has certain comments which, although not strictly accurate, provide what may be called the folklore of the Hamiltons. "Chatellerault left four sons, James Earl of Arran, John, Claude and David. The last three were all frantic, as many since of that family have been, viz., The Lord Evandale, who leaped in a hot lime-kiln, and said if hell were no hotter he would endure it. Francis Hamilton, brother to the late Earl of Abercorn, having been furious at his majority, died in the Chartreuse monastery at Paris. And that Lord Abercorn's sister's grandson, the Lord Seton, the first night of his marriage threw a chamber pot at his wife's bosom, and lay in fetters till he died", p. 86. Sir John Scot goes on to state that the first Marquis of Hamilton "married his base sister to John Hamilton, whom he procured to be made Lord Belhaven who in *anno* 1653 was swallowed up in Solway sands, horse and all, and never seen again".

of his own country. Hamilton would never separate himself from Scotland. In this he differed from his younger cousin Lennox whose single principle was attachment to the King's cause.

After an examination of Hamilton's position that of Lennox may be studied. In order to reach a judgment as to the nature of his influence and the effect that he produced in Scotland it is worth placing him in his setting with some care. There were certain superficial resemblances to the head of the rival line. Without Hamilton's interest in collecting objects of art, the younger man had his antiquarian side, a certain restrained interest[1] in architecture and monuments. Both of these great men married English brides, who were in fact first cousins. Their wives were designed for them by Buckingham and Charles I.

Hamilton had the greater share of the King's affection, but Lennox never forfeited his sovereign's strict approval. Both men were conventionally devoted to the chase.[2] Hamilton understood the Court and had his friends and enemies in that closed circle. The Scottish lords were never sure of him. As a curious contrast Lennox hardly knew Scotland but was always welcome there, even in legend and even to the end. Lennox, however, lacked Hamilton's reserves. His history presents no problem. He was very grand and fundamentally quite unambitious.

It was a misfortune for Charles I that he was so often deceived in the aid that he expected from those men he understood. It was not normally a question of a defect of loyalty. His failure was due to the fact that he could not obtain help from those whom he had moulded. Prince Rupert was in many ways the King's antithesis and he performed great services until at the last his uncle sacrificed him. King Charles was not at ease with men who had a mastering virility. This was one of the reasons why the Marquis of Montrose would always irk him. A certain quietness, in contrast to his brothers Lord John and Lord Bernard Stuart, was a quality that appealed to the King in James Duke of Richmond and Lennox.

An exact impression of the fourth Duke of Lennox is conveyed in his portrait[3] now hanging in his own great house at Cobham which lies on the low chalk downs that slope westwards to the

[1] Cf. An entry under 1 September 1640. "The Lord Duke of Lenox, who went by Beverly to see the old Minster and Monuments", *Diary of Sir Henry Slingsby*, ed. Rev. Daniel Parsons, p. 59.

[2] Lloyd states in reference to the Duke of Lennox that "hunting was both his pleasure and accomplishment", *Memoirs*, p. 334.

[3] In 1877 there were portraits of the fourth Duke of Lennox in the possession of the Duke of Buccleugh, the Marquess of Bristol and the Earl of Denbigh. There is also a portrait of the Duke, described as of the School of Vandyck, in the double cube room at Wilton.

Medway. The picture shows a mild young face, the carriage extremely dignified; he had become a grandee of Spain at twenty-one. A large brindled greyhound nestling against the right leg serves to emphasise his height and slenderness. His shoes have a simple black rosette. The Duke is wearing the star and George of the Garter and has a trifling gold moustache. Cobham Hall meant more to him than those wild lands where Lennox marches with the Campbell country.

It was a great red-brick Elizabethan mansion on the largest scale, the north wing still unfinished.[1] The garden was both stately and exotic;[2] the contents of the house included much fashionable tapestry. All this had been granted to his cousin by King James I, who wished to provide the Stuarts of Lennox with a Hatfield of another man's devising. It had fallen to the Crown on Lord Cobham's forfeiture[3] in connection with the Main Plot in 1603. Everything was provided for the young Duke of Lennox by his royal protector; his house and lands; his marriage; his religion. The King arranged his wedding with Buckingham's only daughter. She was the child-bride of Lord Herbert of Shurland and figures in the great Vandyck picture of the Pembroke family on the west wall of the double cube room[4] at Wilton. Her first husband had died of smallpox, while travelling as a boy in Italy.

The planning of this marriage had been one of the King's domestic preoccupations. There had been many rumours. During Lennox's elaborate travels a Princess of Savoy had been suggested[5]

[1] William seventh Lord Cobham began building Cobham Hall in 1584, but only completed the south wing. He died in March 1597 leaving the north wing uncompleted. Cf. *Archaelogia Cantiana*, col. xi, p. 205.

[2] Holinshead has this comment on Lord Cobham, "overpassing . . . the statelie augmenting of his house at Cobham Hall, with the rare garden there, in which no varietie of strange flowers and trees do want, which praise or price maie obteine from the furthest part of Europe . . . or from other strange countries, wherby it is not inferior to the Garden of Semiramis", *Chronicle*, p. 1512.

[3] The grant was subject to a lease for life in favour of Lord Cobham's widow the Countess of Kildare, who survived until 21 June 1628. In a letter to Sir Dudley Carleton dated 22 June 1622 Chamberlain describes the King as going to Cobham to persuade Lady Kildare to pass that house at a reasonable figure to the Duke and Duchess of Lennox, S.P.Dom., James I, vol. cxxxi, 53.

[4] In the same room there is also a portrait by Vandyck of Lady Mary Villiers as Duchess of Lennox. Mrs. Gibson, the dwarf, is seen beside her holding the Duchess's gloves on a tray. A portrait of the Duchess painted under the Commonwealth was in the dining room at Cobham Hall when the inventory was compiled in 1672, *Archaeologia Cantiana*, xvii, p. 393.

[5] Cf. a letter from Pory to Lord Brooke dated 22 October 1632. "There is now a great present of horses and rich saddles to be sent to the Duke of Savoy, where my Lord Ambassador Weston now resideth, and where his brother-in-law the Duke of Lenox, is to marry the Duke's sister", *Court and Times of Charles I*, vol. ii, p. 186. Also Sir Henry Ellis, *Letters*, p. 186. "The

for him. The Queen was said to have favoured a French match;[1] she did not share her husband's feeling for the ladies of the Villiers[2] family. The bride was only fifteen at the time of this second wedding which took place in the disturbed summer of 1637. She bore a child after twelve years. The Lennox marriage proved one of those contented unions which gave the King such satisfaction.

The young Duke also accepted his royal cousin's guidance in religious matters. The family background may be described as a courtier-like Erastianism grafted upon a Catholic past. The chiefs of the House of Lennox were sensitive to their sovereign's notions; the second and third Dukes had followed James VI's developing preferences very closely.[3] Lennox, himself, had been bred an Anglican from childhood. There had been a slight contact with George Herbert since the Duke's mother, who had been the heiress of Leighton Bromswold, had given a donation to the church at Leighton Ecclesia. Archbishop Laud performed the christenings and marriages for all the family.

There were Catholic contacts on the distaff side; his French grandmother of whom they all stood in awe;[4] his mother who was *mondaine* and extravagant and a convert of the Capuchins;[5] perhaps at a later stage his wife.[6] Three younger brothers were brought up as Catholics so as to inherit Aubigny and be eligible

Duke of Lennox is to marry in Savoy." Robert Baillie indicates the standing of the Duke of Scotland. "We had hopes he might have obtained one of the Palatine's sisters", *Letters and Journals*, i, p. 11.

[1] The Queen is said to have favoured a marriage with Mlle de Bourbon, daughter of the Prince of Condé, Mlle de Saint Paul or Mlle de Rohan, *Strafford Letters*, p. 64.   [2] *Ibid.*, pp. 45-7.

[3] The second Duke had been brought over to Scotland in 1584 aged ten and his brother the third Duke had come to England aged twenty-four. Both had hitherto been educated in France as Catholics.

[4] Catherine Duchess of Lennox *née* de Balsac d'Entragues lived as a widow at Aubigny in Berri from 1583 until 1632. On her character cf. a letter from the Master of Gray to the second Duke of Lennox dated at Paris 9 November 1598. "I remainit vit my Lady your Lordschips mother at Obignie four dayis . . . Sche (the Duchess) is a verie hard voman, yet with good vsage ye may be master of all sche hes", *Cal. Moray MSS.*, Appendix to sixth Report, p. 659.

[5] Fr Cyprien de Gamache, one of the Capuchin Fathers of the Provinces of Paris, refers to the conversion of the Duchess of Lennox, mother of M. d'Aubigny in his *Memoirs*, p. 481. Her second husband James second Earl of Abercorn is referred to by Robert Baillie. "Her husband, mainely by her princely carriage, is more then four hundreth thousand merks in debt" *Letters and Journals*, I, p. 22.

[6] Fr Cyprien de Gamache mentions the conversion of Buckingham's sister the Duchess of Richmond, *op. cit.*, p. 408. It is difficult to find confirmation for this statement.

[7] Lord Henry, Lord George and Lord Ludovic went to France, while Lord John (b. 1621) and Lord Bernard (b. 1623) remained in England as Protestants.

for French ecclesiastical preferment. Clarendon's point made in connection with the Duke's outlook carries conviction. "His affection[1] to the Protestant religion was unquestionable and very eminent; and though his sisters, who had been bred under their mother, were Catholics, yet his brothers (of whose education he had the sole care) were very good Protestants." This is worth quoting because in Scotland the Duke of Lennox was not regarded as a Laudian or as in any way committed to Episcopacy. With a deep attachment to the King he was clearly not a man to speak his mind. He had a royal manner whose courtesy made approach seem easy; in fact he was considerably influenced by those about him and notably by Thomas Webb[2] his secretary and manager.

Certainly there was much for him to manage. In the first place Lennox had his hereditary offices which had come to him through his uncle and then his father. As a boy of twelve and acting through deputies he was already Lord High Admiral and Great Chamberlain of Scotland, Keeper of Dumbarton Castle, Sheriff of Lothian and Lennox. Perhaps in regard to all his posts and lands in the northern kingdom he never gave over acting by deputy. For there were the immediate responsibilities in England and all the perquisites. Sir Robert Gordon, who was an adherent of the House of Lennox and one of the Duke's tutors, gives an impression of how these were looked upon in Scotland. "His Majestie," he writes[3] in describing the kindness of James VI to his near cousin, "took a great care of the young duke his education, according to his birth and qualitie, appoynting his particular and domestick servants. . . . His matie. even then admitted him gentleman of his bedchamber, and allowed him the yeirlie pension of fourtein hundreth pounds sterlin, which his father had obteined befor his death, for his table in the king's hous, as a speciall grace and favour to that familie, which no other subject in Britane had." He pointed[4] out that the Duchess and her young son and after them the next heir of the House of Lennox had been granted a life-rent of £2,100 sterling. This was chargeable on the Court of Wards. It seems that the general effect produced in Scotland was a feeling of respect for such good fortune.

[1] *History of the Rebellion.* i, p. 259. Lloyd describes the Duke as attached to the Church of England and "well skilled in all its points", *Memoirs*, p. 334.

[2] Thomas Webb died in October 1649 and was buried at Cobham aged forty-nine. Cf. *Archaeologia Cantiana*, vol. xii, p. 101. Clarendon was critical of his influence upon his master.

[3] Sir Robert Gordon, *op. cit.*, p. 390.

[4] *Ibid.*, p. 390. Further details are also given. "King Charles (who now reigneth) hath confirmed both his place and the pensions, and followes his father's steps in his love towards that familie, and hath now latelie payed to the Lord Douglas the marriage portion of Lady Anne Stewart, the Duke of Lennox his sister", *ibid.*, p. 390.

His uncle Ludovick Duke of Richmond and Lennox and the latter's third wife, who was by birth a Howard of Bindon, had accumulated gifts from James VI. All these now came to him. A note was set down in 1624 regarding them; the patents of the profits of the ulnage of undressed cloths which would mature in seven years and then had forty-two years to run; the patent of the greenwax; the patent of sweet wines and sugars; the patent of Newcastle coals. These three last grants had each a duration[1] of twenty-one years. Annexed to the patent of the greenwax was a sum of three thousand pounds due as arrearages and payable out of the Hanaper.

A controlling factor in the development of Lennox's life was his uncle's widow Frances Duchess of Richmond. She had been a great figure in the last days of King James carrying herself like a princess.[2] Her intention was to minister to the grandeur of her husband's stock and to re-acquire for it the English dukedom of Richmond, which had died with him. She stressed the royal associations of that title which recalled Henry VII.

With the exception of Cobham, the Duke had no house suitable to his rank. It is notable that he never attempted to build in Scotland or to reconstruct one of the castles which formed a part of the revived Lennox inheritance. His property in the North of England at Settrington and Temple Newsam formed two large blocks of land without a mansion. Lord Clifton's house at Leighton, which had come to his mother, was still unfinished.[3] Lennox's interest was concentrated upon Cobham; he purchased land at Strood and in the neighbouring parishes; he became the chief proprietor in the Isle of Grain. Later he desired and obtained the post of Lord Warden of the Cinque Ports.

---

[1] These details are given in an account of claims and privileges passed by the Duchess of Richmond to the third Duke of Lennox and his son, then styled the Earl of Darnley. The patent of the greenwax is described as worth fifteen hundred pounds a year and it is stated in regard to the profits from the ulnage that "Her Grace hath ffoure and twentie hundred pounds by the yeare for it nowe", State Papers, Dom., James I, vol. clxxi, no. 87. Cf. *Archaeologia Cantiana*, xi, p. 2225.

[2] A letter from Chamberlain to Carleton dated 8 January 1625 refers to the Duchess of Richmond. Her magnificence is much talked of: she went to her chapel at Ely House, with her four principal officers marching before her in velvet gowns with white staves, three gentlemen-ushers and two ladies to bear her train", Cal.S.P.Dom., 1623-5, p. 441. This may be paralleled by a letter written by her husband to Sir Edward Herbert, then Ambassador in Paris, and dated from Newbottle on 28 August 1619. I have sent some merlins (esmerillons) to the King (of France) which will come later than I expected because I stayed in the north of Scotland longer than I intended. If these please him, I will provide him every year earlier, Cal. Powis MSS., p. 380.

[3] Cf. *Archaeologia Cantiana*, xii, p. 51. Lord Clifton died in 1618. For his lawsuit with his son-in-law about land, cf. Cal. Bouverie MSS., p. 84.

The Duchess of Richmond, who had retired to Exeter House in the Strand, did all that she could to aid him. Her mind was set on his mgnificence and on the external glory of the House[1] of Lennox. She had already handed over[2] "three rich coaches, th'one of yellow velvet. Another of yellow satten imbroidered with fflour-delices of black velvet & gould, The third of black & yellow figur'd satten". To these were added the furniture belonging to my Lord's belonging in the Gatehouse at Whitehall with a wrought bed "that had been My Lady Margaret Lenoxes and of her working". There was a fine bason and ewer that "the French King gave my Lord". All this has a definite bearing on a great household seen in movement.

When she died in October 1639 the Dowager Duchess left her nephew £5,000 in ready money,[3] all the arrearages due to her from Mr Mompesson, and the patent[4] of white cloth. She left a massive quantity of jewellery.[5] To these details may be added those taken from a later inventory which will describe the actual background of Cobham Hall. There had always been much tapestry; new Mortlake and Brussels hangings from the time of Charles I; a set relating to Marcus Aurelius; a whole series of old pieces; some rooms had gilded leather hung on cloth. There were many portraits; the wardrobe of pictures was then filled with them. In the last calm years Cobham Hall had been brightened by Vandyck's familiar conversation piece of Lord John Stuart with his brother in amber satin.

This portrait more than the others manifests the intimate share of the Lennox family in that private cultural background which

[1] "I desire addition and increase of blessings to that howse of Lenox in euerie kind. And I give to my nephewe of Lenox and his wife my black and white powdered Ermyn coach with all the furniture belongine to it to mourn for me when God taketh me", extract from the Will of Frances Duchess of Richmond preserved in the Principal Registry of the Court of Probate and printed in full in *Archaeologia Cantiana*, xi, pp. 232-49.

[2] These details are set out in a paper dated August 1624, State Papers Dom., James I, vol. clxxi, no. 87. Cf. *Archaeologia Cantiana*, xi, p. 225.

[3] "I give to my Nephewe the Duke of Lenox the five thousand poundes in a greene sack written upon for him, which from my heart I wish it were twenty thousand", Will printed *ibid.*, xi, p. 237.

[4] The value of the arrearages was calculated to be £5,297 6s. 8d. The patent, which was of small importance and had been granted in the first place by Queen Elizabeth to the third Earl of Cumberland, brought in £620 against which was charged £100 annually for the Exchequer. She also bequeathed to the Duke the sum of £6,200 owed to her by Lady Elizabeth Hatton, *ibid.*, pp. 234, 236-7.

[5] The Duchess of Richmond left to her nephew and niece "my Chaine of pearle which is five hundred and odd . . . my greate coller of redd and white roses of Diamonds and rubies vsuallie called Lancaster and York which blessed King James gave me. . . . The ffrench jewell of Diamonds that wes my Lords. . . . There are two ropes of pearles . . . all these be paragon", *ibid.*, p. 236.

Q

the King and Queen so prized. In a sense the set-up just described
appears as unimaginative; a property not radically solvent but
shored up by new grants and by old King James's monopolies. It
may have been the stiff grandeur and the sense of royal position
that appealed to the Scottish magnates; this, and on Lennox's side
a sense of obligation and on the part of the Scots lords vicarious
pride. Lennox was a stranger in his own country. He was in fact
a Royal Stuart rather than a Scotsman. In consequence he received
from the northern leaders, both those in the General Assembly
and among the peers, the respect that they would accord to one
of his exalted blood who did not interfere with them.

Still, a deceptive solidarity bound together all the heads of the
great houses, Argyll, Huntly, Douglas, Hamilton and Lennox.
They shared a tangled history of half-alliance and long-seeded
enmity. They were an inevitable constituent in the old-fashioned
Scottish kingdom. Even if the individual was destroyed as Argyll
eventually brought down his brother-in-law Huntly, their lands
remained to heir or heritrix. They could not escape from one
another. This was a situation which James VI well understood,
but not his son.

CHAPTER XVII

THE NATIONAL COVENANT

IT is a commonplace that the introduction of the new Prayer Book provided the actual occasion for the outbreak of the Scottish conflict. This liturgy was a long-meditated project, which enabled the opposition to draw together. Still, it is very doubtful if the problem would not have been settled peacefully had it not been allied with the new authority in political affairs that the King had recently confided to the Scottish bishops. Charles I was unlucky in his sources of information for Archbishop Laud was ignorant and the Earl of Traquair timorous. In the latter case allowance must be made for the fact that it was extremely difficult for a minister of the Crown to speak to his anointed sovereign on matters which the King felt lay uniquely within his competence. A man much more resolute than Traquair would have found it hard to argue with his master on a question which Charles I conceived as a part of his religious obligation.

It was the more unfortunate that Charles I should have constituted Archbishop Laud his sole adviser in dealing with the problems of the Church of Scotland since the primate met with hostility from the whole body of Scottish lay councillors. It does not seem that Laud realised this fact; he was long accustomed to confuse respect and deference. A case in point is his correspondence with Lord Traquair, who had been nominated to the treasurership in 1636. The Lord Treasurer appears to have been an anti-clerical Episcopalian, one who would have wished the King to use his natural advisers. A portrait at Traquair House near Innerleithen shows him in his gold-laced robe of office, his right hand on a red cloth of estate with gilded tassels. He is wearing a slight beard and his still brown hair is seen against the background of a russet curtain. It is a serious face but not a strong one. Traquair's exact age is unknown and there are few details of his education. He was considered to be hostile to the bishops; a stickler for the influence of the Council; a half-hearted supporter of the King who had promoted him. In the quiet years he had paid his court to the Duke of Lennox and had acted for him in the business of the Admiralty.[1] He had a sad devoted

[1] Among the Traquair MSS. are two letters from the Duke of Lennox dated 9 October 1633 and 10 January 1633-4. The earlier refers to "ye black horse of Sir John Fenneck's wch. is known to ye Earle of Traquair". There are also several letters from the Duke's secretary Thomas Webb.

wife,[1] who was a daughter of Lord Southesk, an eminently sober connection. It is strange to note that this made him Montrose's brother-in-law.

He embellished Traquair House, an ancient high building resembling a mansion in a wynd at Edinburgh; he surrounded himself with seemly portraits; his estate was always moderate. Later the family was to become both Catholic and Jacobite. In one respect the Stewarts of Traquair were remarkable. They were spared the sufferings which befell their contemporaries. They cannot be said to have been an able race. But they were prudent in their mental processes, cautious and solitary. It was characteristic that Traquair should have contrived to be absent when the members of the Council went to St Giles' Cathedral for the ceremony of the introduction of the new Prayer Book.

There seems something forced in the alarm which Lord Treasurer Traquair inspired among the Presbyterian ministers. They appear to have built up on paper the power of those whom they knew that they would be able to pull down. This is seen vividly in their correspondence. Robert Baillie should be quoted on this subject. His tumultuous verbiage well conveys both the sense of urgency and also the egalitarian approach of the Kirk leaders. The first comment is a fairly mild one in connection with the vacant bishopric of Argyll. "The Thesaurer," wrote[2] Baillie to William Spang on 29 January 1637, "who now guides our Scotts affairs with the most absolute sovereigntie that any subject among us this fourtie yeares did kyth, is for his old master, Mr James Fairley; and he is most redoubted for the greatness of his friend." The Treasurer was successful in this particular candidature.[3] In the same letter Baillie continues on a note of excitement; disentangling the meaning it is clear that the ministers were in two minds about Traquair. The Ross, Glasgow and St Andrews that he mentions were the bishops of these respective sees.

He begins[4] by a reference to Archbishop Lindsay's[5] troubles. "If he (the Lord Treasurer) doe a third like thir (these) two to poor Glasgow, I think he will kill him with displeasure. There is a God We hear the Bishops are confident that Traquair shall be their arme to force the country, by horrible fynes, to obey all their injunctions: they say he gave Canterberrie this assurance at his

---

[1] There is a portrait of the Countess of Traquair at Traquair House.

[2] *Letters and Journals of Robert Baillie*, ed. David Ling, i, p. 6. Dr. Baillie was at that time regent of philosophy in Glasgow University.

[3] James Fairlie at that time minister of Greyfriars, Edinburgh, was consecrated on 8 August 1637 as Bishop of Argyll. After his deposition the next year he became minister at Laswade, *H.B.C.*, p. 216.

[4] *Letters and Journals of Robert Baillie*, i, p. 8.

[5] Patrick Lindsay was Archbishop of Glasgow 1633-1638.

first advancement; but others doe hope that he will be moved to remonstrate to the King the countrie's grievance at the Bishops proceedings: it is evident that he setts himself to crosse their generall designes, and almost professes to doe particular despite to his antagonist Rosse, also to Glasgow and St Andrewes." It is characteristic of Traquair that he would always remain ambiguous.

Then Baillie lays influence on the power of Lennox and Traquair. "Neglect not," he wrote to an unknown correspondent,[1] "to cause Angus and Rothus at least, if no mo, to speike plaine Scottish to my Lord Duke of Lennox and the Thesaurer; what may cost them readilie their life and their lands, all they not use means diligentlie to avert it." It is remarkable how the theme is heightened, each menace and each danger. This appears in a letter in which Baillie sets out his view of the Prayer Book and of the policy that fathered it. The phrases give the climate of opinion and it is well to put them down before considering the actual facts of the situation.

"These," he writes,[2] "which are averse from the ceremonies, whereof there is great numbers, yea almost all our nobilitie and gentrie of both sexes, counts that Booke little better than the Masse, and are farr on a way to separate from all who will imbrace it. . . . God grant I may prove a false prognosticator; I look for the most pitiful schism that ever poor Kirk has felt." He then sets out the Bishops' policy as he conceived it. "Presbyteries, Sessiones, Assemblies, must down; the Bishop and his officiall, the Warden and the clerk, and the Priest of the parishe must up; the new formes of Baptisme, Eucharist, Marriage, Buriell, Prayers, Psalmes, Preaching, must be received under the paines of depositione, excommunicatione and horning; who will not yield, he is a seditious, factious rebell, not only against the Kirk and King, bot God and his fyfte command: Sundrie of them, in their preaching, discourses, and printed books, declareing their mindes for many tenets of Poperie and Arminianisme; none of them shewing any appearance of zeall for repressing of Papists or Arminians at home, for redressing the afflicted state of Protestants abroad; the most of them openlie hunting for advancement, state offices, pensions; casting the modestie, painfull lecture, preaching, and such other

[1] *Ibid.*, i, p. 14. The editor suggests that it is addressed to either Robert Wilkie or John Maxwell, ministers of Glasgow. Another letter refers to the supposed influence of Traquair over Lennox. "Our Thesaurer, they say, is written for to Court: his friends give out it is to persuade the Duke (of Lennox), with whom he hes great credit, to that match with Pembroke's sonnes widow, Buckingham's daughter", *ibid.*, i, p. 11.

[2] *Ibid.*, pp. 4, 5.

ecclesiastick vertues underfoot." This passage is worth considering. It certainly reflects the opinion of the ministers. The next few years would show how far the great Scots lord would endure "ecclesiastick vertues". In general the lords wished for the withdrawal of the new authority in secular matters which the King had granted to the Scottish prelates. They had no intention of replacing the bishops by a domination of the Presbytery both spiritual and temporal.

As Baillie has remarked[1] there was a cold antagonism between Lord Treasurer Traquair and Archbishop Spottiswoode, who held the office of lord chancellor. An attempt had been made to introduce the Bishop of Ross as treasurer at the last vacancy.[2] There was no peer so friendly to the bishops that he wished to see them entrusted with these key posts. This feeling arose only in part from baulked personal ambition and a distaste for the clergy in high places: it was linked to a well-founded suspicion that if the bishops of Laud's choosing held the great offices they would be used as the instruments of direct rule from London.

This development formed part of a policy which was being pressed forward at an increasing pace since the King's visit to Scotland in 1633 for his coronation. On that occasion he had Laud at his side. The project for the resumption of the tithes and their transfer from the landowners to the parishes, as well as the parallel plan for endowing bishoprics with the still intact lands of abbeys,[3] immediately affected the great lords while giving independence to their rivals. It is true that there were contemporary precedents, both in England and Ireland, for the holding

---

[1] Cf. "So it goes to the mids of July (1636), when the King's letters come down to dissolve the Commission for the Tithes, till farder advysement, procured, as most thought, by the Thesaurer to crosse the Chancellor", *ibid.*, p. 17.

[2] Baillie's account will indicate one strand of contemporary opinion on this subject. "The next rubb they (the bishops) gatte wes in the matter of the Thesaurer, fra Canterberrie had gottin the Bishop of London Thesaurer of Ingland. At the word of Mortoun's dimission, Rosse thought himself sure of that office, and so did we all; bot the Duke and the Marques, sett out by a number of our Noblemen, did concur to stirr up Traquair (as he letts out sore against his heart) to make meins for that place, that he might, by his great partes, be a barr to hinder the inundatione of our impetuous Clergie, which wes like to overflow all. This place he obtained in despyte of them and since he hes ever been a thorn in their side", *ibid.*, p. 7.

[3] Baillie sets out his view upon this matter. "The last year, our Bishops guided all our estate, and became verie terrible to our whole countrie: they are now a little lower. The first rubb they had wes in the matter of the Abbacie of Lindores. They had weill near gottin that through, as a first preparative to have made all the rest follow, that all our Abbacies should have been conferred on preachers, that so many new Lords of Parliament should have been erected for the Church. This all the Nobilitie did so band themselves against, that the King's minde was drawn clean off the designe", *ibid.*, pp. 6, 7.

of great offices by churchmen. In Scotland, however, the ruling oligarchy conceived such a move as a threat to their own position implemented by an absent sovereign and engineered by his alien ecclesiastical adviser.

It was the weakness of the King's situation that no group was more deeply opposed to the royal policy of granting offices of state to prelates than the members of the Council in Scotland. In any conflict in which the prelates were involved he therefore could not rely either on the existing members of his Council or on any lord who might be called upon to join that body. This last factor was masked by the way in which the conflict actually developed. In the first months the refusal to accept the Prayer Book by ministers and their congregations could be looked on as a matter of church discipline. In consequence the early pronouncements by the Council were firm enough. It was a feature of the movement against the Prayer Book that it grew in strength as its scope widened. A serious attack on the bishops found the Council in great part on the side of the attackers. It served to unite those who disliked the prelates with those who envied them that authority in secular affairs which the King was determined to entrust to them. They were thus the inevitable scapegoats and all those in the field of politics would gain by their elimination.

Leaving aside the situation in the North East of Scotland, it can be held that their only lay friends of consequence were those who had not experienced their new power, men like Roxburgh who had lived for many years at the English Court. Two other factors entered into the hostility which the bishops, as a body, had aroused. In the case of the more religious lords the guidance of the ministers resembled a Genevan variant of the relation between a director and his penitent. David Dickson had just this hold upon Eglinton's judgment. At the other end of the scale was the "loose-living Puritan" represented in Scotland by Rothes and in England, if Clarendon's testimony is to be accepted, by the Earl of Warwick. Between these extremes stood the bulk of the Scots lords of strict opinions.

A minor element was the hostility of the Catholics and crypto-Catholics towards the prelacy which harried them. It is only in Aberdeenshire that even formal good relations can be detected. The whole body of the lords, except for the few who were in part Anglicized, appear to have been moved by a profound but still hardly conscious dislike of England. It was this that made the name of Laud so clear a rallying cry.

The actual origins of the new Prayer Book were more complex than its contemporary opponents would admit. Dr Laud had originally proposed the introduction of the English Prayer Book without alteration and had shown himself unexpectedly mild in accepting representations from the Scottish bishops. It is possible that, with all his other preoccupations, the question hardly roused his detailed interest. The most important individual contribution was, perhaps, that of Bishop Maxwell of Ross, who may be held to represent at least in part the views of Spottiswoode. Three younger Scottish bishops[1] nominated since the Coronation through Laud's direct intervention fall into a single category. William Forbes first Bishop of Edinburgh was the only one who manifested an eirenic approach towards the Latin Church. He died in April 1634 barely two months after his consecration. Two other prelates may accurately be described as Laudian, Sydserff of Galloway and Wedderburn[2] of Dunblane. Both these men came from that mercantile[3] background with which Laud felt himself at ease, while Wedderburn held preferments in England and used the English idiom. Sydserff, who apparently at one time had been Traquair's tutor,[4] was of less account. He was not an intellectual, but appears to have supported the proposal to introduce the English Prayer Book. Wedderburn had an individual approach. His contribution to the new Prayer Book, and it was not unimportant, is to be traced in changes in the Communion Office. Dr Donaldson in his careful analysis of the composition of this Liturgy states[5] that Wedderburn "had clearly fallen under the spell of the first Prayer Book of Edward VI". It has been the tendency to ignore the "Scottish Canterburian" element.

The work of the Bishop of Ross had a different emphasis. He was the representative of Archbishop Spottiswoode, who made him his executor and would have wished him for his successor as primate. Dr Donaldson has pointed out[6] that senior Scottish bishops also took an active share in the revision. They had in the first place represented that "their countrymen[7] would be much better satisfied if a liturgy were framed by their own clergy than to have the English liturgy put upon them". The discovery among

[1] Bishop Sydserff was born in 1581 and Bishops William Forbes and Wedderburn in 1585.
[2] Bishop Guthry wrote, "By the Archbishop of Canterbury's moyen Mr Thomas Sydeserfe was made bishop of Brechin, and Dr Wedderburn bishop of Dublainie", *Memoirs*, p. 16. Sydserff was later translated to Galloway.
[3] This is stated in *D.N.B.*, xviii, p. 1213.
[4] *The making of the Scottish Prayer Book of 1637* by Gordon Donaldson, p. 81.
[5] Bishop Sydserff was the son of a merchant in Edinburgh and Bishop Wedderburn was the son of John Wedderburn, mariner and shipowner of Dundee.
[6] Donaldson, *op. cit.*, p. 82.
[7] Quoted *ibid.*, p. 55.

the Earl of Haddington's manuscripts of the draft sent north in 1634 enables us to judge the changes made.

As an example the Scottish bishops succeeded in replacing the term "priest" used in the draft of 1634 by the word "presbyter", which is found in the final version. They also greatly reduced the number of passages from the Apocrypha, whose insertion in any form was opposed to the tradition of the Scottish Church. Among the factors which were bound to arouse opposition[1] were the King's insistence on the printing of the Kalendar with the saints' names[2] set out in full, the so-called ornaments rubric and the vestments which this seemed to imply, and in particular the actual phrasing of the royal warrant. The King's words ran as follows: "I gave[3] the Archbp. of Canterbury command to make the alterations expressed in this book, and to fit a liturgy for the Church of Scotland."

It is not possible to discover at what time it was decided to use the order for the reading of the new Prayer Book as an occasion for an act of defiance. The riot in St Giles' Cathedral took place on 23 July 1637, but the actual text of the Liturgy was only completed three months previously.[4] Archbishop Spottiswoode was over seventy[5] and seems to have felt that the actual situation could last his time. He had had an easy relationship with Archbishop Abbot, who was Laud's enemy and predecessor. It seems that in dealing with the new primate he maintained the type of working arrangement which their own high rank and loyalty to Church and Crown required of them. Laud for his part had little in common with Bishop Maxwell, who had hereditary political affiliations in his own country. He was a cousin of James Maxwell of Innerwick, a gentleman of the bedchamber[6] to James I and Charles I, who was later created Earl of Dirleton; he thus also had private approaches to the English Court.

It may be hazarded that it was as much Maxwell's political ambitions as his theology which caused his opponents to attack him. He was a privy councillor; an extraordinary lord of session; a candidate for honours. Among the younger generation of the bishops, he alone showed a clear executive capacity. It was the

---

[1] These points are discussed in detail *ibid.*, pp. 73-8.

[2] Among those commemorated in the Kalendar was St Margaret, Queen of Scotland, *ibid.*, p. 261.

[3] Quoted *ibid.*, p. 55.

[4] On 5 April 1637 Spottiswoode sent a copy of the Prayer Book to Bishop Wren of Norwich.

[5] Archbishop Spottiswoode was born in 1565 and Bishop Maxwell in 1590.

[6] "At the intreaty of James Maxwell of the bed-chamber, Mr. John Maxwell (was) made bishop of Ross", Guthry, *Memoirs*, p. 16.

prelate whose ideas were more Scottish who was the target for reasons which lay within the field of politics.[1]

It is worth considering the extent and limitations of the movement against the Prayer Book. This is the harder to assess because the successful resistance has crystallised into a legend. It seems that as soon as it was obvious that the Bishops were powerless to intervene the resistance was taken up wholeheartedly by the ministers and by the vocal element among their flocks. Beyond this it is difficult to go. A fairer impression of the sentiment of the people can be gathered some six months later when the National Covenant was prepared for their signature.

The summer and autumn of 1637 were occupied in the development of a series of supplications sent to the Council, all of which petitioned for the withdrawal of the Prayer Book. After the riot at St Giles' Cathedral in the presence of the councillors no further attempt had been made to impose the new Liturgy. It was, however, in use in Bishop's Maxwell's chapel at Fortrose until March 1638. With the attack on the chapel in that month the use of the Prayer Book service ceased in Scotland. During this period the diocese of Aberdeen was tranquil. The successful episcopate of Bishop Patrick Forbes had ended in 1635 and his successor Adam Bellenden was not a considerable figure. He was an elderly man promoted from Dunblane;[2] a member of a leading legal family;[3] as a minister he had shown himself anti-Episcopalian.[4] The leading figure in the diocese was the late bishop's son, Dr John Forbes. His public action falls within the period when resistance to the National Covenant was organised. Besides, Aberdeenshire lay primarily in the Gordon sphere of influence and at this stage the Marquis of Huntly was not brought into play.

The King's attitude to the refusal of the Prayer Book was angry, over-confident and uncomprehending. The Duke of Lennox was married during these days at Lambeth Palace by Archbishop Laud and was called to Scotland on his private affairs. The King

[1] Bishop Guthry comments as follows: "Now among these late bishops whom King Charles preferred, none were generally esteemed gifted for the office except Bishop Maxwell, of whom it cannot be denied, that he was a man of great parts; but the mischief was, they were accompanied with unbounded ambition, for it did not content him to be a lord of the secret Council (as were the rest) but he hehoved also to be a lord of the exchequer, and a lord of session extraordinary, and at last to be lord high treasurer, which proved fatal to them all", *Memoirs*, pp. 16-7.

[2] Adam Bellenden graduated M.A. at the university of Edinburgh on 1 August 1590.

[3] His father Sir John Bellenden and his brother Sir Lewis Bellenden, Lord Auchinoul had both held the office of lord justice clerk.

[4] In 1906 he had been one of the forty-two ministers who signed a protest to parliament against the introduction of episcopacy.

instructed his cousin to enquire into the reasons for the Council's neglect to enforce the royal instructions. Lennox's stately youthful dignity was not without its advantages in Scotland. He was as yet unassociated with any policy. A certain slowness of mind helped him to preserve the gift of silence. "My Lord Duke of Lennox," wrote[1] Baillie, "coming down post for his mother's buriall, who had died of a feavor and wes buried the 17 of September in the night without ceremonie; for her husband (the Earl of Abercorn)[2] mainely by her princely carriage, is more than four hundreth thousand merks in debt; My Lord Duke, I say, had the carrying of the King's letter to the Counsell . . ." An account is then given of Lennox's reception in the West of Scotland. "My Lord Duke was carefully sollisted to agent this weighty business, and hes promised to doe his endeavour. In his passage he was magnificently entertained in the Town House of Glasgow,—he hes subscryved, in the Bishop's presence, an ancient band of his house, to maintain that good towne under the King, against all whomsoever to his power." Baillie makes[3] the further comment that "His Grace did avow, that the King was misinformed much about the nature of the business". By this time, too, Traquair had trimmed his sails.[4] He always knew the limits of the possible and was not the man to affront the considered interests of his own class. This becomes clear in the account of Lennox's attendance at the Council. "All, with most earnest affection, commended the affair (of the Prayer Book) to the Duke's Grace. The Thesaurer, his guider, layes it much to heart; and albeit it was greatly feared that he (Traquair) should have been the violent executor of the King's commands, yet he hes given the Noblemen full assurance that he will venture all he hes before our Reverend fathers get our sweet Prince so farr abused, as to losse needlessly the hearts of all his subjects."

Lennox returned to England in October and in the winter Traquair was sent to London by the Council. The King's position was perfectly straightforward. In his view the objections were unreasonable and the Council pusillanimous. He had given his personal attention to the Prayer Book and it was in fact his duty

[1] *Letters and Journals*, i, p. 22.

[2] The Duchess of Lennox had married James second Earl of Abercorn in 1632 and left three sons by this union, in addition to the ten children by her first husband. Abercorn was only nine years older than his step-son.

[3] *Ibid.*, p. 22.

[4] It is worth stating Bishop Guthry's point of view. "John Earl of Traquair, high treasurer (under profession of friendship enough to the bishops) had under-hand dealing with their adversaries, for he conceived a jealousy (and many thought not without cause) that the bishops intended his fall, to the end Mr. John Maxwell, bishop of Ross, might be made treasurer: and therefore in a covered way he did what he could to supplant them", *Memoirs*, p. 14.

to set it forward. He intended to reject the various petitions, but on the other hand he was prepared to take the view that their sponsors had acted in good faith. If they were dropped, he on his part would avoid recriminations. As so often, King Charles's ideas were reasonable on their own plane; the difficulty was that they lacked contact with Scots reality.

Moreover, Archbishop Laud was discouraging even to his own supporters. He had never learned the amenities of episcopal correspondence; he was brusque and discourteous with the Scottish bishops. The letters written to Dr Bellenden are notable for their severity.[1] Even when jocular, he was 'heavy handed. "Then," he wrote[2] to Bishop Maxwell of Ross on one occasion, "if you do not see the Chapel well furnished, the blame for ever be yours." In writing to the Archbishop of St Andrews his tone was high. Bishop Bellenden had again exacerbated him. "Now," he is found exclaiming,[3] "while the King is settling that Church against all things that were defective in it . . . the new Bishop of Aberdeen hath given way to and allowed a public fast throughout his diocese to be kept upon the Lord's day, contrary to the rules of Christianity." These were hard sayings when addressed to a brother metropolitan.

At one time Dr Laud had a certain kindness for Traquair[4] and would criticize the bishops and especially Spottiswoode in writing to him. It was, perhaps, a habit that he had carried over from his frank correspondence with Wentworth about the shortcomings of the Irish prelates. In using this candour he misunderstood Traquair's real standpoint. The position of the Scottish bishops was very difficult. At the English Court their only true supporter was the King. On the other hand Laud demanded an obedience to his orders that they could not give and a courageous resistance that they could not muster.

The management of the opposition, as far as the lay notables were concerned, appears to have been in the hands of the Earl of Rothes, who is one of the key figures of the period. In spite of the benefits of a long minority, his widespread estates were never freed from liabilities; he is a classic example of a leader of the opposi-

---

[1] Cf. Letters dated 14 January 1633, 6 May 1634, 1 July 1634 and 4 October 1634, *Works of Archbishop Laud*, vol. vi, pt. ii, pp. 340-1, 370-1, 383, and 395-6. A letter dated 19 May 1635 is more cordial. "The King hath been acquainted with your care of the Chapel Royal, and is very well pleased with the conformity that hath been there at the late reception of the blessed Sacrament", *ibid.*, p. 419.

[2] Letter dated at Croydon 19 September 1635, *ibid.*, pp. 434-6.

[3] Letter dated 1 December 1636, *ibid.*, pp. 443-4.

[4] Cf. Letters dated 4 July, 7 August and 11 September 1637, *ibid.*, pp. 491-3, 493-6 and 504-6.

tion beset by money troubles. He can be described as a professional opponent of the Government; he had voted against the five Articles of Perth in the year in which he came of age. He was without that continental education which was a commonplace in his class, a cheerful, amorous Scotsman, shrewd and astute and with a vein of hardy eloquence. Throughout life he was threatened by consumption which in the end proved fatal to him. He was a political Presbyterian with a sound Protestant inheritance; the Master of Rothes had killed Cardinal Beaton. It is not surprising that he could not gain the full trust of the ministers, but it was an asset in the circles of the opposition that he had earned the King's personal dislike. He was looked on as the one Scots lord towards whom his sovereign was implacable; it is interesting to speculate how early he had decided that, on terms, he might sell out to him.

In this he should not be judged too harshly. In Scottish history the only way forward had been by submission to the sovereign, to the king free or to the king captive. Rothes was a *bon viveur* and organiser, nothing of a soldier, a diplomat of the camps. The gathering together of a party was his main work. He had few close relatives except that he was married to Mar's sister. At this time he was thirty-seven years of age; the lords who were his contemporaries and juniors and passed as men of strict opinions came to him. These formed a proportion of the rich resident landowners whose estates lay to the southward of the Carse of Gowrie. They were for the most part not members of the Council; desirous of an authority to which they held they had a right; fearful of the inroads that the Crown might make through the policy of regaining the church lands. Rothes had represented them in this last matter. Nothing could have been achieved without a close relation with the parish ministers. This was the last period in which religious phraseology was pleasing to a ruling caste. The lords were guided by a powerful self-interest and knew that they were all Scotsmen together.

In October 1637 an impressive list of signatories had been obtained to a formal Complaint[1] against the Bishops, who were charged with the "ranversing of the gratious intention of the blessed reformers of religion in England". This document, like all that Rothes put forth, was cleverly worded, an appeal from Laud to Cranmer's memory. The list of signatories was headed by the youthful Earl of Sutherland. There were certain veterans like Wemyss and Eglinton who, with his son Montgomery and Loudoun, represented the West Country. There was Ancram's

---

[1] Details are printed in the *Scottish Historical Review* (1925), vol. xxii, pp. 243-7. Cf. Rothes *Relation*, p. 19.

son Lothian and Queensberry's heir Drumlanrig, Elphinstone and his cousin Balmerino, Dalhousie, Yester, Cranstoun, a total of twenty-six. These men belonged to the middle rank among the peerage. Their magnates still held aloof.

In Edinburgh two politicians, both young and with a mastering energy, bent their minds to study the situation, Johnston of Wariston and Lorne, who would soon be Argyll. They were to be the pillars of the Covenant, which was constructed during this winter. Their destinies were to be intertwined until they came in the end to the same death. Both men grasped the crucial significance of the ministers over whom they were to wield an influence that was for long unbreakable. The simple explanation of their power over the Kirk leadership is in this case quite accurate. Both men were dominated by a profound conviction of God's judgments. Wariston had borne the yoke from his youth; Argyll had come to it.

Their natures were very different. Where Wariston was febrile, Argyll was calculating. They were both Levites of a new dispensation with an innate distaste for Sacerdotalism. Wariston would sacrifice everybody and everything, even his ambition, to the interests of Religion as he conceived them. Argyll was to make the same sacrifice with this reservation. He held the duty to preserve intact the interests of McCailein Mor. To this trust none of his house would prove unfaithful. In their different ways both men were solitary, and Argyll changed in character as his theological preoccupations grew on him. He seems to have regarded Wariston as an instrument, while the Lord Justice Clerk, who was not deceived about himself, had a tortured clarity about men's value. They were both very far removed from the Earl of Rothes.

The actual work of planning the next move was undertaken by Wariston assisted on the side of the ministers by Alexander Henderson and David Dick or Dickson. To any experienced observer the immediate objective was not in doubt, only the method. There was a certain remote parallel between the failure to summon Parliament in England and the suspension of the General Assembly in the northern kingdom. The fact that the General Assembly had not met enabled the opposition to maintain that a whole series of actions were without legal warrant. It was clear that a demand for the withdrawal of the new Prayer Book would be coupled with similar requests for the withdrawal of the Book of Canons, which had just been printed, and for the abolition of the Scottish Court of High Commission, which in effect gave the bishops power to order imprisonment and inflict fines. These measures would likewise involve the calling of a General Assembly free from royal influence.

To achieve this purpose it was decided to re-furbish and modify the former Covenant signed in 1580 by James VI during his minority. Such action could be construed as an appeal to history set forth in Presbyterian terms. It recalled the period before the passing of the Black Acts which were associated with the re-establishment of Episcopacy. The proposal had that conservative quality and love of precedent that marked one aspect of Scottish thought. The Stuart kingship had long experienced this tendency to sanctify revolt and to root disorder in legality. The consequences of the proposal were far reaching and this Wariston had intended. Unlike the attack on the Court of High Commission and on the books sent up from England, it brought into question the existence of Episcopacy. The institution of the episcopate could not in fact survive the general adoption of the Covenant. This was the reason for the opposition that the Covenant engendered in Aberdeen.

The preparation for the bringing forward of the Covenant followed the time-honoured sequence; supplication; petition; protestation; lords acting in concert backed by armed force. The last element in this programme was entrusted to Rothes and Montrose. A singular feature of the protest was its exclusive concern with ecclesiastical affairs. All other grievances were left aside. This was in part due to the cast of Wariston's mind and to his alliance with Alexander Henderson. Wariston saw a God-dominated people and a Covenanted King. Henderson was pre-occupied with evangelical values set within the framework of the Presbytery. This narrowing of the field of conflict was also in part due to respect for secular aspects of the royal authority. Only the King of Heaven could be invoked as bearing sway against their own "dread sovereign". Besides, it must also have occurred to Rothes and his colleagues that the bishops were singularly friendless. They had served their turn as henchmen to the old nobility. The new prelates had no claim of clan relationship or personal affinity. No man of substance would be sorry to see them go.

The crisis developed slowly because the Archbishop of St Andrews still held the office of lord chancellor. It was for this reason that the National Covenant when prepared was presented as a document that did not concern the King's Council in Scotland. It was not offered for signature either to councillors or to the Catholic lords. It was intended as a bond through which the King's disquieted Protestant subjects[1] should manifest their union.

[1] The speech of Mr Thomas Ramsay before the Council on 21 December 1637 is indicative of the mood of the opposition. "That ther had been many weightie affaires befoir their Lordships, bot never any of such importance; that he himself had been of tymes before them about papists, and never parted bot with great contentment, which he expected much more being

In December commissioners had been appointed from among the ranks of the petitioners. These were[1] Rothes, Montrose, Lindsay and Loudoun for the noblemen, Auldbarr, Keir and Cunningham-head for the gentry, two representatives of the city of Edinburgh and one for the town of Perth. In addition Alexander Henderson and David Dick were chosen from among the ministers. This was the origin of the body known as the Tables.

Just before the signing of the Covenant a suggestion was made on behalf of the bishops that the latter would be ready to intercede with the King that he would withdraw the Prayer Book and Canons and agree to restrain the Court of High Commission. "They wold," declares[2] Rothes in his *Relation*, "gratifie the Supplicants one crop so they might keip the inheritance. Bot all resolved to stop their ears at these charmes: and as they wer not gathered mutinouslie by one or a few men, bot by God and a good cause." They were in consequence determined to renew the Covenant subscribed by their ancestors with such additions as the time required. The most significant new passage ran[3] as follows. "We promise and swear that we shall, to the uttermost of our power with our means and lives, stand to the defence of our dread Sovereign, the King's Majesty, his person and authority, in the defence of the foresaid true religion, liberties, and laws of the kingdom, as also to the mutual defence and assistance, every one of us of another in the cause of maintaining the true religion and his Majesty's authority, with our best counsel, our bodies, means and whole power, against all sorts of persons whatsoever." Rothes has a comment[4] which is very apposite. "Blessed be the Lord God of Israell, the author preserver, and restorer of this unione and communione." The Covenant was conceived in the idiom of its period as a means to extirpate the bishops, who had gained a new politico-religious influence. As far as Wariston and the ministers was concerned the loyalty here offered was reserved to a Covenanted King.

befoir them about Poperie itselfe, the seids of whose superstition and idola-trie wer thick sawen (sown) in the Service-book, and its hierarchicall tirrany in the Canons and High Commission, that Augustine, on the (110) Psalme, made mentione of thrie sorts of Antichrists, wherof the first was cruel, the nixt craftie, the third and maine Antichrist was craftie and cruell; that in the Service-book was craft, in the Book of Canons crueltie," Rothes' *Relation*, pp. 39-40.

[1] *Ibid.*, p. 44.
[2] *Ibid.*, p. 70.
[3] For S. R. Gardiner's discussion of this matter cf. *History*, vol. viii, pp. 325-348.
[4] *Relation*, p. 70.

THE MARQUIS OF HAMILTON

CHAPTER XVIII

THE GLASGOW ASSEMBLY

THE sequence of events that now occurred followed inevitably from the way in which the National Covenant had been subscribed.[1] The King decided to negotiate on the basis of the withdrawal of this instrument. He took the view that until the Covenant was given up he had no more power than a "Duke of Venice".[2] It was at this stage that he decided to send the Marquis of Hamilton to Scotland. On 8 May 1637 he was nominated to go north as royal commissioner, and for the next two years he was to hold this post at least in name.

It seems that Hamilton's mind worked slowly and, at any rate in the opening months, with tempered optimism. Like the King he was always ready to try persuasion; it was a consequence of his almost royal rank that he would make use of any one. He had no prejudice against nor interest in the ministers; they soon made their view clear[3] to him. The account of the reception accorded to Rothes sets the note for this period in the relations between the King and his Scottish subjects. After coming from a meeting of the Council Hamilton took Rothes by the hand in the dining-room at Dalkeith and within a little space he was brought into the bedchamber and the door closed. The lords remained together for two hours. It is a matter which throws light on both these men.

The interview is described[4] in the *Relation*. Hamilton "spoke much to the commendation of Rothes, as being much wiser and discreeter than any of the rest, and who had given evident proof of his temperate dispositione in the cariage of this bussiness, and who had great power with the rest of the Nobilitie". The Marquis went on to explain "how much it concerned him to endeavour the

---

[1] "Of Noblemen, at home, who are counsellors or papists, unto which it was not offered, I think they be within four or five who hes not subscryved", Baillie, *Letters and Journals*, i, p. 74.

[2] "I have no more power in Scotland than as a duke of Venice", letter from the King to Hamilton dated 25 June 1638 printed in Burnet, *op. cit.*, p. 76.

[3] The ministers expressed the hope that "your Grace shall prove a worthye patriot, faithfull counsellor, good Christian, and a compassionate member of your mother Kirk, mourning under manifold miseries, and sall reap the fruit of a sweit remembrance in efter ages, and a wonderfull peace and strong consolatione when it comes to the breaking of the eye-strings and giving of the last gasp", Rothes, *Relation*, p. 116.

[4] *Ibid.*, p. 136.

R

libertie of religione, which he so much valued; and of this (Scottish) natione, haveing all his estate here, and nothing in Ingland, save a house and a few aikers of ground, which he had purchased immediatlie before his way-coming for keiping of his children, which, being young, were not able to be transported". Very suavely the royal commissioner besought that the Scots lords "might be temperate, and not crave these things which the King could not in honour grant". He believed that his sovereign had decided to accord that which might justly cause satisfaction. He added that this would make Scotland the most glorious nation under heaven. Such words were what his master then required of him. As to Hamilton's own thoughts, he kept his counsel.

It appears that at least from the time of the signing of the Covenant the King had determined to use force to quell his opponents. Meanwhile, he played for time. Hamilton returning to Court from his first journey as royal commissioner was authorised in July to agree to the temporary suspension of the Service book, which was in fact nowhere used, and to the calling of a General Assembly. It was always assumed that the bishops should take their due place in this gathering.

Sir Thomas Hope, whose position as lord advocate gave a peculiar significance to his judgment, refused to agree that the Covenant contained any phrase contrary to Scottish law. Most of the lords of session took the same line; the Covenant was widely signed by leading advocates. At this point Hamilton, aided by Traquair, made a proposal which it was considered would help the King. It was suggested that Charles I should set forth the Covenant of Faith sworn by James VI in 1580. This was in fact the basis of the Covenant without the new additions. The proposal was accepted and the new document was signed, although in some cases reluctantly, by all the Council.

Wariston was from the outset opposed to any such proposition. His view made headway and a Protestation was brought forward against the King's Covenant which had in fact only found wide acceptance in Elgin and Aberdeen. Finally, Sir Thomas Hope produced the not unreasonable judgment that the Confession of Faith brought forward by the King committed its signatories to a clear repudiation of episcopacy. In September the King authorised Hamilton to summon a General Assembly to meet at Glasgow on November 21 and a Parliament on May 15.

As far as Hamilton's prestige was concerned, Glasgow had certain advantages for it lay immediately to the northward of the bulk of his estates. There were, however, other factors. This was the point at which the threat of Campbell power was brought to bear on the West Country. The region was from various causes deeply Protestant. Ayrshire vied with Fife for the leadership of the largest united group of landowning Covenanters. The Mures of Rowallan were the prime example of a stock deeply bound up with the defence of the Reformed Faith in its cultural aspects.[1] Among the heads of the leading West Country families Abercorn and Sempill were the only Catholics. The rest formed a solid Presbyterian phalanx centering on the rival but equally Protestant houses of Eglinton and Glencairn and to the south on Cassilis.[2] The rhyme which exalts the power of the last-named grouping at least serves to indicate the close-knit character of that society.

> "Twixt Wigtoun and the town of Ayr,
> Portpatrick and the Cruives of Cree,
> No man need think for to bide there
> Unless he court with Kennedie."

A study of this period leaves the impression of the Campbell influence exerted over all these western shires. Thus Lorne is seen quarrelling with Bishop Sydserf over a difficulty with the Tutor of Kenmure, who was guardian to his own young nephew. The marriage of Campbell of Lawers with the heiress of Campbell of Loudoun had planted the second figure in the Argyll family as a great landowner in South Ayrshire. Lorne himself made constant progresses.

A co-ordinating factor for the whole region was the university of Glasgow which had long been a centre of Presbyterian thought. This was in turn bound up with Saumur. John Cameron, Robert Boyd of Trochrig and Zachary Boyd had all taught at Saumur before returning to Glasgow. It may be noted that this did not seem to make these men "extreme" when it was a question of opposition to the Crown.[3] The pattern of French Calvinism had

[1] Cf. *The Historical Descent of the House of Rowallane* by Sir William Mure, written shortly after 1657 and ed. by William Muir, 1825. "This Sir Wm. was pious and learned and had ane excellent vaine in poyesie; he delyted much in building and planting. . . . He lived Religiouslie and died Christianlie in the year of (his) age 67 and the year of (Our) Lord 1657", p. 90. He is described as the intimate friend of Mr Guthrie, minister of Fenwick, *ibid.*, p. 95.

[2] In regard to Cassilis there is an interesting reference in Rothes's account of the Articles for the present Peace of the Kirk and Kingdome of Scotland and set forth in April 1638. "The note was drawne by Mr Alexander Hendersone, very smooth sparing to satisfie Cassles scrupulositie", *Relation*, p. 100.

[3] Cf. "Some other clauses also, whilk might have seemed to import a Defence in armes against the King, this I could not yield to in any imaginable case; for the grounds I had learned from Monsieur Cameron I had not yet leasure to try. . . . My Lord Cassills had my scruple anent the Defence with armes. He sent for me; bot I eschewed to confirme him in that whilk he professed he had from Monsieur Cameron", *Letters and Journals*, i, p. 53.

been formed during the period of Jeanne d'Albret and Henri of
Navarre. There was an Erastian element in this system as long as
the prince belonged to the Religion. A similar tendency can be seen
at work in Robert Baillie's account of the reception of the National
Covenant. The professors of Glasgow recognised that Charles I
was invested with due royal authority. "The greatest opposites in
the West to this subscription," he is found writing,[1] "are our
friends in Glasgow: all the Colledge without exception; Mr John
Maxwell, Mr John Bell younger, and Mr Zacharie, they are not
only withdrawers of their hands, bot all of them pathetick
reasoners against it. How this comes I will not say, bot I have
my own thoughts; yet old Mr John Bell and Mr Robert Wilkie
are passionately for it, albeit half derided by the other as simple
fooles: it is like to fall out evil among them. The body of the
Burgesses hes subscryved. My Lord Boyd, old Blair, Keir, Mr
David Dick, Mr Michael Wallace, and I, went in, as Commissioners
from the meeting of Edinburgh, to deal with the Colledge and
Ministers to joyne with the rest: bot I foresaw it was in vaine;
for no reasoning could move any of them to passe from the
smallest of their scruples, which yet they multiplied."

This opposition depended, as Baillie[2] hinted, upon the judgment
of Dr John Strang, who had been principal of the university since
1626. He was a builder and administrator; a man of wealth; a
cadet of Strang of Balcaskie in Fife. He was learned and perhaps
accessible to flattery upon this subject; preaching was not his
forte. Like David Dickson he had gained some local fame by
bringing over leading Catholics[3] to the Kirk. In the end he signed
the Covenant on the understanding that it was not prejudicial
either to the royal authority or to the episcopal institution. It may
be that he was clear-sighted about the part which the lords would
play. Throughout he remained a convinced "clerical". He belonged
to that section of the ministers who were openly opposed to the
intervention of lay elders.

An element of jealousy can be traced among the university
office-holders directed against those ministers who were gradually
becoming predominant, the "ruling few". From this period certain

---

[1] Letter dated 5 April 1638, *ibid.*, i, p. 63.
[2] Baillie has a long letter dealing with the principal's objections. He also
sets out his own view. "Our maine feare to have our religion lost, our throats
cutted, our poor countrey made ane English province, to be disposed upon
for ever hereafter at the will of a Bishope of Canterburie; thir (these) our
feares are builded mainely upon the withdrawing of our brethren's hands and
countenances from us, in that course which we conceave to be most necesare
at this tyme", *ibid.*, i, p. 67.
[3] Among others Lord Erroll's daughter who was married to the Earl of
Buccleugh.

names recur, principally those of Alexander Henderson, minister of Leuchars, Andrew Cant, minister of Pitsligo and in the West Country David Dickson. It is notable that these men represented three different parts of Scotland. None of them were university teachers.[1] They were home products without foreign education. These leaders were close to the great lords guiding them and in turn accepting their proffered help. Dickson as minister of Irvine was Eglinton's intimate adviser. Henderson had an admirable independence of character, but all three and especially Cant and Dickson were in tune with Argyll. Even as Lord Lorne he had sought them out. This summer the old Earl of Argyll lay dying in London. It would soon be clear that his son was free.

To a great extent the West of Scotland, as far as the nobles and lairds were concerned, existed as a self-contained society. The Archbishop of Glasgow was chancellor of the university, but Patrick Lindsay was personally a man of little weight. He was one of the most pliant of King James's bishops and had been translated from Ross in 1633, when he was already sixty-seven years of age. He was of great family, a cadet of Lindsay of Edzell, but primarily concerned to accommodate himself to all the wishes of successive Kings. His predecessor James Law had held the see for seventeen years since he had been nominated to succeed Archbishop Spottiswoode on his translation to St Andrews. The late Archbishop had bequeathed his library[2] to the university. He had been a scholar; a royalist when this was still in fashion; a friend and patron to the western gentry.[3] These came to study at the college in large numbers. The contacts were very close. In 1631 Lord Stirling, then secretary of state, gave £500 Scottish for the building of a chamber or two "within the Colledge of Glasgow bearing my name and armes for the use of my children and such of my house as shall have their breeding therein in all tyme coming".[4] Seven of his eight sons had their education there.

The young men came together and formed a like-minded company. Thus in 1629 Hugh and Henry Montgomery, who were

[1] Dickson did not hold office in the university of Glasgow between 1618 and 1640.

[2] The bequest was dated 25 July 1627 and the list of books has this note "Remember that Joannis Lopez 'Epitome Sanctorum Patrum' is in four volumes", *Munimenta Universitatis Glasguensis* printed by the Maitland Club 1854, vol. iii, pp. 419-21. A list of books bequeathed to the College by Mr Zacharie Boyd is dated 15 November 1637. The only book in French which is mentioned is a French Bible, *ibid.*, p. 424.

[3] Archbishop Law's mother was a Strang of Balcaskie and he was married successively into the families of Dundas of Newliston, Boswell and Boyle of Kelburne.

[4] *Munimenta Universitatis Glasguenis*, iii, p. 467.

among Eglinton's younger sons, had entered the college[1] attended
by their pedagogue and accompanied by the heirs of the Lairds of
Kilbirnie, Lamont, Porterfield, Kincaid and Hunterstone and by
sons of Cunningham of Craigends and Carmichael of Westraw.
The Earl's sons tabled at the "high[2] buird", where they found
Wigton's son and Linlithgow's and their respective pedagogues.

There was a tendency for youths of strict principles to be sent
across from Ireland. James Clotworthy "Anglus", later the first
Lord Massereene, entered[3] in March 1630. A few years later Clotworthy was followed by Sir Charles Coote's younger sons.[4] In
both cases they were children of leading families among the
settlers who were later to maintain their position with Scottish
help. It is probable that a religious motive was responsible for the
arrival of the few English students. Four were admitted[5] in 1631.
As was to be expected the rare Frenchmen seem for the most part
to have been Huguenots from Anjou or Touraine.[6]

The life of the college was marked by a simplicity which appears
in contrast with the elaborate entertainments given for and by the
young Montrose at St Andrews. The masters and students were to
meet at six o'clock on weekdays and at seven on the Lord's Day.
The scholars were to go to sermon once on weekdays and the
masters were instructed[7] to "tak course to try what conscience
each scholler makes of secret devotion, morning and evening".
Each scholar was to have a Bible and wear a gown. They were
ordered in all places to speak Latin among themselves. The
Faculty was charged with securing obedience to this instruction.[8]

Provision was to be made for a principal and five "regents".
These were, to be attended by the principal's servant, the cook,
porter and foreman, the beadle and "economus". There is a note[9]
as to one aspect of the expenses. "Item to the servants that wash
the naperie, keip the Colledge clein, and bring in provision for
the Colledge, so much bread, drink and money as extends to the
sowme of £5 (Scottish)." Details of the charges[10] made for new
building in 1631 enable us to reconstruct the college life. The first
bill covered the "lofting and putting on the roofe on the new house

[1] Ibid., iii, pp. 80-1.
[2] Ibid., ii, p. 530.
[3] Ibid., iii, p. 82.
[4] Ibid., iii, p. 92.
[5] Their names were William Dearlove, Phatuel Fyshe, Thomas Bateson
and "Gulielmus Pullein", who was blind, ibid., iii, p. 83.
[6] Six Frenchmen were admitted in 1622-3. Two are described as from
Touraine, one from Normandy and one from Anjou, ibid., iii, pp. 76-7.
[7] For these details cf. ibid., p. 455.
[8] For these details cf. ibid., ii, p. 465.
[9] Ibid., ii, p. 459.
[10] Account printed ibid., ii, pp. 481-6.

buildit on the north syd of the Inner Close of the Colledge"; the
second the cost of making windows, the third the expense incurred
in "plenishing the chambers, with beds, buirds, formes and
studies". It is clear that rather later in the same period the cost
of the building of grates for fireplaces was to be borne by the
individual undergraduate. Sir Richard Couts allowed his two sons
£54 Scots for "adorning their chamber".[2] There are details of
payments to the gardeners,[3] for binding and dressing the garden
hedges and for looking after the kale and herbs.

Sir William Brereton has left us the impression made by the
college on an English traveller. "There is," he wrote[4] in 1636,
"a good handsome foundation propounded and set out, to add a
good fair and college-like structure to be built quadrangular; one
side is already built, and there hath been collections throughout
Scotland towards the building of this college, and much more
money is collected than is needful to the building hereof. Here
the library is a very little room, not twice so large as my old
closet; that part of it which is now standing is old, strong, plain
building."

It is, perhaps, because Glasgow was then increasing in prosperity
that the town was viewed so favourably by Brereton and other
travellers. "There are," he explains,[5] "about six or seven thousand
communicants, and about twenty thousand persons in the town,
which is famous for the church, which is fairest and stateliest in
Scotland, for the Toll-boothe and Bridge." The same note recurs
in the account by Thomas Tucker, who travelled in Scotland
as a commissioner of excise nineteen years later. "This towne,"
he wrote[6] of Glasgow in 1655, "seated in a pleasant and fruitfull
soyle, and consisting of foure streets, handsomely built in forme
of a crosse, is one of the most considerablest burghs of Scotland,
as well for the structure as trade of it. The inhabitants (all but
the students of the college which is here) are traders and dealers."
Tucker begins by describing the trade for Ireland "with small
smiddy coales, in open boates, from foure to ten tonnes, from
whence they bring hoopes, ronges, barrell staves, meale, oates and
butter". The trade with France is then described and the timber
brought in from Norway. The Highlanders came constantly, in

---

[1] An account of the iron chimneys in the chambers to be paid by the
scholars (1646), *ibid.*, ii, pp. 490-1
[2] *Ibid.*, ii, p. 479.
[3] *Ibid.*, ii, pp. 570 and 572.
[4] Brereton's account of his travels was published by the Chatham Society
in 1844. The references here are to the reprint of the Scottish section by P.
Hume Brown in *Early Travellers in Scotland*, pp. 132-58.
[5] *Ibid.*, p. 150.
[6] *Early Travellers in Scotland*, pp. 176-7.

summer round the Mull of Kintyre and in winter through West Loch Tarbert. To avoid the stormy weather they pulled their small boats across the sandy neck of land into Loch Fyne and then made southwards through Inchmarnock Water. All year long they sold plaidings, dry hides and goat, kid and deer skins, returning home with their provisions.

Traffic was hampered by the shallows of the Clyde and large ships carrying the foreign trade had to unload fourteen miles downstream. Norwegian timber was brought up on rafts.[1] This busy life went forward against a background of strict observance. Bow-butts and archery on the Sabbath were first sharply discouraged and then forbidden. Men and women were censured for playing "Lady Templeton",[2] a game of chance. As a community the traders and gentry had accepted the doctrine of predestination. The will of Thomas Boyd of Pitcon is in keeping with this new age in its firm affirmation of election. "First commit," it reads,[3] "my saule to ye immortale God to be receavit in heavenis gloire appointit for me in the immaculat bluid of Jesus Chryst my blessed redeemer, and my body to ye erthe, to be buryit in the sepulchre of my father, yr to remain to ye glorious resurrectioun." With its scholars and regents and with these religious principles enshrined in the South West, Glasgow was a suitable setting for an assembly destined to reconstruct the Presbyterian authority.

Constant contact was maintained between the university and the leading families in the neighbourhood of the small city. Thus the seventh Lord Boyd was a cousin of Robert Boyd of Trochrig and had been sent to Saumur in 1611 to study under him. He owned property in Glasgow including the Parson's Manse, which was used as a dower house,[4] and tenements on the west side of the High Street.[5] As a stock the Boyds were strongly Protestant,

---

[1] Brereton has a comment on the need for timber. He is speaking of the country around Kirkintilloch. "There is very little or no timber in any of the south or west parts of this kingdom, much less than in England, I have diligently observed, but cannot find any timber in riding near one hundred miles; all the country poor and barren, save where it is helped by lime or sea-weeds", printed *ibid.*, p. 150.

[2] The Session Book of Ayr gives the names of many censured for playing this game, i.e., "28 December 1607. Compeirit Marion Busbie, and accusit for playing ye Lady Tempilton, was purged with Maister Huw Spier, and absoluit", printed in James Paterson's *History of the County of Ayr,* vol. ii, p. 190.

[3] Printed *ibid.,* ii, p. 90.

[4] This was used by Margaret Colquhoun, Lady Boyd. Cf. Contract dated 30 September 1595 preserved in Box 2, item 389, Burgh of Kilmarnock, Inventory of Boyd Papers, General Register House.

[5] These were purchased from Archibald Heigate on 7 March 1598. A tenement at Scotland House Yardhead was purchased in the same year, Box 3, items 439, 440, 494, 495. The description and an account of the site of a "great tenement" passed over by Lord Boyd to his son is given in item 416a.

country nobility, living quite simply. An account has survived[1] of the plenishing of Dean Castle in the year in which the young Lord Boyd inherited from his grandfather. The house then consisted of a single square tower four storeys in height. The great hall had a large furnished chimney in the fire place and two oak chairs. There were stone seats ranged along the walls and also forms. Velvet cushions were laid on the seats of greater quality and rush work carpets upon the rest. The hall was lit by five brazen chandeliers. In the chambers above the curtains were made of cramoisy worsted. The only book mentioned in Dean Castle was "ane meikle bybill".

As a family the Boyds were typical of the western Scottish baronage. They were without contacts with England;[2] local in their interests; markedly God-fearing. They held the patronage of both the high and low kirks at Kilmarnock. In the period under consideration the heads of the house were both short-lived and serious. Robert eighth Lord Boyd succeeded his father in 1628 as a child of ten. He was the youngest peer to subscribe the National Covenant. Two years later, and just before his early death, he was to gain for himself a small niche in Scottish history through the action which he took in connection with the association of "conservative" leaders known as the Band of Cumbernauld. In one respect he was unusual for he was a young man whom the ministers could dominate. He had, of course, his own clerical kinsmen. Zacharie Boyd was his counsellor and also guided his child-wife and his mother. The whole stock form an example of the closely integrated life[3] of the ruling classes in the counties around Glasgow.

In contrast the Stirlings of Keir represent a family much more open to Court influence. They maintained a house at Edinburgh in Bell's Wynd Head.[4] They employed Jameson to paint companion portraits of both husband and wife;[5] their general style of

---

[1] Cf. Inventory dated June 1611 printed by James Paterson, *History of the County of Ayr*, vol. ii, pp. 168-9.

[2] The limit of their interests is indicated by the ticket dated 6 July 1626 admitting Robert Lord Boyd as a burgess and guild brother of Edinburgh, Box 3, item 640, Burgh of Kilmarnock, Inventory of Boyd Papers.

[3] Further detail is reflected in an agreement dated at Brewland of Kilbride in Cunningham on 12 August 1608 between Sir Thomas Boyd of Bollinschaw, Kt, and Lord Boyd his father. They consented to dwell together in his Lordship's house at Badley, the said Lord to provide two bags of meal, malt, flesh, fish, cheese, butter, coal, candle, powder vessels for the table, napery, etc., for their honest householding, and the said Sir Thomas to furnish the third part of these necessaries, Box 3, item 523.

[4] Cf. *The Stirlings of Keir and their Family Papers* by William Fraser, p. 111.

[5] The portraits of Sir George Stirling of Keir and his wife Margaret Napier are dated 1637 and signed "Jamesone pinxit", *ibid.*, p. 54.

dress reflected fashion. Their members had travelled in both France and Italy.[1] At the same time cadets and seniors tended to make Keir their residence[2] and they were faithful to the local university. Three generations had studied there and Sir James Stirling, the patriarch of this line, had been an undergraduate at Glasgow with Zacharie Boyd and with the heirs of the Covenanting families of Kelburn and Calderwood. The list of commissioners sent to persuade the regents and masters of the university of Glasgow to accept the National Covenant included the names of both Sir George Keir and Lord Boyd.

There was little difference of opinion on religious questions throughout this region, except among such stocks as the Sempills, who were avowed Catholics. One family, the Montgomeries of Eglinton, had a dynastic quality which gave them leadership. Still, they entered fully into the preoccupations of their less wealthy neighbours.

Alexander sixth Earl of Eglinton was a man of military temper and strict outlook, the name Graysteel was given him in youth. His wife was devout[3] and he was much attached[4] to her. Together they maintained at Kilwinning a state that was at once dour and elaborate. He had made a great marriage for his heir with the Marquis of Hamilton's eldest sister. Their ardent attachment to the Kirk was a link between Eglinton and his wife and the bride's mother.

Eglinton kept up a correspondence with those ministers whom he esteemed while carrying on a long dispute about church patronage[5] with successive occupants of the see of Glasgow. He

[1] The details of the travelling and personal expenses of Sir John Stirling of Garden during his journey to France from October 1610 until March 1613 are preserved at Keir. Cf. *ibid.*, p. 58. On 26 January 1633 Sir George Stirling of Keir wrote to the Laird of Glorat younger, "Having passed the dead of the winter in Padua, I am nou upon my voyage to Rome and Naples, quilk I shall accomplish, God willing, with all possible diligence that I may be in France before the heats come on in this cuntrie", *ibid.*, p. 482.

[2] There is a note at Keir of the birth of the ten children of Sir John Stirling of Garden and his wife Margaret Monteith. She was delivered at Keir in 1614, 1618, 1619, 1622 and 1628 and at Calder in 1616, 1617, 1620 and 1626, *ibid.*, pp. 472-3.

[3] Cf. Letter from Robert Bruce of Kinnaird to his cousin Anna Countess Eglinton dated at Kinnaird 2 September 1629. "I cannot tell at quhat schole your ladyshjp hes beine at; bot surlie your ladyships last letter smelled of grace & had ane fragrant perfume of the doctrine of the Holie Spirit", Fraser, *Memorials of Eglinton*, p. 223.

[4] A series of letters from Lord Eglinton to his wife written between 1619 and 1632 are printed, *ibid.*, pp. 210-226 *passim*.

[5] On 29 November 1621 a summons was registered by Archbishop Spottiswoode against the Earl of Eglinton for non-fulfillment of a contract and in the following month a counter-claim was made by Eglinton against the Archbishop of Glasgow and others in the matter of the presentation to the parish of Dreghorn, Inventory of Boyd Papers, Box 3, items 624 and 625. A

had a marked feeling for all his scattered kinsmen and corresponded with the Comte de Montgomèry. He had himself been brought up in France and required his son to describe the fortifications[1] in that country. He would engage in recollections of the "old Parisienne familiarities".[2] He was both serious and hospitable, with a sense of authority in his wide lands. There is something a little intimidating in the sentence.[3] "I have not mett as yeit upon our merches with my Lord of Loudoun." The Earl was not a builder and his tastes were old-fashioned. He still placed value on his silver basins, lavers, candlesticks, and on his great gilded salt three tiers in height,[4] all engraved with the arms of Livingstone and Montgomery. There is a reference to his wife's virginals, and it is evident that Eglinton had no contacts with the Vandyck aspects of the English Court. He was some twelve years older than Charles I and among the circles of the opposition he had something of the prestige of an elder statesman. In the West his authority was uncontested. Eglinton was more determined and had wider connections than his only rival Cassilis, who was moreover marked by a vein of eccentricity. The long-standing feud in that country lay between the Cunninghams of Glencairn and the older line of the Montgomeries. There was a sharp rivalry for precedence between these earldoms.[5] The young Glencairn was, however, at this time out of Scotland and played an equivocal part during these years.

The sixth Earl of Eglinton was by birth a Seton and thus the Earl of Winton's younger brother. The Montgomery lands and earldom were devised to him by his cousin and he was "sent for out of France" to accept his inheritance. Although he became a leading Presbyterian, he kept up the closest ties with his Catholic relatives in East Lothian. It is likely that he had a double effect upon the Setons, protecting them from the Kirk and also weaning them from their religion. There is seen in Eglinton's well-documented life that kindness of Protestant[6] to Catholic which has

contract dated 1 August 1614 between the Archbishop of Glasgow and the Earl of Eglinton refers to the teind sheaves of the kirks of Kilwinning, Pearcetown, Irvine, Ardrossan, Kilbride, Kilbirnie, Beith and Dunlop, *ibid.*, item 552.

[1] Cf. Letter dated "Paris 1634" printed in Fraser's *Memorials,* pp. 6-7.
[2] Letter printed *ibid.,* p. 223.
[3] Letter printed *ibid.,* p. 187.
[4] These and other goods were bequeathed by Eglinton his eldest son, testament dated 5 June 1652, *ibid.,* p. 319.
[5] A detailed account of these disputes is given in *The Montgomery Manuscripts* by William Montgomery of Rosemount, ed. Rev. George Hill (1869), pp. 4-6, 12 and accompanying notes.
[6] Cf. Correspondence with Marion Countess of Abercorn and her son James Earl of Abercorn, *Memorials,* pp. 213, 261 and letters relating to Maxwell of Herries, 216-221.

already been noted. It was cordiality on a social level and was due in part to the strong links between men and women of the same rank and lineage but perhaps also to the sense that among the great families south of Forth Catholicism was a dying creed.

Eglinton was a seeker of alliances. Like Rothes he took Scotland for his canvas.[1] He had a special care for his Seton niece, who was married to the young Earl Marischal.[2] His influence helped to keep that youth faithful to the Covenant. When his son Montgomery became a widower he arranged a second marriage for him with Rothes's elder daughter. There was at this period a working arrangement between these lords. In all the policies of the opposition there was a clear understanding between the noble managers. The solidarity of their joint interests reached far back. Rothes and Eglinton had been together in the matter of the five Articles of Perth.

Montgomery's character does not appear with the same clarity as that of his father-in-law and father. He hesitated over taking the Covenant and showed at different times a leaning towards neutrality. It is not impossible that this caution was encouraged by his father. Even in the seventeenth century one is conscious of the doctrine that the interests of the family must not be allowed to suffer from the disturbances between factions in the State. In religion father and son thought alike. They both desired to uproot the bishops. The presbytery of Glasgow chose Eglinton as its commissioner.

The main business of the General Assembly was to be the abolition of episcopacy. It is clear that it was not grasped that this step, if persisted in, made peace with Charles I impossible. However much he might consider England and Scotland separately this was something that he could not tolerate if offered as a permanent solution. If the King had little experience of the dominant factors in the Scottish scene, the lords and ministers in the northern kingdom had still less knowledge of their own sovereign.

To the managers of the opposition it seemed that the only way to check the new episcopate, which the King was building up, was to destroy it completely. There is no doubt that the bringing forward of the doctrine of episcopacy by divine right created a profound effect. The position is set out in a paper which Alexander

[1] Cf. Letter from John second Lord Balmerino at Edinburgh to the Earl of Eglinton. "The Earle Marshalle is either gone with them, or sent all his people. The Laird of Innes and our friends benorth Spey are with them also", *ibid.*, p. 250.
[2] Cf. Letter from Elizabeth Countess Marischal to her uncle the Earl of Eglinton dated at Dunnottar 3 June (c. 1640). "I will asour your lordship ther is no friend he (Lord Marischal) hes in the world that he will follow their adwyse so much as he will doe your lordships", *ibid.*, p. 241.

Henderson prepared for Charles I in later years. "I have," wrote[1] the Presbyterian moderator, "but one word more concerning your piety to your royal father of happy memory, with which your Majesty does conclude. Your Majesty knows that King James never admitted Episcopacy upon divine right; that his Majesty did swear and subscribe to the doctrine, worship and discipline of the Church of Scotland." One cannot underestimate the doctrinal opposition and the fear that the Reformation settlement was in danger.

Settlement is the operative word for the King desired to re-endow the Church and to use bishops as his ministers in the sphere of politics. Men of strict opinions were affected by the religious argument and those with political ambitions were by now alive to this last danger. It was, however, the threat to the land which served to unite the great body of the lords. Even the Catholics and the indifferent and those whose general preferences were Episcopal would join with the stiffest Presbyterians in opposing the restoration to the bishops of land which the Crown had granted to the noble families.

There was a widespread fear that the King was meditating just this policy. It was the kind of quasi-legal action that they had come to look for from him. The kirk lands had been guarded cautiously and in some cases, notably those of the Earls of Abercorn and Lothian, the abbey properties[2] formed the basis of a family's wealth. Already the King had begun by purchasing at a very cheap rate lands of the priory of St Andrews held by the Duke of Lennox to form an endowment for the bishopric of Edinburgh. They feared that their master might in time proceed from compulsory purchase to confiscation. It was not only in the religious sphere that the thought of Dr Laud would prove disquieting.

[1] Printed by Dr. John Aiton in *Life and Times of Alexander Henderson*, p. 617.

[2] It is worth setting down the distribution of the former abbeys, most of whose lands had been transferred as single entities in 1625. At that date the abbey of Dunfermline remained in the hands of the Crown with Lord Dunfermline as hereditary baillie. Six abbeys had been annexed to bishoprics, the rest were held as follows: Arbroath by the Marquis of Hamilton, Deer by Earl Marischal, Dundrennan and Holywood by the Earl of Annandale, Inchcolm by the Earl of Moray, Jedburgh by the Earl of Home, Kelso by the Earl of Roxburgh, Kilwinning by the Earl of Eglinton, Melrose by the Earl of Haddington, Newbattle by the Earl of Lothian, Paisley by the Earl of Abercorn, Baxlmerino by Sir James Elphinstone, Culross by Lord Colville, Inchaffray by Lord Maderty, Kinloss and Lindores by Edward Bruce and Patrick Leslie who held baronies with these titles, and Scone by Viscount Stormont. New Abbey had been granted to Sir Robert Spottiswoode in 1624. This list is printed in the introduction to the *Register of the Privy Council of Scotland* 1625-7, pp. cxliv-vi. With the exception of Roxburgh there is hardly a peer mentioned on whom the King was able to rely.

The great majority of the Scottish lords seemed to have nothing to lose by that policy of opposition which was dictated by their own interests. The days of King James's lavish welcome to the English Court were gone for ever. Very few of them had anything to hope for from their present sovereign. He was at the same time secret and parsimonious. Although careful in regard to gifts and offi:es, he was lavish in granting titles. His coronation in Edinburgh had been marked by a shower of earldoms. There were thus various families which were satisfied but not grateful. The circle of the Scottish lords was not likely to gain much from their present master.

To this generalisation there is one exception, the new Earl of Argyll. The King had hoped to win him over for it was part of his weakness that he never minded where he bestowed his favours. For long he seems to have held the strange belief that office by itself created loyalty. Since he could have gained great office from his sovereign, Argyll was the more determined to attain to power in his despite. In the gathering at Glasgow he always acts as one who sought authority, perhaps his conscience drove him to this. He had a gift of manifesting his moral earnestness to the Kirk that none could equal. He stood apart by his unique position for Huntly was absent and Hamilton the King's Commissioner; he was also the only great man to earn the acclamation of the Kirkmen. It was this last fact that riled the Scottish lords.

In many cases their interests were avowedly political and they had held that the ministers would prove a useful lever. They had come themselves into the Assembly as ruling elders. There could already be discerned at Glasgow the outlines of that alliance between Argyll and the Kirkmen which would endure until they fell together. This is, perhaps, the moment to consider the standpoint of the young Montrose for, whatever may have been his motives, his course was deflected by the Argyll ascendancy.

It is always difficult to attempt a reconstruction in the case of the early life of a national figure, who is remembered by the attributes of his maturity. In this case there is the additional embarrassment of Montrose's legend. Yet during the period in which he acted with the Covenanting lords as one of the leaders of their party his actions were in fact remarkably consistent. He was to prove impetuous on the field of battle; in these years he had only the irritating impetuosity of the council chamber. He was very proud; admirers and enemies agree about this attribute. He had a feeling for his order, which in some ways recalls St Simon. He aspired to be the leader of the group of earls of middle fortune, who existed independently of the Court. This was one of the factors that brought him to the Covenanters and kept him loyal to them. His pride made him intensely jealous of the magnates and he happened not to be of kin to any of them, a matter of some consequence. Hamilton he viewed with grave distrust; Huntly he perhaps despised; Argyll he grew to hate. From one angle the history of Montrose is resumed in these last words.

All his power came later; it was not exercised on his canny equals. It was when he was imprisoned after the discovery of the Band of Cumbernauld that he found what he could not do with his own class. He was not helped by his family except by his brother-in-law and guardian, Napier. His father-in-law Southesk was one of the King's lukewarm adherents. Menteith, the head of the other branch of his stock, was a suspect name. He had been deprived of that title in 1633 for claiming the royal earldom of Strathearn.[1] Montrose had no political adviser and in his early years he needed one.

Another strain was constant in him. Throughout life he showed himself a proud and high-hearted anti-clerical. He entered into all Rothes's feelings about the bishops. Two years later he was the first to take umbrage at the power which had been gained by the Presbyterian divines. He was by instinct and conviction and by his sense of his own noble blood opposed to power in the State passing to any cleric. As far as the royal cause was concerned, he took no decisive step till Laud was gone. All this was present only in the germ as the leaders gathered at Glasgow for the Assembly.

The ensuing eighteen months cover a part of Montrose's early public life known to us mainly through official documents. It is therefore difficult to assess the degree or nature of his influence. Rothes seems to have brought him forward and to have had something of the kindness of an elder brother for him; but in this case it was an elder brother whose own affairs were permanently embarrassed. As far as military authority was concerned Rothes naturally looked to a very different quarter. At this date the minister of Methven had an influence on the young Montrose. He was accessible to religious feeling when this was set within the frame of Scotland's welfare.

The months between the signing of the National Covenant and the meeting of the Assembly had been a busy period for the

[1] William eighth Earl of Menteith had received the earldom of Strathearn by patent on 31 July 1631, but two years later he was deprived of both those titles and was instead created Earl of Airth. He was accused of stating that he was the lineal representative of David Earl of Strathearn, the eldest son of Robert II by his second marriage whose offspring might be held to have a more secure legitimacy than those born of his first union.

opposition managers. The King, on his side, had produced the Confession of Faith signed by James VI in 1580. This step had been taken with reluctance on the partly erroneous assumption that episcopacy, not directly attacked or indeed even mentioned in the National Covenant, could thus be better protected. It was also felt that a document composed more than half a century previously was bound to be sedative in its effects. The bulk of the privy councillors accepted the document; the signatories included a number of men who would in time be "moderate" Covenanters.

The opposition had been using Wariston as their legal adviser and his hand can be traced both in the protests against the use of the Confession of 1580 and in the complaint which the Edinburgh presbytery proffered against all the bishops. This last document accused them of usurping ecclesiastical jurisdiction and was set forward in time to be examined by the General Assembly. It was skilfully arranged that the signatories to this complaint should not be among those elected to go as commissioners to Glasgow. They could then not be accused of being judges in their own cause. Among the nobles who subscribed to this complaint were two who lived remote from the capital, Sutherland and Forbes, and two who were heirs to the heads of their respective families, Montgomery and Elcho. One gains the impression that the signatures were parcelled out among the minor figures: they included the young Lord Boyd.

The next matter was the selection of representatives from the presbyteries; both ministers and laymen would be included. This last factor was of great importance in the composition of a body which would in reality carry through the work which belonged properly to the lords of the articles in the Scots Parliament. Eventually one hundred and forty ministers[1] and ninety-eight ruling elders were sent as commissioners. The laymen included seventeen lords, nine knights, twenty-five landed proprietors and forty-seven burgesses of standing. Apart from the Earl of Wemyss chosen by Perth, the peers all represented presbyteries south of the Tay. They formed the hard enduring core of the early Covenanters of their rank; Home from the presbytery of Chirnside near the Border; Lothian from Dalkeith; Eglinton and Cassilis from the West; Rothes from Dunfermline; Montrose from Auchterarder. The assembly included twelve provosts or ex-provosts of the principal towns. Every commissioner was instructed to bring at least four attendants with him.

It is worth pausing to consider the effect that the lay elders

---

[1] In addition there were two professors.

made on their opponents. A speech by Hamilton,[1] made to the assembly as the King's Commissioner, sets out the argument. It reads now like a debater's triumph. "Let the world judge whether those laymen," he is speaking at this time of the ruling elders, "be fit to give votes in inflicting the censures of the Church, especially that great and highest censure of excommunication . . . and whether all the lay-elders here present at this assembly be fit to judge of the high and deep mysteries of predestination, of the universality of redemption, of the sufficiency of grace given or not given to all men, of the resistibility of grace, of total and final perseverance or apostasy of the saints, of the antelapsarian or postlapsarian opinion, of election and reprobation; all which they mean to ventilate, if they do determine against the Arminian, as they give out they will."

He then turned to arguments of a practical character. "How can these men now elected be thought fit to be ruling-elders who were never elders before? . . . By what law of practice was it ever heard, that young noblemen, or gentlemen, or others, should be chosen rulers of the church, being yet minors, and in all construction of law thought unfit to manage their own private estates, unless you will grant that men of meaner abilities may be thought fit to rule the church, which is the house of God, than are fit to rule their own private houses, families, and fortunes?"

This is an excellent speech, perhaps among the very best that Hamilton ever had written for him. Bishop Maxwell was in Glasgow Castle at this time and possibly it was he who composed it or it may have been the Commissioner's chaplain Dr Balcanquhall. Starting from its own premises it was entirely cogent, but it is likely that there was hardly a man in the whole assembly who agreed with it. Old Mr John Bell had preached inaudibly on "The Seven Golden Candlesticks". The members accommodated in the Cathedral through the seven shortening November days during which Hamilton remained with them had chosen Alexander Henderson as moderator and Wariston as clerk. The ministers, to whom the Commissioner's words were primarily addressed, felt that the laity were showing a reverence for God's Kirk and a readiness to defend its interests.

And Hamilton himself? The Marquis sat on his chair of state with six assessors ranged beside but below him. He made a compact rather burly figure full of dignity, the cheeks of a dark high colour beneath his questing eyes. It was his duty to maintain the King's position and satisfactory that this charge was committed

[1] Printed in Burnet *Lives of James and William Dukes of Hamilton,* p. 130.

S

to the House of Hamilton. Like so many viceroys he was following instructions on a matter which he viewed with deep indifference. There was set down on the manuscript in his hand the words "antelapsarian or postlapsarian opinion". These were notions which had hitherto not engaged his attention. Across the choir and beyond him the opposition sat row on row. They lit the candles in the failing light.

The bishops had recommended the postponement of the General Assembly, but Hamilton had decided to require that they be admitted to take their seats. Wariston produced the registers, presumed to have been lost, of the Assemblies that had met before the influence of James VI became predominant. Everything went contrary to the royal wishes. The Commissioner's six assessors, the Earls of Argyll, Traquair, Roxburgh, Lauderdale and Southesk and Sir Lewis Stewart, were refused the right to vote. In consequence the King had a single vote, while the city of Edinburgh had two. Beside the actual Commissioners were ranged a numerous body of assessors; it was a predominantly lay body armed with swords and daggers. The effort to question the validity of certain elections of ruling elders proved unsuccessful. The Assembly persistently postponed the reading of the bishops' letter declining to recognise the gathering as legal. On 28th November Hamilton declared the Assembly dissolved. At this point Argyll separated himself from the other councillors. "I have," he said, "not striven to blow the bellows. But studied to keep matters in as soft a temper as I could, and now I desire to make it known to you that I take you all for members of a lawful Assembly and my honest countrymen." Hamilton withdrew, while the Assembly continued its sessions, Argyll remaining with them. In effect he came in and took that place of leadership which Hamilton had vacated. All recognised that he was the "great man" and this was also Hamilton's opinion.

Both sides were now moving to an armed conflict. The Commissioner had for some months advised his master as to how this should be carried forward. In Scotland there had been many clashes around this question of the royal authority. Hamilton and his associates looked forward and considered what would happen after these first clashes. Argyll would show a clear distaste for war. All those in Scotland knew far better than the King and Archbishop Laud what would happen when the forces were aligned. Rothes had some months before obtained the hearty support of Field-Marshal Leslie.

CHAPTER XIX

THE SCOTTISH ARMY

AS a contrast to Hamilton there now emerged a man who was born to be successful, and whose significance in the Scottish scene is often underrated, Alexander Leslie afterwards first Earl of Leven. A comment made by Spalding, although not wholly exact, will give[1] the impression of the effect created. "There came out of Germany from the wars home to Scotland ane gentleman of base birth, born in Balveny, who had served long and fortunately in the German wars, and was called by the name of Felt-Marshal Leslie—his excellence. His name, indeed, was Alexander Leslie, but by his valour and good luck attained to this title 'his excellence', inferior to none but to the King of Sweden under whom he served among all his cavalry."

He was, perhaps, the last *Condottiere* on the grand scale; aided by land hunger which had marked the old-time leaders; freed from the trammels of any formal education; spurred forward by his bastardy. There may be something in the story related by Lord Hailes that his instruction in reading did not reach beyond the letter *g*. He certainly had the clear objectives which were lost to the sophisticated general officers of the France of the *grand siècle*. He was essentially a man who would carve out a principality; it is likely that Wallenstein's example influenced him more than he knew. Much stress is laid on Leslie's religious zeal and this need not be doubted. It was in any case to some extent common form in the years before the seventeenth century had settled to its fatigue. He seems, however, mainly to have been concerned both to preserve and to break into the Scotland that he knew. He could not but be hostile to Archbishop Laud and to any Englishman who came north to meddle.

Alexander Leslie's parentage has never been elucidated satisfactorily. He is described as the natural son of George Leslie of Balgonie in Fife, who was at one time captain of Blair Castle in Atholl and was himself descended from the Leslies of Balquhain. His mother is said[2] to have been a "wench in Rannoch". Much stress was laid on his parents' marriage after his birth, but accord-

[1] Spalding, *Memorialls*, i, p. 130.
[2] Cf. Diary of David second Earl of Wemyss.

ing to Scots Law he would only have been legitimated *per subsequentem matrimonium* if he had not been born in adultery.[1]

His connection with the Earl of Rothes was thus remote, although he early worked to gain the friendship of the head of his own family. It seems probable that from the time of his return Leslie was determined to secure an earldom for himself in the old Scotland, that is to say in his country free from interfering southerners. He had had considerable contact with Hamilton, an acquaintanceship begun in Germany and carried on subsequently by correspondence. His earlier letters are almost obsequious, the later less[2] so; it seems that this change was due to his own increasing military standing. This is just one more example of the almost endless ramifications which bound the King's Commissioner to Scotsmen of importance.

In considering the armed preparations that are about to be described one gains the solid impression that the opposition knew that their manoeuvres would prove successful. This view seems also shared by the Scottish privy councillors. It was only the sanguine King who was convinced that he might win by military measures. The result depended mainly on the line of action that Scottish soldiers in the Swedish service would adopt when once the bidding had begun for their support.

The most detailed impression of the soldiers of fortune at that time is that preserved in Robert Monro's account. He draws attention to the consideration with which Scotsmen of standing were always treated. This is mentioned in an interesting comment on his kinsman Robert Monro of Foulis,[3] who "went beyond sea a voluntier with Mac-Keyes Regiment" after he had mortgaged his estates for ten years[4] to pay his creditors. In this account the reli-

---

[1] The writer in the *D.N.B.*, vol. xxxiii, 68, states that George Leslie married his mistress after the death of his first wife.

[2] On 16 April 1636 he addressed Hamilton as "Most noble Lord and Patron" and on 9 May of the same year as "Most honorable and noble Patron". Cf. Letters printed in *The Life and Campaigns of Alexander Leslie* by C. S. Terry, 1899, pp. 33-4.

[3] "The Baron of Fowles comming over a voluntier was allowed a free table to entertaine an Earle, being ordinarily above sixteene persons at table, his visitors, horses, and servants entertained accordingly", Robert Monro, *His Expedition with the Worthy Scots Regiment (called Mac-Keyes Regiment)*, 1637, pt. 1, p. 1.

[4] My Chiefe and cosen, the Baron of Fowles, being in his travels in France a little prodigall in his spending, redacted his estate to a weake point, being advised by his friends timely to looke to the woundes of his house and family, and to forsee the best cure to keep burthen off his estate, having engaged his revenewes for ten years", *ibid.*, pt. i, p. 3.

gious note is somewhat pressed. Foulis died in 1633,[1] after seven
years' service, at Ulm from a wound in his foot caused by a musket
ball. During his later life he showed marked piety, "a true
Christian[2] and a right traveller". Robert Monro concluded his
Expedition with seven pages of notes[3] entitled "The Christian
Souldier going on Service his Meditations".

The enemy did not represent the only danger. "On this expedition towards the Waser streame," writes[4] Monro in an account of
one of his earlier campaigns, "Captain Boswell comming after the
Regiment was killed by a number of villanous Boores ever enemies
to souldiers; the Cavaliers death was much regrated of all that
knew him, and no reparation had for his death. But the Boores
being fled, the Dorpe was burned off." The expressions "Dorpe"
and "Boores" and "Cavaliers" all raise an echo. A reference to
Scotsmen serving with the Imperialists has a turn of phrase which
is very pleasant. It relates[5] to the storming of the sconce at
Beysenburg. "There was also a Scottish gentleman, under the
enemy, who coming to scale the walls, said aloud. Have with you,
Gentlemen, think not now you are on the streets of Edinburgh
bravading."

The medium of communication between the higher ranks was
often French. Thus Andrew Newport[6] explains that the King of
Sweden spoke to him in that language until he changed to German
on "Sir John Hepburn informing his majesty that I spoke High
Dutch". The same writer reinforces[7] the suggestion of a certain
noble freedom that Gustavus was accustomed to employ with the
men of rank who came to him. "Sir John Hepburn took the case
up something gravely, and drinking a glass of Leipsic beer, said
to the captain, 'Come captain don't press these gentlemen, the
King desires no man's service but what is purely volunteer:'"
Newport's *Memoirs* also contain two English tributes[8] to the Scotsmen. The first will give a general impression. "I met with several
gentlemen in the King's army who spoke English extremely well;
besides that there were three regiments of Scots in the army, the

[1] The principal members of this family on foreign service were Robert
Monro and his brother Sir Hector, who were both sons of Hector Monro of
Foulis by his wife Anne daughter of Hugh sixth Lord Lovat; their cousin
Robert Monro the author and Covenanting general; the latter's nephew Sir
George Monro, who was present at Lützen as a young man.
[2] Monro, *op. cit.*, pt. ii, p. 49.   [3] *Ibid.*, pt. ii, pp. 217-24.
[4] *Ibid.*, pt. i, p. 4.   [5] *Ibid.*, pt. i, p. 11.
[6] *Memoirs of the Honourable Colonel Andrew Newport*, ed. 1792, p. 80.
[7] *Ibid.*, p. 70.
[8] Cf. *ibid.*, pp. 70 and 87. The authorship of this work has been disputed
and its attribution to the Royalist Andrew Newport cannot be sustained. It
would, however, seem to be based upon some genuine anonymous original.

colonels whereof I found were extraordinarily esteemed by Gustavus, as the lord Rea, colonel Lumsdell, and Sir John Hepburn . . . he was a complete soldier indeed." The second entry deals with the rate of fire. "The Scottish brigades, giving fire three ranks at a time over one another's heads, poured in their shots so thick, that the enemy were cut down like grass before a scythe."

At the bases where these regiments were equipped, solid merchant houses had been established. Thus Monro[1] refers to Mr Balfour and Mr Sinclair, shipbuilders established at Copenhagen under the patronage of the Danish Crown. The chaplains, who were to be so much to the fore in the Armies of the Covenant, had also appeared in the German wars. "Here," writes[2] Monro, "I must not forget the memory of our Preacher Master William Forbesse, a Preacher for Souldiers, yea, and a Captaine in neede, to lead Souldiers on a good occasion." These points being made we can return to Alexander Leslie.

The King's Commissioner had dissolved the Glasgow Assembly. It had continued in session and passed enactments. Its members were faced with the alternatives of surrendering to the King or bringing pressure on him to induce him to accept its measures and reverse his policy. It is the nature of such pressure that it is intended to lead to reconciliation; it did not occur to Alexander Leslie or to any other Scotsman that men might take away the fount of honour. Meanwhile it was his practice to play the viceroy, and for this purpose he always used his style of Excellency. A little, bent, crooked man he kept up elaborate state in order to maintain his military splendour. Later he would be described[3] as sitting "at table with the best of the nobility of Scotland, at the upper end, covered and they all bareheaded".

General Leslie was in the true sense a soldier of fortune; he had begun as far back as 1605 as a captain in the Dutch service in Sir Horace Vere's regiment of volunteers. There was twenty years of soldiering in Sweden before he became Governor of Stralsund in 1628; he was then a colonel. It is characteristic of the mixed character of the Scottish military experience that at Stralsund he relieved Sir Donald Mackay's regiment which was then in the service of the King of Denmark. Three years in command of the garrisons along the Baltic coast brought Leslie to Frankfurt-on-Oder, where he was appointed governor upon its capture. The

[1] Monro, *op. cit.*, pt. i, p. 87.

[2] *Ibid.*, pt. i, p. 52. At the end of part i Monro prints a four page list of the "Scottish Officers in Chiefe (called the Officers of the Field) that served his Majesty of Sweden *Anno* 1632.

[3] Cf. Baillie, *Letters and Journals*, i, pp. 213-4, Fraser, *Melvilles*.

ingenuous account by Robert Monro[1] shows what the new commander found there. "The fury past, the whole streets being full of Coaches and rusty waggons richly furnished with all sorts of riches, as Plate, Iewells, Gold, Money, Clothes, Mulets and horses for saddle, coach and waggons, whereof all men that were carelesse of their dueties were too carefull in making of booty." There is no doubt that booty was a subject on which the general was well-informed. He acted as second in command to Hamilton during the latter's campaign in Germany and did not return to Scotland until the summer of 1635 on the signing of the Peace of Prague. When at home he received the freedom of Culross and purchased landed property in Fife. More important he arranged the marriage of his eldest surviving[2] son to Rothes's daughter. It seems likely that there was henceforward a working arrangement between Leslie and Rothes; they would aid one another as occasion served.

Slender as is our information as to Leslie's personal life, a certain light is cast on his outlook in a letter written[3] to Hamilton provoked by the King of Sweden's death. Much of his phrasing in praise of his leader is conventional, "the fame of whose valour and love to the good cause sal nevir end". Still, the following sentences appear more personal. "So ar we to our unspeakable greife deprived of the best and most valorouse commander that evir any souldiours hade, and the Church of God with hir good cause of the best instrument under God, we becaus we was not worthie of him, and she for the sinnes of hir children." This was a common Scottish outlook and was reflected by Robert Monro. From the idea that the Kirk was suffering for the sins of her children it was a short step to the proposition that the Kirk must be set free.

There were many prepared to take part in such a work. The war on the Continent was flickering; it no longer offered that stable employment which had been ensured by the King of Sweden's enterprises. The leaders who appear under a slight disguise in Leslie's letters, the "King of Boheme" and Duke Bernard of "Veimers"[4] were now dead. Capable officers were ready to return to Scotland to serve the "good cause" in their native country. Some of them at any rate were given to an apocalyptic phraseology. This is seen in the tributes paid to Gustavus Adolphus. "I dare be

[1] Robert Monro, *His Expedition with the Worthy Scots Regiment* (called *Mac-Keyes Regiment*), 1637, pt. ii, p. 34.

[2] His eldest son Gustavus was born in the first years of his Swedish service, perhaps Leslie attached himself early to the young prince.

[3] The letter dated at Stade on 26 November is printed by C. S. Terry, *op. cit.*, pp. 30-2.

[4] These phonetic spellings as also that of "Duke Ewiene of Lunnemberie" for Erwin of Lauenburg or one of the House of Luneburg throw doubts on the extent of Leslie's education.

bould to say," wrote[1] Monro, "he was a man according to Gods minde, if there was one on earth. Such was our Master, Captaine and King. . . . Was young Tobias mindfull all his days of the Lord, in his heart, and his will set not to sinne? So was our Master, Captaine and Kinge, like unto a stone most precious, even like a Iasper, cleere as Christall ever and ever." This is a strain notable among the Army, at least among the officers, the "will set not to sinne". It made them incomprehensible to Hamilton and to his young brother Lanark, who was now coming upon the scene. It was something that no Cavalier could view without repugnance. At the same time it was just this approach which commended the officers to Wariston and his circle and likewise found an echo in one aspect of Argyll's embracing mind. Yet the ministers and soldiers were not to work easily in double harness. Among the officers this apocalyptic phrasing was not lasting; the dead King of Sweden had inspired it.

There were also two further factors. Leslie was the incarnation of common sense and as a consequence this tended to divide the Army into two factions. Further the whole body of officers had a reverence for the King, whom Leslie had addressed[2] as "his most sacred Majestie of Great Britane, France and Ireland, my most dred soueragne". This last consideration must never be forgotten. The Covenanters had raised an army which purposed to win by a show of strength. Nothing more military was really intended. The Army was bent on reconciliation, but this did not make it the less formidable to the King's policies.

The matter has not been fully studied, but it seems that Leslie's part in gathering the officers was very great. "He has," wrote[3] Baillie, "caused a great number of our commanders in Germany to subscryve our Covenant, and provided much good munition." Spalding enforces the same opinion.[4] "He causit send to Germanye, France, Holland, Denmark, and uther countreis, for the most expert and valiant capitanes, livetennantis, and wnder officiares." To these experienced men were added the sons of the Covenanting families. The question of the soldiers' pay was settled. As far back as March 1638 eight collectors had been named in every county to exact a "voluntary" contribution of one dollar for every thousand merks of free rent.

[1] Monro, *op. cit.*, pt. ii, p. 169.
[2] Letter dated "frome our Leager at Herford the 9th Maii, 1636" printed in *The Melvilles, Earls of Melville, and the Leslies, Earls of Leven* by Sir William Fraser (1890), ii, p. 35.
[3] Baillie, *Letters and Journals*, i, p. 111.
[4] Spalding, *Memorialls*, i, p. 130. He states, however, that these officers "cam in gryte numberis upone hope of bloodie war". It seems much more likely that they came in hopes of remunerative military employment.

Among the officers brought over was "Sandy" Hamilton, the General of the Artillery. In March Edinburgh Castle had surrendered without a struggle. When the Army had formed itself the lords of the opposition were all present "either[1] with whole or half regiments", Rothes, Lindsay, Balcarres, Loudoun, Montgomery, Erskine, Boyd, Fleming, Kirkcudbright, Yester, Dalhousie, Eglinton, Cassilis; this reads like a catalogue of all that was most forward in the high Covenanting world. It can be looked upon as a mass movement guided by a ruling class.

Baillie's well-known account of the Army at Duns Law should be given here for it has certain features whose meaning is not recognised. There was an artillery park of forty cannon. "Our regiments," explains[2] Baillie, "lay on the sydes of the Hill, almost round about: the place was not a myle in circle, a prettie round rysing in a declivitie, without steepness, to the height of a bowshott; on the toppe somewhat playne; about a quarter of (a) myle in length, and as much in breadth, as I remember, capable of tents for fortie thousand men. The crowners (colonels) lay in canvas lodges, high and wyde; their captaines about them in lesser ones; the sojours about all in hutts of timber, covered with divott or straw. Our crowners for the most part were noblemen. . . . Our captaines for the most part, barrons or gentlemen of good note; our lieutenants almost all sojours who had served over sea in good charges; everie companie had, flying at the Captaine's tentdoore, a brave new colour stamped with the Scottish Armes, and this ditton, 'For Christs Croun and Covenant', in gold letters. Our Generall had a royall tent; but it was not sett up; his constant guard was some hundreds of our lawiers, musqueteers, under Durie and Hope's command, all the way standing in good armes, with cocked matches, before his gate well apparelled."

There follows an account of the councils of war held daily in the castle at the foot of Duns Law and the "ecclesiastick meetings" in Rothes's large tent. Attention was paid to the commissariat. "Our meanest sojours[3] was alwayes served in wheat-bread, and a groat would have gotten them a lamb-legge, which was a daintie world to the most of them." The town of Edinburgh sent moneys, Mr Rollock by his sermons moved the Faithful to "shake out their purses", the storehouses of non-covenanters and especially those of Mr Maxwell and Lord Winton were laid under contribution.

The description[4] of the common life is memorable. "Had ye lent your eare in the morning, or especiallie at even, and heard in the

[1] Baillie, op. cit., i, p. 211.   [2] Ibid., i, pp. 211-2.
[3] Ibid., i, p. 213.   [4] Ibid., i, p. 214.

tents the sound of some singing psalms, some praying, and some reading scripture, ye would have been refreshed: true, there was swearing, and cursing, and brawling in some quarters, whereat we were grieved; bot we hoped, if our camp had ben a little settled, to have gotten some way for these misorders; for all of any fashion did regraitt, and all did promise to contribute their best endeavours for helping all abuses." With this there may be set another passage.[1] "Our sojours grew in experience of armes, in courage, in favour dailie; everie one encouraged another; the sight of the nobles and their beloved pastors dailie raised their hearts; the good sermons and prayers, morning and even, under the roof of heaven, to which their drums did call them for bells; the remonstrances were frequent of the goodness of their cause; of their conduct hitherto, by a hand clearlie divine."

One has the sense that they knew that all would come to them, and certainly without a struggle. There is the same idyllic note about the countryside. "Marche and Tevidaill (Teviotdale) are the best mixt and most plentifull shyres both for grasse and corn, for fleshes and bread, in all our land." This was, surely, the happiest moment that the Covenanters would ever know. The flags blew out in the keen air of early summer in Berwickshire, the "brave new colour stamped with the Scottish Armes and 'For Chryst's Croun and Covenant' in golden letters."

The great body of the soldiers came from the southern and south-western counties, "the most of them," as Baillie remarks,[2] "stout young plewmen". They were in bulk the tenants or dependants of the great Covenanting families or of the lairds who followed them. An interesting and very different element was provided by the College of Justice regiment. Robert Baillie, at that time just forty years of age and minister of Kilwinning, was present at Duns Law as a chaplain. He makes this clear[3] in his long letter to William Spang. "It would have done yow good to have casten your eyes athort our brave and rich Hill, as oft I did, with great contentment and joy, for I (quoth the wren) was there among the rest, being chosen preacher by the gentlemen of our shyre, who came late with my Lord of Eglintoun. I furnished to half a dozen of good fellows, musquets and picks, and to my boy a broadsword. I carryed my self, as the fashion was, a sword, and a couple of Dutch pistols at my sadle; bot I promise, for the offence of no man, except a robber in the way; for it was our part alone to pray and preach for the incouragement of our countrey-men, which I did to my power cheerfullie." These were the

---

[1] *Ibid.*, i, p. 213.   [2] *Ibid.*, i, p. 212.
[3] *Ibid.*, i, p. 211.

ancestors of the men who would support the Covenant in the hard times.

Still, it is important to prevent lack of proportion. The presentation of Scottish history is often dogged by rival romanticisms, the legend of Montrose and in its more sober fashion the legend of Duns Law. The Army of the Covenant was to prove such a powerful engine in the field of politics just because there was no other. Its preparation was a triumph of skilful timing. The experienced officers maintained a force in being for the purpose of rendering secure what amounted to a revolution in the politico-religious sphere. The strength of this policy lay in the fact that nothing further was attempted. In a way this was a game of double bluff. The King through the early summer was assembling an army on the Scottish Border. It seems to me that he was clearly aware of Leslie's sense of the dynasty and considered that he would not permit his soldiers to oppose themselves with arms against their sovereign present in person. On the other hand the King had not the military force to compel surrender, while the Scottish leaders confined themselves to seeking the royal sanction for changes which were represented as being strictly within the religious sphere.

Leslie's earlier military actions during this year had been concentrated on efforts to enforce the acceptance of the Covenant. The Marquis of Huntly had received a royal commission to act as lieutenant over the country between the North Esk and Caithness. In 1638 he had been active in securing signatures to the King's Confession of Faith and he had boycotted the Glasgow Assembly. During the second half of March Montrose and Leslie marched north and occupied Aberdeen. The leading churchmen, who had throughout resisted the Covenant, then left the town by sea. Huntly himself opened negotiations and this step resulted in his seizure. He certainly signed a variant of the Covenant apparently satisfactory to Montrose and received a safe conduct from him. This safe conduct was disallowed, presumably under Leslie's influence, and Huntly was brought south to Edinburgh. By the time that the Army had assembled on Duns Law he had been allowed to go to join the King. All that need be said at this point is that Huntly was unprepared to resist attack. It seems likely that his pride was affronted by being offered a safe conduct in his own country and then by finding that the promise was not kept. The whole question remains very obscure. Huntly had received great offers from the Covenanters in return for his support and Argyll had advanced large sums of money to help to pay his brother-in-law's debts. Perhaps Huntly knew himself what line he meant to follow. By the time of Duns Law he personally, as opposed to his sons and followers, no longer counted.

The impression remains that the outcome of the gathering on Duns Law was one that Leslie had long foreseen. The King was in no position to move forward and the Scots were at this time resolved to avoid entering England against their sovereign's will. All was set for the pacification which was signed at Berwick on 18 June 1639.

CHAPTER XX

THE CHARACTER OF THE CONFLICT

AFTER the Pacification of Berwick events moved fast. It was a predictable pattern of the fulfilment by the Scots of their own intentions. It had been agreed that a general assembly should meet at Edinburgh on 12 August and that Parliament should then be summoned to ratify its acts. Traquair sat as the King's Commissioner replacing Hamilton; David Dickson was elected moderator succeeding to Henderson in that office. During the session Traquair promised that he would subscribe the Covenant. The Assembly was dissolved on 30 August and Parliament met the following day. Argyll bore the Crown during the procession for the opening. Sixty nobles and ninety-eight lairds and burgesses were in attendance. The Lords of the Articles named by the Commissioner included Argyll, Montrose and Lauderdale. Their actions consisted of a reassertion of what had been decreed at Glasgow. These measures were now embodied in legal form. Thus an Act was passed rescinding all former enactments in favour of the bishops or episcopacy. This was followed by another discharging the civil powers of churchmen. Finally on 24 September an Act was passed rescissory of enactments giving civil power to churchmen. This Act was retrospective and could be regarded as infringing the King's right in relation to appointments in the sphere of civil jurisdiction. In consequence Traquair demurred to this measure as a violation of the royal prerogative. On 14 November he prorogued Parliament until 2 June 1640. The enactments were in fact a series of affirmations of each detail of the Glasgow policy. The bishops had all gone, and these developments were surely not unexpected. Life in Scotland went forward with a kind of resolute tranquillity.

This is the point at which to consider the position of the individual leaders, and in the first place Hamilton who had been until so recently his sovereign's representative. In the Marquis's apparently anguished complaints of Scotland there appear a dual trend, the resentment of a viceroy at the insults to his king and the knowledge that these would have to be forgiven. Apart from certain of the bishops, there were few men of position who could envisage living outside of their own country and in these troubled

285

times the English Court was not a harbour. The thought of exile was intolerable to the Scottish lords. Thus Huntly would see himself returning with the King's victory; the other magnates had prudently remained on Scottish soil. Hamilton is often criticized for the advice given to the opposition in his quality of "kindly Scotsman". He told them that if they yielded they would be lost, and for this he has been accused of treachery, Another reading is admissible. The sovereign, as long as Archbishop Laud was at his side, had hardly a friend among those Scottish circles where the personality of the English primate had left its impact. The continual influence of the Archbishop was the unwelcome concomitant of the King's perfect victory. This is a factor that Hamilton may have realized.

At the time of the signing of the Pacification the dominant sections were already aligned in three different groupings. Huntly in England[1] alone remained apart from them. Traquair was carefully cast for the *rôle* of scapegoat; he had no affinity to rescue him. There were considerable numbers of "moderate" Covenanters and unmolested conservatives and, placed between them, those accommodating neutrals to be found in every quarrel. Rothes and Leslie may be said to have concentrated on the Army. It was always a body on which Argyll could not rely. Almond, who would be second-in-command, was to be found among his enemies. Argyll and Wariston and the ministers formed a single *bloc*. Hamilton had laid down his commission. One could already trace the indications that he knew that Argyll was a statesman with whom he could, and in fact must, work. Their curious uneasy partnership was coming closer. During this winter of 1639–1640 one can trace a sense in Scotland that among the grandees no one, except Huntly, would be the loser. This carried with it a corollary that the King must pay for all.

One element in the situation served further to insulate the King in his dealings with his Scottish subjects. There was during these crucial years no effective secretary of state. During that winter the old Earl of Stirling, who had held that post since 1626, lay dying in his house in Covent Garden. He was insolvent and for long had been politically a cypher. His duty was to reside at Court to take the King's instructions on Scots affairs. The principal significance of his death lay in the fact that his office was now vacated and in the means that Charles I would take to fill the post.

At the same time the secretary had in his own measure added

---

[1] "Albeit that the Marquesse of Huntly himself wer all the past tyme, after the pacificatione, at court with the King", Gordon, *History of Scots Affairs*, iii, p. 159.

to the burden of the royal unpopularity. Sir William Alexander of Menstrie, who had been created Earl of Stirling in 1633, had been a contemporary of James VI: he came of minor gentry with burgess connections, and was a poet and a friend of Drummond of Hawthornden. He was pliant and had something of the new King's outlook on religious matters; he was bound to his master by many ties and mutual indebtedness. In general he is known as the grantee of Canada and Nova Scotia. In Scotland the town house that he built, Argyll's Lodging at Stirling, is his sole memorial. In his own country he was thought of as the author of the copper coinage. The facts of this matter should be set down for it served appreciably to complicate the King's position.

It had been decided in 1631 to issue farthing copper tokens in an attempt to solve the problem presented by coins of too high a denomination. Each token was to have the value of three pennies Scottish. There were to be penny and two-penny copper pieces, the whole range being intended to provide the country people with small coinage for marketing. The project was also aimed at liquidating the King's debts to Stirling. With this end in view the secretary of state was granted authority to administer this coinage and the right to mint. The transaction was unpopular in the extreme, Stirling having received licence to coin these farthings, known as "turners",[1] to the value of one hundred thousand pounds Scots money.

Gordon of Rothiemay[2] sets out the popular view of Stirling's purpose. "To be some recrute to his cracked fortune, after his former monopoly of selling knyght barronetts patents for New Scottland was growne stale and gave no more pryce, and after the planting of his kyngdome in Alexandria (Nova Scotia) had miscarryed." Men were not slow to criticize the King's careless monopolies.[3]

On this question Baillie has a comment. He is referring to the death of Stirling's son and heir some eighteen months previously. "It Feares me," he wrote,[4] "his death will undo that ryseing House: their debts are great; his Father is old, and extremely hated of all the countrey for his alledged briberie, urgeing of the Psalmes, and the Books for them, overwhelming us with his Black money." Two sets of verses[5]

[1] This name may derive from the French *tournois*.
[2] Gordon, *History of Scots Affairs,* vol. ii, pp. 87-8.
[3] In addition to the permanent difficulty caused by the copper coinage, both the King's salt monopoly and also the project of the soap makers were injurious to Scottish interests.
[4] Baillie, *Letters and Journals,* i, p. 77.
[5] The first satire preserved among the Denmylyn MSS. was printed in Brunton and Haig, *Senators of the College of Justice,* p. 289.

or Argyll as her husband's enemies; that *rôle* was in her mind reserved for such as Pym.

William Hamilton was very young. He was born in December 1616 and had only lately come upon the scene. It is a significant factor that he had no independent fortune and was wholly dependent on his elder brother. The earldom of Lanark,[1] without any estates annexed to it, was provided for him shortly after he came of age. At the same time an admittedly uncongenial marriage was arranged with one of the daughters of Mr Maxwell of the Bedchamber, who was later created Earl of Dirleton. Her father, who was one of King James's surviving Scots,[2] made a very heavy settlement. Before travelling in France Lanark had studied for some years at the university of Glasgow. He was a novice in all that related to his native country. "He had," Burnet admits,[3] "no experience at all in Scottish affairs, but for that he resolved to trust to his brother's informations and advices; which did not only continue till he came to understand persons and affairs better, but that noble pair were all their lives united with bonds of friendship closer than those of their blood." This judgment has not been disputed by other commentators. In the years that followed he was to prove the Marquis of Hamilton's dutiful ally. "He was," wrote[4] Burnet a favourable witness in regard to all the Hamiltons, "of a middle stature, his complexion black, but very agreeable, and his whole air and mean was noble and sprightful." It is understandable that he was the more popular of the two brothers. "He was," wrote[5] Clarendon, "in all respects to be preferred before the other (the Marquis): a much wiser, though, it may be, a less cunning man; for he did not affect dissimulation, which was the other's masterpiece."

Lanark had desired the post of master of the horse to the Queen and moved proudly among his equals. "His discourse[6] was short, but nervous, witty, and full of stings, when he had a mind to reflect on others; but he was soon heated, and kept his fire pretty long." Until his last years he was licentious and there was little to commend him to the ministers. He is described[7] as "a zealous Protestant", but the note that follows would not have impressed Wariston in his favour. "He had a great dislike of churchmen's pretending to meddle in civil affairs, finding it hurtful on all

---

[1] William Hamilton's normal signature was "Lanerick".
[2] James Maxwell of Kirkhouse was created Lord Innerwick in 1638 and Earl of Dirleton in 1646. His wife was French. "It was not without reluctancey that he (Lanark) was engaged that way, but his brother's authority over him was absolute", Burnet, *op. cit.,* p. 530.
[3] *Ibid.,* p. 531.   [4] *Ibid.,* p. 529.
[5] *History of the Rebellion.*   [6] Burnet, *op. cit.,* p. 532.
[7] *Ibid.,* p. 532.

T

hands; and therefore was much for confining them to their own work." As a young man Lanark was painted by Daniel Mytens, but the more familiar portrait is that painted in 1649 by Cornelius Jonson van Coelen, when he had succeeded as second Duke of Hamilton. He is represented seating and discoursing with the Earl of Lauderdale. His heavy features suggest pride and a morose honesty.

It is worth while considering the relationship between Argyll and the Hamiltons for this was now entering on a phase of cordiality. There was, however, a marked difference in their situations. Hamilton and Lanark worked from a position of weakness; manipulation was their sole weapon. Their understanding of the minds of the King and Queen was an asset of steadily diminishing value. Argyll bestrode the field of Scottish politics. The unwavering support of the ministers gave him the position of strength. This was to some extent masked by the deference which Argyll showed at this time towards his "Lord and dear Brother". In addition there was a further factor. Hamilton was a widower with daughters and Lanark, also, had no sons. An alliance between Argyll and the brothers involved the possibility that Lorne might gain in time the whole Hamilton inheritance. There were reasons why they should stand against the world, but it was exactly this union that would rouse a section of the Scottish lords against them.

As for the Hamiltons, the King had a deep and irrational loyalty to both his cousins, which became stronger after the sacrifice of Strafford. Charles I had himself asserted his belief in Hamilton's fidelity when this was questioned. The history of the next two years is in effect that of a series of concessions made by the reluctant sovereign. Argyll was the principal beneficiary. A final comment may be made on Hamilton and Lanark. It is not wise to be the mediators of a king's surrender.

A separate but allied question was that of Argyll's relations with the Gordons. Since the death of his sister the Marchioness of Huntly, he had taken her daughters under his protection and had arranged a marriage between Lady Jean Gordon and the widowed Earl of Haddington, who he had been anxious to secure for his own cause. Argyll had given his brother-in-law Huntly great help in his embarrassments, and he was always smooth and kindly to his eldest nephew suggesting that there was no one who had more care for the prosperity of the House of Huntly than McCailein Mor. It is true that his ancestral ambitions were shot through by the good of religion as he conceived this. Argyll had a burning sincerity in his desire to extirpate the Catholic Faith. To achieve this end when dealing with individuals of rank he would prove himself sweet-tempered as he made with his quiet voice the great offer of his friendship. This was a moment when it seemed that the Huntly Gordons might be gained for the Reformed Religion. Their grandmother the old Marchioness of Huntly had been driven overseas; the two elder boys Gordon and Aboyne counted as Protestants. Argyll had persuaded his niece to abandon Catholicism and to join the Kirk before her wedding.

In the territorial sphere no direct attack was ordered by Campbells against Gordons. The harrying of Strathbogie, which formed part of the "cleaning up" operations of this year, was allocated to Monro. Argyll did not himself go further than ordering the spoiling of the Athollmen and the wasting of the lands of the Ogilvies of Airlie. He was most concerned with his own borders and "his designe to swallow upp Badenoch and Lochaber". Gordon of Rothiemay describes[1] this action. "He (Argyll) had gott some hold upon Lochaber and Badenoche the last yeare, viz. 1639, as a cautionarye pledge for some of Huntlyes debtes, for which he was become engaged as cautioner to Huntlyes creditors. By this meanes his title was legall in caise of breache of conditione by Huntlye." From one angle these were the age-old methods of clan expansion, but it seems fair to suggest that Argyll's original motives were transmuted by the need to establish True Religion. Macdonalds, Camerons and Gordons failed by his strict standards. In this he was at one with Wariston. Surely Argyll saw all these moves as a gradual establishment of the Just Kingdom. Very few other Scots lords shared his views.

This summer of 1640 may be regarded as the final period of solidarity among the Scottish opponents of the King's policies. As far as the great landowners were concerned this was a solidarity that had been maintained on the basis of a uniform objection to the loss of teinds coming from the Church and to the increase of the political power of the Episcopate. Their union was also strengthened by the presence of an external threat. This took two forms, the royal army from England which had been assembled before the Pacification and the suggestion that either the McDonnells or else an army under Strafford should be ferried across from Ireland to attack Kintyre or the south western shires. The project that the Marquis of Antrim should lead a force had never much reality. At the same time the links which bound the Irish McDonnells to their Scottish kinsmen were genuine enough as would be proved later in Montrose's army. Strafford's force presented a real danger, which is indicated by the famous phrase

[1] *History of Scots Affairs*, vol. iii, p. 163.

used to his master, "You have an army in Ireland you may employ here to reduce this kingdom".

The relations between the Covenanters and the leaders of the opposition in the English Parliament, a subject which falls outside the scope of the present study, were cemented by the fear and detestation with which both parties regarded Strafford. This was a powerful motive in the Scots invasion which took place that summer, nor would the danger be removed until Strafford's impeachment in November 1640.

As early as the beginning of the year the English army was assembling under commanders selected on Strafford's advice. The Scots were likewise gathering with Alexander Leslie again in command and with Linlithgow's brother Almond as his immediate subordinate. In April Charles I had summoned an English Parliament for the first time in ten years. In the same month he arrested Loudoun, one of the Scottish commissioners in London, on the charge of sending a letter to the King of France which described the "candour and ingenuity" of the attitude of the leaders of the Covenant to their own sovereign. This was a significant development for it was the first occasion on which an important leader had been confined to prison by either side. Parliament refused to endorse King Charles's view that the document bore a treasonable construction. They also took the step of refusing to grant supplies for the Scottish war. This last move paralysed the ill-paid and unwilling English force. On 5 May the Short Parliament was dissolved.

Under these circumstances it is hardly necessary to stress the weakness of the English. "I," wrote[1] Conway to Lady Devonshire, "am teaching cart-horses to manage (*manège*) and making men that are fit for Bedlam and Bridewell to keep the ten commandments, so that General Leslie and I keep two schools, he has scholars that profess to serve God, and he is instructing them how they may safely do injury and all impiety; mine to the utmost of their power never kept any law either of God or the King and they are to be made fit to make others keep them." In June the Scottish Parliament, which Traquair had prorogued, met without a royal commissioner.

The way in which the Scots concealed their intentions reflects much credit on their planning. As late as 3 August Conway, one of the English generals, was still writing.[2] "Neither do I believe the Scots will come into England; this that they do is only to

---

[1] Letter dated at Newcastle on 28 May 1640, State Papers, Dom., Charles I, vol. ccclv, 38.

[2] Letter sent to Secretary Windebank, *ibid.,* vol., cccclxiii, 11.

brag; but, however, I will look to myself as well as a man may that has no money in his purse. I would send for more of the foot from Selby, but I fear unpaid soldiers more than I do the Scots, and the Devil to boot. God keep you from all three". On 20 August the Scottish forces crossed the Tweed. Leslie soon passed the site of Flodden and the columns concentrated upon Wooler. The guns were carried in "great close waggons[1] bigger than horse litters". They pushed them forward through the summer weather. The only skirmish occurred at Newburn Ford.[2] After an artillery duel, which ended in their favour, the Scots forced the passage of the Tyne in the afternoon of 28th August. The English casualties were about sixty dead, lying mainly about the earthworks which had formed the gun emplacements. The next day the English army withdrew from Newcastle and on Sunday 30th August General Leslie marched in and the Scots occupied that crucial town.

There now began the first of the two periods of occupation by a Scottish army, a force which was for some years to prove as resolutely peaceful as it was expensive. Fighting was over and would not begin again in Scotland until Montrose went north in 1644 with the King's commission. The coal trade with London[3] was throttled at the source as the army settled into winter quarters. The Custom House was occupied by the Scots, who seized the tolls for their own use. A tax of £200 a day was levied on the town. Some Covenanting leaders had moved south; Leslie lay at Anderson Place, a fine town mansion; Lothian was governor with Maddison's house as his headquarters. The Scots admired the massive walls which Lithgow had described[4] as "a great deale stronger than those of Yorke, and not unlike to the walls of Avineon, but especialy of Ierusalem". Negotiations were begun almost at once and by the Treaty of Ripon signed on 26th October the King agreed to pay the Scottish army the sum of £850 a day levied from the four northern counties. The Long Parliament assembled a week later and by Christmas both Strafford and Laud had been impeached. The King's enemies had proved surprisingly victorious.

The stay of the Scottish army in Newcastle lasted for just a year, a period in Scotland during which the implications of the

[1] Contemporary account printed by C. S. Terry in *The Life and Campaigns of Alexander Leslie,* p. 110.

[2] For a detailed consideration of this action cf. *ibid.,* pp. 111-32.

[3] The average annual sale of coals amounted to about one hundred and eighty thousand chaldrons. Eight Newcastle chaldrons were the equivalent of twenty-one tons. For this subject cf. *The Rise of the British Coal Industry* by John U. Nef.

[4] William Lithgow, *Relation,* p. 17.

King's surrender were working themselves out. It is in some ways a difficult time to interpret for the opposition among the Covenanters themselves to certain aspects of their leadership was only germinating. One episode makes clear the very natural Anglo-Scottish tension. The second Earl of Haddington, a man of forty, brought up in a ministerial tradition, the beneficiary of his father's great fortune, had at length come fully to support the Covenant and had been placed as major general in Lothian with his headquarters at Dunglass Castle. It was his duty to superintend the provisioning of the army and to guard the siege train as it moved south. The news of Newburn Ford reached Dunglass on the day after the battle of Haddington had let fall pleasantries on the conduct of the royal troops in the hearing of Edward Parise[1] his English page. Gordon of Rothiemay's account[2] of the disaster that took place between four and five in the afternoon is very vivid. 'Having dyned very jovially with such gentlemen and officers as wer about him, after dinner he (Haddington) was going downe staires, reading a letter which he had newly received, when behold, upone a soddaine, the whole house is suddenly blowne upp with one blast of gunnepoulder." The forepart of the building was thrown down and killed in its collapse a number of soldiers and others standing in the castle yard. Among the dead were Haddington and two of his brothers, his brother-in-law Colonel Alexander Erskine, and Sir John and Sir Alexander Hamilton, together with their intimate household servants.[3] It was supposed that Parise obtained the key of the magazine in the castle vaults and "fyred[4] a parcell of poulder with a red hotte ladle of iron". None of his remains were ever found except one hand holding an iron spoon.[5]

The next months were occupied by the gradual crystallising of opposition to Argyll. This was a natural development consequent upon the power to which he was very gradually attaining. In its simplest form it was jealousy of the mighty subject, who would soon overtop the rest; it was expressed, as so often with such

[1] "The Earle, getting advertishment . . . of the Scottishe victorye at Newburne, did jeere, saying to him (Parise) that his countreymen wer cowardly, or some wordes to that pourpose", Gordon, *Scots Affairs*, iii, p. 262. It should be said that this motive appears inadequate.

[2] *Ibid.*, iii, pp. 261-2.

[3] "And many honest and trusty servants, as Ninian Chyrnside, Alexander Cuninghame, John Johnston, with sundrie others". Entry under 30 August 1640 in the Sessions Records of the parish of Tynninghame printed by Fraser in *Memorials of the Earls of Haddington*, vol. i, p. 198.

[4] Gordon, *Scots Affairs*, iii, p. 262.

[5] Sir James Balfour's *Annales*, vol. ii.

dislike, in terms of the fear that he was aiming at the Crown. The idea is well expressed in an old ballad.[1]

> I give the Great Argyll the praise,
> For he will tak from the Lowland men,
> And he will tak the Crowne perforce,
> And he will cry King at Whitsontide.

Such a notion was uncongenial to the southern lords as they sat at home in their own castles. These men were the "realists" and wished to make sure of certain gains in Scotland. They were not prepared to be a party to the raising up of any viceroy and in particular they disliked the emergence of theocracy. For opposed to a policy of "realism" there stood those who can best be described as the "illumined", Argyll and Wariston and all the ministers.

The idea of a Covenanted kingdom and a Covenanted king was taking root and, as the royal power faded, this new notion seemed less impracticable. A sermon preached in September at a camp a few miles above Newcastle gives an impression of the attitude of the Covenanters. "Good Lord bless our King," concluded[2] the preacher, "and open his eyes, that he may see the truth of our Covenant. Lord Bless the Queen, open her eyes that she may fly her idolatry. Good Lord bless the King's bairns." This has a homely touch, but it shows what they still hoped from him. A rather different approach is reflected in an address made before Newcastle by Leslie's representative Sir William Douglas. The Scotsmen are described[3] as having swords "to defend them from their enemies, who interpose between their good King and them, and had kept them from being heard or relieved in their many former petitions, but not to offend their King, or any of his loving subjects, but that they were ready to lay their hands and their heads under his feet for him to trample on". These sentences are hyperbole, but they leave the impression that it was not difficult for at least one element among the Scots to see their sovereign in the light of a Covenanted king, that is to say a prince who might act as an Elected instrument.

As time passed this notion was bound up with the offer of the Solemn League and Covenant and with the proposition that a Presbyterian form of church government and worship should be accepted in England. The ministers went forward with equal

---

[1] Printed by A. A. W. Ramsay in *Challenge to the Highlander,* 1933, a work which contains an interesting study of the forces and personalities of this period.

[2] Described in a letter sent on 11 September 1640 by John Newport to Edward Nicholas, State Papers, Dom. Charles I, vol. cccclxvii, 31.

[3] Letter from Leonard Pinckney to John Stephens dated at York on 10 September 1640, *ibid.,* vol. cccclxvii, 12.

fervour and acceptance. A letter[1] from Zacharie Boyd to the Countess of Cassilis, who had lost three brothers in the Dunglass explosion, sets the tone. "What God hath done, or permitted to be done, must not be said against. Whatever the instruments have been, we must ever bless the Lord. Job did so after that Sathan in a mighty winde, by the fall of an house, had smothered all his children. As for Job's children, they were at a banquet, in dangers of blasphemie, but your ladiship's brethren, at the very blast, were praising the Lord for a victorie graunted unto Christ's armie; and from that spirituall joy and singing of hearts on the Lord's day, they being Christ's martyrs, went up to heaven, where they shall sing Hallelujah for ever." This was not the outlook with which Montrose felt in harmony. In the month that this screed was written he gathered his friends together in his cousin's house at Cumbernauld.

This meeting is one of the more obscure episodes of Montrose's life. Even the date has never been fixed exactly; it is generally described as "early in August". The purpose of the gathering is plain enough for it was the first move against Argyll's hegemony. A band was set forth and signed by Montrose and nineteen companions. It is not clear how many of these were present at the meeting. The terms of the band remained unknown until a copy was found by Mark Napier; it therefore did not appear in print until 1856. All those who signed were considerable landowners and avowed Covenanters, most were peers. The first section of the band read as follows:[2] "Whereas we under-subscribers, out of our duty to Religion, King, and Country, were forced to join ourselves in a Covenant for the maintenance and defence of eithers, and every one of other, in that behalf: Now finding how that, by the particular and indirect practising of a few, the country, and cause now depending, does so much suffer, do heartily hereby bind and oblige ourselves, out of duty to all these respects above-mentioned, but chiefly and namely that Covenant already signed, to wed and study all public ends which may tend to the safety both of Religion, Laws, and Liberties of this poor kingdom". Montrose was only twenty-eight at this time. It is interesting to consider those who agreed to give their signatures; they tended to fall into two main parties.

There was in the first place Montrose's close relatives and connections, his host the Earl of Wigtown and the latter's young son-in-law Lord Boyd, and Almond, who was Leslie's second-in-

---

[1] Printed by Fraser in *Memorials of the Earls of Haddington*, vol. i, pp. 198-9 and first published in *Four letters of Comforts* by Zachary Boyd in 1640.
[2] Cf. Mark Napier, *Memoirs of the Marquis of Montrose*, vol. i, pp. 269-70.

command. Almond was to play a serious part in the ensuing wars. His equivocal conduct was perhaps partly due to a determination to preserve the House of Livingstone. He is better known as Callendar,[1] his later title. There were also other groupings, for instance the young Earl Marischal and his uncles Kinghorne and Perth. There was Perth's first cousin Stormont and the latter's nephew Atholl. It is no surprise that these last two were ready to combine against Argyll. All these were connected more or less remotely[2] with Montrose, but this is a point which it is unwise to labour given the maze of Scottish genealogy. More important they were, with two exceptions,[3] not young men; they had not been among Montrose's contemporaries in his college days; they seem to have been chosen as peers of standing of the second rank, who found the growing power of Argyll irksome. None were Catholics, nor within a sphere of Catholic influence. The prevailing atmosphere was in a political sense most strongly Protestant. The Band of Cumbernauld itself pre-supposed support for the Covenant, but it is not clear that all the signatories had taken this. Two men were avowed Royalists, Seaforth, who would support Montrose in later days, and Galloway a courtier who had been Stewart of Garlies. It is not easy to account for Home's presence.[4] There was one point that appears to unite them; they all stood apart from both Argyll and Hamilton.[5]

The purpose of the Band remains obscure, what Montrose hoped to do and what induced the other peers to sign it. They were for the most part undistinguished as individuals; not one has left a reputation for caution and sagacity. To this statement there is, perhaps, one exception, James Livingstone Lord Almond. It is possible that he was an *agent provocateur*; he certainly sought advantage from both sides.[6] Presumably all interested parties knew about the Band from the beginning.

---

[1] Wigtown was first cousin to Montrose through his mother and was married to Callendar's sister.

[2] Perth's father Patrick Lord Drummond had three sisters who became respectively Countesses of Montrose, Mar and Tullibardine, the last-named was Stormont's mother.

[3] Marischal was born in 1614 and Boyd in 1616.

[4] Montroses aunt Lady Beatrice Ruthven was married to his grandfather Sir John Home. It was probably a question of private friendship.

[5] It is also true that they had no connection with any Gordon, and Marischal was an enemy of that house.

[6] For an unfriendly estimate cf. Baillie's comment. "That place (of lieutenant general) was destinate for Almond, in whose wisdom and valour we had bot too much confidence; yet in the tyme of our most need, the grievousness of his gravell, or the pretence of it, made him goe to France to be cutted: alwayes when he came there, it was found he needed not incision, so he past to his charge in Holland, wher to us he was as dead in all our dangers, *Letters and Journals*, i, p. 212.

The "discovery", which was the result of some words dropped by Boyd when dying of fever in November, seems very opportune. It is worth noting that it was Almond whom Argyll questioned. Many points are still not clear. How many of the signatories were in the house of Cumbernauld at the time and by what methods did the others add their names? What was the attitude of the Court to the whole matter and why did Lord Napier, who was Montrose's normal adviser, stand aloof? Once the matter was made public, the Band was ordered to be burned by the General Assembly. Argyll had and took the chance to be magnanimous. A certain pattern of opposition within the Covenanting ranks had been revealed to him. One man alone, Montrose, was pursued fiercely. Perhaps from the beginning it was intended so.

During the autumn, when Montrose was with the army at Newcastle, he was accused of corresponding with the King. Such a charge reads strangely and should be interpreted as an accusation of acting with disloyalty to the Covenant that he had helped to promulgate. Argyll was well aware of the difficulty of his own position. In the year preceding the Treaty of Ripon the legal position of the Covenanting lords had not been tenable. In the Parliament of 1639 Traquair, as Royal Commissioner, had chosen the nobles who in their turn had chosen the lesser barons and burgesses. In this way a Committee of the Estates had been selected, and their juridical status imperilled by the absence of the bishops. Later on Argyll's motion it had been decided that each estate should elect its own Lords of the Articles. In June 1640 the prorogued Parliament had reassembled without any representative of the Crown. By the treaty, consequent on the occupation of Newcastle by the Scots, these irregularities had been accepted as temporary and in effect condoned. In the winter of the burning of the Band of Cumbernauld the whole country was profoundly peaceful, even if it was the peace of royal defeat.

Among the documents that throw light upon the situation in Scotland one discovered by Mark Napier has an especial significance. Amid so much that is doubtful it provides a clue to Montrose's mind. It is generally known as the letter on Sovereign Power and appears to have been composed between the autumn of 1640 and the summer of the next year. Written in the form of a dissertation it is undated and unaddressed; it has been reasonably conjectured that it was intended for Lord Napier. In reality it would appear to have been an attempt by the writer to clarify his own still rather confused thought. Montrose was very young and his style pedantic.

A few short quotations will give the drift of his ideas. "In Venice," he explains,[1] "which is a pure aristocracy, laws, war, peace, election of officers, pardon and appellation, are all concluded and done in *Conciglio maggiore,* which consists of principal men who have the sovereignty . . . and the duke is nothing but the idol to whom ceremonies and compliments are addressed, without the least part of sovereignty. So it was in Sparta; so it is in Lucca, Genoa, and Ragusa, and all other aristocracies; and, indeed, cannot be otherwise without the subversion of the present government. If, then, the lords in Republics have that power essential to sovereignty, by what reason can it be denied to a prince in whose person only, and primitively, resteth the sovereign power, and from whom all lawful subaltern power, as from the fountain, is derived?"

The writer then proceeds to definition. "This power is strong and durable when it is temperate. . . . It is weak when it is extended beyond the laws whereby it is bounded; which could never be any time endured by the people of the western part of the world, and by those of Scotland as little as any." He then sets out the alternatives. "The effect of a prince's power too far extended is tyranny—from the King, if he be ill; if he be good, tyranny or a fear of it from them to whom he hath entrusted the managing of public affairs. The effect of the royal power restrained is the oppression and tyranny of subjects; the most fierce, insatiable, and insupportable tyranny in the world; where every man oppresseth his neighbour, without any hope of redress from a prince despoiled of his power to punish oppressors."

The value of Parliaments, considered in the light of seventeenth century usage, is then examined. " 'But,' it may be demanded, 'how shall the people's just liberties be preserved if they be not known, and how known if they be not determined to be such?' It is answered, the laws contain them; and the Parliaments, which ever have been the bulwarks of subjects' liberties in monarchies, may advise new laws against emergent occasions which prejudge their liberties. . . . And if Parliaments be frequent, and rightly constituted, what favourite counsellor or statesman dare misinform or mislead a king to the prejudice of a subject's liberty." Montrose then comes to the core of his reflections on the actual situation. "The perpetual cause of the controversies, between the prince and his subjects, is the ambitious designs of rule in great men, veiled under the specious pretext of Religion and the subject's Liberties,

[1] The letter was first printed by Napier in *Memoirs of the Marquis of Montrose,* vol. i, pp. 280-9. It was also reprinted in Buchan's *Montrose,* pp. 397-406.

seconded with the arguments and false positions of seditious preachers." After this statement there was nothing more to be said. No man could be at ease in the political atmosphere of Edinburgh in the summer of 1641 who held Montrose's strong objection to Argyll and to the ministers.

The King determined to come northward bent on peace. It should have been no surprise to those who knew the climate of opinion to find that Montrose was lodged in prison in Edinburgh Castle when he arrived. There is little reason to suppose that any part of Montrose's programme appealed at this stage to Charles I. The King needed something more subtle for his encouragement, a quiet and sober work which would separate his enemies and dissolve their rancour. In spite of his own probity, he was never ill at ease with dissimulation. The King began seeking aid in a different quarter; he entered into negotiations with Rothes.

This development could have been foreseen. The conflict had developed in quite another fashion from that which Rothes had envisaged. His mind was essentially political and he was repelled and his interests were threatened by the programme which was taking shape under Argyll and Wariston. His wife, who was Mar's daughter, died in May 1640 and he now sought a new alliance. During the winter he formed the project of marrying Lady Devonshire, a step which would recoup his broken fortune and bring another factor into Scottish politics. It was not realised in England that Rothes's health was by now almost destroyed. In any case there was little for him to build upon. Strafford was gone, a statesman who would have understood and, perhaps, have used him. To the King's new advisers, to men like Falkland and Edward Hyde, he was just the insinuating "greedy Scot" to whom they had been so long accustomed.[1] And it is true that Rothes's ideas were old-fashioned and seem to have amounted to a return to the position under James VI in the first days of Dunfermline's chancellorship; he saw himself as the chief minister in Scotland with a body of lords co-operating with him. He must have had hopes of Alexander Leslie. All such projects were bound to break down before the fact of the alliance between the Covenanters and the English Parliament. This was a tie whose strength the King did not appreciate. All through the summer of 1641 he went forward

---

[1] In later life Clarendon summed up his impressions. As he states that Rothes was "little more than thirty", it is likely that he did not know him. "He (Rothes) was of a pleasant and jovial humour, without any of those constraints which the formality of that time made that party subject themselves to; and he played his game so dexterously, that he was well assured, upon a fair composition, that the Scots army should return home, and that they should be contented with the mischief they had already done". Cf. Rothes, *Relation,* appendix, pp. 226-7.

with the plans for a Scottish visit. In that circle which would come in contact with the sovereign, there were few Scots who were not loyal enough to want rewards from him.

The final Rothes episode was brief. Christiana Countess of Devonshire[1] was a daughter of Edward Bruce of Kinloss; a widow who had lived at Chatsworth with her son and his tutor Thomas Hobbes; something of a "blue stocking"; a deeply attached adherent of the Stuart family. Light is thrown on the situation in a letter sent by Baillie to his wife, who was asked to show it in confidence to Rothes's elder daughter, who was married to Eglinton's heir. "The King and Queen begin[2] much to affect him; and if they goe on, he is lyke to be the greatest courteour either of Scotts or English. Lykelie he will take a place in the Bed-chamber, and be little more a Scottish man. If he please, as it seems he inclynes, he may have my Lady Devonshire, a very wise lady, with four thousand pounds Sterling a-year. The wind now blows fair in his topsaile." There had been other rumours[3] of this marriage and of Rothes's new outlook. "His Majesty expected[4] much service in this present conjecture, he having given many assurances thereof." In August there was already reference to his weakened health and danger. The end came suddenly, and on 26 August Thomas Wiseman wrote[5] to Sir John Penington. "The great statesman and Scottish Covenanter, Lord Rothes, died last Tuesday of a consumption at Richmond; who, if he had lived should have married the Countess of Devon." There was for the moment no further effort to build a party for the King.

It is possible that the sovereign himself hardly desired this for he was now bent upon a new experiment. Charles I reached Edinburgh on 14th August and remained there just over three months. He had determined on his line of action. The proceedings have been well characterized as "an austere honeymoon".[6] There was question of an expedition to restore his nephew the Elector Palatine to his

[1] The index in the Calendar of State Papers, Domestic, 1041, 3 confuses Christiana Countess of Devonshire with her daughter-in-law the young wife of the third Earl.

[2] Letter dated 2 June 1641. On the same day Baillie wrote to Lord Montgomery, "For the present, your good-father (father-in-law) is a great courteour: if it hold, he is lyke to be first both with King and Queen; bot sundry thinks it so sudden and so great a change that it cannot hold", Appendix to Rothes's *Relation*, p. 225.

[3] Cf. a letter dated 17 June 1641 from Sidney Bere to Sir John Penington. "Some speech goes that the Earl of Rothes shall marry the Lady Devonshire, and she be about the Queen and he be about the King", State Papers, Dom., Charles I, vol. cccclxxxi, 42.

[4] Letter dated 28 August from the same to the same, *ibid.*, vol. cccclxxxiii, 96.

[5] *Ibid.*, vol. cccclxxx, 91.

[6] C. V. Wedgwood *The King's Peace, 1637-1641*, p. 456.

lost hereditary lands in Germany. The project, could it have been implemented, would have drawn the troops away to a "good cause". This idea soon came to nothing, but the meetings remained tranquil. At the solemn opening of Parliament Hamilton had borne the crown and Argyll the sceptre. The King was attentive to Alexander Henderson and it seems that he made an impression on this Presbyterian leader. There was always a certain majesty attaching to the notion of the King of Scotland; that Charles should have been the Doge of a Presbyterian Venice would have suited Argyll perfectly. By the end of August all the legislation passed in the previous year had received a legal sanction through the royal assent.[1] The officers of state were then proposed; Sir Thomas Hope remained advocate and Lanark secretary; Loudoun became the lord high treasurer. A difficulty arose over the King's proposal that Morton, Argyll's father-in-law, should have the chancellorship. This was rejected[2] and it was clear that the King could not succeed without force behind him.

One matter throws light on the situation, the episode known as the Incident. Montrose was all this time in prison as a result of complicated charges involving Traquair's cousin and servant Walter Stewart. These were charges which could be and were dropped. Whoever was responsible for the Incident, Montrose himself was not at liberty. The gist of the earlier accusations had turned on rumours that Argyll aimed to depose the King and the next stir began with a similar statement affecting Hamilton's loyalty. "My Lord Kerr," wrote[3] Baillie in regard to Roxburgh's young heir, "in God's mercie, makes vent to them in his drunkenness before their maturitie. That very insolent youth, without all provocation, one day, after too much drink, will bot cartell the Marquis of Hamilton as a juglar with the King, and a traitor both to him and to his countrie". The challenge was brought to Hamilton by Crawford, a returned soldier of fortune lately come home to his bankrupt earldom. Crawford, who was in drink, found Hamilton in the presence chamber and the Marquis put him by with courtesy. Parliament put forward a complaint and Hamilton

---

[1] At the opening of the session certain lords who had not yet taken the Covenant subscribed it, Hamilton, Morton, Roxburgh and Lanark on August 18 and Lennox, Annandale and Dumfries the next day, Baillie, *Letters and Journals*, i, p. 386.

[2] Argyll opposed Morton's nomination as a "man unmeet, because of irresponsableness to the law for his debts", *ibid.*, i, p. 390. "The nixt on whom his Majestie pitched was Almond. This motion was also rejected. Argyle had been before allwayes to that man a most speciall friend; bot he said, he behooved to preferr the publick good to private friendship", *ibid.*, i, pp. 390-1.

[3] *Ibid.*, i, p. 391.

"on his knee did supplicat the King for Kerr; to whose father (Roxburgh) he professed his manifold obligations." So far the setting seems a careful comedy.

It was a prelude to further action. "It was noised everie where," writes[1] Baillie, "that Hamiltoun, Argyll, and Lanerick, onlie for companie, should have been called for out of their bed by Almont, as it were to the King's bed-chamber; when they should have come, they were to have been arrested as traitors, and to have been delyvered to the Earl of Crauford, waiting on with armed sojours at the foot of the backstairs in the garden (of Holyrood), by them to be cast in a close coatch, and carried to the shore." They were then to be put aboard one of the King's ships which had lain for some weeks in Leith Roads. This vessel was designed to be their prison until they were brought before Parliament "to answer challenges of the highest treason". It was added that Crawford and his men were prepared to stab the lords should any resistance have been offered. Hamilton, Argyll and Lanark "took a short good night"[2] of the King and then retired to Kiniveill. It was made clear that in their judgment Montrose would benefit from this plot against them.

The work of the Parliament was interrupted and all public business ceased. The King declared his honour to be affronted by this withdrawal as if he was unable to protect his own high officers in his own Palace. The Marquis left Kinneill and moved westward to Hamilton, where he was joined by Argyll and by the latter's nephew Gordon, Huntly's heir. There they "lay quietlie[3] without any convocation of friends". They made a very powerful combination. The notion of the capture of the leaders and their captivity on board an English ship was hard to bear. They daily consolidated their position. Robert Baillie's account is quite convincing in so far as it concerns opinion in the Covenanting circles. "Sure their late danger," he writes[4] of the three lords, "was the meane to increase their favour with the Parliament; so whatever ruling they had before it was then multiplied. The Marquis did not much meddle; bot the leading men of the Barrons and Burrowes did daylie consult with Argyle." A letter came from the King and instructions from the Parliament requiring the presence of Hamilton and Argyll. The matter was composed. "They all returned and at once seemed to have as great confidence in the King as ever."

The episode appears as a typical stratagem of Scottish faction on the ancient model, even the setting at Holyrood. The withdrawal

[1] Baillie, *op. cit.*, i, pp. 391-2.   [2] *Ibid.*, i, p. 392.
[3] *Ibid.*, i, p. 393.   [4] *Ibid.*, i, p. 303.

was admirably designed to expose and exploit the King's weakness; he had not the strength to make resistance. There had been very little forethought on his part. It had not been prudent to bring Lennox with him or to propose Morton's name. The power had passed from him and it now only remained to give rewards. Alexander Leslie became Earl of Leven and Almond was advanced to the same rank. These ceremonies were traditional and splendid. Alexander Henderson became Dean of the Chapel Royal[1] and Wariston received a knighthood. The honour of a marquisate was reserved for Argyll. Projects of an alliance were worked out between Argyll's son and Hamilton's young daughter. Charles I would soon give Hamilton a dukedom, which would pass to Lanark in his turn. All these lords and the ministers and their friends were taken into the King's formal favour. He was about to leave his northern kingdom.

There was an air of calm throughout the country arising from the temporary satisfaction of the victors. The day before his sovereign's departure Montrose was released from his imprisonment. The episcopal question was no longer a live issue; the chance of reopening it had vanished when Laud fell. Various of the bishops were living quietly as ministers in Scotland. Maxwell had been translated to an Irish see. The others had gone to England and two had[2] already died there.

Before the King left Scotland some dispositions had been taken in regard to the former episcopal endowments. The universities of Edinburgh and Aberdeen received the temporalities of these two bishoprics. The college at Glasgow obtained the bulk of the lands of the see of Galloway. On the other hand various gentlemen obtained their pickings[3] and Lennox was granted the Glasgow temporalities.[4] These moves seem to reflect some vague hope in the King's mind that the universities might be brought to favour[5] him. The parting between Charles I and his Scottish subjects was marked by a kind of leaden cordiality.

The Scottish situation was singularly impermanent. None of the

---

[1] He did not escape criticism. "Good Mr. Hendersoun all this while was verie silent, and under misconstruction with the chief of his old friends as if he had been too spareing with his Majestie in these dangerous occasions, and that in his sermones some sentences did fall from him prejudiciall to the States proceedings, Bot surely that man is most gracious", *ibid.*, i, p. 395.

[2] Wedderburn on 27 September and Spottiswoode on 26 November 1639.

[3] Baillie notes as follows: "Argyle, Isles, I suspect to Argyle. Rosse, Murray, and Caithness, are divided to Northland gentlemen and ministers, who are bot of verie small decerving", *Letters and Journals*, i, p. 395.

[4] "Glasgow was pitifullie crossed by the Duke (of Lennox), who must needs have the Temporalitie of that Bishoprick", *ibid.*, i, p. 395.

[5] Richard Maxwell, to ingadge his hammermen to the King, got to their Meddlen (Magdalene) Chappell, the most of Dunkell", *ibid.*, i, p. 395.

alliances could endure and no existing policy would prove successful. Each leader was going forward towards his own catastrophe. Thus not only the King but also the other four protagonists, Argyll and Wariston and Hamilton and Lanark, would all die violent deaths. Lanark was to succumb to his wounds after the fight at Worcester.[1] The others perished on the scaffold, Argyll and Wariston at the Restoration[2] of Charles II, and Hamilton two months after his royal master. In a sense they all died for some conception of the royal authority. Scotland had always been a land without Republicans. Wariston was in effect a believer in theocracy and Argyll in a theocratic polity over which he might bear viceregal rule. Both had a religious conviction of the need for a Covenanted King. Hamilton was to break with Argyll at the time of the second civil war. He became the leader of the "Engagement" in which he was joined by Callendar. A link can be traced between the "Engagers" and some of the signatories of the Band of Cumbernauld. The "Engagement" hardly represented a well thought out position; it was an aristocratic movement opposed to the political domination of the Kirk and it carried Hamilton's hallmark, an optimist expediency. Nevertheless the "Engagers" went out to die in the King's name.

Two leaders stood outside the conception of the King's peace with Scotland, Montrose and Huntly. It was by accident that Huntly was outside the settlement. He was in England and his son was with Argyll and Hamilton. He held to an old-fashioned authoritarian doctrine. Montrose on the other hand was clearly seen as an opponent of oligarchic rule. In the end both Montrose and Huntly perished on the scaffold as maintainers of the King's authority.

After three months in Edinburgh there was nothing more that Charles I could do in Scotland. A rebellion had broken out in Ireland and the Parliamentary opposition under Pym was very menacing. In the morning of November 18th the King left his northern capital in the early hours and before nightfall he was on English soil. Seven years of conflict lay ahead of him, but he never again set foot in Scotland.

[1] He died as second Duke of Hamilton on 12 September 1651.
[2] Argyll and Wariston were executed in 1661 and 1663 respectively.

INDEX

INDEX

F